With loop
Boff

MY REGARDS
TO BROADWAY

A Memoir

*James Fairfax at Redford Park, with Paloma, his Rhodesian Ridgeback
and her offspring Max (background).* Photo: The Australian.

JAMES FAIRFAX

MY REGARDS TO BROADWAY

A Memoir

James Fairfax.
4 - 8 - 92.

📚 Angus&Robertson
An imprint of HarperCollins*Publishers*

AN ANGUS & ROBERTSON BOOK
An imprint of HarperCollinsPublishers

First published in Australia in 1991
This Imprint Lives edition published in 1992 by
CollinsAngus&Robertson Publishers Pty Limited (ACN 009 913 517)
A division of HarperCollinsPublishers (Australia) Pty Limited
25-31 Ryde Road, Pymble NSW 2073, Australia
Reprinted in 1992
HarperCollinsPublishers (New Zealand) Limited
31 View Road, Glenfield, Auckland 10, New Zealand

HarperCollinsPublishers Limited
77- 85 Fulham Palace Road, London W6 8JB, United Kingdom

National Library of Australia
Cataloguing-in-Publication data:

Fairfax, James, 1933- .
  My regards to Broadway.

  ISBN 0 207 17669 8.

  1. Fairfax, James, 1933- . 2. John Fairfax & Sons - Biography.
  3. Publishers and publishing - Australia - Biography. I. Title.

070.5092

Unless otherwise acknowledged, all photographs
are the property of James Fairfax

Front cover photograph courtesy of the Australian

Typeset by Deblaere, Sydney
Printed in Australia at Griffin Paperbacks

5 4 3 2
96 95 94 93 92

CONTENTS

ACKNOWLEDGMENTS

I have divided the people whose help I would like to acknowledge into three groups and I apologise in advance for any inadvertent omissions.

The first group are those concerned with the production of my book and I shall begin with my secretary Janet Finn, whose unremitting efforts and patience were indispensable. My agent Barbara Mobbs (introduced by Patrick White to whom I shall always be grateful), my first editor Jo Jarrah and Gavin Souter also gave invaluable assistance and encouragement. My five research assistants: Catherine Armitage, Alan Dobbyn, Margaret Jones, Alan Peterson and Ted Thomas provided essential and lucid reports on the areas they covered. Lady Edwards was a tremendous help both in searching out and compiling material and in maintaining press cutting books. Tony Clifford-Smith provided and taught me to use my Compaq computer and was available on the telephone wherever I was. Finally I am indebted to my publishers, Collins/Angus & Robertson, also to Lisa Highton, their publishing director, and their editors Garth Nix and Jacqueline Kent.

The second group kindly agreed to be interviewed or talk to me on a number of occasions, in a few cases where necessary by telephone. They are: Chris Anderson, Sir John Atwill, Jim Bain, Elsie Betts, Bill Bland, Fred Brenchley, Mark Burrows, Nancy Carter, Ron Casey, Sir Rupert Clarke, John Dahlsen, Father Davis, Professor Denton, Bob Falkingham, Greg Gardiner, Sir David Griffin, Glen Kinging, Charles Lloyd Jones, Ranald MacDonald, Paddy McGuinness, Angus McLachlan, Rupert Murdoch, Sir Eric Neal, John Pringle, Helen Rutledge, Sue Scarisbrick, Dacre Smythe, Harold Stewart, Max Suich, Trevor Sykes, Greg Taylor and Jim Wolfensohn. John Dahlsen, Sir James Darling, Annette Dupree, John Fairfax, Greg Gardiner, Glen Kinging, Ranald MacDonald, Billy McCann, Angus McLachlan, Roy Napier, Michael Collins Persse, Caroline Simpson and Richard Walker also read parts of the manuscript, for which I am most appreciative.

The third group can best be described as my immediate and extended family, all of whom gave me much understanding and support, as well as their frank recollections. I thank my sisters Caroline and Annalise and my brothers-in-law Philip Simpson and David Thomas — also my brother Edward Gilly and sister-in-law Marie Helène. My thanks, too, to my cousins Vincent and Nancy, John and Libby and Virginia and David McCord and their families. I am particularly grateful to my stepmother Hanne Van de Weil and to her son Alan (Bill) Anderson.

I end with the best advice I received — from that perceptive critic, my mother — her penetrating eye scanned the early chapters and the most significant of the latter ones, to very good effect.

James O. Fairfax

FOREWORD

Probably only the presses that print Argentinian and Soviet banknotes have been responsible for the felling of more trees than the John Fairfax group. As well as their fat, classified ad-full papers, the company and its founding family have had five books published about their activities since 1980. This is the fifth. Do we need another? Can we afford the trees?

Well, yes. All the other books have been **about** the Fairfaxes. No matter how well sourced, all the previous books have struggled to grasp the nature of the family. Rich, numerous, intimate, far-flung and complex, the family has defied persuasive characterisation. This book is by a Fairfax and the authentic and unusual character of the family is here. Nevertheless, this is a memoir by a man of modesty and discretion and the disclosures are modest and discreet.

Curiously, these qualities, for the journalists who worked for him, were James Fairfax's strength as chairman of the media group that encompassed in his day the three most important daily papers in the country, a muckraking weekly, subsidiary provincials and suburbans, the quality commercial radio network and a TV station that pioneered Australian drama and comedy. He was not an egomaniac obsessed with commercial self-interest and convinced of his wisdom, and thus determined to impose his views on the reader or viewer. He was a cultivated, thoughtful and tolerant man who listened to ideas and argument. Tolerance. Whoever heard of a press baron who was tolerant? As the reader of this volume will observe, this tolerance arose from a childhood of hurtful and puzzling parental conflicts and a painful adolescence. I judge that it came in particular from the necessary adjustments James had to make in his adult life both to live up to his inheritance and to live a full, creative life—two lives, really. One was that of the duty-bound Fairfax involved in the company and its affairs and mindful of its responsibilities and influence. The other was that of a man of taste and leisure and a thousand friendships. These lives rarely touched. Their circles were vastly different. These differences perhaps imposed tolerance. However acquired, it was this tolerance that was his gift to the company.

In 1976 he took over as chairman. From that time, with the considerable assistance of his cousin John Fairfax—the only other figure of youth on the Fairfax board—James, with tact and guile, led a group of deeply conservative men to recognise that their responsibilities required them not merely to allow, but to encourage, diversity of opinion, comment and reporting in the extraordinary portfolio of media outlets the company owned.

In 1975 it was deemed a sackable offence to challenge in other Fairfax papers the view of the *Sydney Morning Herald* and its effective editorial director, Sir Warwick Fairfax, on a controversial subject such as the Vietnam war. By 1983 it was board policy to encourage diversity of views in the group's outlets. In 1971 the *Sydney Morning Herald*, after encouraging a police officer, Philip Arantz, to make important disclosures about the disturbing state of the police force, was persuaded by political intervention to abandon its responsibilities and leave him to face the consequences alone—which included an attempt by the police hierarchy to have him committed as insane. In 1981, by contrast, the board instructed the Fairfax papers to live up to their responsibilities and examine and disclose the strength of organised crime and corruption in the justice system of NSW, which they did.

The character of the company that developed in the period under James Fairfax as chairman was not unique. Roy Thomson endowed the London *Sunday Times* and the *Times* with similar independence and his editors, Sir Denis Hamilton and Harry Evans, with similar responsibilities and authority. The Sulzbergers at the *New York Times* and the Grahams at the *Washington Post* have done something similar, though they have been careful to keep much more policy control in their own hands. But in Australia the power and authority thus eschewed was considerably more. In the *Sydney Morning Herald*, the *Age* of Melbourne, and the *Australian Financial Review* Fairfax possessed in a single company influence equivalent, in the Australian context, to that of the *New York Times*, the *Washington Post* and the *Wall Street Journal* combined. It is a power and influence not a thousand miles from the minds of the men who are bidding for the Fairfax group as I write.

To give up power, encourage diversity, tolerate controversy, yet retain responsibility cannot be done without pain and conflict as James Fairfax and his family learned. Not exercising seigneurial authority brought more threats, denunciations and insults—not least from the Wran and Hawke/Keating Labor governments as well as from elements of the corrupt—than its actual exercise might have done.

We can see how much we have lost now that we can observe the new owners of the Fairfax papers.

Max Suich

1

BLOOD TIES AND SEA BREEZES

M y birth on 27 March 1933 was greeted by *Truth*, I am sure inaccurately, with 'Australia's Richest Baby is Born'. The article ended by asking, 'Will the baby justify his great ancestors? The burden awaits him.'

I was naturally unaware of this burden at the time. My first memory is of my third birthday, on 27 March 1936, when I was given a large wooden rabbit on rockers. I swung up and down on it in my mother's bedroom singing out, 'I'm three today'. I cannot claim to have been as original as Granny Fairwater (as we called our Fairfax grandmother). On her fourth birthday she is supposed to have said, 'This is the hottest summer I have ever known'.

My own fourth birthday foreshadowed a brief appearance at Rosemont Play School, first established by Mrs Charles Lloyd-Jones at Rosemont, her house in Ocean Street, Woollahra. The only event I can recall there is my sweeping some two dozen paper cups filled with milk onto a boy who was standing in the garden beneath them. I do not know why I did this, but in return I was stabbed in the arm with a steel pen and shortly after removed from the school. Around this time I was also asked to leave Miss Penelope Cay's dancing class at St Marks Hall as I 'distracted' the girls. I am not sure what form this distraction took.

My elder sister Caroline also attended the school but it did not long survive. By 1938 we were both at Mrs Broinowski's kindergarten, Fairfield, with many of our friends. It was then in Beresford Road (the house is now owned by Mrs Harry Meeks) but moved shortly after to the corner of Victoria and Mansion roads, where I spent the next three years. On my first day I was teased about the golden curls that still, unfortunately, adorned my head and I refused to go back until they had been removed. I regret to say that in our first year we were driven from Barford, our house, along Victoria Road by Hookey, the chauffeur, in the Rolls until we objected and were allowed to walk the short distance.

It was an extremely good school and Mrs Broinowski is rightly regarded as a remarkable educator. She now lives in a converted chapel at Burrawang, near Bowral, and I visit her there as she does me at Retford Park some twenty minutes' drive away. I remember her reading the *Adventures of Marco Polo* and the *Adventures of Vasco da Gama* to an enthralled audience. I also recall her staging a kind of historical pageant of the kings and queens of England, taken from that wonderfully clever and witty book *Kings and Queens* by Herbert and Eleanor Farjeon. The art teacher, Dora Sweetapple, sister of Marion Hall Best (Lady Hall Best, the well-known innovative decorator), undertook the monumental task of copying the illustrations of each king and queen from William the Conqueror to George VI on to life-sized cut-outs, which each performer carried.

To my disappointment, but not unnaturally, the older pupils were given the parts. Caroline was Edward II, who 'was commonly reckoned as one of the feeblest of all our kings'. The significance of some of her later lines was undoubtedly lost on us: 'Favours he lavished on pretty Piers Gaveston, giving him duchies and riches and rings', and later, 'King Ned was mad about this

giddy gadabout but others had had about all they could bear'. The *pièce de résistance* was certainly Susan Potter (Mrs George Bullock) as Queen Victoria: 'Victoria, Victoria was England's pride and joy, when Grandma was a baby and Grandpa was a boy'. My sister, characteristically, still has the program.

Miss Joan de Mestre and Miss Kate Challis were two of my teachers, and I asked them to my sixth birthday party at Barford. Many years later, I met Kate again as the wife of Professor Bernard Smith, then Power Professor of Fine Arts at Sydney University. I used to visit them at their Glebe home and, despite the number of intervening years, she still remembered the birthday party.

On that wooden rabbit, aged three, 1936.

A few years later I was able to recite most of the Farjeon book off by heart, because of my Wilson grandfather's custom of encouraging Caroline and me to learn a poem each week. We would recite to him each Sunday morning as we walked from Yandooyah, where my Wilson grandparents lived, to the confectioner's in O'Sullivan Road, Rose Bay, and the newsagent next door. At these establishments we bought sixpence worth of sweets and comics: at that time *Tiger Tim, Rainbow* and *Comic Cuts*, with *Buck Rogers* still to come. My mother used to say that these weekly walks and talks with Grandfather were far more beneficial for us than Sunday school, as he was an extremely erudite and amusing man with a very down-to-earth manner. I was always irritated when Caroline could not be bothered to learn anything new — she got away with reciting 'The Raggle, Taggle Gypsies' which was one of his favourites.

At ten each Sunday morning, he would walk along Victoria Road waving his stick. We would see him from our windows, where we were waiting, and race down the steps. My grandmother put in a similar appearance, in her case waving a scarf, at two, and down we would go to Yandooyah for games and afternoon tea. Both my grandmothers had a genius for keeping us interested and entertained. Granny Wilson could be fey and scatterbrained but she had great understanding and good nature. Both Caroline and I, as we grew up, found that we could tell her all sorts of things we could not tell anyone else and be sure of a sympathetic response.

The Sunday teas continued until 1942 or 1943 when, to us unaccountably, our grandparents sold the house and lived apart. My grandfather moved to the Astor in Macquarie Street and my grandmother to Gladswood House, then a kind of select private hotel. The residents included Mrs George Macarthur Onslow, man-about-town Gerry Bannister and Leslie Friend, the father of the artist Donald Friend. It was some years before we learned why our grandparents had separated.

I could see Yandooyah, in Cranbrook Lane, from my bedroom at Barford. Barford adjoined an estate, purchased in the early 1850s by John Fairfax, at the top of Bellevue Hill overlooking Double Bay. At the time it would not have been a sought-after place in which to live, being very exposed to what were then regarded as unhealthy sea breezes, and the land itself was largely sand and rock, with a few stunted eucalypts. The only other house on that part of Bellevue Hill was Sir Mark Sheldon's Trahlee, where great-grandfather James Reading Fairfax lived after his marriage to Lucy Armstrong (descendant of First Fleeter Sargeant Small) in 1857. My great-uncles, Hubert and Wilfred, were born there.

The estate was bounded on the north side by Victoria Road, on the west by Ginahgulla Road, on the south by Kambala Road and on the east by 'the cow paddock' which became part of the Barford garden. Over the years portions were carved off the estate, partly to provide land on which other members of the family built their own houses. Thus John's eldest grandson, Charles Burton Fairfax, built Caerleon in 1886 on the site of an earlier house occupied by his nephew Alfred on the corner of Ginahgulla and Kambala roads. Other blocks, part of the Caerleon subdivision, were sold in Kambala Road and Rupertswood Avenue including Danbury, built by my cousin Margaret and her husband Peter Moore in the early 1930s.

Barford was built for my parents after their marriage in 1928. It occupied two or three acres of land, not part of the original John Fairfax purchase, adjoining the cow paddock. Called after the village outside Warwick where the Fairfax family had been established since the early sixteenth century,[1] Barford is a large red-brick house designed by Wilson, Neave and Berry in the American colonial style. Its 'L' shaped bulk had been wedged into the Bellevue Hill dunes and supported by vast concrete retaining walls. The extent of the operation is shown in movie films taken by my father at the time.

When my sister (born 6 October 1930) and I were children, the large garden was bounded by the Danbury and Ginahgulla gardens, Victoria Road and a flight of steps adjoining Quambar, the neighbouring house. The vacant lot between Quambar and Barford, leading to Rupertswood Avenue where the Barford drive emerged, was bought by the Lindsay Bells. It was a truly idyllic setting for two children to grow up in. Not only did we have our own garden, but we were free to roam at will in Ginahgulla's marvellous Victorian garden.

Barford's drive curved down from Rupertswood Avenue to the garages which, with a squash court above them, stood close to the upstairs back door. The drive continued steeply down to the front door, ending in a stone-flagged circle with a large Chinese elm in the middle. This arrangement meant that the household nearly always used the back door, the front door and porch door (in case of rain) near the bottom of the drive being used for visitors.

Below the circular court, the tennis court lay at the foot of a steep flight of steps, and more steps led to Victoria Road. A fountain, from which a lawn stretched out, was the focus of a colonnaded courtyard formed by the square of the 'L'. Most of this side of the garden adjoining Ginahgulla consisted of a large and somewhat unkempt grassy field, known to us as 'The Paddock' — originally the Ginahgulla 'cow paddock' — with a huge Moreton Bay fig near the bottom. Down one side of it, a long path with a herbaceous border gave some formality to the Ginahgulla boundary. Incongruously perched at the end, between both gardens and fronting Victoria Road, was a small wooden cottage occupied by Macleod, Ginahgulla's gardener. The milking sheds and fowl yard adjoined the Danbury garden further up.

All this in the heart of Bellevue Hill seems hard to imagine today, but I cannot say that our having a larger garden than most of our friends, with access to an equally big one adjoining it, had much effect on us. As children, we took the established order for granted in the same way we did the large number of indoor servants. They would be called 'staff' now, but in those days there was no opprobrium attached to the description 'servant'. Until 1941 there were six indoor servants: Miss Anthony, the cook; Davrel, the butler; Elsie, the housemaid; Ethel, the parlourmaid; Eileen, the kitchenmaid; and Carrad, my mother's personal maid. Outdoors there was Hook (or Hookey as we called him), the chauffeur; Hodges, the gardener; and Eric, his son. Finally, with her own small empire, there was Nanny, making ten altogether. I make no apology for this situation, nor would my mother. It was 'the way we lived then' and, indeed, until the late 1930s many old Sydney families maintained this sort of establishment. The way, of course, was changed by the war.

Ginahgulla's garden, for example, was sadly flattened in 1946–47 to provide an additional sports oval for Scots College. After the death of my great-aunt, Miss Mary Fairfax, in May 1945, my two great-uncles, Hubert and Wilfred, sold the property to the school for £20 000 and it subsequently became Fairfax House. It was indeed sad that the original house should pass from the family, and nowadays, ways would doubtless be found to preserve its historic interior and garden. Considering the situation immediately after World War II, however, and the fact that none of the family wanted to live there, my great-uncles' decision is understandable if regrettable.

The ghosts of Auntie Mary's cows must have continued to moo, though, as for some years I preserved the rural atmosphere of the original Ginahgulla cow paddock by keeping six white Leghorns in an enclosure near the fig tree. I regarded providing the household with eggs (and later with the produce from my vegetable garden at the bottom of the paddock) as part of my war effort. Then there were Sir Mark Sheldon's sheep, kept in a steep grassy run next to the Trahlee stables. I am not sure why he needed six or seven, but it was fun scaring them and making them race down to the bottom of the run. It was also fun running after the bread and milk carts, and especially the Chinese market gardener; the horses would move from house to house of their own accord and wait patiently while deliveries were being made.

The last family Christmas at Ginahgulla was in 1944 — indeed, it proved to be the last Christmas the family as a whole were ever to celebrate together. Aunt Mary, eldest child and only daughter of my Fairfax great-grandparents, had six brothers, the third of whom was my grandfather, James Oswald, who

At Woodside, aged two, with Auntie Mary, 1935.

died in 1928. She was the force holding the family together and, had there been someone to step into her shoes, the different branches of the family might have been able to maintain a closer relationship, which could have diminished later divisions. As it was, the passing of both my aunt and Ginahgulla removed the focal point. My grandmother, then in her early seventies, lived alone at Fairwater and did not feel inclined to take on the task, while my two surviving great-uncles, Hubert and Wilfred, died in the next seven years.

So, in 1944 the family foregathered at Ginahgulla with one important exception. To my rage, my mother had not been invited. This was because news of her impending divorce from my father had reached the family and some of them — possibly the great-uncles — felt her presence would not be 'suitable', and prevailed upon Aunt Mary not to ask her. My cousin John and his wife Valerie were also to be divorced, but managed to hold off until after Aunt Mary's death.

My father decided to take Caroline and me to the gathering for the sake of peace and unity and also because I was expected to fill the role of Father Christmas which, as the eldest boy of the fifth generation, I had done for the last five years. My rage had obviously affected my digestion as I decided I felt sick after lunch and returned home through the garden. My mother, however, prevailed upon me to go back and play my part.

There was reason for added excitement that year. For the first time since before the war, we were to be back in the dining room — for the past few years it had been used as a dormitory for one of the women's services — and we children were to be at the grownups' table. In previous years Caroline and I, with our cousin Virginia (eldest daughter of John and Valerie) and in later years her sister Charmian and our cousin Mary-Jane (eldest daughter of Peter Moore, who went down on HMAS Parramatta, and Margaret) sat at a small table adjoining the main table at the end of the long entrance hall with its classical marble statues in alcoves (all discreetly fig-leaved), its marble busts of great-great-grandfather John and great-grandfather James R, palms in brass pots and Landseer prints.

My two great-uncles were kind but somewhat remote figures to me. Uncle Hubert had a forceful wife, Ruth, and a passion for budgerigars which he used to show me as they flew on to his fingers and shoulders at Elaine, the house next door to Fairwater. Elaine had been acquired by Uncle Hubert after the death of his elder brother Geoffrey, who had lived there with his wife Lena. Geoff and Jim, my grandfather, had married two sisters — Lena and Mabel Hixson — who were daughters of Captain Francis Hixson, R.N., Commander of the New South Wales Naval Brigade and his wife Sarah, who was the granddaughter of emancipated convict and leading colonial entrepreneur Simeon Lord.

My great-aunt Ruth, a formidable lady with a twinkle in her eye, had founded the Queensland branch of the Country Women's Association.[2] She had a somewhat hirsute upper lip and Pauline Allen told me that her mother, Mrs Frank McDonald, who was one of Ruth's close friends, suggested she have some depilatory treatment. Aunt Ruth's response was, 'What God has put there no man shall remove.'

According to my grandmother, my Uncle Wilfred, the youngest of the family, used to suck up to his parents, and in later years, my grandmother was determined to outlive his wife, my great-aunt Marguerite, with whom she had

At Sospel, aged three or four, with Caroline, Granny Fairwater (Lady Jim) and my father,
W. O. Fairfax, 1936–37.

a rivalry of sorts. Needless to say, she did. She was the last survivor of her
generation, dying in 1965 in her ninety-fifth year. Aunt Marguerite was always
very kind to me and Caroline, however. Caroline, her husband Philip Simpson[3]
and I enjoyed dining with her at Woniora in her last years. A Christian Scientist
and teetotaller, she nevertheless produced for us musty old bottles of gin and
wine which had clearly been in the house in Uncle Wilfred's time. Her eldest
son, John, who took his own life in 1951, gave a delightful description of
Ginahgulla in Auntie Mary's (as all the family called her) time in his book *The
Story of John Fairfax*, published in 1941. His mother's dearest wish was to have
the book reprinted, which happily I was able to arrange in her lifetime.

The Christmas gatherings also included my grandmother's brother, Uncle
Willie Hixson, and Aunt Janie, his blind wife, and my Wilson grandparents.
The Hixsons lived at Fairlight at the end of Elizabeth Bay Square. Cousin

Margaret and my father's first cousins Vincent and John[4] (on leave from the army) and Mick, together with their wives Nancy, Val and Sue, completed the family. Vincent and Nancy were to become my friends and supporters in many difficult situations and troubled times at the company much later on, but it was 'Auntie Val' I always made a beeline for. She was the most beautiful and glamorous person I had seen and was marvellous with children. From my early twenties onwards, she became a very close friend, as did her second husband Malcolm Carswell whom she married in the 1960s. Visiting them in the various apartments they occupied in Rome after their marriage was always a delightful and exhilarating experience.

As I was nearly twelve when Auntie Mary died, I remember her well. Caroline, Virginia (always known as Tiddy and her sister Charmian as Spiffy), Mary Jane and I often had dinner with her and played everything from charades to Chinese checkers — no one wanted the yellow counters which were referred to scornfully as 'little yellow Japs', preferring the little red Indians and little black Africans.

The Ginahgulla garden was a treasure trove for children. There were mysterious hothouses and greenhouses with cloudy glass, a large covered fern house with a fountain we called 'The Lady in the Pond', and numerous paths and hedgerows leading to enclosed rose gardens, along which all sorts of games could be played. There was Macleod, the gardener, to 'shadow' and otherwise annoy, there was an enormous macadamia tree whose nuts could be cracked and eaten and lastly, the old stone stables still stood at the Victoria Road entrance.

Apart from the garden, I occasionally used to make uninvited visits to the house at weekends when I had a friend round to play. My chief friends were Robert Fleming, son of the actor Athol Fleming ('Mac' of the ABC children's session), Michael Crouch and Donald Vickery, whom my father called Donald Duckery. We used to sneak in the kitchen door, creep round back corridors and sometimes penetrate as far as the long hall. On one such occasion, we tumbled out from behind a curtain at Auntie Mary's feet. She did not look at all surprised, but simply said, in her tinkly little voice, 'Aren't you going to introduce me to your friend?' Needless to say, when Nanny finally found out about these shenanigans, she put a stop to them and I was told to ask properly if I wanted to visit Auntie.

Another thing I loved doing was taking the train with her to Woodside, her country property at Moss Vale, 121 kilometres south of Sydney. Before the war she sometimes used to take me in her large Daimler, which had the excitement of a speaking tube through which I could give instructions to

Comfort, the chauffeur. But the train was much more fun. It had separate compartments opening on to the platform, like the old-fashioned English trains, and Auntie, myself and Nellie (her Scottish maid) would occupy one with an assortment of rugs, thermoses of tea and other goodies, including books, which were seldom read as I was too fascinated by the countryside.

In later years, returning to Woodside was a similar experience for me as Proust's return in time to his great-aunt's house at Combray. Woodside was then owned by my friends Margot and Peter Chambers, whose mother, Helen Tooth, had bought it in the late 1940s. On the outskirts of Moss Vale, it stands at the end of the road leading past the well-known boys' preparatory school, Tudor House, its orange clay drive winding past massive dark cypresses to the mellow red-brick house with its white curved gables, somewhat Dutch in style. Nothing in the house had been changed since my great-grandfather built it in the 1870s, with the exception of an additional bathroom, built to supplement the original which had served my great-grandparents, their seven children and, later on, their sons' wives. There were also two lavatories with fine blue and white porcelain bowls, one downstairs and one outside, which doubtless saw considerable use. The house appeared as the home of the Woolcot family for the television adaptation of Ethel Turner's *Seven Little Australians*.

There were fascinating old Victorian games which, with the garden and farm, were quite enough to entertain me, and I never particularly wanted to go over to Tudor House for cricket when this was suggested. On one of the veranda walls, the heights of all the family members who had stayed there were pencilled in together with dates indicating, in the case of the offspring, their growth over the years. This was thoughtfully glassed in by Helen Tooth and still survives, although the interior of the house has been greatly altered with many bathrooms added by Bill Shipton, the present owner.

Peter and Margot Chambers sold Woodside in 1967, after I had bought Retford Park at Bowral. I have never regretted doing this but, had I not seen Retford at the end of 1963, I might well have bought back the old family country home.

2

BOYS WHO DAILY TAKE THEIR STATION

EARLY EDUCATION, 1939–43

I remember my parents discussing the war shortly after its outbreak. Not long before, they had held a dance at Barford for the Red Cross, the last at Barford for over fifteen years. The sounds of revelry were irrestible, so Caroline and I watched the goings-on from various vantage points. We were particularly intrigued by the 'peep show' in the courtyard, which we saw from an upstairs veranda where we used to play amidst a clutter of rocking-horse, small tables and chairs, games, toys and books. The 'show' consisted of a large panel on which were painted life-sized, fig-leaf-clad figures of a naked man and woman with holes for the heads and arms. The various combinations of guests who posed for photographs in this contrivance caused much hilarity — most of it lost on us.

With the war came the breakup of the household, beginning with the men, except Hodges who was too old for either service or an essential occupation. My father, who turned forty at the time of Pearl Harbor, was in this latter category as managing director of one of the country's leading newspapers. After the Manpower Department had been at work, we were left with Nanny and Elsie, the latter having been turned down by 'Manpower' because of a heart disability. (At the time of writing, she is a hale and hearty eighty-three, living in her Melbourne flat. She returned to Sydney from Victoria in the early 1960s to look after my three nieces for several years and attended the weddings of my nieces Louise and Emily. Her stories of 'Downstairs' Barford life are indeed worthy of a slim volume.)

Nanny — Bertha Mary Tamblin — was a Scot who had looked after the five children of the Marquess of Linlithgow, later Viceroy of India, at Hopetoun House, the family seat at South Queensferry outside Edinburgh on the Firth of Forth. The Earl of Hopetoun, the first Governor-General of Australia, was his father. Nanny came to us in 1931 after some years with another Sydney family, the Molesworths, taking over from Sister Stafford, who looked after Caroline and me in our earliest years. The latter was to look after my half-brother Edward Gilly when he was a baby in Tokyo in 1947–48.

Nanny had all the best qualities of a Scotswoman. She was kind, firm and practical with commonsense, a good sense of humour and a strong religious faith which she imparted to both of us. She was also human and inordinately proud of her Linlithgow links. All over her room there were photographs of the Marquess and Marchioness and their children, to whom she always referred as Lady Anne, Lady Joan and so on. The family remained devoted to her and if any of her former charges came to Australia, they always visited her in retirement at Bundanoon, some fifteen kilometres from Bowral. My mother stayed with the Viceroy and Vicereine at the summer residence at Simla and the three daughters — Anne, Joan and Bunty — remained good friends of hers.

Nanny retired to Wollongong at the end of 1945. Until that time we used to have the evening meal with her in the 'day nursery'; lunch, of course, we had at school. In our younger days, when we had both meals with her, she kept a large wooden spoon beside her plate with which she used to rap us over the knuckles for disobedience. In the 1950s, I occasionally used to drive Granny Wilson, of whom she was always very fond, to see her at her two sisters' houses in Wollongong. Later, I used to visit her at the Linkside Rest Home at Bundanoon (her accommodation was paid for by my father), and before she died in 1965, the matron brought her to tea with me at Retford Park. She remained neat, spry and interested in people and events to the end, carrying the *Herald* round with her in a plastic bag. As the matron said, 'She sets a standard here.'

In 1941 I passed into the hands of another remarkable educator, Miss Van Heukeleman, at Edgecliff Preparatory School. My father had attended a school run by her in Manning Road, Double Bay. For many years EPS (which had been moved to Edgecliff, stone by stone, from Darling Point) was run by 'Miss Van' and 'Sir' — Mr H. M. Butterley, father of the composer Nigel Butterley. It occupied a two-storey stone house with twin gables, almost opposite Ascham, which Caroline and many of her friends attended.

When I began at EPS — I still recall my extreme trepidation on the first day — there were five classes: Miss MacBurnie took the youngest, my own age group had the stimulating and sometimes alarming experience of the principal herself, and the upper three were taken by Miss Lakeman, Mr Mallon and 'Sir'. By 1942, Mr Mallon had gone to the war and his class was amalgamated with 'Sir's'. Towards the end of the year, with the rapid Japanese advance south, many pupils were evacuated to country schools and the rump of Miss Lakeman's class, of which I was one, also joined 'Sir' upstairs. We were very much aware of both the German and Japanese advances as every day Miss Van, with an appropriately belligerent commentary, produced maps with the front lines of both armies in the different theatres of battle indicated by coloured pins.

Other details I recall in my first year include, in her more relaxed moments, Miss Van reading us the *William* books by Richmal Crompton and her passion for poems about British naval victories. An old boy presented the prizes that year, and in his speech he made an apt

On my way to prep school.

comparison by quoting Wordsworth's 'The River': 'Men may come and men may go but I go on for ever'. Miss Van certainly went on for a long time, and her influence must still be with a multitude of her former pupils.

I received a prize that year (I think everyone got one for something) for poetry and reading — the first and last in my entire school career. The book I received, *Skipper, My Chum*, was a prophetic choice as it began a lifelong devotion to dogs.

We concluded with the school song to the tune of 'The Men of Harlech': 'Boys who daily take their station, in this seat of education . . . Soon will come a long vacation . . . Boys today are men tomorrow . . .' being the only lines I can recall. I think our transfer to Sir was accomplished by Miss Van sweeping into the classroom and saying, 'You're going to learn Latin from Mr Butterley. You can all do it — up you go.' So up we went to find *Nauta casam habet* on the blackboard. The motley array of ages assembled under Sir proved to be a very effective class. The older stimulated the younger and the latter seemed not to hold the former back.

Signs that Australia was at war were appearing everywhere. City buildings were sandbagged, windows were given wooden shutters, sometimes the whole ground floor was encased in a wooden barricade, as at the GPO, and troops departed. We watched the 8th Division of the AIF sail through the Heads, bound for the Middle East, from the veranda off my mother's bedroom at Barford. A weeping Eileen — her brother was on board — was supported by her more stoical colleagues.

Two large concrete cylinders, rolled halfway down the Barford paddock and buried, became our air-raid shelter. It was always inhabited by spiders, but only once by us. On 31 May 1942, the night the Japanese midget submarines entered Sydney harbour, the air-raid sirens sounded their singsong warning for the first time in earnest, and we trooped out into the garden to the shelter. While we were there our local air-raid warden, Mr Alan Potter of Llanillo,[1] Ginahgulla Road, called in to tell us the alert was over. Soon after, the 'all clear' sounded, but I think it was a day or so before I knew what had happened. It was not long, however, before two of the submarines were on display at Garden Island naval base and we were taken to see them. I was fascinated that anyone could survive under the sea in such a tiny structure and bought two small bits of the engine room which I still have.

I do not think the concept of an invasion as such concerned me greatly, although my parents discussed getting Caroline and me to Granny Fairwater's house at Leura in the Blue Mountains, 160 kilometres from Sydney. My mother agreed reluctantly — she never got on with her mother-in-law and certainly would not have gone herself — that it would be the safest place should Sydney be subjected to air-raids. At that time she was chairman of the committee running Air Force House in Goulburn Street, where Granny Wilson and Caroline used to go and help make the beds.

For schoolchildren in Sydney during the war years, the basics of life did not change much. I was more concerned with the various problems of school and, for Caroline and me, home and holiday life continued as before. The great day was Boxing Day when we used to pile into the Rolls, or during the war into the Talbot, with a profusion of beach requirements, and head for Palm Beach, 50 kilometres north of Sydney. In our youngest years we were put into Inglewood, a small wooden cottage in Florida Road, with Nurse Craig, Nanny being on her annual holiday with her sisters in Wollongong. Our parents would take a house called Boanbong at the end of the beach. (Nurse Peggy Craig, now 87, recently sent us a kind message saying she remembered us with affection.)

Then, to our joy, we were allowed to come to Boanbong.

This was a rambling, white wooden house, its brown beams giving it a slightly Tudor appearance. It had a steepish drive leading from the end of Palm Beach Road into a lush, tropical, jungle-like garden. It still stands, painted olive-green, with not much jungle left. We used to alternate between Boanbong and Kalua, the house owned by the Hordern family, just north along the road. Kalua was much grander, with lawns sweeping down to the beach and an enormous conservatory at one side. My father used to think the rent, at thirty guineas a week, was very high so some years it was back to Boanbong, but we loved both houses.

Palm Beach was a delightful place in those days and remained so until the building boom in the 1950s and 1960s. There were two beautiful old stone cottages at the beginning of Pacific Road and two elegant pink houses further on, owned by Mrs Scotty Allen and her mother. Further on again was the Carrolls' house, which we took once or twice, and the Rudolph Muellers' stone cottage, where the angophoras spread to the point. All the cottages dotting the peninsula were of stone or wood and were surrounded by bush. The only two-storey houses were the ugly grey structure on the beach owned by a Mr Peters whom we wrongly dubbed 'the Peters Ice cream man' and two further on housing the surf lifesaving club and the ladies' Pacific Club. Now, however, any style from Point Piper to St Ives can be seen, and marble floors are not uncommon. Driving there along the coast was equally pleasant, with each small settlement separated by grassy dunes, the occasional stand of Norfolk pines and scrubby trees.

The social life of the regulars, casual but constant before the war, continued on with a number of the British admirals and senior officers being entertained there. Another occasional visitor was the Prime Minister, Bob Menzies, a friend of several habitues. He would sit on the beach under an umbrella in his dark blue double-breasted suit. Among country and city families I remember, there were the Jim Whites of Belltrees, the Tony Horderns, the Moses clan and the Packers, among others. The younger generation mingled on the beach or at parties at the Pacific Club and I came to know many of the parents well in later years. The last summer we spent there was January 1945.

During the May and September holidays, from an early age, we stayed at Sospel, Granny Fairwater's house in Fitzroy Street, Leura, overlooking the golf course. It was named after a village near Menton in the south of France, where my grandparents had spent part of their honeymoon. They bought it in the late 1920s to indulge their passion for golf and my grandmother's for building gardens, but sadly my grandfather died quite soon after, while playing the eighteenth hole of the Royal Sydney Golf Club. My grandmother and her sister

Lena had been women's champions several times in the 1890s. The garden was created between the late 1920s and mid 1930s, Granny dragging whoever she could muster from family and friends staying there into the bush to retrieve rocks and flat stones. One large, flat quartzite rock forms a natural bridge over the pond, which is fed by a stream flowing down a gentle decline. There are exotic and native trees and formal herbaceous borders on different levels, the whole being surrounded by a dry stone wall. Sospel provided the flowers at the annual Red Cross fete at Fairwater, where Caroline and I were in charge of the pot plants. By the late 1930s it was quite spectacular and known throughout the state, with touring buses stopping to look at it even in those days.

On our visits we were occasionally accompanied by Nanny, but more often we were looked after by Louise, my grandmother's French/Swiss maid who had been nurse to my father and was called 'Lou' by us all.[2] Every morning she took us on a different walk: along bush tracks, across the golf course, to Sublime Point or around the tranquil neighbouring streets. By the time we got back, Granny would be in the garden with Hood, her gardener, planning and happily arguing with him. Granny had a marvellously inventive mind and during the many walks we took with her, she held us enthralled with serial stories she continued while the visit lasted. Her two main characters were Mrs Mackenzie, a good witch, and a boy called Wickedy.

Our favourite game with her was 'Restaurants', set up on the back veranda, in which she used to play about five different people, including groups at other tables, with whom she had the most hilarious conversations. Another more alarming game was 'Stealthy Terror', in which all the downstairs lights were turned out and you had to get from one part of the house to another without touching anybody. She introduced us to the Doctor Doolittle books, reading two chapters a day after lunch and tea. Once, when a pie we were about to eat at lunch was a bit off, she composed during the course of the meal a sixteen-line poem about this unhappy occurrence, which she then sang to the tune of an operatic aria.

There were shopping expeditions to the Leura Mall by bus, with a special request to Mr Peacock, the grocer, for an extra tin of salmon or whitebait for her hungry granddaughter. There were visits to the cinema where we saw everything from *Weekend in Havana* to *Pimpernel Smith*. Of the neighbours down the road, I particularly recall Ruth Hudson and Arthur and Mainie Butcher.

Later, Granny succeeded in installing a nine-hole mini golf course in the garden, one hole of which was a shot over the roof. To her disappointment, and in spite of lessons from the pro, I was never proficient at the game. Caroline was somewhat better.

The house was gutted in the fires of 1957 and with it went a host of childhood mementoes, but not memories. I can still see every room. The garden was largely spared and still exists much as I have described it. Caroline and I made a sad journey up to retrieve a few china ornaments and pieces of crockery from the charred ruins. We visited it several times after Sydney ophthalmologist Dr Claffey bought the property and, with his elderly mother, partially restored the house. It is now, with the gardens, part of the Leura Motel and some of the surviving walls, including Granny's bedroom, form the restaurant.

In August 1942, my father took us to Canberra by train for the first of many holiday visits. We were most excited by the Canberra Hotel (reopened as the Hyatt Hotel Canberra in 1988), the first we had ever stayed at. The rooms were arranged in tiers, connected by open galleries which were spread out like an octopus. They were marvellous to run around in, if ice-cold in winter.

In those days, Canberra was a series of settlements separated by open country, with the Molonglo River flowing through the middle. We had three favourite walks across these fields. The first was to Civic Centre, sitting like a caravanserai in a grassy desert; the second was to the War Memorial, which housed a fascinating collection of relics from the First World War. We saw parts of ships retrieved after action at sea, the first tanks and fighter planes, uniforms ranging from field hospital matrons to Prussian death's head hussars, and dioramas of Flanders battlefields. The third walk was to the Institute of Anatomy with its intriguing collection of creatures (some with multiple heads and limbs) preserved in bottles. Down the road was Parliament House, later to become better known to me, but of embassies there were none. Australia was still a fledgling as far as overseas representation was concerned. I remember a year or two later seeing the US Embassy, one of the first, in the course of construction.

The Canberra scene was completed by the comfortable houses of Mugga Way, with gardens of semi-bush, and, in splendid isolation, The Lodge and Yarralumla, soon to be converted into a suitable residence for the Duke of Gloucester. The only other recollection I have of my first visit is my father singing 'Stormy Weather' with Dorothy Kidder (the Randolph Kidders from America were posted in Australia during the war and now live in Washington and Paris) in one of the bedrooms, and being grouped round a piano with other children to render such current hits as 'In the Mood', 'Elmer's Tune' and 'Deep in the Heart of Texas'.

In the years that followed I returned with my mother, Caroline, a school friend Robert Fleming and the Dunlop and Winchcombe families. Joan Winchcombe achieved the almost unique distinction of being an equally close friend of both my parents. A highly intelligent and amusing Tasmanian, she was a good friend to me, too, and now resides in that remarkable institution Lulworth.[3]

Usually after these Canberra trips we would go on to Bungendore (The District) just to the north and stay with old family friends. Much has been written about these well-known pioneering families and their properties, so my mention will be brief. I could not count the number of times I have stayed at Gidleigh and Currandooley, owned then by the Tom Rutledges and Paddy Osbornes respectively, and now by their children.

Staying with Helen Rutledge and her two daughters Martha and Caroline, both younger than me, was quite a different experience from Currandooley where the twins Pat and Mike, and their younger brother Brian, were all older. At Gidleigh, activities revolved more around the house while at Currandooley, the redoubtable Da Osborne had us riding the ranges, myself unsteadily, and going on deer shoots. 'Thought you said you could ride,' she observed, not unkindly, of my first efforts. With her encouragement, I managed. Da (Marjorie) Osborne's twin sister Dee (Gwendolyn) Ryrie, in the form of *The Squatter's Daughter* by George Lambert, has recently ridden happily into the Australian National Gallery. This work was painted by Lambert in 1923 at Micelago, the Ryrie family's property near Canberra. Fellow guests at Gidleigh and Currandooley were often Lorimer[4] and Margot Dods with Rosemary and Robin. Both houses were beautifully run and the traditions continue, as indeed they do elsewhere in the district.

The Forbes Gordons were at Turalla, now owned by Bill Davy and his wife Dimity. While at Manar, near Braidwood — later to pass to the Forbes Gordons — was Mrs Deuchar Gordon, Bill's grandmother. I remember having long talks with Mrs Deuchar, who was always very kind to me. At Bowylie, Ingrid Davis is running the property formerly owned by her parents, Bedford and Mollie Osborne, and the Brett Falkiners are at Foxlowe. Returning to these Bungendore establishments, whether for notable family events or a quiet visit, is always a joy.

The visits to Canberra alone with my mother were to prove the most memorable, and they really began my political education. She took me to see Prime Minister John Curtin and Treasurer Ben Chifley in the former's rooms at Parliament House in 1943. I recall discussing Agatha Christie with Mr Chifley, as I was a recent fan and had heard he read her books for relaxation. Mr Curtin (the first of thirteen serving or former Australian Prime Ministers I have so far met) kindly lent us his car and driver to visit the Cotter River dam. He also provided us with passes for the Speaker's gallery on the floor of the House of Representatives.

We both became fascinated watching our legislators at work. I was familiar through press, radio and talks with my father with the names and reputations of the members of the Curtin Cabinet, but here they were in the flesh on the Government front bench. It was certainly quite a line-up. Next to the Prime Minister and Treasurer were Dr Evatt and Messrs Calwell, Ward, Dedman, Beazley, Makin and Forde. The Curtin Government's relationship with the *Sydney Morning Herald*, graphically described by Gavin Souter in *A Company of Heralds*, was an up-and-down affair with the censorship crisis evoking a notable battle against Calwell, as Minister for Information, which resulted in victory for the press. The *Herald* had brought on its head much criticism for its support of Curtin following the fall of Menzies and Fadden in 1941, and my father in particular bore the brunt of this from his conservative friends — there were stories of him being cut in the Union Club. I was to find myself in a similar situation exactly twenty years later.

Arthur Calwell, who by that stage was Leader of the Opposition, was the only one of the above I was to get to know. In the Federal election of 1943 the *Herald* advocated support of the best candidate regardless of party in an attempt to break across party lines at a time of national crisis. The result was a Labor landslide and, as Souter says, while the *Herald* could hardly claim credit for that and had not supported Labor as a party, its electoral advice had been the least conservative in all its long commentary upon the Australian political process. In this election the opposition United Australia Party and Country Party were decimated.

In 1943, apart from Menzies and Fadden, I recall Billy Hughes crouched in his seat with hearing aid, the dignified Dame Enid Lyons and the uniformed Air Commodore White. With us in the gallery each day was Mr Makin's father, aged ninety, and we witnessed many exciting clashes, as well as speeches which sent us from the chamber. We thought of the lines: 'When Mr Menzies makes his speeches, I think of grouse and brandied peaches, When Mr Curtin warns the nation, I think of crumbs and cold collation'. It ended with 'But when I hear from Mr Forde, I go to sleep and praise the Lord' — our position exactly. We often met Bob Menzies walking along the alleyways of pines between Parliament House and the hotel. Sometimes he accompanied us back, his urbanity and wit unaffected by his defeat. He was to remain a lifelong friend of my mother, in spite of several serious breaches with the *Herald* in the later years of his second long period of office. He used to call on her at her London flat for a martini and a gossip about his current political doings which she always found riveting.

I have never felt there was any substance in stories of a personal feud between

Menzies and my father. In the early days they got on well, but they were separated by the increasing vehemence of their political differences. Menzies always made a point of talking to me when our paths crossed in future years and was possibly aware that I was, with Angus McLachlan, a voice for him — albeit not always a particularly successful one — in the intensive political discussions at Broadway.

After his retirement I saw him in Melbourne several times and we had lunch, together with Dame Pattie and Charles Lloyd-Jones, in his Collins Street office after Harold Holt's funeral. The solemnity of the occasion in no way dampened his spirits, nor did it affect the excellence of the repast. The last time I saw Bob Menzies was when I called at his home in Haverbrack Avenue about six months before he died. The long passage leading to his study was lined with every cartoon portraying him that had ever appeared. He had had a stroke but his comments as we drank our whiskies were as witty and trenchant as ever.

My mother and I covered most of Canberra by bicycle at Mrs (later Dame Pattie) Menzies' suggestion. Indeed, she arranged to get the bicycles for us. I have retained an affection for the 'bush capital', as Jack Lang's 'Century' used to call it, ever since. On almost the last day of our last visit we were sitting utterly alone in the lounge of the Canberra Hotel — everyone else had gone to meet Mrs Roosevelt — when my mother noticed a distinguished foreign-looking man in uniform who was the only other occupant. Thinking he might be lonely, she got me to ask him to join us for coffee, but had to admit later on that her kind gesture had been misinterpreted by the gallant Dutchman — she had a great deal of difficulty shaking him off.

3

FORTUNE'S BUFFETS AND REWARDS

CRANBROOK, GEELONG GRAMMAR,
SYDNEY UNIVERSITY, 1944-52

The first blow in what had been an idyllic childhood fell in 1944. During the course of that year the family became aware that my parents were contemplating divorce. My father had already moved from Barford to Quambar (now part of the Packer estate with the house demolished) around this time, although I think this was initially described as a temporary measure for reasons of health. I had noticed increasing arguments and coolness between them over the last few years — doubtless Caroline had too but we did not talk about it — and we never did anything together as a family, always going on outings with one parent or the other. It was usually with my mother, as my father was going through a period of bad health around this time. When he was not occupied with the wartime problems facing the *Herald*, he usually wanted to rest and recover from them.

Before he left Barford, he often barricaded himself behind the double doors of the library, while my mother's dinner parties went on in the dining and drawing rooms. However, he sometimes came to stay at Sospel when we were there, or he would come to Palm Beach and my mother would return to town. Every couple of weeks I used to walk across the bottom of the Lindsay Bells' garden to have dinner with him at Quambar, where he was being looked after by Davrel, who had been released from the Air Force for health reasons. For a while I accepted this state of affairs but two other important factors, or I should say people, were coming to my notice.

My mother, like a number of her friends, frequently entertained the commanders and senior officers of visiting ships, or sometimes fleets, anchored in Sydney harbour on their way to or from various theatres of war in the Pacific. I recall handing round savouries at Barford to Admirals Sir Bruce Fraser, Sir Philip Vian, John Eccles and Charles Lamb (the latter two later knighted), among others. I was always told that it was Sir Philip Vian who said at dinner on board *Indomitable*, with my mother on one side and Val on the other, 'But I meant to ask the good Mrs Fairfax!' Thereafter Betty, Val and Nancy, cousins by marriage, were sometimes known as 'The', 'The Other' and 'The Good'. It's a good story but I understand it is apocryphal.

The Americans, and occasionally the French, came into port as well. Capitaine de Frégate Pierre Gilly came from a seafaring Breton family. His father had been an admiral commanding the French fleet in Eastern Mediterranean waters, particularly looking after French interests in the Levant and dealing with the Ottoman Empire, before World War I. Pierre was second-in-command of *Le Triomphant*, a vessel I came to know quite well, and was subsequently promoted to *capitaine de vaisseau* or full captain of the same ship. I became progressively aware of his presence at Barford and conscious of his growing importance in my mother's life until, finally, she told me she 'liked' him more than any of the others. Pierre used to try to coach me at football on the tennis court — he had been a star player in his youth — with as little effect as the Leura golf pro, and in other ways attempted to break down the barriers I was subconsciously raising.

At the same time I began to hear of a Mrs Anderson. I was aware that my father had an attractive blonde companion and understood she was Danish. Hanne Anderson's family lived in Copenhagen. Her father, Emil Bendixsen, was a forester and timber expert and her mother Elna was a well-known artist whose family had been distinguished in the arts for many years. She was a direct descendant of the first director of the Royal Copenhagen Opera. Hanne had married an Englishman, Donald Anderson, who worked for the Shell company in Malaya. He was transferred to Shell Aviation in Bangkok, where they were with their recently born son, Alan, when war broke out. Hanne and her baby were flown to Singapore with the other wives and from there evacuated by boat to Sydney. Her husband became a prisoner of war in a Bangkok prison camp.

Hanne took a flat at Mosman, where she was befriended by the Hynes family. Curiously enough, my grandmother had other Danish refugees staying with her at Fairwater for the duration of the war: Sigrid Fough and her small daughter, Eva. Hanne was also befriended by the Danish consul, Dr Erik Fischer, to whom she had a letter of introduction from her parents, and his wife Ellen. Under her professional name of Helene Kirsova, Ellen had established the Kirsova ballet company. Erik and Ellen used to invite Hanne out on their boat, together with ballet friends and artists. On one of these outings Hanne met a ballet enthusiast named Warwick Fairfax.

Hanne's name used to cause occasional misunderstandings on my part. When my parents referred to Hannah Lloyd-Jones, I often assumed they meant Hanne Anderson, resulting in several awkward moments. The most awkward of all, however, was walking with my parents in the Barford garden when, precocious little wretch that I was, I said, apropos another couple they had been discussing, 'If Mummy didn't like Daddy, Daddy would marry Hanne and Mummy would marry Pierre'. My father subsequently told me it was one of the most embarrassing moments either had ever had. Other difficult moments used to arise at Fairwater when, with childish indiscretion, I would describe my visits to the *Triomphant*. I learned not to after one such occasion when, with both grandmothers present, I said a nice Frenchman had given me a cigarette. Once, Charles Lloyd-Jones and I, then aged ten, were invited to lunch in the ward room and after some tentative sips of wine during lunch, I was presented with a cigar. I gave this to Charles who took it home and, after smoking half of it, had to spend three days in bed with nicotine poisoning.

Plans for divorces and re-marriages were proceeding. Hanne would eventually obtain a divorce from Donald Anderson, but not before she had made an unsuccessful attempt to revive the marriage when he visited Sydney at the end of the war. My mother was proposing to marry a Frenchman whose family had never met her and who could strongly disapprove. To put it bluntly, she could not be sure the marriage would take place. In due course the situation was explained to my sister and me and we adjusted to it as best we could. Life would not be the same again, and the first chapter was drawing to a close.

I believe my relationship with my father was normal for a boy of ten, but with possibly more restraints than in many such relationships, and I was naturally much closer to my mother. He was certainly a stern parent when I transgressed and, until his departure, made genuine efforts to do things with me. After that it was not really until my stepmother Hanne (they were married in 1948) encouraged us that I felt a relationship began to build up again. Caroline was similarly closer to her father and felt his departure much more keenly than I did, though as it turned out she spent much of her adolescent years overseas with our mother while I, being educated in Australia, saw her much less frequently. The result of this was to create a bond between my sister and me and make both of us more self-reliant at an early age. Perhaps, too, it gave us a greater awareness of the problems our elders had to face in life.

Departure of W. O. Fairfax and Hanne from Harrington Park after their marriage on 1 May 1948.
From left: Willi Perndt, Nancy Fairfax, James Fairfax and his godfather Hugh McClure-Smith,
Mrs Hynes, Granny Fairwater and Vincent.

In 1944 I began the first of two years at Cranbrook, both of which I enjoyed very much. Edgecliff Preparatory School boys were expected to go on to Sydney Grammar, but even so I never understood why Miss Van told me Cranbrook would be 'two years out of my education'. Nor, indeed, did I understand why I was removed from Cranbrook except that I had been 'put down' for a 1946 start at Geelong Grammar, my father's old school, and J. R. Darling had a considerable reputation as headmaster. I recently reflected that times had indeed changed when I heard that my half-brother, Edward, and his wife Marie-Hélène were discussing with their two sons whether they would like to complete their pre-university education at schools in England and America.

The two years passed pleasantly and uneventfully and, to my surprise, I was elected form captain in the second. I remember with gratitude the grounding I obtained in Latin with K. B. Felton, in ancient history with A. C. Child and English with C. A. Bell. A nice old German called Dr Heinemann taught us raucous English and German student songs, and Eric Wilson, the art master, awoke in me the glimmerings of a later passion. A small Paris street scene by him was the first painting I bought — in 1945, from the Macquarie Gallery. It joined a Van Gogh print of *Sunset in Provence* from the Notanda Gallery in Rowe Street. There was also the benign and birdlike Reverend F. T. (Polly) Perkins, the first headmaster and then in his last year as chaplain. Over all, presiding benevolently and capably, was the headmaster B. W. Hone.

Outside school my interest in the theatre had been aroused by the Gilbert and Sullivan operas, of which my grandfather was a devotee. I saw Ivan Menzies and Evelyn Gardiner in all of them, together with Richard Watson, Max Oldaker, Gregory Stroud, Marie Bremner and Elva Blair. Then, of course, there was Gladys Moncrieff in *Rio Rita*, *Katinka* and *The Maid Of The Mountains*. My mother took me to all the movies she wanted to see, as well as those considered more suitable for my relatively tender years. I was fascinated at the situations portrayed, applying them with vivid imagination to scenarios closer to home. She also took me regularly to the Minerva Theatre, run by Kathleen Robinson, where Alec Coppel and Myra Morton were the stars.

My father's interest in the arts varied in direction and intensity during the course of his life. His entry in *Who's Who* for many years showed 'The arts and cattle breeding' as his recreations. His interest in the visual arts was fairly constant. He bought the study for William Dobell's celebrated portrait of Joshua Smith at the time of the court case, and in 1944 he arranged for the *Herald* to sponsor Russell Drysdale on a tour of outback areas badly affected by drought, from which some notable paintings emerged. He also bought paintings by Sydney Nolan, Justin O'Brien, Lloyd Rees and Sali Herman at early stages in their careers and, in particular, gave financial support and friendship to Francis Lymburner at a time when he greatly needed both. Later, influenced by my stepmother Hanne, he was to acquire an important collection of French Impressionist and early nineteenth-century paintings.

At this time, however, ballet was a consuming passion, encouraged by his friendship with Helene Kirsova. She had come to Australia in the late 1930s with Colonel de Basil's *Ballet Russe de Monte Carlo* and, in common with a number of its members, had been stranded by the war, to the great future benefit of ballet in Australia. So, from an early age I was exposed, too, to ballet and was taken to see Tatiana Riabouchinska, Tamara Toumanova and David Lichine. At the age of five, after seeing Toumanova dance Odile in *Swan Lake*, I was plonked on her knee while she took great amusement in fixing her long false eyelashes to my own eyes. We were loyal supporters of the Kirsova company and must have seen every program at the Conservatorium during the war years. The period was vividly brought back to me by a recent exhibition at Grace Bros' Blaxland Galleries of photographs by Max Dupain of the de Basil, Kirsova and Gertrude Bodenweiser companies. I recognised with pleasure Strelsa Heckelman, Rachel Cameron, Helen Black and Henry Legerton. My father possibly let his loyalty affect his better judgment when, acting as critic for the *Herald* at the rival Borovansky company, he described the chorus as a row of sheep. As a result the *Herald* was banned from the Borovansky's performances for some time.

In 1944 my father acquired the country property Harrington Park. This surprised his family, and probably his friends as well, as he had never shown much interest in possessing a country property. The company bought it on his behalf for £32 610; in 1956 he bought it from the company for £97 937. It is situated on a gentle rise surrounded by trees, at Narellan (near Camden), sixty kilometres from Sydney. With its kitchen wing dating to 1815, the main house was built in 1825 and an upstairs storey and semicircular sitting room at the back were added in 1870. It was greatly in need of restoration. After some haggling with its elderly owners, named Swan, it was bought with its two thousand acres for just under £17 an acre. My father resisted Caroline's suggestion to commemorate both the previous owners and Toumanova by changing the name to Swan Lake.

The early days in this tumbledown place were great fun. The Swans' furniture was falling apart, there was a chip heater in the bathroom and each morning we milked the cows. As the polled Hereford herd — later to become a flourishing stud — expanded, with bulls and heifers imported from the famous Vern stud in Herefordshire, we would set off in the morning to ride round parts of the property inspecting the animals with Scott Garland, the manager. My father rode an elderly mare named Bertha while I had Percy, a pale chestnut gelding. One of the things I liked doing best was roaming the ranges alone with him. He lasted all my school years and died while I was at Oxford.

We had many happy times at Harrington Park, which was completely restored by John Mansfield in 1949, with furniture acquired from both Ginahgulla and Woodside. The garden was landscaped by Sorenson from Leura; my grandmother maintained that he had acquired a lot of his knowledge from her and that she had assisted him in the laying out of Everglades in Leura, which he did not always acknowledge.

My mother married Pierre Gilly in March 1946 and they left for China, where he had been appointed naval attache to the French military mission at Chungking (then the headquarters of General Chiang-Kai-Shek). The only clergyman my mother could find who was willing to marry a divorcee was the Reverend Alan Tory of St Stephen's, Macquarie Street. Archbishop Mowll, a friend of the family, refused. The only witnesses were my grandparents, Caroline and myself. I can still see my grandfather at the conclusion of the ceremony, as the bridegroom kissed each of his new family, stretching out his arm in alarm to ward off the approach: 'Don't do that to me!' he said.

My mother's remarriage and departure, together with my transfer to Geelong Grammar in February 1946, brought my childhood years to an abrupt end. It is not my intention to spend much time on the tetchy and temperamental years of adolescence, as few things are more tedious than reading about someone's unhappy schooldays — even Alec Waugh, writing about Lancing, causes the spirits to sag.

I am determined to be positive about Geelong Grammar School. In my day the school had many excellent aspects, and this is even more the case in the current enlightened era of co-education. The first of these was, of course, its headmaster, James Ralph Darling.[1] An awe-inspiring but never remote figure, he used to descend on the junior school once a term to read our reports, eyeing each of us as he did so.

My first year at Barrabool House involved a kindly housemaster, B. R. A. Coulter, and an occasionally explosive but intellectually stimulating form master, A. Todd. However, after the friendliness of Cranbrook I was unprepared for the comparative roughness of my reception. In retrospect, I can see that the combination of priggishness and reserve I seemed to exude served only to stimulate my schoolmates against me. Barrabool, though, was a haven of peace compared to Manifold House where I spent the next four years. The mockery prevalent there took varied and ingenious forms and although I was by no means the only victim, I always felt that I got more than my fair share. Of course it

With Caroline and our parents at Barford in 1946.

was my own silly fault, as one or two well-intentioned friends tried to point out to me, and I would have had a much happier time if I had made myself conform to the accepted standards.

My housemaster was quite unpredictable in his attitude to his house and its inmates and on one memorable occasion, when he had taken off with a few cronies from among his prefects to one of his seaside haunts, there was a near-riot back at Manifold House which had to be quelled by JRD himself. I recall with pleasure the blessed escape provided by the music school, where I spent hours practising the clarinet in a successful effort to join the school orchestra. It had excellent facilities, as did the art school, presided over by the renowned Bauhaus artist Ludwig Hirschfeld-Mack, rescued by JRD from a prisoner of war camp. He was a delightful man and I am grateful to him for keeping alive the flame kindled at Cranbrook by Eric Wilson.

Other happy memories are the English classes of the witty and eccentric P. L. J. Westcott. No one was better at inspiring interest in the glories of Keats, Shelley and Byron, or at ridiculing the more idiotic poems that had found their way into our textbooks. One of them began, 'Booth led boldly with his big bass drum Are you washed in the blood of the Lamb?' The second line was repeated at regular intervals and as Westcott said, if you asked that question in a

Melbourne pub the reply would be, 'No, I use Palmolive'. The devotion to Keats
he inspired in his class surprised his colleagues. On one occasion, his students
were all seen walking round the school, heads buried in a book of Keats' poetry.
In fact we had all been given twenty-four hours to learn 'Ode on a Grecian Urn',
as a punishment for trespassing on his good nature and neglecting to learn
something else. I can still recite it from start to finish.

I have always been grateful to my father for insisting that I learn Latin and
Greek. The study of both provides an indispensable insight into the English
language and both were particularly well-taught at Geelong. At various times
I had as Latin masters K. C. Masterman, J. F. Gammell (on exchange from
Winchester) and R. G. Tanner from the University of New England, Armidale.
John Gammell was a very good actor. He played Falstaff in the school production
of *Henry IV Part I* and, as well as inspiring us with his rendition of the *Aeneid*
and the *Georgics*, gave spirited performances of the major speeches in *King Lear*
and *Othello* in his English periods to the same fortunate class. Surprisingly, he

was equally successful at portraying
Jane Austen's Emma, her stupid
father and extraordinary aunt.
Godfrey Tanner had a beautiful voice
and a wicked sense of humour, both
of which he employed with great
effect to the *Aeneid*, the *Odes* of
Catullus and — one of Cicero's
stranger defences — *Pro Staieno*,
which involved a complicated
Roman murder by poisoning.

My Greek master was J. B.
Ponder, a softly spoken man with a
sly sense of humour whose nickname
of 'Leopard' seemed very appropriate. He persuaded JRD to
establish Greek as an alternative to
chemistry and shepherded his class
of two through to matriculation,
although I later wished we had had
a more exciting play than Euripedes'
Hercules Furens, presumably chosen
because there was no murder, rape or
incest in it.

With Granny Wilson en route to Romano's, 1946.

'Lady Jim' (right) with Lady Mary Ward (left) and Ruby Warry at the 'coming out' dance given at Fairwater for Caroline on 16 December 1949.

The acting palm, though, would have to have gone to JRD, who every now and then decided to read a play to the combined sixth forms. I particularly enjoyed his playing every part in *The School For Scandal*, and can still hear him do Lady Sneerwell. A talent for acting must surely be one of the qualities inherent in a good schoolmaster.

Another teacher I must mention is the friendly, methodical A. J. Spear, who struggled manfully and eventually successfully to get me through Leaving Certificate physics. Thereafter I was able to absorb myself more rewardingly in the humanities. Athletic prowess, as the reader has probably gathered by now, eluded me, although I achieved some modest success in swimming and sprinting. The only trophy I ever won was for the sack race.

The chapel was central to school life, made more so by JRD's justly famous sermons, some of which were subsequently published. Unfortunately, he never did get round to all of the seven deadly sins. I recall the Archbishop of Canterbury, resplendent at JRD's suggestion in golden cope and mitre and preceded by the Canterbury Cross, processing up the aisle to the indignation of our evangelical chaplain.

Halfway through my last year I was allocated, in an act of kindness by my house master, to the sanctuary of study passage, which made life much more comfortable and enabled me to devote more time to my work. I matriculated in 1950 with second class honours in Latin and French and passes in English expression, English literature and Greek.

Strangely enough, I seriously considered returning to Geelong for a second sixth form year, then not unusual, as JRD was form master of the top sixth form. He recommended in my report that I should do this. In many ways it was a pity I did not, as 1951 was to prove a largely wasted year — a fact I am not proud of. My father's idea was that, after five years at a school in Victoria, I should get to know the city in which I was to live and work, and also some of his friends and business acquaintances. I would also attend Sydney University for a year before going to Balliol College, Oxford, in the Michaelmas term of 1952.

The first objective was achieved, but the second proved to be a miserable failure. In spite of much kindness and encouragement from Hanne, who made me feel very welcome at Barford, with many of my friends still at school or in Melbourne I was unsettled and felt no real incentive to work very hard at my Arts course of English, Latin and philosophy. Towards the end of May I went to Paris to see my mother and stayed until the end of June. I conceived the idea of either staying on and working in England or returning briefly to Sydney to sit for the University exams. Then, so I thought, I could get back to England and prepare for Oxford. However, when I returned I discovered that, through

The Black and White Ball at the Trocadero, October 1951. James Fairfax with Christine Wincott, Frank McDonald and Barbara Potter. Photo: Daily Telegraph.

missing several tutorials, I had forfeited my right to sit for the exams. I then had to persuade the university authorities to let me sit for exams I did not think I could pass anyway. I should have made a clean breast of it to my father straightaway. As it was, I waited with resignation for the cataclysm which soon followed: failure in all three subjects.

My only confidant had been Granny Wilson, who seemed to understand some of my difficulties, but it was a different matter trying to explain them to my father. I was helped in this by JRD with whom I stayed at Geelong for a weekend and whose advice I sought. (He and his wife Margaret had been fellow passengers on the *Stratheden* with my father and Hanne when the latter were on their honeymoon in 1948, and had made friends with them.) I drove to Harrington Park to receive the predictable and deserved hauling over the coals, although my father later took the trouble to go to Geelong and see JRD about his errant son and returned in a more understanding frame of mind.

My sister Caroline's education had followed rather an erratic course. She left Ascham early in 1947 to join my mother and Pierre in Tokyo and attended a convent school there before going on with them to Europe in 1948, where she went to what was then called a 'finishing school', run by our cousin Colleen Norman[2] near Interlaken in Switzerland. She was never a particularly diligent pupil at Ascham, but many years later, when her own daughters Louise (now Mrs Gary Dobson), Alice, and Emily (now Mrs Jerome Ehlers) were there, she became a most enthusiastic supporter, producing with Annette Dupree a most interesting and lively history of the school and its many celebrated old girls for its centenary in 1986. In 1949 she was back in Sydney for her coming-out dance at Fairwater. Before leaving for Paris early in 1951, she left me her Morris Minor coupé (which two years later I was to wrap round a lamp-post in London's Hyde Park). She also left me with instructions to make friends and mingle with my own age group (lists of suitable contemporaries were provided), not hers, which I largely ignored. Her parting act was to organise me into a party for the Matrons' Ball which, in common with others like it, was a breeding ground for matchmaking.

I have always enjoyed the society of older people and still do, so by the time my disastrous university year was drawing to a close, I had made a number of friends in Caroline's group. The first half of 1952 was indeed spent very pleasantly with Prue Bavin, Juliet Winchcombe, Beverly Belisario, Barbara Potter, Christine Wincott, David Burns, Bruce Kirkpatrick, Andrew Clayton, Frank McDonald, Bruce and John Arnott and John Dangerfield. These friendships were to continue after my three years at Oxford, with the addition of husbands and wives, although our bridge-playing became less intense. My future brother-in-law, Philip Simpson, who was somewhat older, I did not come to know until after Oxford.

I had been taught bridge at Sospel by my grandmother, who often argued across the table with my father, and in Hanne's time we played a lot both at Harrington Park and Sospel. My grandmother continued to play until she was ninety, her table getting younger as her contemporaries died. One of the most redoubtable of these was the marvellous Lady Reading,[3] (Mabel) who used to tick me off whenever her daughter, Sue Crossing (Mrs Anthony Scarisbrick), took me to the Davis Cup when I should have been at a lecture. Another friend who kept a kindly eye on me was Pauline Allen who, with her husband Dick, lived at Edgecliff Square and had a house at Palm Beach. I always loved going to both places and experiencing the acerbic wit of my hostess.

There was also dinner and bridge with Nesta and Gwendolyn Griffiths at their Silchester flat, the fourth player being carefully selected from the group mentioned above. These two remarkable ladies were very fond of my mother and in her absence 'adopted' me, although I had been going to Silchester with Caroline since I was a small child. They used to take us on all sorts of excursions when we were young — swimming at Nielsen Park (they both swam there as long as their health permitted) and to zoos and museums.

Many have taken up the pen where Nesta left off, but her books on the history of important early New South Wales houses reawakened Australians' long-dormant interest in their architectural and historical heritage, which spread beyond this state. Nesta tended to be idiosyncratic in her choice of families about whose houses she wrote, notable architecture and historical factors not being her only criteria. Gwendolyn, a highly intelligent woman with a nervous giggle and a devotee of Proust, outlived her younger sister whose mind sadly failed in her last years. I recall their last dinner party at the Macquarie Club, which was a great gathering of the clans. Gwendolyn lived long enough to come to lunch at my Lindsay Avenue house with her American niece Valerie Brannon and cousin Valentine Adams.

The first wedding I remember attending as a child was that of Philippa Stephen to Denis Allen in 1943, but after leaving school the first was Susan Watt to Laurence Street.[4] In my ignorance and to my mortification, I turned up at St Mark's at 6 pm in a suit and had to race home and change, with some difficulty as I had only just acquired them, into white tie and tails, arriving at the reception perspiring and bursting out of unaccustomed starched dress shirt and wing collar.

I shall return to the Sydney scene in later pages, but before moving briefly to my Oxford years, I must mention the three overseas trips which so far I had taken.

Being subjected at the age of eleven to the traumatic experience of one's parents' divorce may present emotional problems, but it certainly also presents the opportunity for travel if either of them lives overseas. Ever since my mother had described to me her trips to Europe by KLM in the 1930s, the prospect of travelling to all those exciting and glamorous places had been my dearest wish. In 1946 she had wanted me to visit her in China (at that stage she and Pierre had moved to Peking) but my father, to my lasting regret (although perhaps understandably on the grounds that it would unsettle my first year at a new school), had put his foot down. By Christmas 1947 it was a different story and early in December I set off at midnight from Rose Bay in a Sunderland flying boat bound for Singapore via Batavia, farewelled by an anxious father and grandmother. The cabin was divided into a series of compartments holding four, with bunks for the women on the upper deck.

At Singapore I was met by Arthur Goodwill and his Italian wife, who drove me to their house at Tanglin where I spent three happy days. At Bangkok a somewhat distracted French ambassador had been asked to look after me and I was driven round that then delightful and romantic city by one of his officers. In Hong Kong the charming Jobez family took me to their bosom for five days while I waited for an RAF plane prepared to take me as 'luggage' to the air base at Iwakuni in southern Japan. Each day, travelling part of the way by rickshaw, I ascended the Peak to the French embassy for a delicious lunch with kind Madame Jobez, her daughter Michelle, who showed me around, and sometimes the ambassador. More prosaically, I had tiffin in the evening at Kowloon's Arlington Hotel, long since pulled down.

A Sunderland stripped for cargo finally took about six of us to Iwakuni. The temperature in the cabin was below zero and we spent most of the time running up and down trying to get warm. On arrival, however, I was whisked off to a very comfortable Japanese house where Air Vice-Marshal Boucher, the RAF commander in Japan, was living with an exceptionally beautiful French lady. The next day I was put on the train for Tokyo and as we passed Hiroshima, I was reading John Hershey's brilliant and moving account of the bombing.

I was met at the station by Pierre and Caroline, my mother being in hospital awaiting the birth of my brother Edward two days later, on 21 December. They took me to Nagaoka House, not far from the Imperial Palace, which turned out to be a slightly art deco two-storey building in creamy-white brick with a good-sized garden. It had been requisitioned for my stepfather from the former Marquis Nagaoka, from an ancient Kyoto family, who was living with his wife in a wooden cottage at the back. The head of the French mission was General Pechkoff, a short man with one arm, bright blue eyes and a bristling moustache. He was an illegitimate son of Maxim Gorky by a titled Russian lady. His aide-de-camp was the fat, outrageous Roger Pignol, who became our particular friend.

James Fairfax with Binzuru-sonja, a god of healing, at Todai-ji Temple, Nara, Japan, January 1948.

He ended his days as *sous-préfet* of Nontrons in the Dordogne, where I was to stay with him twenty years later.

My mother, in spite of being in her forty-first year, soon recovered from the birth and we set off for Kyoto by military train, the four of us sharing a compartment, to stay for a few days in the faded grandeur of the original Miyako Hotel. We were almost its only occupants and certainly the only tourists in Kyoto and Nara early in January. At the Todai-ji temple in Nara, the Buddhist deity Binzuru-sonja, a god of healing, cured an outbreak of boils on the back of my neck.

Being the only mission wife resident in Tokyo, my mother was called on to do a great deal of entertaining, which usually took the form of cocktail parties. General MacArthur, who had been appointed commander of the occupation forces in Japan, and his wife seldom attended any kind of social gathering, but I recall General Eichelberger, his deputy, being there. My mother, with other diplomatic wives, used to go to tea with Mrs MacArthur and met the general several times. In fact we only once saw MacArthur, entering his office at the Dai Ichi building between lines of bowing Japanese. Tokyo had sustained a fair amount of bomb damage and there were few tall buildings standing. Frank Lloyd Wright's Imperial Hotel had survived the war and earthquake of 1927 only, sadly, to be pulled down after the war.

I can recall driving past many old wooden houses to the Meiji shrine and the Asakusa and other temples and old cemeteries. I went twice to the war crimes trials, a fascinating experience where I saw Tojo among the defendants. Other regular expeditions were to the PX stores and to the movies, in the raucous atmosphere of the Ernie Pyle Theatre. I was interested to see, late in 1988, that

General William C. Chase, who showed me over the Seventh American Cavalry Division, had died, well into his nineties.

I was totally reconciled to my mother's remarriage, and Pierre was very kind to me both in Japan and on my first visit to Paris. He took me to stay at a *ryokan* (an ancient and traditional Japanese inn) at Hakone, a marvellous experience and one I was unable to repeat until I stayed at the Tawaraya in Kyoto in 1984. All too soon it was back to Iwakuni and a two-day wait, this time in a room at the barracks, while a Lancaster bomber was made ready to convey a mixture of British and Australian military personnel plus myself to Sydney via Manila and Darwin, the nine of us sitting in a row along one side of this very narrow plane. It broke down for two

M. E. Fairfax and Pierre at Edward's christening, Tokyo, January 1948.

days in Manila and we were not allowed to leave the base. We seem to have spent most of the time playing a card game called Ricketty Kate. So ended my Japanese adventure. It instilled in me a love of travel that has never left me.

A fifteen year-old schoolboy's first impressions of Paris would probably be of doubtful interest to most readers. My main reason for mentioning the trip is that I first met Pierre's remarkable mother, who became 'Grandmère' to Caroline and me, and 'Ma Mère' to my mother. In December 1948 I took a Constellation to London with overnight stops in Singapore, at Raffles Hotel, Karachi and Rome, accompanied by the *Herald*'s London correspondent, Irvine Douglas, who later joined the *Mirror*.

My mother and Pierre had an apartment at 124 Avenue Victor Hugo, off the Etoile, with the faithful Elsie in attendance. It was not long before Grandmère turned up, enfolding us with affection and presents, accompanied by Pierre's sister, Fanny. Grandmère's own apartment in the Square du Rôule, off the Rue St Honoré, had floors and walls covered with Turkish and Persian rugs acquired by her husband, the Admiral, and every piece of furniture was loaded with objects from the Near East. She was a woman of great culture and discernment, who remained devoted to us after her son's marriage broke up. In later years I used to walk from the Lancaster Hotel to her apartment, 'vers cinq heures', and spend the next two and a half hours with her, neither of us drawing breath. Paris I loved as soon as I saw it and we rocketed all over it by metro, but it was never quite the same after Grandmère's death.

Perhaps the other event worth mentioning was an evening at the Club des Champs Elysées, where Josephine Baker was appearing. Before we left for it my mother said, 'Now remember, darling, the only thing that will be between you and Josephine Baker will be a banana skin and your mother.' Unfortunately, Josephine's banana skin days were over, but she gave a great performance and was vociferously applauded by us all, including Orson Welles and a gaggle of lesser stars whom I was taken over to meet. Pierre took me one evening to what were clearly some of his old haunts in Montmartre, where we were joined by two 'ladies'. One of them had to struggle to entertain me but I did my best to respond before Pierre decided we had better go home.

On this trip, too, I first met the glamorously zany Sheila Fourcaud, a first cousin of Val Fairfax (Sheila was described by Joy Packer in *Pack And Follow* as having the face of Greta Garbo and the character of Harpo Marx). Her husband Pierre — M. Le Colonel, as we called him — was a Français Libre friend of Pierre Gilly and half Russian. They lived in a beautiful ground floor apartment, with its own garden, in the Avenue Charles Flocquet near the Invalides.[5] Here I went to the twenty-first birthday party of her stepdaughter, Annie, where I met cousin

Valerie's sister, Betty, married to Comte Henri de Janzé. Sheila became one of my mother's closest friends and was to figure largely in our European life.

By my 1951 trip, my mother and Pierre had moved to a rather grander apartment in the Rondpoint Bugeaud, just off the Avenue Foch, with nurse Margery Timms looking after my brother Edward, then four years old. Caroline was there too, and as well as the usual excursions, we went to night-spots such as the Folies Bergères and the Lido, both of which I loved. The Bal Tabarin, to which I had been introduced on my previous visit by Baptistine Augustin-Thierry, a lively and amusing friend of Pierre's, was the place to go. But it was on this trip that my mother and I, sent by Caroline to a restaurant where a famous

At Maxim's, Paris. James Fairfax with Prince Hansel of Pless, Caroline and M. E. Fairfax in 1951.

guitarist was playing and whom we scarcely noticed, had our first heart-to-heart chat. Curiously, we had never been together long enough, nor had I been old enough, for this to happen before.

Among the subjects discussed was my grandparents' separation. When I asked why this had occurred, my mother replied, surprisingly but logically, 'Because they never should have married each other in the first place.' Religion and belief was another subject. Until then my mother had had no particular devotion to the church, but she told me she was facing a certain crisis. She did not want to discuss it further at that stage but I guessed it concerned Pierre. She had become involved with the Moral Rearmament group, which surprised me, but was delighted to discover that I also had the solace of the Christian faith. In fact, after a period as an Anglican, she later became a convert to the Catholic faith, but that is another story.

I returned to Australia worried by the situation I had left in Paris. There had been no indication from Pierre that anything was wrong but he was away for most of my visit. My forebodings were to prove correct as, not long after, my grandparents and I received letters saying that the marriage had broken up because he had resumed seeing a lady with whom he had previously been involved. My mother was naturally devastated as she was still very much in love with him and had had no idea about this involvement. A little later I was staying with Helen Rutledge at Gidleigh. The day I was leaving, she had stayed in bed with a cold and when I went to say goodbye to her, I noticed a letter from my mother in her hand and *The Blessing* by Nancy Mitford lying on the bed. It was an ironic coincidence which also gave some amusement to my mother, unhappy though she was. My grandparents were wildly indignant: 'Dreadful bounder' said Grandfather. My grandmother, who was of Irish Protestant descent, was inclined to blame it on Pierre's Catholic background, even though he was a professed atheist.

Any plans I had made about a quick return to England, I soon realised, were impractical. They would have required my father's consent which it was now clear would not be forthcoming. After my disastrous performance at the university exams later in 1951, over which my father was finally much more understanding than I deserved, he decided I should have private tuition in history from a university lecturer called Ken Cable, who was going up to Cambridge for the Michaelmas term early in October when I was due at Balliol College, Oxford. My father mapped out a course covering, in the main, eighteenth and nineteenth-century English history and I spent the first half of 1952 doing an essay for Mr Cable every ten days or so, when he would come to Barford to hear me read it and assign the next one. It was, in fact, a forerunner of the Oxford tutorial system, which was usually a far more arduous two essays a week. I cannot therefore claim that my 'course' was particularly demanding, and I see from my diary that my social life continued apace, largely with the earlier-mentioned group. Prince's and Romano's seemed to figure prominently.

Visits to friends in the country alternated with Harrington Park and Sospel, where my grandmother still had hopes, not to be realised, of turning me into a golfer. In January I laconically recorded 'Bushfire' during a stay at Gidleigh with Andrew Dangerfield. The night spent on a mountain range fighting the fire under the sometimes alarming direction of our kindly but occasionally irascible host, Colonel Tom Rutledge, returned vividly. I lost both Andrew and the colonel during the course of the night, but managed to get a lift back on a truck to the Gidleigh gate towards dawn and faced the long walk to the house. The next night Andrew and I went to dinner at Currendooley where, during a game of charades, I afforded some amusement to the Paddy Osbornes and their guests by imitating Tom Rutledge directing the firefighters.

I recall the first dance I attended at Camden Park, given by Sir Reginald and Lady Stanham. Lady Stanham, born Helen Macarthur-Onslow, had inherited the historic old house from her father, General 'Jim', under circumstances that caused a family feud, of which there are occasional rumbles even today. I arranged to stay at Harrington Park with Prue Bavin, Juliet Winchcombe and Frank McDonald, chaperoned by my cousins Vincent and Nancy as my father and Hanne were away. It would have been unthinkable to stay there unchaperoned.

As the year drew on, my father and I often had talks about life at Oxford as we walked round the Leura golf links. He regarded Oxford as one of the most important experiences of his life. It established his intellectual qualities and gave him some independence from his mother. JRD had told me, while I was staying at the headmaster's house on a return visit to Geelong, that the first two terms would be singularly lonely but the remainder could be among the happiest and most rewarding of my life. I was to learn the truth of his statement, even though academic rewards continued to elude me.

I was booked to fly to Vancouver by BCPA on 2 August. The previous week was taken up with farewells to my numerous elderly relatives. I was taken to lunch at the Yacht Club, Kirribilli, by Granny Wilson, with whom I lunched almost once a week at Romano's or the Macquarie Club in Bligh Street, and her elder sister, my great-aunt Claire. The latter had a crackling sense of humour (her late husband was the tennis player, Dudley Webb, who often partnered Norman Brookes, husband of Dame Mabel, the well-known Melbourne hostess and charity worker).

Then there was lunch with my grandfather at the Australian Club, dinner with my grandmother at Fairwater and a visit to my recently widowed great-aunt Marguerite at Woniora. Vincent and Nancy gave a splendid dinner for me at Prince's, where I had been the previous night with Joan and Dinger Bode and Sue Playfair (Sue was to marry John Atwill while I was at Oxford). There were farewell bridge evenings at the Griffiths with Prue Bavin and David Burns and at Beverly Belisario's house two doors from Barford. Even though we had been neighbours from childhood we first met properly at a dance at Rosemont where, gazing myopically at a signed photograph of Pandit Nehru, I apparently said to her, 'Jesus, it's the Pope!' I also went to lunch at the *Herald* office with my father, Rupert Henderson, Angus McLachlan and Hugh McClure Smith.

This was the life I was to leave for over three years before returning for my thirty-two year association with the Fairfax company.

4

A CIVILISED GUIDE TO LIFE

On 2 August 1952 I departed as arranged for Vancouver with stops at Fiji, Canton Island, Honolulu and San Francisco — an inordinate number by today's standards — and on the evening of my arrival next day, I caught the Canadian Pacific Railway to Montreal. We crossed the Rockies in a carriage open to the elements at the back of the train, a scenic experience only equalled by the gorges of the Yangtse river many years later. After leaving Banff I recall only endless wheat and corn fields as we travelled through Calgary and Winnipeg before arriving at Montreal, where I caught the *Empress of France* to Liverpool. On that cold Atlantic crossing I was mistaken for the Earl of Dundonald and introduced to the delights of bingo.

My mother and Caroline met the boat train in London on 15 August and conveyed me to the Cadogan Hotel in Sloane Street, notable for having accommodated Oscar Wilde before his arrest in 1895. The next day I was put into a morning suit and taken to Miranda Casey's wedding to Gerald Selous, at which Caroline was a bridesmaid, and the following day we drove to Paris, stopping briefly to see five-year-old Edward who was spending the holidays with nurse Margery's parents in Canterbury. He was not to accompany us to Majorca — 'Poor little Edward never goes anywhere,' Nursie said reproachfully — where we were to share a villa with some French friends of my mother. The day after we arrived in Paris we headed south, carefully selecting 'one turret' hotels at Brive and Narbonne from *Michelin*.

In pre-public company days, we were all three habitually short of money. My mother was struggling with the expense of keeping up the apartment in

Our flat at Elm Park Gardens (ground floor right) with Caroline, M. E. Fairfax and Edward, early in the 1950s.

the Rondpoint Bugeaud, to which Pierre, who had now moved out, made only sporadic contributions. I was on a modest Exchange Control allowance, out of which I had to pay my university and college fees. It was around this time, too, that the private Fairfax company decided to pass a dividend that made our situation even more sticky.

We crossed from Barcelona to Palma over rough seas in a leaky old car ferry and saw, to our joy, Sheila Fourcaud waving to us from the dock with her adopted daughter Xenia. They were staying outside Palma, but we drove to Cala d'Or, an hour away up the east coast, over roads so appalling I seemed to spend a lot of time changing tyres and taking them to be patched at sleepy garages.

Sharing the house with us was Francoise Goussault, whose first husband, Lord Ashley, had been killed in the war. His first wife, Sylvia, had married Clark Gable, allegedly largely because of her resemblance to his late wife Carole Lombard. Francoise's two children — Anthony aged fourteen, and Frances aged twelve — were also there. Anthony bore his father's courtesy title and was to succeed his grandfather as Earl of Shaftesbury. The family seat, which I visited many years later, was one of the great Dorset houses: St Giles House at Wimborne St Giles, with its central block attributed to Inigo Jones and its magnificent collection of Chippendale furniture and other treasures now sadly dispersed (although the Shaftesbury family still live in part of the house). The original Ashley, together with Clifford, Arlington, Buckingham and Lauderdale, had been one of Charles II's cabal, a useful new word they contributed to the language, and the great reforming Earl of the nineteenth century was also a forebear.

A member of the household at Cala d'Or was a charming, startlingly attractive and statuesque blonde called Arlette Boucard, whose father, a famous doctor, had invented several patent medicines. She clearly had many admirers, some of whom turned up from time to time at our villa. Considering Francoise and my mother were fairly recent friends and Caroline and I had never met the household before, we all got on well. The villa was beautifully situated on a rocky promontory, with a stepladder descending directly into a crystal-clear sea.

Anthony and I, together with the occasional other male guest, slept in a small house down the road. The first room I occupied had a lavatory perched prison-like next to a washbasin. Cistern and basin both crashed to the floor the first night. I thankfully escaped from this curious Spanish arrangement and moved to another room with less plumbing. We stayed there for a month, with Francoise and family departing after the first two weeks.

Among the visitors who stayed at the local hotel were Sir Walter[1] and Lady Monckton. Sir Walter was a fascinating and amusing man. Stimulated by Spanish sun and *jerez*, he told countless anecdotes of his interesting and varied career. He was also a Fellow of Balliol, and I saw him a number of times at dinners or lectures during my time there.

Majorca's most distinguished permanent resident was the writer Robert Graves, who used to greet the few visitors to his tiny fishing village of Deya with great courtesy and charm. We chatted to him a number of times, lunching there at the little *chiringuito*. Not far away was the villa where Chopin lived for a time with George Sand.

It was in Palma that I saw my first bullfight and I must admit to being carried away by the colour, atmosphere and excitement, and the combination of courage, skill and cruelty. Far better writers than I have described this curious feature of the Spanish character and tradition. I have enjoyed bullfights on many subsequent trips to Spain though I am the first to admit that this sits oddly and inconsistently with a passionate devotion to animals and wildlife, and certainly I have never been able to come to terms with the part played by the picadors. At its best a bullfight should be a duel between man and beast on equal terms before the inevitable; at its worst, it can be a very messy spectacle indeed.

In preparation for my Modern History course I was supposed to be reading Bede's *Historia Ecclesiastica* in Latin, which our idyllic surroundings and the *jerez* and other wines of Spain did not make any easier. On the way back to Paris Francoise very kindly arranged for us to stay a night at her converted mill, Le Moulin, beautifully situated with its millstream at Condrieu near Vienne, and then it was back to England for me.

On 9 October I presented myself at Balliol and moved into a nice set of rooms on the top floor of staircase 20 (now demolished), with a view across the inner quad to the chapel, library and Master's lodgings. What I had not realised was that, being a Freshman and Commoner, I would be sharing the sitting room. Exhibitioners also shared in their first year but not Scholars. In my case it was with Bill Podmore, a small, earnest man from Manchester with a good sense of humour. Our contrasting personalities seemed to hit it off quite well and, by the time of the Hilary term after Christmas, I was participating in a number of activities with a group drawn from our own year. Most were from the Modern History faculty, which was the largest, with some from the PPE (Politics, Philosophy and Economics) and English.

At this stage we joined far too many clubs and societies devoted to all sorts of interests: academic, cultural and political. They ranged from the serious to the frivolous. In the former category was the Dervorguilla, for historians, named after the woman who jointly founded the college with her husband, John Balliol, in 1263. About midway between was the Arnold, whose members conducted two or three debates a term, drank a great deal of port and wore red corduroy bow ties. About halfway through my time, a group from public-school and county-squire backgrounds broke away from the Arnold and revived a former society, the Brackenbury. It was quite a bitter split. One or two leaders of the young Turks were bored with some of the more establishment Arnold figures, and the result was the green stock of Brackenbury. A not always friendly rivalry existed between the two clubs and once, during the course of a rather bibulous Arnold meeting, I was asked to remove my guest, who was chairman of the

Brackenbury. Both Matthew Arnold and Miss Hannah Brackenbury — the latter the most munificent of the college's 'pious benefactors' — would have been startled at the tenor of some of the debates, but some years later both clubs amalgamated to more serious purpose.

One often joined clubs to hear the speakers: the Liberal Club produced George Santayana, Salvador da Madariaga and, surprisingly, Dr Hewlett Johnson, the 'Red Dean' of Canterbury. The English Association featured David Cecil and Rose Macaulay. Her discourse, titled 'A Man's Woman and a Woman's Man', was about the capacity of writers to portray convincingly the opposite sex, and after giving a brilliant introduction she encouraged her audience to participate with questions and examples. I was sorry in retrospect that I had yet to read Proust and Patrick White.

We followed enthusiastically the debates in the Oxford Union where wit was considered preferable to bombast and cool-headed argument defeated vehemence and indignation. Passionate argument was a rare occurrence, even in a debate on the Irish Question which included the fiery Foreign Minister from Eire, Sean MacBride. In fact a curious feature of my three years at Oxford was the lack of political ferment among undergraduates, which indeed reflected the mood of the country. These were the last years of the second Churchill administration and the great man had instructed Walter Monckton, his Minister for Labour, that industrial disputes were to be settled at all costs, a policy that caused a few problems for his successors.

On the international front, America was preoccupied with the activities of Senator McCarthy and the inability or unwillingness of Eisenhower to do anything about them, while Russia was, in 1953, to go through the trauma of Stalin's death, the effects of which would keep her busy for several years. On the evening of the day that the bloodthirsty Russian ruler was called to his reward, a few of us were having coffee in someone's rooms after Hall when one of our number with known communist sympathies burst in and announced in a stricken voice, 'The master is dead'. We looked at each other in shock and confusion, assuming that he was referring to the greatly liked and respected Master of our college, Sir David Lindsay Keir, rather than the monster of Moscow.

The Korean war had ended in 1953, while the Russian invasion of Hungary and the Suez crisis occurred the year after I went down. A repercussion of the Korean war caused the only potentially nasty scene that I can recall. A woman member of the British Communist Party was to address its Oxford counterpart on alleged atrocities she had seen committed by Commonwealth and US troops in South Korean prison camps, and the Dean of Balliol had unwittingly given permission for a lecture room in the college to be used. We glared in silence at the lady when she arrived and then piled into the lecture room. The Oxford party members attempted to eject us, as we did not have invitations, but we insisted on our right to be present and all hell broke loose. Finally there was grudging acceptance that they could not force us to leave a room in our own college and we stayed for the lecture, making appropriate interjections at what we regarded as the traitorous garbage we were listening to.

The invasion of Hungary by Russia in 1956 was to cause Christopher Hill, one of my history tutors who succeeded Keir as Master, to leave the Communist Party, an act he made public. It was truly the calm before the storm; I cannot think of any period since that has been so free from international tension. The rearmament of West Germany through the European Defence Community was one major issue; as the New Statesman put it, we were caught between the devil and the EDC.

Universities were far less politically minded then. Oxford did not so much reinforce such political beliefs as I then held, as not discourage me from holding such beliefs. I never went through a socialist phase and it is interesting to note that, of around twenty first year Modern History undergraduates in my year from all kinds of backgrounds, there were only two socialists and one communist. In the development of my own beliefs, there was a gradually awakening inspiration but in no way an instantaneous conversion to anything.

I suppose that I and a lot of my contemporaries, other than those involved in the political clubs and societies, adopted something of an apolitical attitude. It is hard to recall whether we were aware of our good fortune at the time. There must have been a few Cassandras around, but they failed to shatter the tranquillity of our little world. The atmosphere induced, in me at least, a somewhat casual and inconsistent attitude towards my work, something I now genuinely regret. While I certainly gained greatly in a number of ways from my Oxford experience, unlike my father, I failed to take full advantage of the intellectual opportunities it offered.

Of my tutors, Dick Southern, later Sir Richard and Chichele Professor of Modern History, was passionately involved with Anglo-Saxon and Medieval England, a passion I was unable to share at the time. Softly spoken with a gently malicious wit, he dropped a few pearls to Freshmen, but reserved his energies for those who pursued the early medieval period and the excitements of studying monastic life and rent rolls.

Christopher Hill, another of my tutors, is still renowned as one of the foremost historians of the Stuart period and, when I later told him that this period turned out to be one of my scheduled gaps, his characteristic reply was, 'Why the hell didn't you tell me, then we could have gone to a pub?'.

With the Australian Hugh Stretton[2] I was totally absorbed in nineteenth-century England. I should, of course, have persevered in studying the periods I found less interesting. My absorption in the eighteenth and nineteenth centuries would then have had a proper balance, possibly resulting in second-class honours instead of the third with which I emerged after a twenty-minute viva, an indication that I was a borderline case. (The viva is an oral examination held after 'Schools', the main exams, and it can last two or three minutes or half an hour.)

My first two terms were spent on a study of the aforementioned Bede, a curious hotchpotch described as Historical Geography, and a choice of Locke's *Essays on Human Understanding* or Maine's *Ancient Law*. It transpired that I was the first person to choose the latter for quite a number of years and, according to Stretton, I produced a good paper on it in the Preliminary exams conducted by the colleges.

My tutor for the eighteenth century was a bluff hearty character called A. B. Rodger, who had a passion for naval and military history and whose hero was Napoleon. Unfortunately, he regarded the civilisation and refinements of the century as too trivial to rate much interest and he was even relatively unmoved by the fascinating period of the 'Princes Éclairés', that remarkable trio Catherine, Frederick and Joseph. Of course, the really enlightening biographies had yet to be written. Apart from the *Dictionary of National Biography*, our sources were the Oxford and Cambridge histories — indeed Sir Maurice Powicke (author of *The 13th Century 1216–1307*) at nearly ninety was still perambulating gently in and out of Balliol. Nancy Mitford was in Paris but her perceptive and entertaining studies of Frederick the Great and Madame de Pompadour were some years in the future. I never found Rodger a particularly sympathetic character and, as a result, the bits of the eighteenth century I delved into tended to be of my choosing rather than his.

His successor as Dean was the college Chaplain, the Reverend Francis Leader MacCarthy-Willis-Bund, who was inclined to conceal a true devotion to his calling behind a somewhat eighteenth-century attitude to life. He had a marvellously wicked sense of humour but his sermons, beautifully composed and delivered in his melodious Anglo-Irish accent, were a tribute to the Age of Reason. He was, in fact, the head of a branch of the Irish clan MacCarthy, his title being The MacCarthy Reagh, and the Willis-Bund had been added by a family inheritance. He became a particular friend of mine, and consented to be patron of a dining club several of us formed called L'Ancien Régime, the purpose of which was to have one dinner a term and in a vague way uphold the best

Dinner of the Ancien Régime, Balliol College, 1955. **Front row from left:** *Keith Robertson, Tom Devas, Michael Persse, John Keegan (token revolutionary), Jeffrey Wickham, Hon. Richard Bigham.* **Back row:** *James Fairfax, Simon Wyndham-Lewis (guest from Magdalene), Rev. F. L. McCarthy, Roy Napier, Dermott Cross, Stephen Younger, Peter Stein, David Landale.*

principles of pre-revolutionary France. We used to dress for the dinners in an approximation of the late eighteenth century, but there were sometimes some very strange variations from other periods. We held one dinner at the Hotel de Paris at Bray and when we marched in, headed by the Dean and Chaplain of Balliol wearing a high evangelical clergyman's collar, the inmates burst into applause.

I mentioned earlier that I gained greatly from my Oxford experience, even though I failed to take sufficient advantage of the intellectual opportunities Balliol provided. I find this hard to put into words without sounding self-indulgent or apparently out of touch with realities, but for those lucky enough to be there and willing to seek it out, Oxford could provide a civilised guide to a well-rounded future life, whatever one's particular discipline or interests happened to be. Of course other seats of learning provided the same thing, but to old Oxonians there was something special about Oxford, its atmosphere, background and way of life. As Dornford Yates said, 'and so we sat in the shady old quadrangle and talked of Oxford and of the time that a man wasted there, which is profitable beyond measure'.

I differed from many of my fellow undergraduates in that I would be joining a family business rather than having to go through the rigours of interviews, after Schools, with the talent scouts that many major companies sent to the universities. But remarkably few undergraduates were obsessed with their degrees to the extent that they missed out on the broad humanising influence of the place itself. In spite of the increasing encroachments of many aspects of modern life and the greater demands made on today's undergraduates, I believe Oxford still preserves its own unique ambience and contribution.

My passion for travel had already been increased by several trips and during term time at Oxford I managed to explore the surrounding countryside, particularly the Cotswolds, by dashing out to lunches at such places as Burford and Chipping Campden. There were occasional expeditions to Stratford, on one of which we saw a magnificent *Antony and Cleopatra* with Peggy Ashcroft and Michael Redgrave, and I also visited the scenes of John Fairfax's birthplace and early days as a newspaper proprietor in Warwick and Leamington. These included the little village of Barford outside Warwick where the family is first recorded early in the sixteenth century. By tradition, although not by firm evidence, the Warwickshire Fairfaxes came from the much older Yorkshire branch which produced the parliamentary general and Cromwell's commander-in-chief 'Black Tom', the second Lord Fairfax of Cameron.

Not far away at Old Tudor Place, a much restored Tudor house outside Reading, were my good friends Rada (née Penfold Hyland) and Paddy Russell with whom I spent a number of hilarious and bibulous weekends. Late one night I got trapped in a folding door and had to be rescued by Rada's mother, Gladys Penfold Hyland, who emerged from her bedroom in an elegant, pink nightgown in response to my cries for help. Rada's daughter Rebel (Mrs Stuart Quin) was born at Old Tudor Place in 1954 and I recall going to her christening there.

There were also occasional jaunts to London for theatres, Noel Coward at the Café de Paris and sometimes dinner or supper at Rico Dajou's Casanova Club, which I could not really afford. I sometimes recklessly signed a cheque there, which the long-suffering ANZ bank manager, Mr Guy, used to wave indignantly at me when I paid him a visit. The cheques were pink with heart-shaped designs, decorated with silhouettes of scantily clad ladies.

My Balliol days were also enlivened by Beverly Belisario (Mrs Owen Grose) who was working for Lever Brothers in the somewhat depressing surroundings of Birmingham. Her job was to instruct a group of salesgirls in the psychology of creating enthusiasm for the qualities of various brands of soap. She visited me a number of times at Balliol, including for the annual ball, and we made an epic journey to Bayreuth in 1954 to see Wieland Wagner's new and epoch-making production of the *Ring*. She arrived late at the Festspielhaus and was admitted on the arm of Herr Wagner. We travelled on to Interlaken where we met Australian violinist Brenton Langbein who was to perform the Brahms violin concerto in a large, popular cafe bar, all the cups and glasses being thoughtfully provided with rubber bases. He is now the leader of the renowned Collegium Musicum and Zurich Kammermusiker in Switzerland.

A new friend in my life at this time was Diana Dawson (Mrs Sam Walder), who I met in dramatic circumstances at Kitzbuhel, Austria, in January 1953. I had just skied unsteadily (I was a very late beginner) down a gentle slope when there was a swish and whirl of snow and I was nearly knocked over by an attractive young lady whom I had not met and who said: 'Oh there you are, darling!' She was being pursued by a skiing instructor to whom she said: 'I've just found my husband!' This, alas, was not to be the case, but we had a high old time drinking martinis with Annie, the barmaid at the Weisse Rossl, and we also won a charleston competition there. Together with her travelling companion, Carol Forbes (Mrs Trevor Rowe), and an English friend, Geoffrey Earle, we made up a very jolly foursome. My mother, Edward (aged five) and Caroline were scattered in different accommodation in the village and I recall Edward's name being blared over the loudspeaker after he had broken his leg in a skiing class. His mother, blissfully unaware, was in the local church, the one place where the loudspeaker did not penetrate. Di's daughter Samantha and Beverly's daughter Caroline are my goddaughters.

The spring vacation of 1953 took me and my Morris Minor to the Lake District. In March, in the early 1950s, there was practically no one there. I established myself at Crook, near Lake Windermere, in a nice little hotel called the Wild Boar, and set off each day with sandwiches to hike round the lakes and up some of the gentler slopes. Reading the names in my diary — Ullswater, the Old Man of Coniston, Hard Knott, Buttermere, Borrowdale, Hawkshead, Wastwater, Ambleside — I can recall it all perfectly. I spoke to no one in the daytime but looked forward to my evening chat with the barman at the Wild Boar and the occasional local or visitor. It was a totally satisfying experience mentally and physically, and one I often wished I had repeated when I had some particularly difficult problem to sort out, or wanted to reflect on which direction my life might take. I drove on to Durham, York and Cambridge before joining my mother and Caroline in the Rondpoint Bugeaud.

The great experience of my Oxford years was discovering northern Italy which, with trips to Germany, Greece, Egypt, Syria and Lebanon, was to comprise my vacation wanderings. Until my mother left Paris for London in 1954, however, Paris was really home, and our summer holidays spent in the south of France continued sporadically for a number of years. I have already mentioned my mother's closest friend in Paris, Sheila Fourcaud, and her cousin

Betty de Janzé. Others in the 'group' included Betty de Broglie, married to Prince Philippe de Broglie and formerly Betty Lamb of Sydney; Rita Essayen, the daughter of Calouste Gulbenkian; Jacqueline de Galant-Béarn and her husband Hector; the Goussaults and our very good friend, Sir Keith Officer, who represented Australia in an impeccably civilised way at the eighteenth-century Embassy in the Rue Las Cases near the Invalides. He had brought over from a boarding house in Melbourne his mother, then in her late eighties. Over one hundred years old, she outlived her son, ending her days in the house to which he had retired at Beaulieu in Hampshire. Keith, a bachelor, used to exercise

Dancing at the Summer Sporting Club, Monte Carlo, James Fairfax, Sheila Fourcaud, Caroline and Paul Jones, in the late 1950s.

his labrador, Crumpet, in the Bois de Boulogne. On one occasion he was surprised to find, at a large dinner given for him in a provincial capital, a place set by the ever-gallant mayor for 'Madame Crumpette'.

My mother's Paris friends were always extremely kind to me. Rita Essayan took us to see her father's vast five-storey house on the Avenue d'Iéna, each floor of which was crammed with incredible treasures. Rita herself lived in a tiny apartment in the Rue Barbé de Jouet, and when her father died all her possessions, down to her bedside clock, were swept back into the estate. The collection is now housed in the beautifully designed Gulbenkian Institute in Lisbon. Visiting it years later, when I had learned a little more about such things, I was astonished at the excellence of everything in it. Also, of course, in Paris there was our beloved Grandmère and the always amusing Fanny, who had been decorated for her work with the Resistance. Fanny married fairly late, lived for a number of years in Phnom Penh and, on her husband's death, resumed in Paris her old profession of piano teacher. She is a most individual character.

During my Oxford years my mother and Sheila Fourcaud took houses in

At La Falaise, Rocquebrune-Cap-Martin, James Fairfax, Sheila Fourcaud, M. E. Fairfax, Paul Jones, Edward, Jacqueline de Galant-Bearn and John McDonnell (seated left). Photo: C. Simpson.

various parts of the Côte d'Azur, according to the state of our joint finances. The first was in Cap Brun, an unfashionable but quiet resort outside Toulon. We progressed to Cavalière where Sheila's husband, Pierre, owned a villa in an attractive position on the point. It was while we were staying there that Caroline and I recalled that my father's first cousin, James Griffyth Fairfax, and his wife, Rosie, lived outside Monte Carlo in a house built by his mother. I had the odd experience of ringing up and saying it was James Fairfax wanting to speak to Mr James Fairfax; we were immediately invited to lunch.

Sous la Madône is a pink villa with green shutters set in a large garden in an estate called L'Hâmeau, outside Rocquebrune-Cap Martin, its view extending from Menton to Monte Carlo. Cousin Jim, a former captain in the British Army, had been Conservative MP for Norwich City from 1924 to 1929 and had published books of poetry over the years. His father, Charles Burton Fairfax, was my grandfather's eldest brother and the builder of Caerleon, next door to Ginahgulla. Early in life Charles had decided that newspaper publishing was not for him and had taken his wife, Florrie, to live in the south of France. He decided that life with Florrie was not for him either, and spent most of the rest of his time at the Negresco Hotel in Nice, leaving his wife and their small son at their recently built villa.

We immediately took to Jim and Rosie, who was sweet and zany but 'not nearly as mad as people think me', and over the years they became very good friends. Indeed, of all the family, Jim was the one I felt most attuned to and with whom I had the greatest rapport. He lived to be ninety and told his daughter, Benita, that I was the son he never had. After a career that could only be described as exotic and adventurous, cousin Benita, who has three sons and one grandson, now lives at Sous la Madône with her third husband, Aldo Biso, and they are just as kind and welcoming as her parents were.

Like a number of houses in the south of France, Sous la Madône had been occupied by German officers during the war and as was often the case, it was left in immaculate condition. Jim and Rosie were in the famous 'last boat' to leave with such distinguished expatriates as Somerset Maugham. In later years we alternated between two villas at Rocquebrune-Cap Martin: La Falaise, with its beautiful garden and view across to Monte Carlo, and the more modest Dacha.

Sheila Fourcauld was an inveterate gambler and we used to have to search her bag to see whether the much-needed housekeeping money was being carted off to the casino. She played roulette on instinct with a surprising degree of success — the problem then was to get her out of the casino while she was still winning. Caroline and I would virtually carry her to the door while she was scrabbling round for a last concealed chip to toss on an 'en plein'. Her mother,

Jim and Rosie Fairfax at Segovia, Spain, 1960.

Mrs Hooper, a distinguished old lady who sensibly kept her hands on the purse strings, each year paid for a cabana for us at the Monte Carlo Beach Club where we took a picnic lunch prepared by Sheila's cook, Marie-Louise (whom we called Mary Mouse owing to her resemblance to a well-known character in a children's book).

These holidays in France with the delightfully eccentric and glamorous Sheila and the numerous friends who came to stay, together with the odd characters she seemed to attract, were the greatest fun; one could get around the Riviera in those days without being in an endless stream of traffic. After my return to Australia in September 1955, I was able to rejoin my mother and her friends several times over the following years.

It was not until July 1988 that I finally rented my own house in the South of France, to which I went to continue writing this book after beginning it at Koshihata, in Japan. This was the Chateau des Aspras in a concealed valley just outside the little village of Correns in the Haute Var, a fifteen minute drive from the autoroute at Brignolles. The square nineteenth-century Provençal manor house with simple garden in the local style, swimming pool and beautiful view across the valley to the hills, is owned by London merchant banker Julian Baring and his Australian wife, Isla, the daughter of Lady (Viola) Tait. The only other habitation in the valley is the Domaine des Aspras, where the redoubtable Lisa Latz makes excellent wines and keeps a friendly eye on the Chateau, sorting out any problems that may arise. It is a beautiful corner of France and I happily returned there two years later in 1990 to absorb its comforts, marvellous cuisine (Christophe, formerly with the Relais de Toutours not far away) and interesting surroundings.

My Finals, however, were looming at Oxford in June. I thought I might have scraped a second and I recall walking from the private hotel where I used to stay in Onslow Gardens to the newspaper stand on the corner and finding myself among the thirds. The thought of a third had not stopped me from farewelling Balliol at a party given with three friends — Roy Napier, Michael Persse and Keith Thomas — at the college cricket pavilion. A number of our friends among the dons were present with their wives, together with those of our respective families who were within range and friends from other colleges and London. It was an uproarious success, partly due to a punch made from white wine, a particularly lethal Kent cider called Merrydown, and some other ingredients including 94 per cent export gin. The Australian artist Paul Jones, who was making his name as an outstanding botanical painter and was a regular with us in France, had promised to do the flowers, to be provided by Michael. On arrival, he was handed a few rather tired bunches of Iceland poppies, which taxed even his ingenuity.

I have kept in touch with all of my co-hosts: Roy joined the steel industry and now runs his own building maintenance company,

James Fairfax after receiving his Bachelor of Arts degree, Balliol College, 1957.
Photo: M. E. Fairfax

Michael continues a distinguished career as a master at Geelong Grammar (he was also an effective if occasionally eccentric president of the Junior Common Room) while Sir Keith Thomas is president of Corpus Christi College and Professor of Modern History.

My thoughts were turning with some trepidation to my future career and how I would begin it. I set sail from Southampton on the *Strathmore* in September 1955 with Michael Persse as travelling companion. He was returning home to Queensland before starting his career as a schoolmaster. I remember very little about our fellow passengers, apart from those at our table. These were a pleasant English couple called Greaves with a bright son of about eleven, a solid, jovial, middle-aged Australian woman whom we christened (from the menu) 'Mortadella', and an immaculately groomed lady of indeterminate age who volunteered no information about herself at all other than her name — Miss Cleary. She remained a total mystery for the whole voyage. Years later I discovered from a newspaper article that she was a Woolworths executive.

After half a day at Port Said, Mrs Greaves had the answer to the whole Middle East question. It did not favour Israel and some disparaging remarks about the Jews, later retracted, sent Michael from the table in a rage. At Colombo we shared a car to Kandy with two women who had no interest in the temples but only wanted to get back to the shops. On to Adelaide, where we lunched with Greta Lewis, mother of Tom, former Liberal Premier of New South Wales; Melbourne, where I was taken to lunch in the Dandenongs by an Oxford friend, Bill Flintoft; and finally Sydney, where my father and Hanne were at Pyrmont to meet me.

It was very strange seeing him again after three years and I remember being aware of his moderately Australian accent which, after my Oxford years, seemed quite broad. Back at Barford, I was put into Nanny's old room overlooking the courtyard as my stepbrother, Hanne's son Alan, then fifteen and at Geelong, had not unreasonably moved into mine. There I remained for the next nine months.

5

BAGPIPES FOR BEGINNING

JOHN FAIRFAX LTD AND
THE GLASGOW HERALD, 1955-57

I had come back not knowing how I would start work or what my duties would be, although at no stage had I ever contemplated doing anything but joining the family business. There was no parental pressure over this, nor was it necessary. I had been brought up to believe it was both my destiny and my duty and I had no interest in any other career. I was aware, however, that my first period of newspaper work in Sydney would be brief, because of the accepted plan for me to work for a newspaper organisation in England.

In reply to my enquiries from England, Warwick (I shall refer to my father by his name when writing about company matters) had said that we would talk about it on my return. In the event it was decided that I would start as a special *Herald* writer, working directly for the editor, John Pringle. I had known the *Herald* building in Hunter Street since childhood when I watched processions, usually of our armed forces, from the balcony outside the general manager's semicircular office. During each school holiday when my godfather, Hugh McClure Smith, was editor, I always went to lunch there and so had known Rupert Henderson, now managing director, and Angus McLachlan, now general manager, for some years.

From 1951 on, I was aware of Rupert Henderson's dominant role, to some extent from my own observation but largely from my mother. There had been strong disagreement between Warwick, now governing director, and Rupert[1] over some controversial religious articles entitled 'Ethics and National Life: the Need for a New Basis' which appeared in the *Herald* in late December 1944 and early January 1945. They resulted in Rupert submitting his resignation, as he felt they had offended many traditional *Herald* readers. Warwick was alarmed at the prospect of losing his general manager although his attitude in this regard was to change radically twenty years later. I have a dim memory of Warwick telling me at various times about 'difficulties with Mr Henderson' but in 1955 I was quite unprepared for the form future difficulties between them would take.

On my first day, towards the end of October, I found myself at the desk in what had been Vincent's office, next to Warwick's, overlooking O'Connell Street and feeling somewhat alone in the high-ceilinged room. Among those who made me feel welcome were Philip Palmer, the company secretary; Bill Gibson, the chief messenger; and Miss Leemon at Enquiries. The charming and elegant Constance Leemon had known me for many years, particularly when, during school holidays, I used to sign an occasional chit for £5, being unable to find my father to ask him directly. John Pringle received me in a friendly way, although I think he was sceptical about the results the arrangement might achieve. He was certainly very helpful and carefully chose a variety of assignments to which he felt my total lack of experience in this field might respond.

The first one was to investigate the state of an important colonial house called Macquarie Fields (at Ingleburn, just outside Liverpool) which was falling into disrepair, and the possible involvement of the New South Wales branch of the National Trust, then in its infancy with little public or private support. The first person I saw was my old friend Nesta Griffiths who put me on the right track.

Other assignments followed rapidly, although they tended to be in non-controversial areas. Reg Foster was to say to me later, when I reported to him at Broadway, 'Don't you write about anything except culture and good works?' I do not think this is a reflection on Pringle, who must have had to scratch around a bit to find subjects he thought I could handle, and I probably should have pushed myself more.

The acquisition of Associated Newspapers had taken place while I was at Oxford, although there were still a few legal leftovers. The sale of the Hunter Street building and the purchase of the Broadway site were also dragging on. Gavin Souter has vividly described the move to Broadway,[2] which had been taking place between June and November, culminating in the setting of the last issue of the *Herald* at Hunter Street on 21 December 1955 and its printing at Broadway the same evening. Souter rightly says that no one could have accused either John Fairfax and Sons or Stuart Brothers, the builders, of putting form before function — the Broadway, or back side, of the building has been an eyesore ever since it was built. I have never been convinced that the exigencies of the site or the requirements for the building need have resulted in it being erected back to front, even allowing for the fact that some of the properties on the Broadway side were not to become available for some years.

The reverberations of some of the tussles between Warwick, Hanne and John Mansfield (the exterior architect)[3] on the one side and Rupert, on the other, were still evident on my return. There were continual differences of opinion over the exterior and the fourteenth floor, whether offices should be panelled, and so on. At any rate Rupert was still growling about 'That bugger Mansfield' when we were in the building ourselves some time in January 1956. Anyone who opposed him or got in his way was temporarily referred to in that way, and if there was the remotest connection between the person so described and yourself, then it was, 'Your friend, that bugger so-and-so.'

When we first occupied Broadway, the executive offices were on the sixth floor, later moving, as the building was completed, to the fourteenth. There was a suggestion that they remain on the sixth floor, to keep us close to the editorial fifth floor, but up we went to the 'bloody' or 'ivory' tower as it has frequently been called since. I was often present at the executive lunches, although at this time they were held in a temporary office with a decor of metal drums and leaking pipes.

At these lunches Pringle was indeed sometimes reduced to fury by Rupert (as Gavin Souter describes it in *A Company of Heralds*) but it was by no means always speechless fury. I recall him saying on one occasion that the *Sun* could be counted among the world's worst newspapers. It was probably here that I got the feeling that I would find it hard to work with him, which I expressed to Warwick once or twice when asked. At that stage I did not have sufficient experience to appreciate the changes Pringle had made and was making to the *Herald*, or the degree of talent and expertise he brought to it. However, I was a strong supporter of McLachlan's action in bringing Pringle back in 1965 and was able to play some part in persuading Warwick to agree to give him authority over the whole paper.

My impression during these first nine months was that Warwick was not attending the office very regularly and in his absence Rupert increasingly talked to me about the problems we were facing. This absence, unlike during the war years, was not due to reasons of health. Nor do I think it was due to marital difficulties with Hanne (which were soon to emerge if they had not already done so). Rupert and I came to the conclusion that he was preoccupied both with the book he was writing on philosophy and religion[4] and Harrington Park. This was the first time Rupert held forth to me on a theme that was to become a refrain over the next nine years: the difficulties posed by the chairman's irregular attendances. It was usually some variation of 'How can you run this place when the chairman ambles in at midday?' In January 1945, at the time of the religious articles drama, he had written to Warwick in the following terms:

> *From time to time I have stressed to you the difficulty of management due to your absences, and I think it is desirable to emphasise that now. I do not know what the solution is but certainly the position is not helped by the fact that during your limited attendance in the office a substantial amount of your time is devoted to writing special articles.*
>
> *Last year was the most critical and difficult in the history of the paper. Decisions of the greatest importance had to be made repeatedly. You were ill or absent practically throughout the whole period and at times unavailable. Yet I do not know one occasion when a matter of importance was decided without your knowledge and approval.*

Warwick's attendance was to remain a problem to some degree until the years of the Committee of One and R. P. Falkingham's appointment as general manager in December 1969, when difficulties of a quite different kind would arise.

Early in 1956, Rupert began to tell me about the plans to establish a public company, which had been under consideration for almost a year. As a private company John Fairfax & Sons no longer had the capacity to finance its activities. It needed capital for development in connection with the Associated Newspapers purchase, for new plant, newsprint and its proposed entry into television through Amalgamated Television Services Pty Ltd,[5] which was granted a Sydney licence in March. I was kept informed by Rupert and company secretary Philip Palmer of the various negotiations they and the company's consulting accountant, F. E. Trigg,[6] were having with the Melbourne underwriter Ian Potter.[7]

The resulting proposal establishing the public holding company, John Fairfax Ltd, was adopted by the private company board on 27 March, my twenty-third birthday. Warwick left it entirely to Rupert to explain to me this vital decision — one of the most important in the company's history — and showed no concern at the possible effects on future control of bringing in a fifty per cent public shareholding, an issue that later become an obsession with him. I was very pleased when I learned that Vincent would be offered a seat on the board, as I felt he had been treated unfairly in being asked to resign from the private company in 1953 after accepting a seat on the Bank of New South Wales' board.

As I mentioned earlier, it had been generally accepted that later in the year

I should return to England for a period of training on a newspaper there. As it turned out, it was a Scottish one. I had been quite keen on London and, in retrospect, I think I would have learned more in the melée of Fleet Street than in the relative backblocks of Glasgow. Hugh Cudlipp had told me I would get the best training on the *Daily Mirror*, of which group he was managing director, but Rupert had dismissed this, saying he ran his newspapers in the same way he would run a pickle factory.

Warwick, however, possibly fearing I would be too close to my mother's influence in London, held out the alternatives of the *Manchester Guardian* or the *Glasgow Herald*. He had nothing to fear from my mother, who had never done anything but encourage me to take up my inheritance in Sydney, not least so that I could keep an eye on the Trust set up for her in the new public company, which substantially increased her income. In the end I chose Glasgow, partly because I had friends and family connections in the vicinity and partly because I thought it would be a more interesting place to live than Manchester, although this was based on hearsay as I had never been to either city.

On arrival in Glasgow I checked in to the Central Hotel for a few days and reported for duty to the somewhat antiquated offices of George Outram, the owning company, in Buchanan Street. Mr Byles, the editor, seemed a little bemused as to what to do with me. After a friendly chat he told me to report back on Monday at 2 pm. I also met Mr Stephens, the manager, who was very helpful with advice and put me on to an agent to arrange accommodation. This I found almost immediately in Loudon Terrace, Hillhead, along the Western Road, with handy access to the west coast. The door had a brass plate with 'Macbeth' on it, this one proving to be my very nice landlady who lived outside Glasgow. I took the pleasant ground floor with sitting room, bedroom and bathroom, together with the pitch-black basement containing dining room cum spare bedroom, kitchen and Mrs McIntosh, the caretaker, in another corner.

I settled in over the weekend and when I duly arrived at the *Herald* on Monday and discovered the reporters' room, I found it in a state of uproar. A triple murder had just come to light in one of the suburbs and everyone seemed to be running round in circles either allocating reporters to cover it or trying to get themselves allocated.

I eventually discovered that my assignment was to report a speech by the Moderator of the Scottish Church at the University at 2.30 pm and was told which bus to take. By the time I had found bus, University and auditorium, the speech was over and the Moderator having tea with various academic dignitaries. However, he kindly filled me in sufficiently to enable me to file my first report.

Thereafter assignments varied: the courts, where I usually accompanied the regular reporter, the meetings of the City Corporation and occasionally its dinners which were great fun with bagpipes, haggis and plenty to drink, reviews of Jimmy Logan at the Alhambra, Bill Haley and the Comets when the audience nearly tore the theatre apart and the Celtic-Rangers matches at which they often tried to tear each other apart. The Inquiry into the Redevelopment of the Gorbals everyone was more than happy to leave to me and I spent hours listening to pub owners and shopkeepers staking their claims to be part of the 'centres' to be included with the soul-destroying blocks of flats that were to replace the slums.

A number of times I was even attached to the triple murder squad, investigating the deaths of a woman, her sister and her daughter, who had been found shot in their suburban home. The husband, driving a red Vauxhall and accompanied by a black labrador, had been on a weekend's fishing on one of the western islands and the case hinged on the evidence of two different ferrymen who said they had seen such a car heading back to Glasgow at certain times. The husband denied any involvement in the murder but, pending the inquest, he had to report daily to the local police station, whence he and the labrador in the red Vauxhall were sometimes pursued relentlessly to their home by us reporters. He was never charged with the murders and was clearly judged to be innocent. I have a recollection that a link was established with a series of so-called tow-path murders in London later but have been unable to verify this.

I had a permanent invitation to join the George Outram board of directors for lunch every Wednesday. The chairman was Sir John Spencer Muirhead and the directors included Messrs Andrew MacGeorge, Bryce Morrison (managing director) and Robin Gourlay, together with the editor-in-chief, James Holburn. I had been warmly welcomed by these men and I retain the happiest memories of the lunches there and up the street at the Western Club where I had been made an honorary member. I worked as a reporter for three months and then moved to the sub-editors' table for two, repeating this process with the *Evening News* where the hours suited me better, leaving the evenings free.

When the Suez crisis broke in October, James Holburn in the *Herald* strongly supported the Eden Government. I took this view myself and wrote Warwick one or two sabre-rattling letters which seemed to accord with his and Rupert's views but not with those of Pringle.[8] At the time I agreed with the supporters of the action taken that the greatest mistake was to stop before the operation was completed. After the political tranquillity of my Oxford years, Britain, already shaken by the Russian invasion of Hungary, was now divided to an extent that many felt surpassed the Abdication crisis and the policy of appeasement in the 1930s. I can recall dinner parties in London breaking up in disarray when the subject was raised.

Perhaps they took things more calmly in Scotland. At any rate, social life at weekends was interrupted mainly by petrol rationing. I had three Australian links: Moira Brady of Sydney had married Bill Broadhurst and they often had me to stay at Clathick, Crieff, near Perth. The Elliot Carnegys of Lour, Forfar, in Angus, were also very hospitable. Colonel Elliot Carnegy's parents had commissioned Horbury Hunt to build Fairwater in the early 1880s, on what had been part of the Cranbrook Estate. At that time it was a compact sandstock brick house before my grandparents' additions on the harbour side, which one has to admit were not entirely in character with the original house.[9] My third link was Diana Scott-Waine, part of our 'group' in Sydney. She had married Alastair Thorburn, whose family had knitting mills in Peebles, and they lived in Edinburgh.

I was also to get to know the Earl and Countess of Glasgow at Kelburn Castle, Fairlie, Ayrshire, and the Colquhouns of Luss, on Loch Lomond. The Wakehurst connection provided me with several interesting and enjoyable experiences. I had known them since what I can only describe as the 'hunt-the-slipper' days at children's parties at Government House in the 1930s. I can still see Peter Lubbock, in a circle of about forty of us, playing hunt-the-slipper and other games in the entrance hall.

Lord Wakehurst was Governor of Northern Ireland and I stayed twice at Hillsborough in County Down, the first time being buffeted mercilessly in a little steamer across the Irish Sea. The second time was for the opening of the Northern Irish Parliament at Stormont Castle. The Lords-Lieutenant of the six counties were also staying at Hillsborough, among them the Duke of Abercorn and the Earl of Enniskillen. 'The Troubles' had temporarily subsided and my job was to record the occasion on His Excellency's movie camera. The Cabinet, headed by the Prime Minister Sir Basil Brooke, advanced in rows of three up the central aisle of the chamber, stopping and bowing to His Excellency after each three steps. I do not know where this custom originated. At the reception at Hillsborough afterwards, we were joined by a small and extremely vituper-ative group of Maltese MPs from the Labour opposition, who did not contribute to the atmosphere.

One other feature of Hillsborough I recall was the parish church where the house party attended morning service the next day. It had retained its seventeenth-century box pews and His Excellency's pew — formerly that of the Marquess of Downshire whose seat Hillsborough had been — was like a large panelled room with no ceiling, just below the pulpit. Here we all sat on benches round the walls, looking at each other and, with the exception of the vicar when he was in the pulpit, quite unable to see the rest of the church. It was an odd sensation. John Wakehurst was a very wise and good man, also rather shy, and particularly on my first visit, when I was the only guest, I enjoyed the long after-dinner chats with him on everything from appeasement to Covent Garden, of which he was then chairman.

Peggy Wakehurst, now Dame Margaret Wakehurst DBE, turned ninety in 1989 and published a book about her most interesting and colourful life and family, called *In a Lifetime Full* . . . Her father was the remarkable Sir Charles Tennant, whose daughter by a previous marriage, Margot, married the Liberal leader and Prime Minister Herbert Asquith, later Earl of Oxford and Asquith. John Wakehurst's mother was a daughter of the Duke of St Albans, who was descended from the ancient de Vere Earls of Oxford when the title was created. Peggy has remained a devoted friend, particularly to my mother during her London years, as did her brother Peter Lubbock. Peter, the kindest and most hospitable of men, welcomed to his house in Chapel Street, off Belgrave Square, streams of Australians over the years. He died in 1987.

Lady Wakehurst's sister Kay, later Baroness Elliot of Hawick and still, at ninety, attending debates in the House of Lords, was married to Walter Elliot, then Conservative MP for Glasgow, Kelvin. They had a house at North Berwick near Edinburgh where I had to accompany my host for his morning swim in the Forth. It made me wish I had struggled harder with those early golf lessons at Leura. On one pre-Suez weekend, Sir Maurice and Lady Violet Bonham-Carter (the daughter of Prime Minister Herbert Asquith by his first marriage) were staying, as was Peter Lubbock. There was much talk about how to revive the Liberal party, with reminiscences from Lady Violet. It was just as well it was not post-Suez as she was violently opposed to the Eden Government's action and gave me a blast about it later in London.

6

IN AT THE DEEP END

A SEAT ON THE BOARD IN
THE HENDERSON YEARS, 1957–64

arly in 1957, I caught the *Queen Elizabeth* at Southampton for New York, farewelled by Simon Wyndham-Lewis and his mother. Alan Moorehead[1] was also on board and we used to have lunch together in the restaurant each day, escaping from our allocated tables in the dining room. Other celebrities I met briefly on this marvellous ship were the film star Robert Taylor, author Frances Parkinson Keyes and the health food enthusiast Gaylord Hauser, an interestingly diverse trio.

As this was my first visit to the United States, I could hardly have been given a better introduction to it than by Abe Rothman, the company's editor and manager in New York. He was a fund of wit and wisdom on anything American, all of it imparted with his slightly cynical, Jewish sense of humour. He was totally devoted to Rupert Henderson, whom he called 'Boss', and was a good friend to the whole family, having sometimes to deal with potentially delicate situations which he did with consummate tact. Rupert, who always enjoyed being in America and used to come back with hair-raising stories of his dealings with movie tycoons, relaxed and unbent with Abe in a way that he did with no one else who worked for him. In later years I stayed several times with Abe and his wife, Marion, sipping his lethal mint juleps on the back porch of their Strawberry Hills farm in upstate New York.

I had written to my father from Glasgow saying I felt the time had come for me to get a flat of my own in Sydney, as I would be twenty-four when I got back. Accordingly, when I returned to Sydney in April, I was temporarily accommodated in my old day nursery at Barford while I looked for a furnished flat.

The atmosphere at Barford could have been cut with a knife. Something had clearly gone wrong with my father's second marriage. Not long after my return, Hanne departed on a lengthy visit to Denmark, during the course of which my father asked Rupert to act as go-between, sounding Hanne out on a possible divorce settlement.

Shortly after my return, Caroline and several of my friends asked me whether I had heard of or met Mary Symonds, so there was clearly some awareness of my father's friendship with her at that stage. I understand that he and Hanne met Cedric and Mary Symonds through US consul Dougherty and his wife Ruth. At any rate the Symonds came to Barford to dinner before Hanne's departure and this was my first meeting with my future stepmother. I recall discussing with Hanne and Caroline in a semi-humorous way how Mrs Symonds had been very taken with my father and had been 'playing up to him'. My father, while half denying it, seemed pleased to have made a hit with her.

Meanwhile, I had found a flat in Drumalbyn Road, Bellevue Hill, owned by Miss Felicia Garvan. It suited me ideally and I took it for six months while I looked for something permanent.

The company I came back to had just been through its first year as a public company and had held its first Annual General Meeting the previous October. Warwick was chairman (he had been governing director of the private company), Rupert was managing director, McLachlan was general manager and Vincent had rejoined the company as a director. Print activities were largely confined to New South Wales with the *Sydney Morning Herald*, *Sun* (evening), *Sun-Herald* (Sunday) and the *Australian Financial Review* (daily across Australia). The opposition was provided by Frank Packer's *Daily* and *Sunday Telegraphs* and Ezra Norton's *Mirror* (evening). Both Fairfax and Packer held interests in AAP and Australian Newsprint Mills, while in the electronic field, we both held interests in television stations in Sydney and Fairfax had its Macquarie radio shareholding. We both published national magazines — the most important being Packer's *Womens' Weekly* and our *Woman's Day*.

As soon as I got to the office I had a discussion with Rupert about my future role in the company. He thought I should join the board and become involved with the decision-making process staightaway. Both he and Warwick agreed there was little point in my occupying executive positions in different departments, as Vincent had done. Rupert argued for the board appointment partly because he liked to keep the Fairfaxes under his eye and partly, I think, because he already foresaw the probability of trouble with Warwick. While he did not necessarily see me as an ally at that stage, he felt it would be helpful to have another family director who understood the management point of view in the event of future disagreements. In later years he sometimes questioned whether he had been right in dragging me into such disagreements from the start but, always concluded that it was unavoidable.

A seat on the board was considered incompatible with an executive position; had I not joined the board immediately, I might well have been more detached from the disputes that were to arise. Also, in an executive position I think I would have had a more satisfying and rewarding start to my career than the role which I found myself increasingly forced to fill. The events leading up to Warwick's temporary resignation early in 1961 provided an unsettling background, even if they did not affect the progress of the company.

When I attended my first board meeting in May 1957, the company had surmounted its liquidity crisis of the previous December, which Rupert described to me, in his usual vivid way, as 'Hawking a bloody bag round Melbourne to find the week's wages'. In fact the before-tax profit for the 1957 financial year of £929 000 was more than double the previous year's and at the first annual general meeting I attended in October, a rise in dividend of 1 per cent to 7.5 per cent was announced. It did not stop a garrulous shareholder from making a lengthy and inaccurate comparison of Sydney and Melbourne papers, to which the chairman got the managing director to reply. This taught me two things: never allow anyone to speak for too long and always answer yourself as chairman unless, of course, specialised legal or financial information was required.

In some ways my early years with the company were frustrating, but I was feeling my way and gradually gaining experience to be stored away for future use. I cannot claim to have played any major part in the various deals that resulted in the expansion of the company between 1958 and 1964. There was no conscious policy of empire-building, but where does self-protection cease and territorial ambition start? As Souter says, it is often hard for outsiders to discern. However, the problem is universal, and depends on an individual or subjective view of motivation. The acquisition of Truth and Sportsman Ltd from Ezra Norton in 1958 was to stop the Melbourne *Herald* group getting a foothold in Sydney through the *Daily Mirror*.

The *Canberra Times*, secured by Rupert through the agreement with Arthur Shakespeare,[2] was a natural acquisition for Fairfax as sooner or later someone was bound to start an opposition paper in the national capital (as Murdoch did with the Australian in 1964). One extremely advantageous side effect of this particular deal was that it brought John Pringle back to Australia (from Britain) in 1964 to become managing editor of the *Canberra Times*.

There was also the incredibly complicated ATV deal, which ended with Fairfax buying its Australian assets for £2 600 000, selling some for £2 930 000, with

With my father, Caroline and Philip Simpson, at Fairwater, following their wedding on 17 April 1959. In front is the silver Epergne given to John Fairfax by his daughter and three sons, together with his son-in-law and daughter-in-law on 24 October 1855, after 'fifty winters have passed over your head'. Their letter and his reply are quoted in The Story of John Fairfax *by John F. Fairfax. Photo:* Sydney Morning Herald

*Farewelling the bridal car at All Saints Church. **From left:** Donald and Paddy Rankin, Pauline Allen, Nesta and Gwendolyn Griffiths, Joan Winchcombe, June Hordern, Cherry Gordon, Sue Scarisbrick, Anne Fairbairn, Juliet Winchcombe (Kirkpatrick), Sylvia Dowling and Lady Knox.*

the remainder being valued at £3 520 000. Rupert's last 'Bonzana' (one of his malapropisms) resulted in a tax-free capital gain over four years of £3 850 000.

The only one of these deals that was not followed through to its logical conclusion was the acquisition of the *Daily Mirror*. In more recent times, the incorporation of the *Daily Mirror* into the *Sun* would be regarded as a natural consequence, provided suitable arrangements were made for the *Mirror* staff. As it was, the shelf company O'Connell, which had been provided with finance by Fairfax to run *Truth* and *Sportsman,* was always regarded as being controlled by Fairfax, and we got the worst of both worlds. Rupert was doubtless genuine in his belief that it was in the public interest to have two competing evening papers in Sydney, but given his time again, I do not believe he would have organised things the same way. The suggestion has also been made that he wanted to help the young emerging Murdoch on his way, a quixotic act of which he might have been capable. As far as I am aware he never acknowledged this as a motive to anyone.

Interestingly, I do not recall any serious consideration being given to closing the *Daily Mirror* in spite of its financial and circulation losses, but when the Murdoch offer came it seemed an ideal way out of the situation at a good capital profit of £500 000.

During 1958 Warwick was preoccupied both with his personal affairs and his book, *The Triple Abyss: Towards a Modern Synthesis*, and this continued until his marriage to Mary, just after midnight on 3 July 1959, when Hanne's divorce decree became absolute. His close involvement with editorial policy was maintained, but apart from consultation, he was content to leave the business decisions to Rupert.

After Murdoch had made his offer for Truth and Sportsman Ltd, Warwick told Rupert in London in late April/early May 1960 that he was against it. When it was clear that we in Sydney were in favour of the deal Rupert in fact tried to contact Warwick by radio-telephone as the *Orion* steamed from Fiji to New Zealand, but being unable to get through, characteristically decided to go ahead and take the consequences. In this he was supported by McLachlan and myself but not by Falkingham, who would have preferred to go ahead with the original concept and form a public company.

Four generations at 14 Clairvaux Road, Vaucluse; my grandfather, David Wilson, Caroline with Louise, and M. E. Fairfax, 1960.

The first thing Warwick said to me when the ship docked in Sydney was to ask why the decision had been taken without his knowledge; he clearly did not regard inability to contact him as an adequate explanation. In fact, of course, it was not and I recall Rupert offering to try and get out of the deal, but the majority view was that we were committed. It is quite true that this incident was a major factor in the cooling of relations between them that followed Warwick's third marriage and I must certainly bear my share of the responsibility for it. It is, however, an over-simplification to argue that this was the foundation on which Murdoch built his Australian empire — that already existed in Adelaide. The later purchase of the *Telegraphs* from Frank Packer was of far greater consequence and anything might have happened in the hypothetical situation of a *Daily Mirror* as part of a public company or merged with the *Sun*.

During this time I seem to have accepted what Gavin Souter describes as the management's curious faith in England's ability to provide better editorial timber than was available locally; Warwick certainly held this view. It was unfortunate that Colin Bingham[3] did not succeed Pringle in August 1957, as the three-year editorship of Angus Maude[4] was really a period of marking time both for the *Herald* and Maude's own career as a British MP. As Maude has said himself, he stepped quite easily into the Australian political scene, although he found New South Wales politics 'almost unbelievable'. However, it was asking too much to have expected him to reconcile the Hendersonian blasts at lunch in the directors' dining room at Broadway and the lengthy sessions with the chairman, often at Barford or Harrington Park. He attempted to satisfy both men, which he managed initially, but by the end of 1960 he was satisfying neither. At an early stage, perceiving some of his difficulties, I asked him to lunch to talk about them and gave him what advice I could on how to handle Warwick and Rupert, for which he seemed very grateful. Some time later, I tried to repeat the process, but he quite clearly did not want to discuss it.

In order to involve me more deeply in the editorial decision-making process, Rupert had arranged for me to see Maude every afternoon to discuss the leaders. Sometimes he would ask me to convey his views on a particular leader, thus creating another management 'line' through to the editor. Warwick, correctly thinking that I lacked experience, did not accept my role in this regard, and he continued to direct the editor himself, which often created difficulties. Rupert's rejoinder on the question of experience was 'If he doesn't start he'll never get it'. But it was another way of bringing the situation between himself and Warwick to a head and possibly forcing Maude to make more of a stand.

I remember the arguments that raged in the thirteenth-floor dining room and sitting room at the time of the 1958 federal election. Rupert used the quotation 'A plague on both your houses', a phrase he employed again in 1961 and 1963. McLachlan and I both felt that we should give a clearer indication of support for the Menzies Government which, with all its faults, was still the best prospect for the country. The end result was that the *Herald* tried to get the best of both worlds by giving lukewarm support to the Government on the grounds that Labor could not be trusted on socialism and defence, but it advocated a loss of seats for the Coalition which would shock it into action on the economy. The question of the degree of support a newspaper should give in an election or to what extent it should advocate a vote for one party or another — an issue which also arose during our discussions — was to occupy me a lot during my term as chairman.

After Warwick and Mary's departure on their honeymoon in July 1959, my role in discussing editorial policy with Angus Maude became much more positive. I gained more experience and got on well with him as long he was there. I also enjoyed both his and his wife Barbara's company on numerous social occasions, for they had wide-ranging interests. Angus Maude resigned by mutual agreement in May 1961 and, having been paid for his unexpired two years, returned to England. Both Fairfax and he misjudged his ability to make the transition from House of Commons to editorial chair and we parted without rancour.

In returning to the events which resulted in Warwick's brief absence from the chairmanship early in 1961, I would like to emphasise that I did not know Mary's former husband, Cedric Symonds, had issued a Supreme Court writ against Warwick in February 1959, alleging that he had induced Mary to leave him and claiming £100 000 damages, nor do I recall hearing about it until some time in 1960. Warwick himself did not mention it to me until the time of his resignation in January 1961. I should have pushed past the barrier and spoken to him about it, but found it very difficult to do so. Had we been able to speak about it, Warwick's resignation might have been avoided, and both he and Mary would not have been able to use it in their allegations in August 1976 that there was a conspiracy to get rid of him. For this I blame myself, but in January 1961, we were certainly acting in the best interests of the company on the information available to us.

There had been considerable gossip before the marriage and it continued through 1960. We were aware, through more official sources, that Cedric Symonds could make allegations that would reflect adversely on both chairman and company. Indeed, it was always our intention that Warwick should return to the chairmanship when the litigation resulting from Symonds' assertion had been settled, but in the heat of that meeting on 5 January, when he kept questioning my own and Rupert's motives and future roles, it was not easy to put that point positively. His parting words to me were: 'Go and do your dirty work.'

In the ensuing days, when tempers had cooled, Warwick and Rupert discussed the circumstances of his possible reinstatement. At Warwick's request, I gave a written undertaking about the disposition of the Kinghaven shares[5] which I believe satisfied him about my future intentions. Written undertakings from Rupert contained the following sentences:

An important aspect of our recent discussions has been your functions and activities in the office. If and when you return as Chairman it will be necessary to have a clear understanding of your functions, and it may be that the board will decide to define these. I undertake that I will exercise my votes in an endeavour to ensure that any such definition of your functions is not decided until you have returned as Chairman and are present at any meeting which may discuss the matter.

McLachlan, then general manager, had also been drawn into the matter by a summons to Barford where he was asked by Warwick for assurances of support. When he said he could not give any assurances, but would always act in what he regarded were the best interests of the company, Mary said angrily, 'That's no use for my husband.' McLachlan believes Mary's hostility to him began then. Warwick's request for reinstatement would have to be 'timely and appropriate' following the withdrawal or settlement of the litigation and a definition of these terms depended on any undue embarrassment caused to the company by the litigation.

When I telephoned my grandmother on the weekend after the meeting with Warwick, she refused to let me come and see her to explain the situation, which of course upset me. About two weeks later, obviously upset herself at the breach, she telephoned me and I went to see her at Fairwater. She said her main concern was that the family should be reunited and, after I explained to her the reasons for forcing Warwick's temporary resignation, she accepted that my motives were proper but disagreed that the action had been. I told her I would contact my father to try and heal the breach.

When I saw Warwick at Barford, I apologised for words said in the heat of the moment but maintained both the correctness and propriety of my action. If he thought I had said there was no place for him in the office, this had never been my intention. He agreed that the situation might not have occurred if he had taken me more into his confidence and blamed himself for not having kept in closer touch with me. He also felt that I could have various resentments and misconceptions going back over the years which he could clear up and he suggested that we should talk about these. Unfortunately, whether this was true or not, we never got round to it.

One weekend in December 1958 there had been an altercation at Harrington Park when, in response to a question from Caroline about Christmas arrangements, Warwick said that the fact that his family refused to receive his future wife made it difficult for him to answer. I referred to the harm that the gossip and speculation were doing to the company and this resulted in my returning to Sydney sooner than I had intended. We were following my grandmother's lead in this matter as she had been equally concerned at the gossip around the town and felt Warwick had not kept her informed. In fact she only agreed to meet Mary shortly before the wedding, when we all had dinner at Barford. She did not stay for the ceremony just after midnight; neither did Caroline or I. But the two of us were among the party who farewelled the bridal couple on the *Oriana* the following morning. Also present were Philip, Sue Du Val,[6] Lady Braddon (who was one of Mary's closest friends and a witness at the wedding), and Mrs Erwin, Warwick's and my secretary. The Harrington Park incident had

With Philip, Mary, Caroline and my father at the sailing of the Oriana *following the Barford wedding on 4 July 1959. Photo:* Sydney Morning Herald

been quickly patched up but the problems did not cease with the marriage and honeymoon.

To return to my Barford meeting with Warwick, I believe he genuinely accepted my assurances that we had never intended him to leave permanently. He certainly did so in my case but the seeds of doubt had been sown in the case of Rupert, although with no justification, and there they germinated. Mary continued to maintain that the whole exercise had been an attempt to get rid of Warwick, although I was not aware of this until many years later. She referred to it several times in correspondence with me during her son Warwick's 1987 takeover proceedings, usually bracketing it with the 1976 'deposition'.

In a letter written on 30 March 1988, she describes me as siding against my father to try and remove him for 'such a spurious reason', and goes on to say quite wrongly that Warwick then persuaded my grandmother to bypass him and make the Bridgestar arrangement with me to save death duties. My grandmother was supposedly loath to do so because of my action in forcing his temporary resignation. In fact Rupert had arranged the Bridgestar sale between her and me during the honeymoon.[7]

Sadly, my own relationship with my grandmother never totally recovered from this incident and there was something of a constraint between us even though she had accepted my bona fides. She did not regret the Bridgestar sale but related it quite unjustifiably to Rupert's subsequent action, and it soon became clear he was someone she and I could not discuss. She continued to blame Rupert for what had happened, an attitude possibly shared by Warwick, although when he returned to the office following his re-election on 9 March, he said we should all put it into the past and work together for the future. Unfortunately, working together for the future never included the board defining the functions of the chairman, which was relegated to the 'too hard' basket. Indeed, they were not to be defined until the 'Committee of One' decision at the end of 1969, which resulted in a degree of ambiguity.

Colin Bingham was appointed editor in succession to Maude in June 1961, and I continued to attend the daily editorial conference, from time to time contributing a leader. Colin Bingham (he was 'Mister' to me at first, while he appropriately called me by my Christian name) had the appearance and manner of everybody's favourite, benevolent uncle. While genuinely jovial and kindly, he had strong views and when angered, his blue eyes would flash and he could be very formidable, as I witnessed a few times at the conference. Guy Harriott, the associate editor and defence expert, was an extremely amusing and witty man behind his formal military exterior, and his conservative beliefs, when he eventually became editor in 1970, coincided with the chairman's perfectly.

Another attribute they had in common was to become ice-cold when annoyed, although Warwick had a very rarely seen flashpoint beyond this. Harry Kippax, the foreign affairs writer and theatre critic, had a quirky sense of humour, but also a flashpoint that would erupt suddenly and subside equally suddenly, sometimes provoked by the earnest and slightly pompous financial writer Roger Randerson, who would turn puce with rage after one of Kippax's more outrageous forays. The fifth member of the team was the quiet and studious Bob Bell who wrote on state government matters and 'everything else'. Tom Fitzgerald, the financial editor of the *Herald*, would attend from time to time, usually if there was a major economic issue coming up.

It was an extraordinarily interesting experience for me seeing Bingham — and in his absence, Harriott — run these daily conferences from beneath his map of a divided Germany. (I once asked Bingham if he really thought Germany would ever be reunited. He said the map was a symbol, but I could not help thinking of it nearly thirty years later.) Bingham and Harriott both had the capacity to outline the major issues of the day, get a specific view from the writer whose subject it was, and then get the general feeling of conference before laying down firmly the line to be taken. These four years were to be invaluable to my own chairmanship. The most important questions of all, such as the *Herald*'s policy concerning federal or state elections, were ultimately decided by Warwick and the editor, following often lengthy lunchtime discussions at which Rupert, McLachlan and I were present but not the editor. Such discussions had originally been between Warwick, Rupert and McClure Smith.

I regularly attended the normal lunches with Pringle for part of his first term and then for Maude's term and I was gradually getting more confidence in my ability to make a positive contribution. But when Bingham was appointed as editor, he was no longer invited to our regular lunches. This might have been due to some mutual antipathy between him and Rupert which was to have unfortunate results. The election policy sessions were extremely important, providing the one occasion when we could have a joint discussion that, ideally, enabled the chairman to take a consensus to the editor. The chairman still adhered firmly to the view that the family, as majority owners, ultimately decided policy and that he, as senior proprietor, was the final arbiter. The board very rarely considered editorial policy as such, although it was sometimes referred to in general terms, and details such as changes of format or layout, and senior editorial appointments would be discussed. This left Vincent out in the cold and at this stage he did not make a board issue of it, although he sometimes complained privately.

The fact that the only view heard by Bingham was Warwick's did not create

With the Herald-Sun *rugby league team, premiers in the Business House Competition in 1962.*

a crisis in 1961, as Rupert finally accepted Warwick's proposed support of the Labor Opposition led by Arthur Calwell, but it did in 1963 when he was totally opposed to what he regarded as an inconsistent 'switch' back to Menzies. In fact, Rupert must bear considerable responsibility for Warwick's 'conversion' to Labor between 1958 and 1961 because he argued so vehemently against the Menzies Government's repressive economic policies. He and Warwick both felt strongly that the private sector needed stimulus, and when Calwell gave an undertaking not to raise the question of nationalisation during the life of the next parliament, Warwick went over the jump while Rupert reined in on the other side.

In his autobiography Calwell wrote that Rupert said to him late in October 1961 that he disagreed with the paper's decision to support Labor but his boss, Mr Warwick Fairfax, had told him to implement it. If this was so, I was not aware that we were definitely supporting Labor until I read the 1 December article in the paper. In fact, Calwell said afterwards that he never expected final endorsement from the *Herald* and that it might have been better for Labor if it had stopped short of this.

Interestingly enough, in this election Warwick consulted Rupert on the night of publication, after McLachlan refused to print the article without Rupert's endorsement, while in 1963 the leader went in without Rupert seeing it, for which I was remiss. Some days after the 1961 election, I had complained to Warwick that he had not consulted me about the leader, and he said he was aware that I was opposed to the support of Labor but, as senior proprietor, the final decision was his. In 1963 I was shown the final election policy leader, but Rupert was not. I must confess I was surprised at the violence of his reaction to the *Herald*'s support of the Menzies Government. All the indications were that the chairman thought Menzies had learned his lesson in both the economic and defence areas, where the *Herald* had been most critical. For my own part I welcomed this and could not disagree with Warwick's assessment, but I was worried on grounds of consistency about an all-out endorsement a mere two years after our commitment to Labor. However, my objections were swept aside.

Tom Fitzgerald, Maxwell Newton and Lou Leck were very upset by the pro-Menzies leader and were contemplating resignation. In his heyday Fitzgerald had a unique reputation in the world of financial journalism throughout Australia. In days when company law was much less strict, he exposed all kinds of nefarious activities, collecting for the *Herald* innumerable writs for defamation, all unsuccessful. Souter says that at one time four people who had issued stop writs against him were all in gaol together.[8] He wrote on economic matters with unrivalled distinction and clarity and brought wit and humour to enliven an often drab subject. It would be a crushing blow to lose him but in April he put in his resignation and for the second time was talked out of it.

The brilliant but rambunctious Maxwell Newton, who first put the *Financial Review* on its feet and had been its editor since 1960, would be an equal loss; he could not be dissuaded from resigning in March that year. I was shaken by this turn of events, more so when Leck, Fitzgerald and Newton came to see me during the course of the week. I had great respect for Lou Leck, who had been McLachlan's right-hand man, first as news editor then as assistant to the general manager for a number of years. Unfortunately my opinion was not shared by Rupert, whose views were clouded by the 1944 journalists strike.[9]

Leck was a man of total loyalty and integrity, down to earth in a humorous way (he once described the publishing room to me as being the arse of the industry) and a very able editorial executive. He resigned in January 1963 but was persuaded by McLachlan to let it remain ineffective for the time being. In brief, Leck was anguished, Fitzgerald distraught and Newton outraged — I can still see Max bursting into my office red in the face and gasping for a glass of water.

When the chairman himself turned up, he and Rupert had a monumental row. For the first but not the last time, I could hear them shouting from Warwick's office through the connecting door to mine. Rupert afterwards said to me, 'I thought the bugger was going to job me'. Warwick had called him 'Mr Henderson', as he was to do again in 1976. When things had cooled down somewhat, I passed on to Warwick details of my own sessions with Rupert, Leck, Fitzgerald and Newton, but he was in what I can only describe as one of his 'I am right, everyone else is wrong' frames of mind and refused to budge against the combined weight of evidence that the *Herald* had done itself harm by its advocacy of Menzies' return. Many years later, the subject was still like a red rag to a bull and he would always get very indignant at any suggestion that the *Herald* had been inconsistent.

Quite apart from these other problems, I had failed myself to realise what the implications of the *Herald*'s action might be, particularly in regard to Fitzgerald and Newton, so another lesson was learned. I think Souter is dead right in suggesting that Rupert and McLachlan's resentment was partly, if not largely, a symptom of wider apprehension at the way the chairman was asserting himself, not only in the company's editorial affairs but in its management generally, as he puts it. Indeed, the six months from March 1964 were to be very much taken up with this question in relation to a resignation of greater significance than any other — that of Rupert Henderson as managing director.

After Warwick's third marriage, a coolness developed between him and Rupert, although it is very difficult to pinpoint the time it began or, indeed, the time when there was a permanent breach. Rupert was able to influence Warwick until after the events of 1976, and it was really only his final retirement from the Fairfax board in October 1978 that effected a permanent break in the sense that neither of them, for differing reasons, I believe, tried to maintain contact with the other.

Warwick may have eventually decided to blame Rupert more than he blamed me for his departure from the chairmanship, particularly as the time of his gesture of reconciliation in 1980 drew near. For his part, Rupert would not attempt to keep any kind of contact going unless he felt it would be fully welcomed. Even though Mary was to replace Rupert as the major influence in Warwick's business life — because of the nature of the business, it included family — I could not identify a time when this happened although I could see when it was complete. Between 1960 and 1976, there were times when Warwick appeared to be struggling with the two influencing forces. None of this is necessarily to condemn Mary's attitude towards her new husband's job. In working for what she conceived to be Warwick's interests, part of which was the restoration, as she saw it, of his personal control of the company, she either had to get Rupert on side or replace him as an influence. It was important to Warwick that the 'twin influences' should not only get on with each other but collaborate as well. As Warwick wrote to Rupert in January 1960, after Rupert had visited them in Rome: 'The fact that you and Mary got on so well and I believe got each other's confidence, has given me more pleasure and confidence in the future than I can say.' This atmosphere, to the extent it existed, was damaged by the temporary resignation in 1961, which must have hardened Mary in her attitude to Rupert's resignation. At any rate, control had become the key issue by 1964 and she clearly encouraged and developed Warwick's interest in its assumption.

Following Warwick's return to the chairmanship in 1961, Caroline and I, while not feeling close to Mary, had an open mind and every reason to hope that she and Warwick would be happy and that we would have a good relationship with our new stepmother. Caroline had not been involved in any way with Warwick's temporary stepping-down and any problems I was to have with Mary were entirely to do with business matters. Our personal relations, apart from the 1976-80 period, were always friendly. This also applied to the Vincent Fairfax family, who although being occasionally critical of some of Mary's activities, maintained friendly relations.

It seems that I started the ball rolling on Rupert's retirement by passing on to Warwick a casual remark Rupert had made to me about it at the end of 1963. Had I foretold the alacrity with which it would be taken up, I would have been a bit more cautious. Coincidentally, in 1965 Rupert would complete fifty years' service with the company, having been employed as a copyboy by my grandfather in 1915. Nevertheless I had no reason to believe Rupert's general intention to retire was not genuine and I also thought that McLachlan, as heir-apparent at fifty-six, should have been thinking about taking on the top job, for which he was well equipped. He was indeed thinking of it and I was soon plunged into the crisis caused by the letter he wrote to Rupert in April 1964:

Dear Mr Henderson,

Fitzgerald's resignation this afternoon has shocked me beyond words and I am in despair. You have told me often over recent months that you wish to retire soon, and I have assumed that I have been thought of as your likely successor. If this is, in fact, your intention and my assumption about myself correct, I am reminded of Weygand's remark on the eve of the fall of Paris, 'They have handed me a disaster'. Weygand would have been well advised to have gone away and grown turnips instead of agreeing to accept the great and hopeless burden, and I am convinced that I would be well advised to do just that.

What is it that Newton and Fitzgerald have said to us as the senior members of the management? It is simply this. They say, 'Thank you for all the help, advancement, encouragement and inspiration you have given us. We trust you, we have been glad to work for you, but we don't think you count any more. And so any assurances, any encouragement you may give us, any enthusiasm you may try to inject into us, can't overcome our feeling of disillusion, inertia and dismay'.

Leck has said precisely this to me. He has remained here solely on a personal assurance I extracted from him when I returned from abroad, and the pledge must be redeemed before very long.

Fitchett in Canberra has, by implication, conveyed to me much the same message as Newton and Fitzgerald have expressed more directly. Management can have no meaning, much less give any leadership, if it is to lose, or at best be patronised and pitied, by the limited number of men of character and intelligence that we have in the organisation. The Newtons and Fitzgeralds are not the end of the story. The drones and mediocrities, of whom we have too many already, will stay; but the men of brains and heart and spirit who, because they value their self-respect and independence of thought must be nurtured and cultivated, have lost faith in the paper and in us.

I don't think I am lacking in courage, but the future outlook for the organisation and, less important, for myself, daunts me.

Yours sincerely,

A. H. McLachlan

I had never seen Rupert in a worse state than on that April morning, and I thought I should get out to McLachlan's flat as soon as possible. I found McLachlan calm — indeed, I have never found him anything else — but determined not to accept the position of managing director unless his executive powers and responsibility to the board were specifically defined and this included the chairman not exercising executive authority. I had no difficulty with that, nor with his insistence that Rupert stay on the board, which I always assumed he would. I was sceptical, though, that the chairman would cease dealing directly with executives, whatever resolutions were passed. Warwick, who did not seem deterred by the spate of resignations, actual or threatened, did not make an issue of these points fully when talking to McLachlan. He simply carried on the way he had always done, so the question was not resolved until it blew up again, as it was bound to, in August.

After the April letter, McLachlan also spoke to Vincent, who was most indignant at his cousin Warwick's concept of himself as supreme arbiter of the company's destinies by virtue of his being the senior proprietor, and who promised full support in asserting the board's authority. Warwick was still in fact leaving the running of the company to Rupert, but the disruption of the 1963 election was in his mind, and in pursuing the retirement he doubtless thought he could dominate McLachlan. However, in a letter to Henderson on 13 June, McLachlan wrote:

> . . . *the Chairman either is determined to take over the active management of the Company, a role he is of course perfectly entitled to assume with an appropriate title, if the Board, as the custodian of the shareholders' interests, so decides; or he has failed completely to comprehend the issues of managerial authority and responsibility vis-a-vis the Chairman and the Board which I tried to put to him . . . I now feel that when you get home I will have no alternative but to ask you to arrange for my release from the trap in due course.*

The actual cause of McLachlan's submitting his own resignation on 7 August was a meeting the chairman held with senior advertising and circulation executives. He had proposed that this be done on a weekly basis, with me attending too, when McLachlan succeeded as managing director. Not unnaturally, McLachlan had strongly objected to this proposal as undermining his authority and what possessed Warwick suddenly to spring it I do not know. I

was given no advance warning and felt unable to avoid attending the meeting. Rupert, still in an emotional state about his retirement and the state of the company, said to me in a despairing voice after receiving the letter of resignation, 'What have you two done to McLachlan?' Rupert dealt with the chairman himself on McLachlan's conditions for taking on the job. This followed an intense discussion between Warwick and McLachlan, during which the unwilling candidate would not give an inch. Warwick finally conceded to acceptable terms, expressing extreme irritation with McLachlan in the process.

On 18 August, the board passed a resolution stating that the managing director was responsible only to the board of directors for the management of the company. However, the two vital points — that the chairman had no executive powers and that in the event of disagreement between him and the managing director, the board's decision would be final — were contained in a letter from Rupert to McLachlan. This placed them on record, but they were not the subject of a board resolution. I was relieved that McLachlan's succession had been settled, but apprehensive about the future. The prospective chief executive was even more so. As he said in reply to a letter of congratulations from my mother, he had never in his life undertaken a job more unwillingly.

My next task was to persuade Rupert to accept a farewell dinner upon his retirement in December 1964, which he was most reluctant to do on the grounds that he could not in the circumstances say what he really felt. I urged him to

At the retirement dinner for Rupert Henderson at Broadway on 19 January 1965. **Top table** *from left:* Lou Leck, John Laforest, H. E. Dadswell, Bob Falkingham, John Pringle, James Fairfax, Rupert Henderson, Warwick Fairfax, Angus McLachlan, Vincent Fairfax, Colin Bingham, Sam Trigg. **Centre left:** *Irene Thirkell and Harry Chester.*

be as frank as he liked, then hoped all would go as well as possible. When the dinner took place, the three main participants — the guest of honour, his successor and the host — were seen at their best. Warwick was generous, McLachlan was witty and humorous and Rupert was indeed frank, but not disastrously so:

> *The formation of the public company nine years ago was the inevitable consequence of growth. It had to come but with it came a number of subtle and quite inescapable changes . . . One regrettable consequence, and the one that added enormously to my worries, was that it changed the ownership and the final responsibility from a family to a large and impersonal group of shareholders. The Fairfaxes cannot own a public company. They can and do control it. But they are not the owners and in law are just as subject to restraint and are as responsible to the shareholders as you or I. This of course is very difficult to adjust oneself to. Frankly I haven't. Equally I don't think the chairman has . . .*
>
> *I believe that the principles of the* Herald *are as high as they ever were. It is in their application and their implementation that I think there is room for questioning . . .*

James Fairfax, Rupert Henderson and Warwick Fairfax at the retirement dinner.

Rupert masked any direct criticism of Warwick's attitude by combining it with the difficulty they both had in coming to terms with the change from private to public company. He said neither of them had done so, which was true, but even though Rupert sometimes ran the company as though the public shareholders did not exist, he was always aware of them, while Warwick regarded them as an unfortunate means necessary for providing finance for the expansion and development of the family company. In these early struggles with management for control lies a clue to Warwick's later attitude to the capital-raising schemes and borrowing as an alternative.

Rupert went on to be extremely critical of the *Herald* — I can still see Colin Bingham's somewhat moon-shaped face impassively taking it in with a slight smile — and Warwick's only comment to me afterwards was: 'It's surprising he should be so critical of the *Herald* when as chief executive he was responsible for it'. This seemed to ignore his own editorial input.

Before he left, I gave Rupert a Godfrey Miller landscape as a gesture of appreciation for what he had done for me personally in the ten years I had been there. After having obtained his early art education from Leon Gellert, Rupert had developed a surprising feeling for non-figurative paintings, which coincided with the years when artists such as Passmore, Fairweather, Olsen and Coburn were reaching prominence. In accepting it, he thanked me for the loyalty I had shown to him personally as well as the support I had given to the management in often difficult circumstances. While I certainly was loyal to Rupert, I should have tried harder to bridge the growing gap between him and Warwick and indeed to create the sort of relationship with Warwick that would have made unnecessary the conflicts of loyalty that then existed and were to intensify. Perhaps it was an impossible goal to achieve. I had indeed supported the management, too, because I thought this was the correct way to run the company and my concept of the role of the family and the chairman was developing as a result of the various crises through which we had passed. The role of the board, always a concern of Vincent's, but one he was to push with increasing strength and confidence, was to become crucial at the end of McLachlan's term of office.

7

WHEN ONE PLUS ONE IS WON

MCLACHLAN, FALKINGHAM AND SIR
WARWICK'S LAST REIGN, 1965-76

My own relationship with the new chief executive was one of complete trust and confidence. Before his new appointment, I used to go to McLachlan's office around nine each morning and we would spend fifteen or twenty minutes discussing the day's *Herald* or other matters, usually editorial, before going into Rupert for a session which might have been over in ten or fifteen minutes or might have lasted an hour, depending on events. Rupert would sometimes ask me to stay on if he had something else to discuss, often his problems with the chairman.

In my daily talks with McLachlan I learned a great deal about newspapers from a master of the craft — news values, layouts, popular appeal, advertising ratios and the economics of increasing editorial space, the use of special features or sections to attract new readers, and whether such new readers were likely to become permanent subscribers. I also saw how he handled Rupert. He used to say it was all a question of timing. Certainly several executives who had lost their jobs in the morning had been reinstated the next day without ever having been aware of the threat hanging over them beyond a suggestion from McLachlan, after they had been confronted with their transgression, that they were lucky to be employed there still.

Now the sessions with McLachlan were much more concerned with the running of the company, and Falkingham often joined us. It is quite true that McLachlan would not take the sort of risks in the pursuit of growth that Rupert did, for example, in the ATV deal referred to in Chapter 6, but there was no doubting his determination when the vital interests of the company were at stake.

In 1967 Sir Warwick (he had recently been honoured with a knighthood, which had been warmly welcomed by the whole family) embarked on a seven-month holiday with Mary and their six-year-old son, my half-brother Warwick. They were anxious to have more children but, after Mary had suffered several miscarriages, the danger to her health was considered too great. They decided to adopt two children, Charles and Anna Bella, and remained in England until the end of 1968 in order to establish resident status, one of the adoption law requirements. Warwick in these years was a withdrawn but friendly enough child with one or two nervous mannerisms which became more pronounced until adolescence. He showed most enthusiasm and response when I took him to a movie — he was enthralled by *2001: A Space Odyssey* and the James Bond films. The only other incident I can recall is Warwick, with great excitement, collecting five-cent pieces thrown over the veranda at Lindsay Avenue by Dorothy Edwards who was working there that day (she has been doing my cataloguing, filing, sorting and photographs for twenty-one years now).

As far as Sir Warwick's relationship with McLachlan was concerned, I could

David Thomas, Sir Warwick Fairfax, Annalise and Warwick at Retford Park, July 1976.

only hope for the best and be prepared to intervene if necessary. His absence overseas lessened the possibility of the issue of the board's control turning into a crisis, but it was always there. When I was in London in May and June 1968, I went a number of times to the house he and Mary had taken in Charles Street, off Berkeley Square, and relations between the three of us were happy. Occasionally I met Sir Warwick at our Fleet Street office in the Reuters Building before lunching with him at the Carlton Club. (I was intrigued at his choice of the Carlton, which he had recently joined, having years before been a member of the Oriental. He was certainly back in the Tory bastion, which he was not again to abandon. I had joined the Carlton Club in my Oxford days and enjoyed using it for many years until I became a member of the Garrick where I now find, on my regrettably rare visits, the combination of stage, law, literature and media more to my tastes).

At these lunches he was very critical of McLachlan for allowing the *Sun* to become more sensational under its doughty editor Jack Tier. Tier tended to follow the Clinch[1] tradition of vigorous, popular journalism, particularly in its treatment of crime stories, to meet the competition of the *Mirror* which was some 11 000 ahead in circulation. Numerous front pages were thrust at me as evidence of this, and Sir Warwick did not accept my argument that you can have a different perspective when you are not in the heat of the battle. He was also critical of what he described as McLachlan's failure to take action in several areas concerning the *Herald*, including changes in format and editorial salaries. In July, when he sent a long memorandum to McLachlan, with copies to directors, giving his views on both papers, I guessed we could be in for a stormy time on his return.

John Pringle had begun his second term as editor of the *Herald* on 1 June 1965 with full control over the whole paper, a condition he had quite rightly insisted on. Sir Warwick put up quite a lot of resistance to Pringle being given full powers, but eventually agreed after several intense sessions in the thirteenth floor dining room. I am quite sure the decision was correct, even though the divisions between editor and chairman, and eventually between editor and board, were to be far greater during Pringle's second term than during his first.

After the chairman's return from England in December 1968, he clashed with Pringle on both nationalism and the monarchy, and permissiveness and film censorship, while the *Herald*'s continued support for the Vietnam war increasingly presented a problem for Pringle, who to a large extent shared the growing opposition to it. Sir Warwick's firm assertion of traditional *Herald* policy on the monarchy certainly had the support of the board. When Pringle wrote a leader suggesting there were virtues in Australia becoming a republic, there was a violent reaction and he agreed to write another reversing his stand.[2] I think there was a growing uneasiness among us all about where the *Herald* was heading under Pringle. The tragedy was that he could have achieved far more in his second term if he had handled the chairman differently, which he seems to admit himself.

The issue that proved to be the breaking point was the Easter Saturday 'humanist' leader in April 1970. Sir Warwick rang me at my Bilgola Beach house on Easter Sunday in what was clearly a state of considerable upset and concern that the traditional Good Friday leader on the significance of Easter had for once been omitted and a humanist approach taken. I found it difficult to see why he was so upset about it, although Pringle, quite apart from traditional policy, should have consulted him in advance on a subject about which he must have known the chairman felt strongly. Unhappily, the conflict resulted in Pringle's departure a week later, ostensibly on leave. It was a great pity things were allowed to happen that way even though, in December 1969, Pringle had in fact already given notice of his intention to retire on the expiry of his term a year later, which Sir Warwick had accepted with regret. Certainly it should not in itself have been sufficient to cause Pringle's going without any attempt being made to arrange a formal farewell to express the company's gratitude for the very real contribution he had made to both the quality and circulation of the *Herald.*

Sir Warwick's reaction to the Easter leader must be taken in context with earlier disagreements, and certainly he had the general support of the board, but it is interesting to compare it with the stand he took twenty-five years earlier as the author of the controversial article 'Ethics and National Life: The Need for a New Basis' which had caused such a ruckus with Rupert — not to mention many eminent churchmen of all denominations.

No doubt a major confrontation would soon have occurred between the chairman and managing director following Sir Warwick's return had McLachlan's heart attack not altered the situation. McLachlan had complained to me about the manner and tone adopted by Sir Warwick when discussing Pringle's leader on the monarchy. He talked him down and would not listen to any viewpoint other than his own. This had happened in other areas, too, as I was aware.

I was in Melbourne when McLachlan suffered the attack on Thursday 30 January 1969. When I called him the following Monday, unaware of what had happened, his secretary Miss Thirkell,[3] beyond saying he was in hospital, clearly did not want to give further details over the telephone. I could tell by her manner that it was serious and returned to Sydney the next day to find Sir Warwick assuming control at the office. I did not question his move at that stage as he obviously intended to involve me in any decisions, but it was not long before

I got a call from Rupert saying that he had urged Lou Leck, then editorial manager, to return from his holidays and act in McLachlan's absence. In Rupert's view, it was essential that the board should meet before the chairman started acting as chief executive. Leck duly returned and with customary tenacity refused to obey the chairman's instruction to resume his vacation, saying that only the board could give such a direction and that he always acted in McLachlan's absence. Philip Palmer, company secretary since 1944, confirmed that the chairman could only perform executive acts if authorised by the board, whereupon Sir Warwick called an informal meeting of all directors, except McLachlan, for 12 February.

Before the meeting, Rupert suggested to Palmer that he and Miss Thirkell should see McLachlan and obtain written instructions for Leck. They were the first visitors allowed the patient other than his sister, Miss Elsie McLachlan, and he authorised Leck to act in cooperation with Falkingham on all journalistic and financial matters, referring matters of policy to the board. He also appointed Leck his alternative director. Rupert had consulted Vincent about obtaining instructions from McLachlan and I was aware that this was being done without knowing their precise nature. I was not aware, however, until the morning of the meeting, that Sir Warwick would put forward a draft resolution giving him full powers to administer the affairs of the company subject to the board and until such time as the board might determine.

The meeting was not an easy one. We were handed copies of McLachlan's letter to Leck as soon as the meeting opened and the chairman then read his draft resolution. Vincent and Rupert were totally opposed to giving the chairman any formal powers. Rupert pointed out that, as McLachlan was now well enough to receive callers and take telephone calls, serious conflict could result. He also pointed out that the chairman had already made three executive decisions: not to recall Leck (which had not been effective), to increase editorial salaries and to change the make-up of the *Herald*, both of which McLachlan had wanted to delay. If McLachlan were stripped of his authority, he said, employing some hyperbole, it could kill him.

Sir Warwick repeated his earlier criticisms of McLachlan for failing to act in the two areas under discussion and insisted that he, the chairman, was the only person with the qualities required to act in McLachlan's absence.

I had felt from the start that a compromise could be achieved whereby the chairman could act on an informal basis without special powers from the board, although as a tactical move I initially supported his draft resolution with some qualifications, being fairly sure the others would not. I had every confidence that both Leck and Falkingham were more than capable of resisting undue encroachment by the chairman, but it was a temporary solution dependent on McLachlan's future.

Sir Warwick was quite as prepared to resort to hyperbole as Rupert, and one of the arguments he put forward against Leck's return was that he 'wouldn't have his blood on his hands'. This was a reference to Leck's own wish to retire, partly for health reasons. Had it not been for the fear that he would use any formal transfer of powers, if only on a temporary basis, as a stepping stone to the assumption of full executive control, there was a great deal of logic in Sir Warwick's proposal.

On a recuperative trip to London in June, as well as attending a Reuters meeting, McLachlan consulted a physician who, after intensive tests, told him he could work only in a serene and enjoyable atmosphere. It had never been serene and was now scarcely enjoyable. McLachlan made his decision not to return to the managing directorship and, even though he did not write formally to the chairman until 11 December, Falkingham, being aware of it, sent a memorandum to McLachlan, with a copy to Rupert, urging his own candidature as chief executive.

After the receipt of McLachlan's letter, Vincent told Sir Warwick he would not agree to McLachlan's resignation until a successor had been chosen and he thought it should be Falkingham. So the stage was set for Act II of what was to be a four-act drama extending over twenty years. (The final act has just run its course.)

Sir Warwick, Rupert, Vincent and I met to discuss the situation before the board meeting of 18 December. Sir Warwick told me that morning that he should be executive chairman and it was on that basis that the four of us began our discussion. He pointed out that there had never been a chief executive without a journalistic background. Rupert said he would never agree to Sir Warwick becoming chief executive at the age of sixty-eight, while Vincent thought Sir Warwick should resign as chairman if he wanted to be chief executive. Accepting that Falkingham should be general manager, not managing director, it became clear in my mind that the problem was how to construct a role for the chairman that would meet his obviously valid point about responsibility for editorial matters, quite apart from any other powers.

I had, in fact, thought from the start that Falkingham should be chief executive but, again, as a tactical move, was not going to say so, partly to give due consideration to Sir Warwick's objections and to his own proposal, and partly because it would appear as if the three of us had ganged up on him. We went down to lunch after a singularly trying session, which lasted most of the morning and seemed to me to have resolved nothing.

When we resumed over coffee, and it looked as if we again were getting nowhere (Rupert said it was the most difficult day he had spent since he joined the company), it occurred to me that it might be possible to get Sir Warwick to agree to Falkingham's appointment if a formula acceptable to everyone could be achieved concerning his own powers. Vincent had already said he would agree to having a general manager, rather than a managing director, if McLachlan stayed on the board, so I presented myself as a convert to Falkingham. McLachlan should stay on the board and none of this was incompatible with a formal definition of the powers which the chairman was already exercising de facto.

I could not for the life of me see how such a definition would be achieved but, to my relief, my suggestion was accepted. It was agreed that Alastair Stephen, the company's solicitor, should be consulted. Alastair, as well as being the senior partner in the old established firm of Stephen, Jaques and Stephen (now Malleson Stephen Jaques), was my godfather and the brother of Helen Rutledge. He was a very good friend both to the company and myself and I valued his wisdom and advice for many years. With characteristic skill, he came up with a solution to our dilemma — Sir Warwick could be appointed a committee of one in accordance with Article 91 of the company's articles of association.[4]

I was not to learn of this proposal until the following Wednesday, Christmas Eve, as on the morning of the 21st, a utility filled with vegetables for Frensham Girls School, driven by one of the Franciscan Sisters who grew them, collided with my car at the intersection of Old South Road and Range Road near Retford Park in Bowral, while I was on my way back to Sydney. After a tremendous bang on the right-hand side of my Mercedes coupé, I felt a violent pain and lost consciousness. I came to almost immediately, finding myself spreadeagled on the front seat with the most excruciating pain I had ever known right across my torso. Bending over me was a nun, whose only apparent injury was to her nose, which was dripping blood onto my chest. Fortunately, as we were miles from any habitation or telephone, a local taxi passed, driven by Neville Young. He went for an ambulance to which I was transferred with the assistance of Neville and the nun. It was the most awful performance as every movement was agony.

After an examination at Bowral hospital, I was taken by ambulance to St Luke's in Sydney where I found a reception committee of both parents (it was the first time they had met for a number of years), Caroline and, in the background, my friends Richard and Marie Blanche Walker and their small daughter. At that time, St Luke's did not have a fully equipped operating theatre so my doctor, Ian Thompson,[5] had me transferred the next day to the intensive care unit at Sydney Hospital, with the six broken ribs and punctured lung I had sustained in the crash.

This was a real eye-opener for me. After I had had a tube put in my lung — to my slight alarm, this was done under a local anaesthetic watched by a dozen trainees — and emerged in a happy state from the prescribed dose of morphine, I could take in my surroundings. All around were people who had sustained serious injuries, or who were to go into or had come out of major surgery, and I could not have been more impressed by the skill and dedication of the doctors and the nursing staff.

As the least serious case there, I could talk to some of them about what they had to cope with. Opposite me was a man with a broken back who was strapped to a sort of St Andrew's cross which had to be raised, turned over and lowered at regular intervals. As I left to recuperate at St Luke's in my wheelchair, I remember thinking that, if ever something really serious happened to me, that Sydney Hospital was the place to go.

My father and Mary visited me in St Luke's and when I asked him if the succession problem had been solved, he said 'Yes, thanks to you'. I was reassured by this very rare praise. The bond between us, seldom acknowledged by either, was still there, and he also talked of increasing my responsibilities. I spent Christmas Day in St Luke's and, having graduated to crutches, Richard and Marie-Blanche drove me to Retford a few days later, stopping at Harrington Park for lunch. (I should add that a charge against me of driving without due care and attention was withdrawn when the circumstances at the intersection were examined. The 'Frisky Sisters', as they were sometimes called, including their 'Flying Nun', were also withdrawn from their convent farm to Melbourne, a year or so later, and the intersection at 'Nun's Corner' was appropriately remodelled.)

Nineteen sixty-nine ended with the board confirming Sir Warwick's powers. Whether he had coveted this for most of his life is another matter. Certainly, since his marriage to Mary and the cooling of relations with Rupert, it had assumed a prominence that might have been dormant in the best days of their working partnership. The question of whether his pursuit and achievement of control was ultimately in his own or the company's best interests must be asked but there is another, more immediate question. Who, during the seven years of the committee of one, was in fact in charge?

There is no doubt Sir Warwick thought he was, but in all matters concerning finance and administration, Falkingham, as general manager, regarded himself as chief executive and he dealt with the board accordingly. The board took a similar view of Falkingham's role, but was not called upon to make a ruling on it until Sir Warwick's incursions into the management field precipitated a crisis concerning the chairmanship that came to a head in 1976.

In the earlier years, in fact, the arrangement worked reasonably well, but in July 1972 the general manager sent a memorandum to the chairman, with copies to directors, complaining in strong terms that Sir Warwick had counter-manded certain of his instructions. Sir Warwick gave way on this issue and said he had not been aware of the instructions.

The major preoccupation during this period was rising costs, caused largely by the explosion in wages as a result of the Whitlam Government's policies, and falling advertising revenues, which occurred when the government finally had to cut back the economy because of the high rate of inflation. This situation struck most forcibly in the 1974–75 financial year when the Fairfax profit fell from $13 453 000 to $7 177 000. Even though it recovered to $12 512 000 the following year, this was only after the most stringent economies, including a staff reduction of over ten per cent and the elimination of many colour features, the Saturday *Sun* and promotion expenditure.

In order to raise its cover prices and advertising rates, the company was subjected to what proved to be the only hearing ever held on the media industry by the newly established Prices Justification Tribunal. The brunt of this fell upon Falkingham, who was conspicuously successful in obtaining, in two separate appearances, $7.2 million out of $10 million unrecovered costs.

On the editorial side there were no problems in general regarding *Herald* policy. Chairman and editor (Guy Harriott) were as one on most issues, including the castigation of the Whitlam Government for its handling of the economy, defence and foreign policy, an attitude shared by the board and general manager. The only conflict, but a major one, concerned Suzanne Baker, the editor of the women's section from 1971 to 1973. Baker had for the first time given women something intelligent, provocative and socially relevant to read, other than the society round, by introducing such subjects as illegitimate children, abortion, birth control and women prisoners, but the traditional conservatism of the chairman and some directors made them critical of her approach. It was true she brought a campaigning zeal that gave a quite different emphasis to those pages, but it was a great pity that a way was not found to accommodate both points of view. Her resignation deprived the *Herald* of potentially valuable readers in young age groups that it has been trying, with varying degrees of success, to attract ever since.

The two other important developments of the early 1970s were the continued growth in reputation, influence and sales of the *Financial Review*, and the launching of the *National Times*, both under the aegis of Vic Carroll. These two events gave birth, not without blood and pain, to a degree of editorial independence in different Fairfax publications. Carroll was to pay the price for his defiance of the gods by being chained to the Promethean rock of Sungravure, but his time was to come.

The *Financial Review* was expected to follow the general editorial line of the *Herald* on major issues, while having the freedom to interpret them in its own way. There had been problems in the past with Newton, over the EEC, for example, and he had finally resigned after the dramas of the 1963 election. Carroll had already had a few brushes with Sir Warwick — he described them as 'getting the cuts' — but the view was gradually taking shape that editorial strength lay in diversity not unity. While I am sure he was not conscious of a deliberate change in attitude, Sir Warwick seemed to be accepting the concept of diversity, probably assisted by the convulsions suffered by the recently born (7 February 1971) *National Times*.

If we had known the problems the *National Times* would cause us or the amount of time, particularly in my own chairmanship, that would be taken up dealing with them, we might have been less enthusiastic about launching it. But now, after its sad demise following Warwick's takeover, there can be no doubt that the effort was worth it, as were the losses sustained. The original concept of a weekend publication devoting equal space to politics, business and the arts was soon to respond to the issues of the day and these, in the lead-up to the 1972 election, were increasingly political. The Whitlam years and his sacking by Sir John Kerr in 1975 were made for a new and struggling publication, as were the bitter divisions in politics and society caused by the dismissal. It is a tribute to Trevor Kennedy, the first editor, that he struggled so successfully to maintain its progress in the first eighteen months on relatively few resources, but it was under Max Suich, who succeeded Kennedy, that the paper really came into its own as an investigative journal.

In its short life of seventeen years, it infuriated prime ministers, premiers, businessmen and many people, prominent and less prominent, who had something to conceal. It caused lasting enmities that extended to board and personal levels and that undoubtedly put the company at a competitive disadvantage as far as the present federal Hawke administration and the former Wran administration in New South Wales were concerned, since Packer and Murdoch usually supported the government. It affected the course of Murdoch's takeover of the Melbourne *Herald* group and may have been a factor in Warwick's takeover, which resulted in the break-up of the Fairfax group. This result was much welcomed in certain federal and state political circles, as well as by some prominent business figures and our competitors.

At the same time, I was always quite surprised at the ready acceptance by the business community of the *National Times* — apart from the few who had crossed swords with it — and their understanding both of the need for such a publication and the role it was trying to fill. Of course, there were errors of taste and judgment, but Sir Warwick had no major cause for displeasure until the Evan Whitton articles of April-May 1975 that, contrary to the *Herald*'s consistent attitude over the last ten years, questioned Australia's commitment to the Vietnam war. They produced a veritable explosion comparable to the *Herald* Easter leader of 1970. Sir Warwick telephoned me one Sunday morning in April, and this time, having been somewhat shocked by the article myself, I could be more supportive as I totally agreed with the line the *Herald* had taken.

At the 30 April board meeting, the chairman strongly refuted the views expressed in the article and drew attention to the responsibility of Carroll as managing editor, Such as editor and Bowman as group executive editor with responsibility for publications other than the *Herald*. The board supported the chairman but fortunately did not adopt Rupert's recommendation to get rid of Bowman, Carroll and Such. It instructed Bowman to convey its view to Carroll. Carroll and Such stuck by the accuracy of Whitton's article and, interestingly enough, his second and third articles went in virtually unaltered. The chairman demanded the publication of an article — B. A. Santamaria[6] was selected to write it — giving the board's (or orthodox *Herald*) view of the conflict, but once again the concept of adhering to the *Herald* line had been successfully breached.

The only victim was Carroll, who in fact wanted to move on. He embraced his new post as manager of Sungravure with muted enthusiasm — the difficulties of the magazine company were only to be resolved by the kind of drastic action which at that stage was not contemplated. The position of executive editor was abolished early in my chairmanship when Such was appointed chief editorial executive with authority over all Broadway publications in 1980.

The *Age* provided the second testing ground for the concept of editorial independence. The aim of the Syme partnership with Fairfax was to maintain David Syme Ltd as an independent organisation, and there was an arrangement whereby Fairfax would not support any resolution at a shareholders' meeting opposed by the Syme partners, as long as they held ten per cent of the ordinary shares. The partnership deed did not define editorial matters, although I always took the view that the eventual determination of policy was a matter for the Syme Victorian directors. The definition contained in the deed seemed to me to bear out this intention.[7]

During Ranald Macdonald's time as chief executive of the *Age,* and when I was a director of the company, Macdonald always informed the board what line it was proposed to take in a federal or state election. He often arranged for the editor, Michael Davie and later Creighton Burns, to attend the relevant board meeting and directors had every opportunity to question the editor and express their opinion. Both these editors also regularly attended board lunches.

After Macdonald's resignation in 1983, the editorial policy was the responsibility of Creighton Burns, to whom directors had regular access at board lunches. It was clearly the Syme board's view in 1972, as recorded in a board minute of 29 February, that the board exercised responsibility for editorial policy through the managing director. Indeed, both Syme and Fairfax boards were united on this question.

In the 1972 federal election, Macdonald had committed the *Age* to the support of Labor before his board had had the opportunity to comment, thus causing considerable resentment among both Syme and Fairfax directors. In 1974 they were determined not to let this happen again. When Macdonald tabled a report from the new editor, Graham Perkin, advocating, on grounds of consistency and because of the Opposition's misuse of its numbers in the Senate, continued support for the Whitlam Government, Sir Warwick led the attack against Whitlam and urged support for the Snedden Opposition. The board agreed with him, whereupon Macdonald threatened to resign. Later, Perkin also said that he, together with some of his senior staff, would resign unless a compromise was reached. Curiously, it was Rupert Henderson who solved the impasse by discussing some draft editorials with Perkin in Sydney, the end result being an unenthusiastic recommendation by the *Age* to vote for the Opposition.

The next year the *Age* was to attack trenchantly the Whitlam Government and call for its resignation but, in striking contrast to the *Sydney Morning Herald* it declared itself firmly opposed to Sir John Kerr's dismissal of the Government. Over the space of four years the *Age,* the *Financial Review*, the *National Times* and the *Canberra Times* all challenged the primacy of the *Herald* as the fount of all wisdom and, in spite of the retreat by Macdonald and Perkin in 1974, the concept of editorial diversity had been established. Indeed, the right of the chairman and board to impose a uniform editorial policy from Sydney had been successfully challenged and this concept of diversity, which was more clearly spelt out during my chairmanship, was something I encouraged.

Perkin's untimely death in October 1975 robbed the group of an executive of great potential significance. Rupert had been cultivating him and he had suggested both to Vincent and myself the possibility of his coming to Sydney. I believe he had in the back of his mind the idea that Perkin could be a future chief executive, thus obviating the necessity for the committee of one.

The actions of the committee of one were causing increasing concern both to the board and to the general manager. The Henderson-McLachlan combination had worked so well because each always knew what the other was doing in the management of the company, but Sir Warwick frequently gave directions to executives without consulting Falkingham beforehand, or informing him afterwards. In October 1975, Falkingham came to me with the proposal that he be made managing director, with Sir Warwick retaining a role in editorial matters. He also consulted Rupert who dissuaded him from persevering with it, I think probably because he regarded it as only a half-solution. At any rate, from then on, when an issue arose with the chairman, Falkingham used to reiterate to me his belief in the inevitability of a general showdown with him.

There were three other main reasons for the showdown when it came. The first had to do with the way Sir Warwick handled board meetings, increasingly, in the view of directors, cutting short discussion on important matters and becoming intolerant of criticism.

The other two reasons involved Mary Fairfax, one directly and one indirectly. Not long after they returned from their honeymoon in 1960, she had complained to me about the traditional Fairfax policy of not mentioning any of the social activities of members of the family in the company's publications. Her argument was that reporting activities concerned with good works, or the raising of funds for charitable, educational or cultural ventures, brought credit to the company. The management and other members of the family adhered to the traditional rule, and this became a bone of contention. Eventually, she contacted editors and social reporters directly, causing embarrassment to them and to the management. Difficulties were also created by her tendency to campaign on policy matters about which she had strong — though doubtless, perfectly genuine — feelings.

The final cause of the showdown was a proposal Sir Warwick put forward to restructure the company. Philip Munz, a solicitor from Rivers, Dickinson, Stirling and Munz, who had been introduced to Sir Warwick by Mary, prepared the proposal in association with a friend and advisor of Sir Warwick's, Willi Perndt of Price Waterhouse. This had been done without the official knowledge of the board and general manager, although, in October 1975, Sir Warwick had asked Vincent, John and me to a meeting with Munz and Perndt to explain the scheme, which involved a return of capital to shareholders and the issue of debentures. It was difficult for us to refuse to attend a family meeting, although we could have insisted on our own advisers being present. Later, the Fairfax board turned down the proposal on the advice of Sam Trigg, its financial adviser and also a partner in Price Waterhouse, largely because of doubts in the funding of the debentures, but the exercise carried an ominous warning.

In retrospect, it could be argued that none of these four major concerns, either in isolation or together, warranted such drastic action as a change in the chairmanship, but the effect over time was cumulative and, in the end, none of us felt that trying to deal individually with them as they arose, would solve the problem of the control of the company. Was control to be exercised by the chairman with the board as an adjunct, or by the board through its appointed chief executive? This was the issue we were now facing and, in August 1976, it came to a head through a matter small in itself but ultimately with considerable significance.

I can honestly say that I had little idea on Wednesday 18 August, when Vincent and I met Rupert in his office in our Hunter Street building to discuss Sir Warwick's salary, that the meeting would lead to an immediate confrontation with him — although at the back of my mind I felt it could be the cause of later confrontation. I had been hoping that some way would be found of dealing with the chairmanship, short of forcing a resignation, but as I was certain he would not accept any of the points on which directors were critical of him, I was not optimistic. In short, I knew the question had to be faced but I had no strategy in mind to resolve it successfully.

The July board meeting had increased the general manager's salary and it had been agreed that the other directors should meet before the August board meeting set for the 19th to discuss that of the chairman. As soon as the three of us met — McLachlan being back in hospital with a mild recurrence of his heart problem — Rupert said it was impossible to discuss Sir Warwick's salary without considering the whole position of the chairman. Any increase would consolidate his claim to be chief executive and signify approval of the existing state of affairs.

I was aware that for some time Vincent had thought the younger generation of Fairfaxes should take on major responsibilities in running the company. I was then forty-three and had been chairman of Amalgamated Television Services for two years while my cousin John, the manager of Federal Capital Press (*Canberra Times* and *News*), was thirty-four.

Rupert detailed all the things he thought were wrong with the office including the control, staff morale and the falling circulation and advertising volumes of the *Herald*. The ball was clearly in my court. Vincent and McLachlan, who had been consulted in hospital, both wanted me to state my position, as did Rupert. Without trying to be overdramatic, it came to me very suddenly that it was now or never — whether it was action to solve the issue, or a continuance of useless bickering, now depended on me. I told them I would take on the chairmanship if the board could effect Sir Warwick's resignation.

After some discussion, it was agreed that Rupert should see Sir Warwick immediately. I was not entirely happy with this as I thought it would look as if I was relying on someone else to beard the lion in his den before having to face him myself. However, I had the faint hope that Rupert, because of his long association with Sir Warwick, might somehow achieve the desired result without too much bloodshed. In this I was wrong, as I soon realised.

Back at Broadway, half an hour later, I could hear the shouting from the chairman's office as I sat in my own, waiting for the encounter. After the exchange with Rupert, Sir Warwick had gone straight down in the lift, but while Rupert was telling Falkingham and myself what had happened, he came back up again and, seeing me, called me into his office. This was the first of two unpleasant sessions I had with him. I was much more in control of the situation than I had been in 1961, but his coldness and relative calmness seemed to make what he said far worse.

He asked me whether I thought he was doing a good job as chairman, and did I not think his reputation both in the office and the community was very high. I said it was certainly high in the community and he had over the years performed valuable services for the company, but there had been much criticism more recently. Anyway, the community was hardly in a position to know the internal affairs of the company.

He referred to my own reputation in the city and said I would be a laughing stock as chairman, it being widely assumed that I was more interested in art collecting and travel than the family business. He said further that from the time and effort I had given to the company, people had every right to make that assumption.

I replied that if there had been times when I was less than wholehearted in enthusiasm and application, he had done very little to encourage me or, indeed, to discuss any major problem with me. He accused me of a lack of nerve in getting Rupert to confront him first. I referred to an emotional block between us, which I said he had not attempted to help me break down. He dismissed my point that I genuinely thought it was in everyone's interests for Rupert to make the initial approach. He asked whether I thought he was getting too old and in reply I used the expression 'over the hill'.

So it went back and forth, until he quite suddenly terminated the discussion on no particularly conclusive note. In fact, as I said a few days later to Vincent, Rupert and McLachlan, I thought I had made a mistake in not speaking to him first myself. In retrospect, it is the one thing I would have done differently, although I do not think it would have affected the result or his subsequent attitude to me in any way. He certainly would have used all the means in his power to dissuade me from my course but I would have had to stand firm, as I did for the next four years.

The board meeting the next day was something of an anticlimax — Sir Warwick asked me to conduct it and McLachlan was still away — but over lunch Vincent, Rupert and I talked about the start of an new era.

On Saturday at Retford Park, Sir Warwick telephoned and arranged to see me in his office at 11 am the following Monday. This meeting was more unpleasant than the first as accusations of betrayal and disloyalty were to the fore. At this point I feel I should quote Gavin Souter's description of what he, as an impartial commentator, conceived Sir Warwick's feelings to be.

It was not hard to appreciate Sir Warwick Fairfax's feelings at this time and for weeks to come. He saw himself as having been betrayed by his fellow directors after almost seven years as the committee of one — a period which, as he believed, had been the most fruitful and signif- icant part of his long chief proprietorship and chairmanship. No one had done as much as he to keep the Herald *and its associated publica- tions true to the company's traditional principles. Twenty years previously, he had owned or controlled 74 per cent of the private company's shares. In the meantime, partly at Henderson's urging, he had transferred such a proportion of his shares in the public company to James Fairfax that his own holding had dwindled to 12 per cent compared with James Fairfax's 18 per cent and Sir Vincent Fairfax's 14 per cent. And now Henderson was saying that the directors wanted him to go! As his friend Willy Perndt was to tell Henderson a few days later, Sir Warwick was like a wounded tiger.*

It was at this second meeting that Sir Warwick told me he had given his son Warwick, then aged fifteen, the full story, so that he would know the sort of man his brother was. I was, he said, motivated by ambition — the most astonishing charge in view of my extreme reluctance to take any action regarding the chairmanship. He was particularly interested in finding out who had been primarily responsible for taking the action to remove him, but got no satisfaction here from any of us. I certainly was not going to dob Rupert in. He might have put the match to the gunpowder but we were all equally involved. Vincent and McLachlan were also subjected to an interrogation, obviously along less personal lines, and both firmly held their ground. Falkingham, too, was in the gun. When Sir Warwick asked him if he had known about the meeting on the 18th, he replied, with meticulous honesty, that he had, even though he could not have known what form it would take or what its outcome would be. Sir Warwick, who regarded this knowledge as disloyalty, was to hold this against him on future occasions.

As soon as I had left Sir Warwick's office after our second session, he came into mine and said that, in spite of what had occurred, he and Mary were keeping their undertaking to lend me her cottage at Blackheath, which by chance had been arranged for the weekend twelve days later. They appeared both surprised and annoyed when I decided to go ahead, but not to do so seemed to me to be a sign of weakness as I in no way regarded myself as the guilty party.

I had arranged to go to Melbourne for a few days on the 24th with Sue Du Val, who knew something was up but sensibly did not question me about it. Neither did my hosts Guilford Bell and Denis Kelynack, who were the soul of kindness and tact with their preoccupied guest.

During this time Willi Perndt, who was a good friend of Sir Warwick and someone we could trust completely, was acting as go-between. He told us that if the board meeting called for 1 September to give effect to the directors' intentions went ahead, Sir Warwick would seek an injunction on the grounds that his dismissal from the chairmanship was illegal. He believed he had 'saved' the company when Rupert was incapacitated by age and McLachlan by heart trouble. But Perndt had arranged a meeting between Sir Warwick and Rupert for Sunday the 29th, and in the course of their three-hour talk at Fairwater, Sir Warwick asked 'incapacitated old Rupert' to return as chief executive and work with him as they had before. He went back over the fifty years of their close association in a way that Rupert, an emotional man, found deeply affecting. 'By God, he was brilliant', he said to me later. 'The bugger nearly had me on side!'

While negotiations with Perndt were continuing, I flew on to Canberra to decide the winners of the poetry section of the Marten Bequest with David Campbell, who had arranged a lunch at his property, and then drove on to Bowral. It had been agreed that Sir Warwick would surrender his executive powers, and the negotiations now converged on the payment of a satisfactory retiring allowance and the timing of the retirement, which was agreed as six months hence.

On the 1st I caught the early train from Moss Vale, which Chief Justice Sir Laurence Street, coming from his property at Canyon Leigh, almost failed to catch. He sat chatting to me for a while, not aware, as he later said, that I was about to attend such a momentous meeting.

The meeting, in fact, was almost an anticlimax. Sir Warwick arrived twenty minutes late, prompting speculation on whether he would turn up. He apologised, though, and immediately enquired about McLachlan's health. The meeting was soon over: Sir Warwick dissented from the first two resolutions rescinding his executive powers with immediate effect, and his office as chairman from 1 March 1977, on the grounds that they were not in the best interests of the company. Other resolutions passed concerned his vacating his office and being provided with one in Hunter Street together with his furniture, a car (his Rolls) and driver. I was appointed deputy chairman and there was a proposed retiring allowance of $250 000, to be approved by shareholders at the AGM.

Sir Warwick said he did not regard the amount as generous but Rupert, with the agreement of us all, said that any sum greater than this could subject both the company and family to damaging criticism. Sir Warwick asked that the matter be discussed further with his advisers but in the event, that was the amount finally paid.

Two more resolutions provided that Falkingham would continue as general manager, but subject to the control and direction of the board as a whole, and not to the chairman as previously; and that I would be appointed chairman of directors when Sir Warwick ceased to hold that office.

He closed the meeting with the words 'That is all the business,' and departed, symbolically closing the door behind him. As we left, Rupert grabbed my arm and said, 'It's all over bar the shouting'. This was true but the shouting was to take some curious forms, extending over the next few months, and a lot of it we were only to hear second-hand.

Richard Walker drove me back to Retford Park in torrential rain and I began to feel the effects of the traumatic two weeks. My wise and witty friend Walter Pye came to lunch one day from his house at Burradoo and cheered me up and I finally drove to the much-discussed Blackheath cottage where Morson Clift, Harold Hertzberg and Schofield Mitchell joined me for the weekend. I tried, with their assistance, to put it all out of my mind. The weekend concluded on an almost surreal note with a Sunday barbecue lunch, for which Richard Walker and his wife Sandie[8] drove up, that saw us sitting outside on the veranda, muffled up to the eyebrows, with snowflakes falling on our heads.

After my return to Sydney, I sent the key back to Mary with a letter of thanks. Rupert had said to me, after his three-hour session with Sir Warwick, that he was 'reasonably certain' he could restore some sort of relationship between us. This proved to be an over optimistic judgment as it was four years before Sir Warwick spoke to me again, except about office matters at board meetings or board lunches. Caroline and Philip were also ostracised by Warwick and Mary for this period because of their support for me, but Annalise, while giving basic support and comfort to her father, was careful to maintain friendly relations with us, and we tried to explain to her why the deposition had occurred. Her parents having been divorced when she was eight, she had considerable self-reliance and had grown up with a strong Christian attitude and belief. She was greatly helped by the commonsense and good nature of her husband David.

Twice, towards the end of this period, I went to Sir Warwick's office at his request to discuss company matters, although on the second visit family affairs were involved too.

The board had agreed that no announcement, apart from my appointment as deputy chairman, would be made until the AGM in October (at which, interestingly, Sir Warwick announced that he was 'leaving' the chairmanship, refusing to use the words 'resign' or 'retire'). Falkingham told me he regarded me as the chairman now and certainly Sir Warwick, other than presiding at board meetings in a fairly formal way, was not active in company affairs, nor did he appear to be spending much time in the office over the six-month period before his retirement.

Only later, by degrees and with the helpful information of a few friends, did we learn that he had been active in other ways involving the company, engaging in intensive discussions with a number of people in an attempt to avert the inevitable, and raising the issue of a takeover. This was to result in a further confrontation at the first board meeting I took as chairman the following March. Also, his membership of the Syme board had not been settled and was to come up in February.

From the middle of October, though, we were mainly occupied with the sixty-day strike, begun on the 21st, by the PKIU (Printing and Kindred Industries' Union) and other production unions. As deputy chairman I became involved, partly in a morale-boosting way, with our efforts using staff and executive labour to bring out all our publications. The fact that this was success-fully achieved, apart from the technical advances in computer typesetting that made it possible, was due to the incredible endeavours of everyone involved under the most difficult of circumstances.

Since Tom Farrell, then executive manager (assistant to the general manager), first submitted his proposal to investigate the acquisition of a computer typesetting system in April 1975 (which resulted, eight months later, in the purchase of the Arsycom system for an outlay of $7 million over five years), we were very much aware of the industrial implications. Implementation of the proposal could result in the displacement, either elsewhere in the company or through retirement, of between three and four hundred employees. Consequently, the PKIU had been formally presented with a proposal designed to protect the interests and livelihood of all the company's employees.[9] Nothing like this had happened before, but the future economic viability of the newspaper industry depended on its success and the John Fairfax group was the first in either the UK or Australia to attempt it on such a scale.

The PKIU had called a twenty-four-hour stoppage on 21 October 1976 because of the management's refusal to accede to demands, made in response to the technological changes, for a thirty-five hour week, a $20-a-week pay increase, Medibank contributions to be paid by the company and a guarantee of no retrenchments. Falkingham reported to the board that few retrenchments would be involved except for employees taken on after September 1975, who were regarded as temporary. The $20 increase was clearly outside indexation guidelines, however, and the majority of PKIU employees worked under thirty-five hours a week already.

The Broadway building was picketed and confrontations often degenerated from verbal to physical forms in spite of the presence of the police, who were both firm and restrained in their actions. It was worst in the publishing docks where the *Sun* drivers and newsagents collected their papers, and violence sometimes ensued. I went down there from time to time to give encouragement to Grahame Wilkinson, the editorial manager, who was valiantly performing his task of directing the trucks in and out. We were all subjected to verbal abuse whenever we entered or left the building, and edging one's car through the scrimmage to the car park was sometimes a daunting experience.

The directors' dining room was thrown open, at lunchtime and for part of the evening, to all executives and there was a great feeling of camaraderie as we related to each other various incidents. The television stations were covering the strike fully and, as some of the day's events were shown on the evening news sessions, offers of help came in and there was considerable public support for our stand. A typical offer of help came from Neville Goodall, a family friend who, with a group of his friends retired and living at Palm Beach, was prepared to run the gauntlet of abuse. Unfortunately, it was not practicable to make use of such offers, but they were greatly appreciated.

We had often berated governments and industry in our leading articles for giving way to union pressure and now we were being put to the test ourselves, not for the first time but never for so long a period. I made a brief announcement for television and was then the subject of a cartoon in a PKIU handout. I was amused to see that the cartoonist had captured perfectly a habit, which seems to afflict me when making speeches, of using mainly the right side of my mouth.

The strike was finally settled on 20 December with the company agreeing to amend the definition of a temporary employee to one who had joined after 21 December 1976. This, indeed, was the only concession gained by the production unions after all the hardships their members had undergone during the sixty-day strike.

Another condition of settlement, which was of vital significance to the newspaper companies, was that the PKIU agreed to accept arbitration by the Industrial Commission on the use of the video display terminals used in the computer typesetting process. This was to result in the celebrated judgment of Mr Justice Cahill, on 3 August 1977, which stipulated that journalists should input all editorial material to the VDTs. Only contributed editorial material, such as letters to the editor and articles by outside writers, would be put into the Arsycom system by the PKIU; telephoned classified advertisements would be keyboarded by the clerks. This important decision meant that the company could use the new technology to its best advantage, and following severance agreements negotiated in 1978, the printers agreed to the new system.

Having won the right for sole use of the VDTs, the journalists made a number of claims, the majority of which involved training and health checks. These were generally accepted but the sticking point came with their claim for a $50 weekly operating allowance. Before Mr Justice Alley of the Arbitration Commission, counsel for the Australian Journalists' Association (AJA) made a somewhat extravagant submission about the traumatic and radical changes to journalism resulting from the new technology. In reply, the newspaper companies submitted that the use of a VDT had no bearing on the professional skills of a reporter in obtaining and writing his or her piece, nor did it add to the skills required for a sub-editor.

The judge attempted to have the best of both worlds. He did not feel the operation of the VDTs constituted a significant addition to the work requirements of reporters; nevertheless, the cumulative effect of the changes, together with mental pressures, did amount to a significant addition to work requirements. When he awarded the journalists $5, the AJA banned the use of the VDTs and, following dismissals at News Ltd and Fairfax for refusal to operate them, a national strike began on 13 May 1980 which was to last thirty-one days. Strikes involving the journalists tended to become more emotional than production ones simply because of the nature of the beast — creative talents are nurtured by volatile temperaments — and this was the first strike since the 'down-grading' strike of 1967, which was itself the first to be initiated by journalists. Strikes by journalists also impose a greater strain on resources, as it is virtually impossible to produce all publications using exempted editorial staff and anyone else in the building with pretensions to writing ability.

I recall a certain amount of horse-trading going on behind the scenes with the AJA, but finally, a six per cent increase for those operating VDTs plus three extra days' annual leave were accepted nationally by 1781 votes to 558, Sydney voting against by 416 votes to 364. Following the return to work, Falkingham's humane side, exemplifying the traditional Fairfax attitude towards its employees, was seen at its best in the memo he sent to editors, advocating that:

> . . . *for reasons of common humanity we need to establish and maintain immediately after their return a normal and natural relationship . . . Some employees will have been through and will continue to go through a period of acute financial distress and . . . we need to help to restore a normal way of life . . . We do not want to be charged with retrospectively financing the strike but humanitarian and employee relationship considerations must be paramount.*

8

TAKING THE BATON

A   MOVE   TO   THE   CHAIR,   AND   DEFENCE   OF
THE   HERALD   &   WEEKLY   TIMES,   1977–80

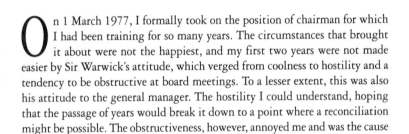

On 1 March 1977, I formally took on the position of chairman for which I had been training for so many years. The circumstances that brought it about were not the happiest, and my first two years were not made easier by Sir Warwick's attitude, which verged from coolness to hostility and a tendency to be obstructive at board meetings. To a lesser extent, this was also his attitude to the general manager. The hostility I could understand, hoping that the passage of years would break it down to a point where a reconciliation might be possible. The obstructiveness, however, annoyed me and was the cause of a number of sharp exchanges.

The first board meeting at which I presided was on 17 March. Following my words of welcome, which expressed confidence that board members would continue to work together in the best interests of the company, and to which Vincent responded, it had a very stormy start indeed. Late in 1976, Sir Warwick had held discussions with Ranald Macdonald, allegedly about mustering support from several friends to make a takeover bid for the Fairfax company. Among those who confirmed that this approach was made are Ranald Macdonald, Sir John Atwill and Jim Wolfensohn. Sir Warwick had also summoned a number of friends in the weeks following the August decisions and the board meeting on 1 September, but this, I gather, had been mainly for purposes of comfort and consolation, as well as to complain about the conduct of myself and my fellow directors. One or two who were also close friends of mine, such as Charles Lloyd Jones, were put in a position of divided loyalty, which they handled with impeccable fairness. Indeed, it was Charles Lloyd Jones who agreed to act as an intermediary, to see if

I would agree to see Jim Wolfensohn on Sir Warwick's behalf.

The meeting took place at Rosemont (Lloyd Jones' Woollahra home) one morning early in December, and after some preliminary talk about the chairmanship, Wolfensohn said Sir Warwick was prepared to accept the situation with good grace, and resume friendly relations with us, if we would agree to him being given an honorary title such as president or chairman emeritus, and to him retaining an office at Broadway. My immediate reaction was that it would be wrong to try and 'buy back' a relationship and that it would put the whole thing on a false basis, leading to confusion and unnecessary difficulties. My fellow directors entirely agreed with me, and I informed Wolfensohn accordingly.

The question of Sir Warwick's retaining his seat on the David Syme board had come up at the February board and while everyone agreed that I, as the new chairman, should join the Syme board, Sir Warwick was unwilling to relinquish his seat, which meant that either McLachlan or Falkingham would have had to step down. He said he had been largely instrumental in bringing about the agreement with the Syme family and that he felt his influence with them was very great. Rupert was clearly of the opinion that Sir Warwick should step down in favour of me and it was decided to leave the matter over until the next meeting.

At the March board, Sir Warwick made it clear that he had understood 'next meeting' to mean 'annual general meeting', although this was not the understanding of Vincent, Rupert, McLachlan or myself as we all saw the issue of Syme board representation to be one of some urgency. As the minutes record (in this abbreviated version):

> *Sir Warwick said he had already stated that he would not resign and the Board could discuss it as long as they liked. It was in the best interests of the company and the* Age *that he should remain on the board. He also said that if he did not resign the matter would have to be left until the next AGM, to which Mr Henderson replied 'not necessarily'.*
>
> *Mr Henderson went on to say that he had indicated at the last meeting his feelings that the interests of the company would be best served if Sir Warwick stood down from the* Age *board in favour of the new Chairman. Sir Warwick had expressed unwillingness to do this. Since then a lot more information had come to hand that made it essential to press for his resignation from the* Age *board.*
>
> *Sir Warwick had engaged in discussions with Mr Ranald Macdonald concerning a possible takeover of this company . . . and Mr*

> *Henderson said that he had had confirmation from a number of people, among them Sir Philip Jones, Mr Wolfensohn, Lord Barnetson, Murdoch and Sir Warwick's own solicitor. There had been certain activities detrimental to the company. The arrangement made and undertakings given were subject to some conditions. Sir Warwick must honour them. Failure to do so must inevitably influence the board in its consideration of two important matters:*
>
> > *The recommendation to shareholders of payment of a retirement allowance to Sir Warwick as retiring chairman.*
> >
> > *Sir Warwick's continuation in office as a member of the present board.*

According to Rupert, his advice to the other directors would be to refuse to pay a retiring allowance, or to allow Sir Warwick to retain a seat on the board, unless the board received firm assurances on his future activities. This led to Sir Warwick complaining about the amount of 'notice' he had been given, at which point I said, as chairman, that if he did not want to reply to the allegations, the board should proceed to consider who should be on the *Age* board. According to the minutes, 'Mr McLachlan said certain allegations had been made that Sir Warwick, as a director of [both the Syme and Fairfax boards] had had discussions of a particular nature with the managing director of one board without the knowledge of other directors on either board'. He said he himself was a director of both boards and would have expected to be told of these discussions if the allegations had substance.

With the chairman's permission, Rupert moved 'that it be noted that it was the board's wish that Sir Warwick resign from the Syme board and that the Fairfax directors on the Syme board should be Mr J. O. Fairfax, Mr A. H. McLachlan and Mr R. Falkingham'. The resolution was put to the meeting and carried by two votes to one, the chairman and Mr McLachlan abstaining and Sir Warwick dissenting.

At no stage did Sir Warwick specifically deny that he had been having discussions about a takeover — he simply refused to answer the charges and said that there was no evidence. He argued that his position on the Syme board had nothing to do with the so-called charges and should be considered separately; he reiterated that he would stay on that board until removed. Rupert, on the other hand, linked the information we had received not only with the Syme board but also with Sir Warwick's position on the Fairfax board and the various arrangements that had been made with him, including the $250 000 retirement payment approved by the AGM.

At the end of the discussion, which took place in a calm although tense and rather unpleasant atmosphere, I was left with the clear thought that Sir Warwick might have put himself in the position where he could not properly remain a director of the Fairfax company. Fortunately this did not come about.

Apart from difficulties with Sir Warwick, one of the most vexing questions we had to face during the first three years of my chairmanship was the profit of the five Sydney publications: the 1976–77 figure was a horrendous loss of $3 million. The group profit of $15 532 000 had been sustained by a rise in television profits from $351 000 in 1974–75 to $4.5 million in 1976–77. The obvious way to remedy the situation was to raise advertising rates and cover prices. This would require, to some degree, that the strong (the *Herald*) sustain the weak (the *Sun* and *National Times*) but to nothing like the same extent as ATN was sustaining the whole group. Unfortunately, two directors — Sir Warwick and Rupert — proved to be firmly opposed to taking these steps, although for different reasons. At the March 1977 board meeting Sir Warwick said that it was quite proper for the Sydney papers to be allowed to run at a loss, carried by television, the *Age* and the country papers.

A month earlier, Falkingham had proposed raising the cover price of the *Herald* from twelve to thirteen cents, to equal that of the *Telegraph*. This followed strong representations for an increase from the Newsagents' Association, which was pushing the *Telegraph* at the expense of the *Herald*. Both Rupert and Sir Warwick had resisted the proposal, claiming that we were seeking profitability and not looking to the quality of the product. Falkingham's view was that the increase would prevent our sales being eroded by the newsagents' action and would return some of the $9 million costs unrecouped since 1974. I supported Falkingham but no decision was made for a further month, by which time the position had worsened to the point where unrecouped costs could amount to between $12–14 million if nothing was done.

Rupert conceded that the newsagents had a case and when, during the March board meeting, a message arrived saying that the *Telegraph* had gone up to fourteen cents, all increases were agreed on. Over the next two years, however, it was a continual struggle to get appropriate increases through the board, with Sir Warwick and Rupert inevitably forming an alliance against them. McLachlan finally said to Rupert that he was playing into Sir Warwick's hands by constantly siding with him against the management and being critical of Falkingham, who was doing a very competent job. I totally agreed with this and was to have a certain amount of difficulty with Rupert myself as the time came for him to relinquish his various directorships, although it was finally achieved amicably and harmoniously.

It is hard to know why Rupert persisted in what both McLachlan and I regarded as unjustified criticism of Falkingham. He could have had difficulties in coming to terms with the fact that he had lost some influence in the company, and he took it out on the person who was in fact running it. The trading losses of the Sydney papers improved by $1 million in the next twelve months but the figures still had to be turned around. Falkingham persevered in his efforts with another memo to the board:

> . . .*it has been suggested that I am obsessed with profit, to the detriment of the quality of the* Herald. *I know of no instance where the* Herald's *quality is being unreasonably affected for the sake of profit . . . Past experience dictates that we should have a profit objective. This will become more important as we move into new technology: if we are not careful we will find that the company carries the risks while readers and advertisers reap the benefits of new technology.*

He also included a memo from Greg Gardiner. As administration manager second to Falkingham, he was playing an increasingly important part in the company, and would have been well aware that Falkingham would reach his sixty-fifth birthday in 1980.

> *Basically our poor profit performance derives directly from our positive decision not to recover even the bare amount of cost increases that have been forced upon us . . . I would suggest that the board's policy of not recovering major cost increases as they occur is probably unique in the land . . .*

These arguments seemed unanswerable to me and with the greater confidence I was developing as chairman, I was able to give stronger backing to Falkingham. While the five Sydney papers were still not making their proper contribution, as a group they were back in profit in 1978–79, and we were finally on the right track.

The composition of the board was also of early concern. From the beginning of my chairmanship I had been particularly anxious to appoint two 'outside' directors to the company — in other words, to appoint, for the first time, directors who were not members of the family or former chief executives. While the shareholders had always accepted the family's control as being beneficial to their own and the company's interests, I felt that, as a public company with a fifty per cent public holding (including staff funds), they should have the opportunity to be represented by directors with broad commercial experience from elsewhere in the community. In addition, bringing in new blood to a board that the community could regard as being somewhat incestuous — particularly in the case of a media company where regular contact with the business community was essential — could not fail to be of benefit. In general my fellow directors shared my view, with Rupert and McLachlan adopting a more cautious approach.

In 1977, there were two vacancies on the board, which otherwise consisted of Sir Warwick, Vincent, Rupert, McLachlan and myself. In the course of several informal discussions that took place in the directors' thirteenth-floor sitting room towards the end of the year, we all put forward names and commented freely on the possible drawbacks of individual candidates, such as their being part of a particular lobby, or subject to pressure to push a special interest. One of the advantages of the existing board was that nobody had any outside interests apart from cultural, community or charitable, with the exception of Vincent, who was scrupulously circumspect in defining his obligations as a Fairfax director, as opposed to those he had with other companies.[1] However, we all accepted that a candidate with the necessary qualifications, unless he was an academic or from the legal profession, would have links with the business community and would soon become acclimatised to the way the company was run.

We ended up with a short list of three (one of whom turned out to be unavailable), and in December 1977 Sir David Griffin and Arthur Lissenden accepted invitations to join the board. Sir David, who attended his first meeting the following February, was a friend of Sir Warwick's and it took all his skill gleaned from his experience as a lawyer, former Lord Mayor and chairman or director of several major companies to steer a diplomatic course between the conflicts and tensions existing on the board at this time. Neither he nor I was assisted by Sir Warwick asking him to lunch to give him a rundown on the defects of the new administration and the terrible way it had come about. He soon learned the ropes but I think at first his methodical mind found some of our customs (such as the fact that traditionally we did not discuss editorial policy at board meetings) a little strange. Even though there were opportunities at lunches and informally to exchange views, he chafed at this restriction — with some justification — until, a few years later, I inaugurated regular dinners for this purpose.

He also found it strange that newspapers devoted to the free enterprise system did not consistently support the non-socialist parties. He accepted the fact that our prime purpose was to enunciate general political principles rather than elect a specific party, but not unreasonably wanted to know what those principles were. We managed to put them on paper some years later. Sir David was to become an extremely valuable member of the board.

Our other appointment, Arthur Lissenden, knew both the newspaper business and the major personalities in it through his many years with the Bowater Corporation. He was a longstanding friend and business associate of Rupert, and knew the rest of us quite well, so he was in a better position than Sir David to appreciate exactly what he had let himself in for. He, too, was given Sir Warwick's views on myself and the company over lunch, but I think he was able to give them somewhat shorter shrift than Sir David. His death in March 1985 was a great loss to the company and I lost a good friend and supporter.

Towards the end of 1979 I had several discussions with Falkingham about his impending retirement as general manager in 1980. He would be sixty-five in May and, having completed ten years in the post, did not want to extend his term beyond the normal retirement age. I agreed to support his election to the Fairfax board in place of Angus McLachlan, who had indicated to me that he wished to retire from it that year.

McLachlan's leaving would be a momentous occasion for me, even though he was to remain on the board of AAP until 1981 and of ATN until 1982, and I was to continue to benefit from his wisdom and advice, as I do to this day. We had been through a lot together, his friendship meant a great deal to me and the understanding and robust commonsense — he never pulled his punches if he thought he should be critical of me — he showed from my earliest days, were of the greatest importance to me. I would greatly miss his presence on the board. Nevertheless, I welcomed the appointment of Falkingham, as he was of proven loyalty and I thought his considerable knowledge and fighting spirit would be of great value to the incoming management. I did not realise how difficult it would be to obtain the consent of some of my fellow directors, nor could I have foretold that his directorship would terminate in the unfortunate way it did a year later. As far as the incoming management was concerned, Falkingham's view was obviously extremely important and I thought it would be a great help if he and I were in agreement before I had any discussions with the board, although for tactical reasons I would not necessarily make that agreement clear.

On my return to the office in January 1980 after the Christmas break, it became evident that we both thought Greg Gardiner was the obvious and logical successor. Since joining the company as administration manager in 1975, he had become an increasingly valuable deputy to Falkingham, which was culminate with his work on the successful Herald and Weekly Times (H&WT) deal in 1979.

The claims of Tom Farrell could not be ignored, however. Originally a distinguished journalist, he had risen through a number of editorial management positions in which his steadiness and sound judgment had helped surmount several crises, and his recent major contribution had been on the technological side. It was subsequently suggested that he missed out on the top job because of the failure of the Arsycom computer typesetting system which he had largely chosen. In my view, Farrell could not have been expected to shoulder the blame in this exceedingly complex and, at that stage, experimental area. As a board we had accepted his recommendation and the buck had passed to us.

For the future chief executive of the company, though, Gardiner had the expertise in the areas of corporate finance which were vital to its future. At thirty-six, compared to Farrell's sixty-two, he also had youth on his side, with the drive and ambition that often accompanied it. Nevertheless, it was a bitter blow to Tom Farrell when I finally told him the board's decision. He accepted it with customary stoicism and, with characteristic loyalty, continued to serve the company in a number of capacities.

Our next problem was how to deal with editorial control. Following my succession as chairman, Falkingham and I had a totally satisfactory arrangement with each other on the editorial side. But, as I shall detail in Chapter 12, when Farrell became assistant general manager, the position of executive editor — occupied firstly by David Bowman and then by Bob Johnson — carried with it some congenital difficulties. Falkingham sent me a memo that, amongst other things, suggested establishing an editorial position with direct access to the board.

It proposed a dichotomy. A chief editorial executive (this was to become his title) would report to the chairman and attend board meetings but would also be under the basic authority of the general manager. There had been a forerunner of this arrangement in 1969, following McLachlan's heart attack, when Falkingham as treasurer and Lou Leck as editorial manager had acted in their respective spheres under the authority of Sir Warwick. This temporary arrangement had worked quite well until the establishment of Sir Warwick as a Committee of One and Falkingham's appointment as general manager, but how could such a dichotomy work? Clearly it would depend very much on the character and ability of each executive, particularly their ability to work with each other. We would be taking something of a gamble with both.

The candidature of Max Suich for the editorial post was soon established, but no discussion of any editorial post could fail to include the two men who, since the death of Graham Perkin in 1975, were the other major editorial talents in the country: Vic Carroll and Max Walsh. Carroll was at that time chief executive of Sungravure while Walsh was managing editor of the *Financial Review*, but the mix of qualities required, in our view, put Suich in front. Whether this would be the view of the board was quite another matter, and I arranged what was to be the first of three long and often gruelling meetings.

It took place on 14 February in stifling conditions, the air conditioning being ineffective, in the directors' thirteenth-floor sitting room. At a distance of ten years I shall not attempt, let alone trespass on my readers' patience, an account of the many ins and outs the discussion took over the three meetings before a decision was reached. Generally speaking, the atmosphere was reasonable, although Sir Warwick's increasing propensity to interrupt when others were speaking made me feel that I was sometimes acting like a schoolmaster.

I had to sell both the concept and the candidates, which I eventually did, not without natural misgivings being expressed by all directors. Sir Warwick finally agreed to Suich but held out against Gardiner to the end, Farrell being his preference. He said he would vote against Gardiner but as we walked upstairs to the boardroom for the formal meeting, he said he would abstain. It had been quite a struggle and when I recounted the story to Falkingham afterwards, and thanked him for suggesting the concept, he congratulated me on the outcome. We were both very confident of the future progress of the company.

Gaining directors' assent to Falkingham's replacing McLachlan on the board had also presented some difficulties. Apart from Sir Warwick's personal hostility, some others felt the former chief executive's presence might inhibit the performance of his much younger and untried successor. Having had experience of the former chairman on the board I had some sympathy with this view, but it did not alter my opinion of Falkingham's value. At any rate I was able to allay their fears.

The meeting to approve the appointments of Gardiner and Suich was held on 27 March 1980 — my forty-seventh birthday — and Sir Warwick duly abstained, to my regret. I had failed to convince him of the correctness of the proposed new management structure, but he was later to concede that it was working well. Gardiner's appointment was to date from Saturday 1 November, following the AGM on the previous Wednesday, while Suich's was to be arranged by Falkingham and myself — in the event it was 21 July.

I confirmed that the group general manager would have overall responsibility to the board and that if matters arising between him and Suich could not be resolved in consultation with myself, they would come to the board. I felt that such an event would be unlikely.

A few months later, a momentous event occurred — my reconciliation with my father. In July he telephoned me at the office and asked if I would meet him at the offices of our legal advisers Stephen, Jaques & Stephen (now Malleson Stephen Jaques) as there was a portrait there by Brian Westwood of Alastair Stephen that he wanted to look at (Westwood was the artist chosen at my suggestion to do portraits of Sir Warwick and Vincent for the boardroom for the *Herald*'s 150th anniversary the following year).

During the telephone call there was a perceptible pause and he suggested, in a slightly awkward way, that perhaps we might have lunch afterwards. With scarcely a moment's hesitation I agreed, thinking that this could be the breakthrough — there had been one or two signs at a meeting at his office earlier in the year that indicated he was anxious to end the rupture. We duly met and, after looking at the portrait, went to the Brussels Restaurant in Paddington. After some stiffness, lunch proceeded amicably and we caught up on a lot of news, including family matters. It was not until he had paid the bill that I said, 'Thank you for that lunch. It has helped to heal a breach of four years.' He replied, 'I was hoping you'd take it that way'. Outside we shook hands and as we parted, visibly moved as indeed I was, he turned and gave me a curious little wave. Subsequently, on 16 July, I attended a dinner at Fairwater.

I cannot deny that our breach had weighed heavily on my mind over the four years and I hoped the change, quite apart from the personal aspect, would lead to a new era of teamwork on the board. This was to be the case for four years until we became embroiled in the capital raising question in mid-1984. Sir Warwick accepted the Gardiner and Suich appointments when they took up their posts, and cooperated well with them. He voted for Falkingham's election to the board and managed to treat him in a reasonably amicable way for the year he was on it.

At the board meeting on 27 March, we had also discussed the vulnerability of the company to takeover threats and the position of the family holding as a defence against such attacks. Gardiner said the retention of family control was enormously important as the company's investment in the H&WT (see below) would not, in the next few years, make a significant contribution to its income or progress. We then discussed our capital requirements, the issue that became one of the most difficult and demanding that Gardiner had to face during his period as chief executive. He said the company had not made a public issue since 1964 and we needed an injection of at least $10 million. Our ratios were approaching the upper limit at which the lending market was prepared to lend unsecured, and secured borrowing would impose all sorts of formal restrictions. It was essential to convert our short-term borrowings. A preference issue would be too expensive at a time of high interest rates and, of course, an ordinary equity issue posed problems for the family in keeping its percentage intact. At that time, the impetus for our concern in this crucial area stemmed from Rupert Murdoch's attempt, four months earlier, to take over the H&WT.

Outside of television and magazines, the basic confrontation and most fierce competition in Australian media at that time was between John Fairfax Ltd and Murdoch's News Ltd. The H&WT and Fairfax were more partners or associates, particularly in television, newsprint and the provision of news services, although, apart from this relationship, we always regarded the H&WT's independence as being of fundamental importance from the point of view of diversity of competition and the gross imbalances that would result from a Murdoch takeover. Never in its history had the Fairfax company launched an aggressive bid against another publication or company, and would not until the final act in the H&WT drama, which was near the end of its own life as a major public company. As Souter puts it, Australia's principal newspapers had been herded by instincts of attack and defence. An attack by A upon B could lead to defensive action by C, which might consider itself threatened by any change in the balance of power; in these circumstances, defence might well resemble attack.[2]

The battle began on the morning of Tuesday 20 November 1979, when Falkingham received a phone call informing him that Murdoch was about to announce a takeover bid for the H&WT. He immediately called Keith Macpherson, the H&WT's chairman and chief executive, to be told that Murdoch and Sir Kenneth May (the managing director of News Ltd) had just left the building. After Falkingham assured Macpherson that we would do all we could to help the H&WT preserve its independence, he discussed the situation with Gardiner and me and we agreed to start buying H&WT shares.

The largest single shareholder, other than Queensland Press and *Advertiser* Newspapers, was the AMP with 3.5 per cent, and Gardiner was able to obtain an undertaking from that company that it would not sell without first letting him know. Before flying to Sydney to see Falkingham and myself, Murdoch called Ranald Macdonald and told him that if he won control he would honour existing agreements between the H&WT and David Syme. It is important to note here that Macdonald was opposed to a Murdoch takeover from the start, both on the grounds of dominance of the industry and of problems that could arise in industrial negotiations and with the *Sunday Press* agreement, in which David Syme was in partnership with the Melbourne *Herald*.

When Murdoch and May arrived at my Broadway office, Murdoch made his quoted remark to Falkingham: 'Falkingham is not laughing', to which the latter replied, 'No, but I've been laughing all morning'.[3] This was a reference to our arrangement with the AMP, of which Murdoch was evidently unaware. Murdoch had a very confident air and assured us he would preserve all relationships we had with the H&WT. Relationships JFL had with H&WT included joint control of Australian Newsprint Mills and the joint 95 per cent shareholding in Australian Associated Press. There was also our partnership in the Seven Network. He was curiously coy about television, however, saying that he had not given it much thought. As the Broadcasting and Television Act stood then, he would have had to sell two of the four television stations owned by the H&WT and he said he was thinking about this.

The following morning, several important things happened. Firstly the H&WT made a defensive move by announcing a bonus issue of one for two and at the same time a record profit of $20 million. This move, which Murdoch had predicted at our meeting, raised its issued capital from 63 to 95 million shares. Secondly, Sir Warwick, who was on a six-month overseas trip, rang from London to stress the importance of buying as many H&WT shares as possible to frustrate the bid. In pursuit of this aim, and in response to a request from the AMP for an immediate bid for its shares, we (my cousin John, who had joined the board in February 1979 following Rupert's departure in October 1978, Falkingham and myself) had to make the decision to buy in advance of the board meeting arranged for three that afternoon. The sum involved was nearly $10 million with an escalation clause in the event of another bid.

When the board met, Falkingham presented three contingency plans, two intended only as illustrations. The first involved action by the H&WT subsidiaries in Adelaide and Brisbane and the second, interestingly enough in view of events six years later, was a takeover bid for the whole company. However, the third plan, which involved an outlay of $38 million to acquire a fifteen per cent shareholding, was clearly the one to pursue.

The two major factors influencing the board were the company's competitive position, given the enormous strength and richness of assets that acquisition would bring to Murdoch, and the question of public interest. Apart from the possible damage to the profit and liquidity of Fairfax's assets, the board felt strongly that it would be a scandalous situation if Australia was left with only two newspaper groups, and that attempts by both political parties to regulate the activities of the press could result from such a situation. Judging by their reaction to the successful Murdoch takeover of 1986-87, this could have proved to be an over-sanguine estimation of both parties' concepts of public interest.

On Wednesday 21 November, it was finally decided to buy up to five per cent of the H&WT shares and to go to fifteen per cent if this would guarantee its independence. On the same day, the Trade Practices Commission (TPC) requested Murdoch to stop buying H&WT shares while the Commission studied the implications of the bid.

The following day Gardiner organised the share purchase, and he and Falkingham flew to Melbourne to see Macpherson and John Dahlsen, the H&WT's legal representative, to inform them of the board's decision. Both greatly appreciated our offer, especially as we would have to make sacrifices in relation to our television stations.[4] They described our action as a 'wonderful gesture'.

At 11 am the same day, Murdoch announced the withdrawal of his bid and the sale of his shares. The next day, the *Australian* claimed that News Ltd had 'outfoxed the Herald and Weekly Times camp by selling through a broker which had not been involved in the affair, while at the same time maintaining one of its known brokers in the market'. In fact, in building our holding up to 14.9 per cent we were aware of the possibility that the shares we were buying could have been those sold by Murdoch, who could have been manipulating the market to keep the price up. Gardiner was aware that the takeover had effectively collapsed before Murdoch's announcement. He had emerged with a modest profit but had failed to gain the prize — it was hardly the 'share market coup of the decade' proclaimed by the *Australian*.

The board was still keen to go ahead with the 15 per cent share purchase and sell it into friendly hands as soon as this could reasonably be arranged at an appropriate price. Apart from a reduction of our television interests, it would mean, as Falkingham explained to the board, that borrowings would increase by $25 million, there would be a profit loss of $800 000 after tax, and the investment holding would be overvalued.

Offset against disadvantages would be the very powerful protective benefit of the acquisition of a fifteen per cent holding in the Herald and Weekly Times and the knowledge that Queensland Press, already one of the two largest H&WT shareholders and 'friendly' to Fairfax, also had 15 per cent. In addition, we had reached an agreement with Queensland Press whereby each would have first option to buy the other's shares should either decide to sell. We were well satisfied with the outcome of our labours in a very dramatic week, and welcome words of encouragement came from Sir Warwick in London, who said that the operation had been brilliant in concept and execution.

The next Fairfax board meeting, at 8 am on Monday 26 November, was a historic occasion as part of it was attended by the chairmen of H&WT and Queensland Press, Messrs Keith Macpherson (later Sir Keith) and William Leonard, together with John Dahlsen. Falkingham outlined the three major areas where the company was acting to protect the interests of the shareholders, employees and public, and it is worth reiterating these.

1. *Control of the Herald & Weekly Times by Mr Murdoch would create political and public disquiet. This would lead to repressive legislation and press controls which would make it difficult for us to perform the role we see for ourselves in the community.*

2. *News Limited would become capable of making very large profits outside New South Wales and using them to the detriment of Fairfax's earning capacity.*

3. *News Limited would become this company's partner in Australian Associated Press and in Australian Newsprint Mills Limited. News Limited would be able to fix the selling price of newsprint to the detriment of ANM and ourselves.*

He referred again to the $800 000 decline in profit after tax and said there was no doubt that the decline would have been much greater if Murdoch's takeover had been successful. The board accepted all proposals and the Melbourne *Herald* men were invited in to hear the decision. Macpherson gave warm thanks for our support and Leonard said we had reached an agreement that Queensland Press had never dreamed would be possible. I replied in appropriate terms, expressing confidence that the three companies would work together in harmony in the future. It was certainly the high point in our relations with the H&WT.

However, there was to be a singular lack of harmony in another quarter. It had, of course, always been our intention to inform Ranald Macdonald of the deal before the public announcement, and by chance he rang Falkingham on Monday morning suggesting lunch. Falkingham asked him to call back at 4.45 pm, when he would have 'something interesting' to tell him. When Macdonald duly called back he was told the outline of the deal and replied 'Good, good, good', which Falkingham took to indicate approval. It is true that he sometimes used this expression to indicate interest or that he had taken the information 'on board', which he maintained he had been doing on this occasion, but its use certainly gave the wrong impression.

I had said in my public statement that we did not have or seek to have a controlling interest in the Melbourne *Herald* or any of its activities. We had not actively sought to make any acquisition but, apart from the interests of our shareholders and employees, had acted in the public interest to ensure as wide a degree as possible of independence and diversity of reporting and comment.

During the course of the following day, Macdonald had telephone discussions with colleagues at the *Age* and came to the conclusion that our shareholding in the H&WT would be detrimental to the independence of the *Age* and its ability to compete forcefully with the *Herald* group. The H&WT would be regarded as being under an obligation to Fairfax — we had invested $50 million for our 14.9 per cent shareholding, which was 70 per cent of our own market valuation, and we already owned 57 per cent of David Syme with the H&WT having built up a 14.5 per cent holding in that company. *Age* readers would not accept that their paper was independent or had freedom to compete and he feared that the careers of journalists would be limited as they would in effect have only one employer.

None of these fears was realised, although I am sure they were genuinely held by Macdonald, but they prompted him into an impetuous and ill thought-out act followed by public statements which I believe were damaging to the *Age* and, in a lot of companies, would have cost him his job. Competition between the two companies was not affected nor, despite a number of alarums and excursions among the journalists, was the independence of the *Age* compromised.

Early in the morning of Wednesday the 28th, Macdonald telephoned me and asked if he could call and see me on the way to the airport. In a fifteen-minute meeting, he expressed the above views and said he had been asked to see the Trade Practices Commission in Melbourne that afternoon. He gave me a letter proposing that if we would agree, by 4.30 pm, to sell our Syme shareholding back to Victorian interests, he would tell the Commission that, in his view, our purchase did not involve dominance of the Victorian market or the loss of freedom to compete; otherwise his evidence would be to the contrary.

I was flabbergasted by the threat but repeated the arguments in my statement, together with the additional assurances that we would not be represented on the H&WT board nor have any knowledge of its proceedings. I was due at an ATN board meeting at 10 am where I could consult with Falkingham and MacLachlan, but I told him I could not conceive that we would dispose of our Syme shareholding under his ultimatum or indeed at any other time. I said I would get back to him before 4.30 pm.

When I got the reply back to him through my secretary, Eleanor Foskett, at Broadway, he dictated a second letter to her which made it clear that it was the Syme family who would buy back the shares. He made the additional comment that, in the event of our failing to agree, the matter 'will need to be escalated into a public debate as it is obviously in the area of public concern and interest'.

In retrospect it is hard to believe that Macdonald really thought we would submit to his ultimatum. I have already said that I do not doubt the sincerity and, indeed, strength of his views, but it is difficult to avoid considering the possibility that he also visualised using the situation to what he saw as the *Age*'s advantage, forcing, through public action, a diminution in our Syme shareholding. Macdonald strongly denies this interpretation. The *Age*'s editorial on Thursday 29th took a rather more balanced view, conceding that our 14.9 per cent was preferable to Murdoch's 50 per cent and pointing out that we could be outvoted by companies closely linked to the H&WT. It went on to comment, 'Even if Fairfax were in a position to dictate editorial or commercial policy to the *Herald* chain, there is little in past experience to suggest that it necessarily would. The same could not have been said with any confidence if Mr Murdoch had won the day.'

It went on to express deep concern, though, about any concentration of media ownership, ending with the Sibylline utterance: 'While Mr Murdoch is around, it is unlikely that Australia will be subject to a national press monopoly, but there is no doubt that the events he precipitated last week have brought us closer to an effective press duopoly'.

At the Fairfax board on Wednesday the 28th, a brief statement in reply to Macdonald was issued and McLachlan reminded the meeting that Fairfax had purchased Syme shares

> *. . . to ease the cash problems of the Syme family who were not then entitled to their shares from the David Syme estate. Fairfax undertook to buy these share in advance . . . the Fairfax interest had built up from about 47 per cent to 57.5 per cent [because] Syme family interests had sold their shares from time to time and under the purchase arrangements we had been forced to buy them. Notwithstanding the disparity in the two shareholdings [Syme owning 15 per cent], each party was entitled to be represented by three directors on the board until the family interest fell below 10 per cent.*

A special meeting of the David Syme board was called by Mrs E. H. B. Neill (Nancy Syme — Macdonald's mother and one of the three David Syme directors) for Tuesday 4 December. We had no idea what Macdonald was proposing to do at the board meeting but, in discussions we had the previous day, I told directors it seemed to me that as our advice was that legal challenges would fail (the TPC had announced on the 30th that we had not contravened the Act), he would be left with two choices: to accept defeat and attempt to make the partnership work, or to continue to use methods of attempting to break up the partnership arrangement by public and political activity.

We agreed that we should avoid a situation in which we would have to call for Macdonald's resignation, but this must depend on his future conduct. To this end we would endeavour to carry four motions. These could be blocked by a three-all vote, but Macdonald could not vote on matters affecting his contract of employment. The motions would be: firstly, that no legal costs be incurred without board approval in relation to the matters covered in recent comment by the managing director; secondly, that no legal action related to these matters be continued or commenced by David Syme unless authorised by the board; thirdly, that the managing director should not make any further public statements in his capacity as an employee of the company unless authorised to do so by the board; and, lastly, that no public statements be made by any director about proceedings of the board.

When we arrived at the Syme office the next morning, we were besieged by waiting journalists who seemed convinced that we were about to sack the managing director. At the opening of the meeting I read the strongly worded statement in a tense and uncomfortable atmosphere. It traversed the history of the partnership agreement, showing how our holding had built up to 57 per cent through sales by the Syme family at their own request and on advantageous terms. There had also been a share issue to Fairfax to help finance the building Syme had acquired in Spencer Street which had increased our holding by 10 per cent. I reiterated that we sought no H&WT board appointment, that on no occasion had Fairfax directors on the David Syme board acted in the interests of John Fairfax & Sons Ltd in priority to those of David Syme & Co. Ltd, and that, having regard to the history of those directors on the board, it would be extreme to suggest that their deliberations on the Syme board would now be influenced by a desire to protect the interests of the Herald and Weekly Times Ltd.

I went on to express our concern about the widespread and long-lasting detrimental effects to David Syme of the managing director's attacks: creating fears and doubts about the standards and integrity of the press in Australia, encouraging an inexorable move towards government intervention in the freedom and activities of the press and creating, amongst the company's own employees, fear and doubt, of which there was no sign until Mr Macdonald spoke out.

It was not a pleasant task having to read my statement. Eventually, our four motions were put to the meeting by Falkingham and Gardiner, who was attending his first meeting in place of McLachlan. Three were lost 3–3 but the fourth, concerning public statements by directors about board proceedings, was carried unanimously. At the next Syme board meeting, on 11 December, Macdonald replied to my statement in terms of his earlier comments and it was clear that the question of whether or not our purchase was disadvantageous to the *Age* was one on which we could not agree.

The meeting ended on a better note, passing unanimously Mrs Neill's motion 'that the *Age* is and will remain a strongly independent newspaper in unrestricted competition with other newspapers circulating in Victoria and that David Syme & Co Ltd itself will remain a strong and independent company'. After this meeting we all went to lunch at the National Gallery of Victoria, where the winner of the 1979 Graham Perkin Memorial Award for Journalism was to be announced. To the surprise of many guests, Fairfax and Syme directors and executives mixed with each other in a friendly fashion over drinks.

I felt confident that our relationship with Macdonald could be restored but the burden of debt we had undertaken concerned me. Extinguishing it, by a sale into safe hands such as Queensland Press, was in my mind until it came to pass in July 1981.

At our January board meeting, the future of our holding was discussed following an inquiry by Macpherson, who was keen to know our intentions. One aspect that worried him was the possibility of the control of John Fairfax changing: some members of the family might sell or Murdoch might make a takeover offer and acquire 35–40 per cent, thus putting the independence of the H&WT in jeopardy again. We had to decide whether to refinance our borrowings short-term or long-term but, provided the independence of the H&WT could be guaranteed, it would be better to get our money back on the investment. This would necessitate Macpherson making watertight interlocking arrangements between all his companies in Melbourne and the other capital cities and we would have to press him to do this. It was agreed that it would have tremendous public impact if we could say that we were withdrawing from the H&WT because our objective had been achieved.

9

HARMONY IN HAZARD

RELATIONS WITH RANALD MACDONALD AND
THE DAVID SYME COMPANY, 1966-84

The relationship between Ranald Macdonald and the John Fairfax board had never been easy. Although it reached the lowest point with Macdonald's display of outrage in November 1979, subterranean strains were a continual source of concern to the Fairfax board and senior management both before and after that public eruption. Most of the arguments were over the quality of investments made by the David Syme board at Macdonald's urging, and over the meagreness of information on their progress. Other points of friction were Macdonald's reluctance, as chief executive of a Fairfax subsidiary, to give information directly to the parent company; the Syme board's refusal to accept that Syme and Fairfax should have the same auditors; Macdonald's role as instigator and witness in a board of inquiry into press ownership; and Macdonald's acceptance of outside appointments at a time when the Syme company was beset with problems.

The Syme-Fairfax partnership, established in 1966, resulted in the voluntary sale of shares by Syme family members to the extent that, by 1972, the Fairfax interest in the Syme company rose above 50 per cent and the company became a Fairfax subsidiary. By 1979, the Syme family members had reduced their holding to about 15.5 per cent while the Fairfax holding had risen to 57.5 per cent.

Under the agreement, the Syme family had voting rights equal to the Fairfax company, despite the disparity in shareholdings, as a safeguard of the *Age*'s independence and of the Syme family's influence. This arrangement would continue unless the Syme family interest fell below 10 per cent. Meanwhile,

Fairfax was obliged by the agreement not to support a resolution at a shareholders' meeting if the Syme family opposed it. This provision, together with the equal division of Syme board seats, meant that Fairfax itself could not achieve the passing of any resolution, either at a meeting of shareholders or a meeting of directors. Nor, as this chapter will show, could Fairfax do much to curb defiance of its wishes by the Syme chief executive. Goodwill on both sides was needed to make such a partnership work properly and, in the late 1970s and early 1980s, Fairfax directors often felt that goodwill on the Syme side was lacking. The focus of their dissatisfaction was Ranald Macdonald, great-grandson of David Syme and the last of the family to have an executive role in the company.

Macdonald had been managing director of David Syme and Co Ltd since his appointment on 14 October 1964, at the age of twenty-six. His achievements had been considerable. Not least, he played an energetic and resourceful role in forging the Syme-Fairfax partnership, achieved in the face of attempts by Rupert Murdoch's News Ltd and Sir Frank Packer's Consolidated Press Ltd to frustrate it. Then, having chosen the gifted Graham Perkin as editor in 1966, Macdonald oversaw a radical redevelopment of the once-stagnant *Age*. A return to the reformist attitudes of the *Age*'s early years under David Syme was accompanied by a successful reach for a wider and younger audience through livelier appearance and content. Macdonald's steadfast support of Perkin, the trust between the two and their shared idealism were crucial to this revolution.

Macdonald saw to it that the editorial advance by the *Age* was matched with innovative marketing policies and — following a badly needed move from antiquated facilities in Collins Street to new headquarters in Spencer Street — production developments that included offset colour printing, computerised typesetting and the preprinting of sections of the *Age* to enable it to cope with a prodigious expansion of classified advertising. Regular weekday supplements, introduced under Macdonald to draw new readers and new advertisers, were to become a model when the strategy was later taken up by the *Sydney Morning Herald*.

Other achievements of the Macdonald era included a venture into audio and video tape production in 1974 through the purchase of two companies that became AAV-Australia Pty Ltd. This grew to be the Syme group's largest and most profitable subsidiary, providing facilities and production services to the radio, television, music, advertising and entertainment industries, as well as to industry, commerce and the government. It provided for Syme a rewarding route to participation in the television industry, from which it was barred as a broadcaster because of the Fairfax television interests. The Syme suburban newspaper interests flourished and expanded, while in the country a notable and highly profitable acquisition was the *Warrnambool Standard*, a daily with a history reaching back more than a century.

In radio, the Melbourne station 3XY prospered with Syme as half-owner of its operating company for eleven years from 1968, rising in the ratings from bottom to top. It was still at the top when the lease agreement between the owners of the 3XY licence and the operators was ended. A later venture in radio, fifteen per cent participation in the syndicate awarded the licence for Melbourne's 3 Fox-FM, also proved highly profitable.

In spite of all this, as Fairfax directors increasingly questioned Macdonald's judgment in his later years as managing director, they found it easier to recall his failures than his successes. Chief of the failures had been the launching in 1969 of *Newsday*, a lightweight tabloid evening paper pitched against the entrenched broadsheet Melbourne *Herald*. *Newsday* closed after seven months with losses totalling between $3 million and $4 million.

Syme embarked on two troublesome and unrewarding ventures in 1978 — Syme Media Enterprises, formed to publish trade magazines in Hong Kong, and an investment in Computicket, an Australian ticket agency network. By September 1979, the Fairfax board was aware that Syme Media Enterprises threatened heavy irrecoverable losses, but the company limped on until 1984, when its magazines were sold. Computicket, in contrast, operated for less than seven months before going into liquidation on 12 February 1979 with a deficiency of $2.6 million. Its failure reached the proportions of a national scandal and the two subsequent trials dragged out the Computicket story until May 1982, when Harry M. Miller, executive chairman of Computicket Australia Pty Ltd, was sentenced to three years' imprisonment for aiding and abetting the company in the fraudulent misappropriation of money belonging to concert promoters.

Miller had been in good standing in the Australian business community at the time he invited Syme to join in — a director of Qantas, head of the Royal Jubilee Committee and special advisor to the Federal Government on Australia's bicentennial celebrations. After investigating a number of feasibility studies to assess the market and the technology, Macdonald was convinced that Computicket was a sound investment when he put it to the Syme board on 13 December 1977. The Fairfax directors resisted it but finally, 'in the interests of harmony', as one of them put it later, they agreed to Syme's buying 125 000 (12.5 per cent) of the shares in Computicket Australia Pty Ltd for $125 000 and putting in $125 000 more as a loan. Other main shareholders were Harry M. Miller and Co. Pty Ltd (350 000 shares), The Myer Emporium Limited (150 000), Computicket Pty Ltd of South Africa (100 000), David Jones Limited

(50 000) and Efftee Broadcasters Pty Ltd (30 000). Except for the South African company, all the shareholders, like Syme, agreed to lend funds equal to the amounts paid for their shares.

Computicket opened in Sydney in August 1978 and in Melbourne in November. A wide range of entertainment and other ticketing and subscription activities was signed up, bearing out the investors' assessment of the market. But as early as September, it later emerged, the company was facing a cash crisis. Nearly all the working funds were gone and ticket sales lagged far below the level at which transaction fees would cover outgoings. Macdonald knew the business was in trouble before Christmas, and in January he authorised a further loan of $260 000 to Computicket, an action requiring later endorsement by the Syme board. I was not told any of this until Macdonald came to see me in Sydney, on 8 February, four days before the company closed down.

There was strongly expressed discontent at this lack of communication when the Fairfax board met a week later. Falkingham reported that the Syme investment was in a disastrous position, with a threatened loss of $500 000 to $1 million, with little of it, if any, tax deductible. Syme would undoubtedly lose the initial investment of $250 000, plus the further advance of $260 000. It had agreed to make an amount available to the pool of ticket creditors in proportion to its shareholding. This was not a legal responsibility but a moral one, Falkingham said, and all the greater because of the circumstances of the failure.

Where had all the invested funds gone? Two months after the collapse, the liquidator's report to creditors showed that none of the money paid for shares in Computicket Australia had gone to that company. The incoming investors had in fact bought their shares from Computicket Holdings Pty Ltd, a company owned by Miller. The only cash available to Computicket Australia had been the $800 000 lent by the shareholders, funds 'completely inadequate for the intended scope of the company's operations'.

During the six-week trial, Macdonald gave evidence that before Syme agreed to invest, Miller had told him he was backing Computicket, his major achievement, 'with his own time, his own money, and substantial amounts of money.' It was basic to his recommendation to the Syme board that Miller put in a substantial sum — $700 000, half in loan and half in capital. Had he been aware that Miller was not putting in any of his own capital 'I would not have recommended putting a cent into it'.

Barely three months after Computicket collapsed, I was surprised to receive, as chairman of John Fairfax Ltd, a letter from Mary Fairfax, as a shareholder, proposing Macdonald as the next chief executive of the Fairfax group on

Falkingham's retirement in 1980, and for a seat on the Fairfax board if McLachlan's ill health obliged him to retire as a director. Praising Macdonald for his 'track record of increased circulation and increased classifieds,' she conceded that *Newsday* and Computicket were blemishes on his investment record. But he could be restricted in the investment area, she said, 'so that he can concentrate his efforts in the area where he excels, that is, in the established newspaper operation sector.' She argued for 'Fairfax family decision' (underlined twice) on the crucial question of who should be chief executive. 'We need someone,' she said, 'with enough proven ability and toughness to cope with Murdoch and Packer.'

My brief reply said in part:

> *Any shareholder has of course the right to express a view to the Chairman — some have the opportunity to gain more knowledge of office affairs than others — but I am sure you will recognise that it would be wrong for me to discuss in any detail internal office matters which are the concern of the Board. I shall confine myself therefore to saying that I am not in agreement with the proposition you put forward.*

It was clear to me at that time that no member of the Fairfax board — except, perhaps, Sir Warwick — would have considered for a moment making Macdonald chief executive of our group and there would have been difficulties working with him as a director on the Fairfax board. There was deepening concern at our deteriorating relationship with the Syme partners and, because of Computicket, renewed doubts about Macdonald's judgment. Within six months these doubts were to be emphatically confirmed by Macdonald's behaviour in the H&WT drama.

Mary's letter, it seemed to me, stemmed from a special relationship which she and my father had formed with Macdonald. Macdonald and his wife dined with Sir Warwick and Mary from time to time during the period after Sir Warwick had been obliged to resign from the chairmanship of John Fairfax Ltd. It will be recalled that Macdonald was among those with whom Sir Warwick discussed a possible takeover of the company.

When I raised these discussions with Macdonald some time later, he passed them off lightly. He did not think it improper or even odd that he, as chief executive of a Fairfax subsidiary, should have been consulted in such a way by a Fairfax director. I concluded that Macdonald felt that the takeover scheming would come to nothing and that there was therefore no breach of duty in his listening to Sir Warwick out of simple courtesy.

Four months after Mary's petition on Macdonald's behalf, the Fairfax board needed to appoint a new director of the Syme company to succeed McLachlan. The choice fell on Greg Gardiner, administration manager of Fairfax and the man who would, in fact, become Fairfax's chief executive on Falkingham's retirement. The need to keep a close watch on Macdonald was raised by Vincent in backing Gardiner's nomination. If it was a choice between a top journalist and a top financial and administrative executive, he said, the way was clear. There was no need to worry about editorial expertise at Syme and, indeed, we should not involve ourselves too much in the question of what went into the *Age*. However, there did appear to be a real need to supervise Syme financial activities and proposals. It appeared Syme had done some bad deals because of inadequate investigation.

During 1980, as the reverberations of the H&WT uproar died away, the Syme partners complained about Fairfax purchases of Syme company shares on the market. It was pointed out that we were not buying aggressively — in fact, our purchases in the past year had amounted to only 0.3 per cent of the capital. Six months later, the Syme partners wrote to the Fairfax board, asking John Fairfax Ltd and its associated companies and funds to refrain from buying Syme shares outside the partnership. They were concerned that such purchases would reduce the number of shareholders and the number of shares available for public trading on the Stock Exchange. The Fairfax directors agreed that we should not commit ourselves to any specified limits on further buying, bearing in mind that the Syme family had allowed their holding to dwindle and might eventually decide to quit the company altogether. It was a mark of the strain between us that our reply to the Syme partners went to our solicitors for checking before it was sent.

A decision of the Victorian government to order an inquiry into ownership of Victoria's newspapers, announced in October 1980, set the stage for Macdonald to renew his attack on the investment in the H&WT as a threat to press freedom, and to air his case for Fairfax to divest itself of its shares in David Syme. The inquiry, under retired Supreme Court Judge John Norris, QC, was to examine the existing concentration of newspaper ownership and control, and to assess the desirability, in terms of public interest, of regulating ownership and restricting the number of shares and votes that any one person or group of associated persons could have.

Macdonald welcomed the inquiry, recalling his own repeated pleas for a Royal Commission into media ownership. Among Fairfax directors there was deep concern that the actions of a director and chief executive of a Fairfax subsidiary had, as we saw it, opened the way for possible government interference

James Fairfax with Sir Philip Jones, Chairman of Herald & Weekly Times, at Bob Falkingham's retirement dinner in October 1980. Between them can be seen Sir Philip's successor, Sir Keith Macpherson.

in the press. We foresaw a considerable expenditure of money and executive hours on Fairfax representation at an inquiry which could have no useful outcome.

Our irritation was not diminished when, at the November Fairfax board meeting, we learned it had come out that Rupert Hamer — the Liberal Party premier who had chosen Norris — had telephoned Macdonald privately to ask whether he thought the chairman of the Australian Press Council would be a better choice than Norris to conduct the inquiry. Falkingham reported that Macdonald, when asked at the last Syme board meeting why he had not relayed the conversation to the board, replied that it had been confidential. Falkingham said he then told Macdonald that he could not, as chief executive, keep information from the board.

At a Fairfax board meeting three weeks before the inquiry hearings began on 9 February 1981, Gardiner (by now general manager of Fairfax as well as a director of Syme) said Macdonald had been advised that if he appeared, he should do so as an individual and not as a representative of the Syme company. His observation that Macdonald had been in London for a week brought a comment from Falkingham that Macdonald's 'unapproved absence' was typical. Macdonald had not made any mention of it to the Syme board. At this stage, said Gardiner, Fairfax's costs at the inquiry were already $30 000 to $40 000 'with a lot more to come'.

Fairfax presented the most detailed written submission, 112 pages, arguing that the legislative controls foreshadowed in the terms of reference would amount to a special system for licensing newspapers, 'a system that was tried centuries ago and found to be productive of great abuses'. We said controls would work against established principles, could not be justified as a way of correcting existing or potential anomalies, would be difficult and expensive to administer, and might present consitutional difficulties. We submitted that the combination of existing legislative controls and market forces provided adequate protection of the public interest. If a regulatory law were to create a distinction between what might be read in Victoria and in other parts of Australia, 'it would be contrary to public interest and would be condemned by the Victorian public as obnoxious'.

The board of David Syme Ltd in 1981. **Left to right:** *Greg Gardiner, Mrs E. H. B. Neil, Ranald Macdonald, James Fairfax, David Hayne, Bob Falkingham. Photo:* Age

The Syme board did not make a submission but Macdonald, the first witness, proposed a statutory body to which amalgamations, mergers and acquisitions would be compulsorily referred. He thought it possible for such a body to examine current ownership. He saw nothing wrong with the body's being able to order divestiture of ownership as long as there were clear guidelines. Divestiture would enhance freedom of the press by increasing diversity. He could see no problem for the Syme company if Fairfax was ordered to divest its shareholding in the *Age*.

As for the Fairfax warning about licensing, 'I think that is an emotive word used quite deliberately to make it seem as though the alternatives are the devil or nothing.' Later, in a written submission, Macdonald proposed that acquisition of shares in the capital of a major newspaper proprietor by another major newspaper proprietor should be illegal and void, unless a press amalgamations tribunal was satisfied that the transaction was in the public interest.

After the hearings ended on 12 May, Tom Farrell, assistant general manager of Fairfax, reported to the Fairfax directors a strong feeling that Norris would recommend the tribunal Macdonald wanted. He was astonished that Macdonald had lent himself to the proposition, particularly as the inquiry report might well be for a Labor government to handle. It was felt that Macdonald had placed himself, and the company for which he was responsible, in a most invidious position. He had damaged his company and his shareholders by taking independent and irresponsible action.

As foreseen, Norris did recommend a Press Amalgamations Authority. He found, inevitably, a very high degree of concentration of ownership and control, with two companies, the Herald and Weekly Times Ltd and David Syme and Co Ltd, controlling just over 80 per cent of Victorian newspapers. He therefore proposed legislation to establish an independent authority 'to whose scrutiny would be submitted certain transactions involving the acquisition by corporations publishing newspapers, or by persons with a substantial interest in such corporations, of interests in other newspapers.' A substantial interest was defined as ten per cent. Any transaction would be deemed contrary to the public interest, the report said, unless the applicant showed that the further concentration involved was not contrary to the public interest. In that event, the authority might give its consent. Otherwise the transaction would be void.

The Victorian Liberal government, now led by Hamer's successor, Lindsay Thompson, had less than seven more months to run when Norris presented his report on 15 September. The Thompson government did not act on the recommendations, and neither did the Labor government of John Cain which came to power in April 1982.[1]

In June 1981, six weeks after the Norris hearings ended, Macdonald again raised the issue of Syme board chairmanship, a source of longstanding disagreement as the Sydney directors, while agreeing that the chairman should come from the Syme side, could not accept one person as both chairman and chief executive. Now, Macdonald's solution — which, he wrote, would 'work to everyone's advantage' — was that he should relinquish the title of managing director and become executive chairman, 'with, of course, no erosion of my current authority'. He outlined the advantages as he saw them, expressed his desire 'to improve the relationship between the two companies' and reiterated his 'hope that the time will come when there is some means of communication through me to your board on matters of mutual interest . . .'

His proposal foundered, though, on the Fairfax view that if he became executive chairman, this would in fact be another way of combining the position of chief executive and chairman. He and Mrs Neill accepted this in discussions with Gardiner and me. It was agreed that the system of Syme directors rotating as chairman should continue.

The unease among Fairfax directors at their lack of control of the David Syme subsidiary was reinforced in 1982 when the Fairfax auditors, Kent Brierley and Barraclough, expressed a parallel concern. At Syme the auditors had been unchanged since the company's incorporation in 1948 and were now part of Arthur Andersen and Company. Kent Brierley and Barraclough, noting their liability as group auditors and the increasing statutory demands on them, put to Fairfax that they were in a difficult position when they did not have full access to the 21 per cent of the group which was Syme. They could go to Syme and inspect the audit working papers, but this just scratched the surface and if more was done, the Syme audit fee would be doubled. They asked to be given the Syme audit to give it 'the direct attention it should have'.

Fairfax had previously suggested this change of auditors without success, but this time the Fairfax board passed a formal resolution asking the Syme company to consider appointing Kent Brierley and Barraclough. The request met with stiff resistance from all three Syme family representatives on the Syme board, and no agreement could be reached. Fairfax accepted defeat for the time being, Gardiner suggesting that we should keep the matter alive without exerting too much pressure. Under the partnership agreement there was nothing else we could do, he said. The agreement was based on goodwill, but the rejection of our request 'showed total lack of goodwill or worse by the Syme family partners'. In the upshot, the change of auditors had to wait until Fairfax achieved full control of Syme.

At this time there was also some concern about Macdonald's commitments outside the company. As leader of a group of seven campaigning to replace the committee and president of the ailing Collingwood Football Club, Macdonald featured on the news and sports pages of the Melbourne papers, including the *Age*, in a way disturbing to Fairfax directors. Macdonald gave assurances that there was no conflict of interest and that he had always been careful about outside activities — among offers he had turned down, he said, was a university chancellorship.

Macdonald took over the Collingwood presidency on 16 September 1982. He claimed, in reply to concerns expressed by Fairfax representatives, that the appointment would not impinge on the effort and time he gave Syme or his attendance in Hong Kong to see to Syme interests there — his Collingwood meetings would be on Monday mornings and Thursday nights, and he would attend matches on Saturdays. The confidence of this answer seemed to be underlined when, two months later, he added to his outside responsibilities the chairmanship of Victoria's 150th anniversary celebrations.

Early in 1981 David Syme had made its first move into television broadcasting, buying an interest in Hong Kong's Rediffusion Television Limited, operator of the lesser of the colony's two stations. Syme, through its Melbourne subsidiary AAV-Australia Pty Ltd, was already successfully involved in videotape and audio-visual production, but the Broadcasting and Television Act's restriction on its broadcasting here rankled with Macdonald and when the opportunity came to buy a controlling stake in RTV he responded with enthusiasm.

With the help of the newly licensed Australian Bank, Syme found two other Australian companies, Henry Jones IXL Ltd and CRA Ltd, to come in as equal partners in a consortium to buy 61.25 per cent of Rediffusion Television Limited. The shares came from the British-owned Rediffusion (Hong Kong) Limited, which had tired of RTV's unbroken history of losses since it began in 1973. For the time being, Rediffusion (Hong Kong) retained a 20 per cent holding, with other Hong Kong shareholders owning the balance.

There was no enthusiasm at Fairfax for the venture, which Falkingham referred to as 'another Computicket', but the Fairfax representatives on the Syme board voted for it. Our decision was influenced in part by a wish to promote some much needed harmony in the Syme-Fairfax partnership, and in part by our judgment of the merits of the proposition put by Macdonald. The investment turned out to be far worse than Computicket. Over its three years it cost Syme more than $6 million in losses. As well, it absorbed the energies and time of Macdonald and other Syme executives while recession was eating into the *Age*'s earnings and the rival Melbourne *Herald* was thrusting into real estate classified advertising.

The investment was fateful for Macdonald personally and for the Syme-Fairfax partnership. The deepening troubles in Hong Kong through 1982 and into 1983 put a heavy burden on him, and it seemed to us at Fairfax that they played a part in the timing of his departure from David Syme and the ending of the partnership. Macdonald, however, strongly denied, both in a conversation with me and by letter, that this issue or any other problems faced in his last years were a factor in his decision to sell.

Despite the change of ownership and further injection of capital, ratings did not improve, the rival station continuing to out-rate it by at least four to one. A new partner was sought and a relaunch planned for May 1982, but by this time the Fairfax directors were already looking at any cash injections solely as a means of protecting our investment until we found a way to withdraw, and CRA had decided to commit no further funds.

By the end of May the Deacon Chiu family of Hong Kong had come in as half-owners. The Chius, Macdonald told the Syme board, were well respected in Hong Kong. Controllers of the Far East Bank, they had substantial finance and extensive experience and interests in the film industry. On completion of the deal, Deacon Chiu became chairman and his young and inexperienced son Dennis became deputy to the Australian managing director, a preliminary to taking over the post.

The misgivings at Fairfax deepened as problems continued: the lift in ratings was short-lived and financial projections by Dennis Chiu, now acting managing director, proved over-optimistic, although there was, 'as far as could be traced', a profit in October 1982. Even by July, there had been a strong feeling on the Syme board that our investment, which had cost $9.7 million, should be sold as it now stood.

The Fairfax board looked again at the situation in February 1983 against a backdrop of falling Syme profits — down 26.2 per cent in the first half of 1982-83, with a loss expected in the second half. Apart from the troubles at ATV (Rediffusion Television had been renamed Asian Television), heavy losses were continuing in a Syme subsidiary, L&S Educational Supply Company, another investment we had originally opposed. We were worried that, if Syme had to write down the value of the two investments in the annual accounts, the whole Syme profit could be eliminated.

To try to be fair to Macdonald in an atmosphere increasingly hostile to him, I reminded the board that we did not go into Hong Kong television 'just to be nice' to the Syme partners. There had been a logical argument for going in. We could not have known it would be a disaster, but we were conscious of the risks and were all responsible for having accepted them. Fairfax directors feared that

John Fairfax Ltd board at Australian Newsprint Mills, New Norfolk, Tasmania, in December 1983. Left: John Fairfax, Vincent Fairfax (fourth left), Arthur Lissenden, David Griffin, George Foster (company secretary), Ron Cotton (chief financial executive).

a write-off by Syme would reflect on Fairfax. Gardiner agreed, saying, 'Analysts will say, "You have 60 per cent of Syme but you do not control them. How often are you going to let David Syme do this sort of thing?"'

In April 1983, the Fairfax directors held a long and troubled discussion of the flaws in the Fairfax-Syme relationship, with some questioning the capacity of Macdonald to carry on as Syme managing director. There was a feeling that we must act to change or dissolve the partnership after Hong Kong was settled, whatever the outcome there, although if there was to be a break with the Syme partners and a change of chief executive at the Syme company, it must happen without a confrontation. We had to find a way that would not revive Victorian antagonism of the kind so successfully stirred by Macdonald after our Herald and Weekly Times defence.

Gardiner said the size of the ATV problem probably would not be known until August, but the company would run out of its present supply of cash before then. Macdonald just did not look at things in proper commercial and concrete terms. He also said there had been trouble with Syme over preparation of the 1983–84 group budget. All other managers in the group took instructions and communicated well, but after budget papers had been sent to Syme for completion, word came back that Macdonald had said there was no need to complete them; it was too difficult and they would be looked at in July or August.

Summarising the hazards of the relationship with Syme, Gardiner said he knew all parts of the Fairfax group precisely except Syme. Because communications were not good, no formal statements came from Syme and there was always concern that the full story was not being told. As group chief executive he felt exposed, and as a consequence John Fairfax Ltd was exposed. 'In one move by Syme,' he said, 'all the profit we have worked for could disappear'.

Unexpectedly, Macdonald himself handed us the solution. Although he had been optimistic about the outcome of a special two-day ATV policy meeting scheduled for June, he told Gardiner, with the crucial meeting still in preparation, that he wished to offer his David Syme shareholding for sale to Fairfax and to pursue a new career away from Syme.

In spite of their long association, Macdonald first approached Gardiner through David Block, a merchant banker known to them both. At first Gardiner thought Block was saying that Macdonald wished to discuss the sale of the Fairfax holding in Syme. He told Block there was no point in talking as Fairfax, as a matter of principle, would not be interested in selling. He remembers Block saying, 'Greg, I'm sorry I didn't make it clear . . . What I mean is for you to buy, for Fairfax to buy Ranald's shares . . .' It was a reply, says Gardiner, that 'really floored me.' I was equally floored when Gardiner rang me in London with the news. Macdonald had not told other Syme family members or the other Syme representatives on the Syme board of his approach.

Direct talks with Macdonald followed. Several Fairfax directors were concerned that our purchase of the shares held by the family, let alone the remaining 25 per cent in outside hands, could bring damaging publicity in Melbourne. It was essential that negotiations with Macdonald, and through him the rest of the family, should be handled delicately, and that when the deal was done, control should finally pass to Fairfax in an atmosphere of goodwill. We were determined that there should be no Sydney takeover of management, that the new chief executive should represent continuity rather than revolution. In this we were fortunate in having within the Syme company an obvious choice, the able and respected Gregory Taylor, then fifty-one, who had served as editor of the *Age*, editor in chief and group operations manager.

Before Macdonald went to the rest of the Symes with his proposal, there was a period of more than two months in which he and Gardiner held talks in complete confidentiality. The negotiations went smoothly and so did the family meeting on 14 September at which the members present agreed to sell nearly all their shares — 13.54 per cent of the David Syme capital out of 15.31 per cent held by the family. Important elements in the success of the operation were Macdonald's determination to go as quickly as possible, his shared concern with us that there should be no fuss, and our offer of a price markedly above the level required under the partnership agreement, enabling Macdonald to put to the family that he had negotiated a good deal for them.

'The final sale,' Macdonald later said, 'was the result of a number of Syme partners wishing to sell and being satisfied with a price slightly above the market value. It was not possible under the terms of the partnership to continue to finance the purchase of their shares and, with the prospect of the Syme interests dropping below 10 per cent, I decided to sell my shares as well.'[1]

Writing six years after this ending to a period of strain between Ranald Macdonald and the Fairfax directors, my judgment of the Macdonald era at Syme is that the pluses distinctly outweigh the minuses. The bulk of this account dwells necessarily on our exasperation at things we felt went wrong. Therefore the achievements listed near the beginning of the chapter need to be weighed to arrive at a rounded and fair view of this determined, idealistic and, at times, impulsive newspaperman. As a Syme he, like the Fairfaxes, had pride in a family tradition of serving the public interest through the press. This pride and an attendant jealousy of the *Age*'s independence were elements in his make-up that would have guaranteed some friction between our two companies, however well the partnership worked. Whatever our quarrels with Macdonald's actions, there is no doubting the sincerity of his motivation to serve the interests of the Syme company and the ideal of a freely competitive Australian press.

The Victorian Premier, John Cain, at first reacted sharply to the Syme sale to Fairfax. He said his government would consider options open to it, including legislation, 'to stem this unhealthy trend of concentration of media ownership'. Within two weeks, however, after discussions with the Fairfax company, he said he was confident that the public interest would continue to be served by the *Age* as an independent and Victorian-run newspaper. Sir John Norris (knighted since his inquiry on press ownership) expressed regret at the sale of the Syme family shares.

Here was an irony. Macdonald had argued at the inquiry for a tribunal to examine transfers of newspaper shares, a proposal adopted in the Norris report. No such tribunal was set up, but if it had been, Macdonald (as well as Fairfax representatives) would have had to go before it to justify the deal Macdonald himself had initiated.[2]

Although full control of David Syme had been achieved smoothly enough, the route to 100 per cent ownership proved long and bumpy. After the Symes' sale we held 75 per cent of the capital. To move to compulsory acquisition we needed 90 per cent of the shares remaining outstanding and 75 per cent of the outstanding shareholdings. Confident we would get the Herald and Weekly

Times' 14.1 per cent of the Syme capital, we foresaw little difficulty, but our efforts stalled when Robert Holmes à Court's Bell Group intervened in mid-October, offering $5 a share for the H&WT holding. The H&WT accepted neither the Bell offer nor ours and when our formal offer closed at the end of 1983 we held only 83.77 per cent of Syme.

We let fifteen months pass before returning to the task in April 1985 with an offer of $6 a share for the 16.4 per cent of shares then outstanding. With Holmes à Court buying, bidding soon carried the price above $9. Most of the H&WT holding, one million shares, was then sold at $10.20, but brokers acting for us and brokers acting for the Bell Group argued over which was the buyer. The row went to the Victorian Supreme Court which said the Melbourne Stock Exchange should decide. The Exchange ruled for Fairfax. We then won the remaining 5.67 per cent of Syme held by the H&WT, again at $10.20, to take our stake to 97.72 per cent.

But Holmes à Court was still not finished. Eighteen days later, on 17 May, his Bell Group Ltd announced an unconditional bid of $12 for Syme shares. 'My first hope,' he said, 'is that Fairfax will sell me their shares and I can get 100 per cent, but I don't regard that as highly probable.' We, of course, had no interest in Holmes à Court's offer. It seemed simply a last-minute attempt to hold on to a minority stake in Syme by securing enough of the still outstanding shareholdings to prevent Fairfax from moving to compulsory acquisition. We extended our $10.20 offer from 24 May to 28 June, and on 1 July were able to announce that we had received acceptance from more than 75 per cent of the outstanding shareholders and that we then owned, or were entitled to, 98.02 per cent of the Syme capital. Compulsory acquisition went ahead.

David Syme's involvement in Hong Kong television had only six more turbulent months to run at the time Macdonald revealed to us his intention to resign. At the special meetings in late June 1983 to set new directions for ATV's management, the Australian directors, unhappy with the performance of the twenty-four-year-old Dennis Chiu, succeeded in having his powers restricted. They also saw to the adoption of strict cost cutting to bring expenditure in line with income. In the wake of these decisions the David Syme board agreed to inject a further $700 000 to allow the station, as Gardiner put it, 'to live for another day'.

Conflict grew between the Chiu family and the Australian consortium, with both sides discussing which should buy the other out. 'Immense difficulties' were reported to the Syme board in September and losses continued, particularly bad results in two months resulting, according to Syme's ATV director, from board level disputes which led to neglect of trading activities. The end came on 12 January 1984 when the Chiu family signed an agreement to buy out the Australian consortium for $HK40 million ($A5.7 million). Taylor told the Syme board that this was clearly the Chius' top price. They had agreed to it only after the consortium had prepared legal documents for the winding up of the company. The effect to be shown in the Syme half-year results would be a loss of $4.27 million. Summing up for the Fairfax board in February, Gardiner said the total loss on the venture was $6.2 million — enormous by the group's standards.

10

BOMBSHELLS AND BANNERS

The appointments of Gardiner and Suich were the most important events of 1980, a year that saw us preoccupied with two major problems: the declining condition of the *Sydney Morning Herald* and the large losses being sustained by our magazine company, Sungravure.

Sungravure, the old Associated Newspapers company acquired with the *Sun* in 1955–56, had long been a bottomless pit into which much executive talent had vanished without trace. Gardiner has described it as a historical hangover which (in 1979) should have been closed five years previously. Its outmoded rotogravure presses required enormous print runs to cover their overheads, while the much more efficient offset process had already been adopted by Murdoch for *New Idea*, and Kerry Packer's Consolidated Press was to abandon gravure shortly after we did, leaving only the Melbourne *Herald* using the old process.

The restrictions on size and format imposed by gravure meant that the factory rather than the consumer dictated the type of product. The flexibility of offset and the consequent improvement in editorial content had pulled *New Idea* well ahead of *Woman's Day*, while at Sungravure the less efficient process stifled attempts to raise editorial quality.

The other problem was on the industrial side where all sorts of restrictive practices had built up over the years. In Gardiner's view there were only two choices: closing down the plant or a massive reinvestment in new technology. In the latter case, quite apart from the economics of such an investment in our highly geared state and a situation of intensive competition in a market that was certainly not undersupplied, the appalling union problems would simply be transferred from the old plant to the new. Falkingham had always been totally opposed to any suggestion of plant closure, convinced the problem should be solved without depriving the company of our own production facilities and throwing more than three hundred men out of work.

During 1979 the question of Sungravure had come up at a number of board meetings. On 9 August, John was appointed chairman, a move suggested by Falkingham and welcomed by Sir Warwick, and there was some strong criticism of Vic Carroll, who had been Sungravure's chief executive since 1975. In October and November, budgeted losses of $750 000 and $250 000 were predicted, reversing a profitable trend over the previous few years and in December Carroll resigned, saying he did not have the energy to meet the challenge. We should have dealt with this situation earlier, but in December, Fred Brenchley was moved from the editorship of the *Financial Review* to become the new manager.

The position continued to deteriorate, but Brenchley merged *Woman's Day* with *Woman's World* in February 1980 and in May Falkingham was able to state firmly that the effect of the new management and the merger, together with a move into supermarket distribution and the appointment of Malcolm Stening as national advertising manager, had to be assessed over a period before any decision could be made about Sungravure's future. At the same meeting, Sir Warwick said we would have to consider closure.

At the July 1980 board meeting, Gardiner outlined the available options, including closure (which would cost $2 to $3 million in redundancy payments to seven hundred staff) and various possible mergers or cooperative arrangements with John Sands, the Herald and Weekly Times, Dai Nippon, the Hearst Group and Consolidated Press. Gardiner said his recommendation was that no decisions should be taken until the new management had had time to implement changes and improvements, and the board agreed with him. Losses for the 1980 year were estimated at $4.6 million and for 1981, following improvements, $1.5 million and re-equipment with modern plant would cost in excess of $10 million.

Over the next six months various of the options were pursued. Kerry Packer had made an offer to buy *Woman's Day* for $3 million and a merger with John Sands, owned by the American company, Textron, was turning into a decided possibility. By March 1981, Packer's offer had risen to $4.5 million but we would need $6.6 million to break even and it was resolved to merge with Sands. This would have been a totally acceptable outcome but, by June, most unfortunately, the deal had broken down, partly because of difficulties over Foreign Investment Review Board requirements and partly through a spoiling offer by Packer. Gardiner reported this to the board on the 18th, with the news that the

Sungravure chapel had been on strike for three weeks and there had been damage to cars, windows and buildings.

The situation that then eventuated was the most difficult I had had to face since the confrontation with Sir Warwick in 1976. I had gone to England early in June, expecting all to have been settled and, after doing my television rounds in London, had gone to Spain with my mother. Falkingham was also away at this time, on holiday in Canada. Whilst at the Ritz in Madrid, on 20 June, I had a call from Gardiner telling me the Sands deal had fallen through and that the strike had worsened. The PKIU had refused to cooperate in any way towards improved efficiency despite being warned that this could lead to closure. Their actions had become increasingly violent, and now they were attacking the homes of supervisers and cutting off the water supply at the Rosebery plant with axes. There was also a possible involvement by the local Labor Party branch.

We went through the issues involved in closure: costs would be saved but we would lose colour pre-print facilities for our dailies. The most serious question was the industrial pain it would cause to the men on strike and the hardship to their families. I said I would think about it and call him back the next day. There had been some compulsory retrenchment on our acquisition of Associated Newspapers, but not on this scale and never during a strike. I agonised over it and called Gardiner to say I agreed with closure. He was going to recommend severance pay of three weeks for each year of service.

I flew on to Marseilles, meeting Mervyn Horton and driving to stay a few days with Roderick Cameron (son of Lady Kenmare, formerly Enid Lindeman of Sydney, a member of the winegrowing family) at Ménerbes in Vaucluse. There I got the bombshell from John. As acting chairman in my absence, he had telephoned Falkingham on 28 June to get his final views on the proposed closure which was to be put to the board the following day. Falkingham's reaction was violent. He said the whole thing was a racket, a fraud and a conspiracy, purposely timed while he was out of the country. Gardiner had deliberately fomented the strike to give himself an excuse for taking the action he had always wanted to take. The board was being made the subject of a confidence trick and if he had been able to attend the meeting, he would have moved a motion of no confidence against the general manager.

I was totally stunned by this. We all knew the strength of his opposition, but neither of us could imagine what had got into him to make such allegations. Falkingham had already sent his views, without the allegations against Gardiner, in time for the board to consider, but John felt bound also to report their conversation. I did not suggest any other course, but I thought in retrospect that if I had had the conversation with Falkingham, I would have avoided telling the board until his return, in the hope of getting him to retract the allegation. It would have involved a little subterfuge but it might have prevented his resignation. He said he would resign from the board if the closure went through, making his reasons public. After a long discussion, at which Brenchley was present, the meeting resolved unanimously to accept the proposal for the closure of the printery. Vincent was absent but had indicated prior approval with reservations.

When the board met again on 23 July, after my return, I asked Falkingham to speak about his views and the accusations he had made in the conversation with John. In the course of a long statement, Falkingham's defence of his position focused on three points: the way the meeting had been arranged and conducted with three directors away, what he saw as the inadequate information and figures presented concerning the proposed closure, and John's reporting to the board details of a private conversation between two directors. On the third point there was general agreement that John had no alternative, although there could have been a misunderstanding. Certainly Falkingham denied that he had used some of the expressions quoted, including 'conspiracy'. John, on the other hand, was not in any doubt that the purpose of the discussion had been to ascertain Falkingham's views and convey them, in their entirety, to the board although, had there been more time between their conversation and the board meeting, John might have been able to put them to the board in a more acceptable form. As it was, he was still in a state of shock when he rang me in France, and the board was similarly shocked when they heard them.

I won't recapitulate further what was a long and occasionally emotional discussion. We kept returning to the question of confidence: if Falkingham no longer had confidence in the chief executive, whose recommendation had been supported by the rest of the board and in whom the board had complete confidence, he should resign. Vincent, in a notable contribution, questioned Falkingham's concept of his role as a former chief executive who had become a director, and paid tribute to the great contribution he had made in the former capacity, but felt he had been unable to make the transition successfully. Therein lay the tragedy. The meeting ended unsatisfactorily: Falkingham expressed regrets that his views and his way of putting them had caused offence, but he did not withdraw them and would not agree to resign. I already understood from Gardiner that, under the circumstances, it would be very difficult for him to work with Falkingham in the future. The ball was right back in my court.

Following this meeting I went to see Falkingham at his office in the Macquarie building. We went over the Sungravure situation again. There was less emphasis on the allegation that Gardiner had engineered the whole thing, but he was firm in reiterating that it was not in the company's interest for him to resign. Shortly after this I had lunch with Sir Warwick who, in his turn, reiterated the impossibility of Falkingham's remaining on the board, saying that with his departure we would be a 'happy' board — something I had begun to feel was a contradiction in terms. Falkingham then went to see Rupert and McLachlan to seek both their views and support. The board discussion had convinced me, most reluctantly, that it was in everyone's interests — including the company's — for Falkingham to resign. I went to see McLachlan and Rupert, at their request, in the latter's Hunter Street office and related the whole story as factually as I could, which took nearly two hours. Following Falkingham's visit they were inclined, at first, to sympathise with him. When I had finished, however, Rupert turned to McLachlan and said, 'The best service you and I can do for the company is to persuade him to resign'.

They accomplished this service with great skill and tact, with the result that Falkingham came to see me in my office to submit his resignation, effective from the October AGM. I was pleased that, during the course of our meeting, he stated that he thought I had acted with complete propriety. It was a sad end to a distinguished career, an end that genuinely distressed me. All the directors, with the exception of Sir Warwick, had paid tribute to Falkingham's contribution during the board discussion, and I believe they felt the same way I did.

Falkingham's great achievement, after joining the company as chief financial officer following the financial crisis at the end of 1956, was to establish a firm financial basis for the company as it struggled to adjust to its public status. The creation of a sound budgetary system, the funding of acquisitions and expansionary moves, together with capital expenditure, proceeded smoothly under his direction. Perhaps his major accomplishment during these years was his coordination of the brilliantly successful ATV deal, which resulted in a tax-free capital profit of £3 850 000 in 1964–65. His handling of the successful H&WT defence against Murdoch marked another high point in his career.

He was an ideal foil for the mercurial Rupert and then for the more cautious McLachlan, and, despite the problems, he worked well with Sir Warwick until the mid-1970s. My own relationship with him was ideal — apart from Sungravure, I can recall only two significant disagreements — and I enjoyed his surprising sense of humour at lunches. It was a tragedy that his sometimes aggressive personality flared up in such a way that the damage could not be reversed. It is no reflection on my fellow directors to say that there were times in the future when I wished that his strength and formidable debating powers were still with us.

Two years later, I invited him to lunch at the Union Club. He was quite complimentary about the progress of the company but extremely critical about what he regarded as the gross permissiveness, if not licence, obtaining in the *Herald*, with which he felt the board could not possibly agree. Six years later again, I had another long talk with him and he still strongly believed that the closure of the Sungravure plant was deliberately rushed through in his absence because of his known opposition to it. He maintained that, up to that time, the board had always achieved a consensus of opinion before making a major decision. The forced resignation of Sir Warwick from the chairmanship was, in a sense, the exception that proved the rule, although this was as a result of an agreement between the other directors, outside the boardroom.

I have to agree with him that it was highly unusual for a major decision to be taken in the absence of a director who was known to be opposed to it — indeed, I cannot think of another instance — but this does not necessarily substantiate his conviction that it was done deliberately. I did not believe it at the time and must still disagree with him on this point. I believed that circumstances justified the action being taken but a director, whom events had rightly or wrongly made predisposed to be critical and possibly suspicious, could certainly mount a case that the decision should have been delayed.

Falkingham was also critical of the way the failed Sands negotiations had been handled and said Gardiner had not wanted them to succeed. He said the board had not been given adequate information both on this and other matters. If this were so — and I do not believe it was — it would also be an indictment of me as chairman.

Falkingham told me that he did not feel that he defended himself as well as he could have at the board meeting on 23 July and it has been suggested that he had a health problem at this time, exacerbated by his overseas trip. If this was so, it would certainly go some way to explaining his uncharacteristically violent reaction. He said he was outraged at the tenor of the meeting and he described the atmosphere as one of 'unadulterated venom'. I would use his own expression, 'outrage', rather than venom, to describe the mood of the directors. As an example, he cites Sir Warwick's remaining in the vestibule until I took the chair, in order to avoid being at the same table with him.

By agreement, he did not attend any board meetings after the July one, but he expressed surprise to me that no one had wished him well and that he had not been invited to lunch after the annual General Meeting at which he resigned. In retrospect I think I could, with some difficulty, have arranged a friendlier parting, after such regrettable events. (Interestingly, in light of what was to come, he said he would have supported Sir Warwick in opposing the PIPS capital raising scheme proposed in 1984, although not entirely on the same grounds. He believes that the board's decision to force a vote on the PIPS proposal, and then proceed with Sir Warwick dissenting, was one of the root causes of Warwick's takeover although, as will become evident, I do not believe we had any alternative. Carried to its logical conclusion, Falkingham's attitude on consensus would result in no resolution being carried if any director dissented.)

The Sungravure closure was the first crisis John had had to handle as acting chairman. He had become a director of the company in February 1979, having been manager of Federal Capital Press Pty Ltd for three years. He had joined the company as a cadet journalist in 1961, coincidentally during the period Sir Warwick had stepped down temporarily from the chairmanship because of the Symonds legal action. This in itself had caused a rumpus when I informed Sir Warwick at lunch just before his return. I had no idea he would object but, perhaps with memories of earlier difficulties with his two uncles, Hubert and Wilfred, he told me it had been done behind his back and that I was 'laying up trouble' for myself in the future. The reverse was to be the case as the support I got from John, who developed as a forceful character with a fund of common-sense, was to prove invaluable during my chairmanship, despite occasional differences of opinion.

John had been through a good training period, having been a journalist in the Canberra bureau and the London office; he had then worked in the advertising and circulation departments before becoming personal assistant to Falkingham in 1971. In addition, he had done the short Harvard Business Course in Switzerland. He had been a good manager of the *Canberra Times* and could well expect to climb up the executive ladder, possibly to the top position.

As an executive and director, however, it was clear that possible conflict could prejudice his effectiveness in each capacity. The advantage of making him a part of top-level discussions and decisions, in view of possible continuing difficulties with Sir Warwick, was apparent — but were we, at the same time, depriving him of the opportunity of developing to his full capacity at an executive level? Inevitably there was some discussion about his potential as a future chief executive. The final decision was a compromise and, like many compromises, not totally fair to one of the parties — in this case, John.

He would join the board as a working director and would be constantly involved with various projects and problems that would give him the necessary daily workload. I genuinely believed that this arrangement, which had not worked in my own case for reasons I have attempted to describe, would succeed in John's with the active support of both chairman and chief executive. While acknowledging that John would eventually join the board, Sir Warwick would have preferred to see him continue in an executive position. For a time the arrangement worked well, although John had not given up the idea of becoming a future chief executive and within a few years he was to become restive with his role.

Fortunately, other events in 1981 afforded far happier circumstances than had the closure of Sungravure. In fact it was a most important year for us, being the sesquicentenary of the *Sydney Morning Herald*, an event we had planned for several years. Tom Farrell, as assistant general manager, had chaired a committee which had been allocated a budget of $1 million to fund a variety of schemes, from providing something permanent for posterity to the purely ephemeral. The greatest credit is due to Farrell and this committee for coming up with two ideas that have made and will continue to make a major contribution to the well-being of the citizens of Sydney and its many visitors.

Herald Square, in front of Goldfields House, was established with the cooperation and assistance of the then Lord Mayor of Sydney, Alderman Nelson Meers, and the City Council. The negotiations were complicated but were resolved with the goodwill of all concerned, and the opening, on Thursday 16 April, was one of the most successful events we had. It was a beautiful autumn day with city and harbour looking their best and the scene was enlivened by the presence of lunchtime crowds and office workers from Goldfields House leaning out the windows. In my speech I recalled that the Sydney *Herald* was first published on 18 April 1831 in a small house in Redmond Court, backing on to the Tank Stream halfway between Bridge Street and Circular Quay. I ended by saying that I hoped, when people thought of Sydney now, they would sometimes say 'Give my regards to Broadway, Remember me to Herald Square' — to quote the well-known song by George M. Cohan. The occasion ended with a very festive luncheon cruise on the John Cadman.

In the second major contribution, the State Government cooperated in providing a suitable site to be dedicated as public parkland, with the company contributing a sum which would cover landscaping, planting and maintenance. After several possibilities were considered, a magnificent site on North Head, beyond the quarantine station, was agreed on, with the Minister, Planning and Environment, the Hon. E. L. Bedford, being particularly helpful.

The best way I can indicate the scope of our sesquicentennial celebrations is by briefly describing the events as they occurred, the most significant perhaps being the dinner held on Wednesday 15 April with the Governor-General, Sir Zelman Cowen, as guest of honour. The first event was in fact the opening of the Heritage Photographic competition in association with the National Trust of Australia (New South Wales) at the S. H. Ervin Gallery on 7 April. The object of the competition was to create, for the future, a wide-ranging pictorial record of the heritage — both natural and man-made — of New South Wales and the

With cousin Nancy and the Governor-General, Sir Zelman Cowen, at the dinner to commemorate the 150th anniversary of the Sydney Morning Herald *on 15 April 1981.*

Australian Capital Territory as it appeared it 1981.

The next day the thanksgiving service was held at St Andrews Cathedral, an appropriately ecumenical occasion. It gave me something of a jolt, however, when I discovered I was totally unused to the Bible currently in use in churches. I had rehearsed the lesson I was to read in my King James version, which was quite different. I have never since thought the revised version an improvement — nor, indeed, the new *Book of Common Prayer* an improvement on Archbishop Cranmer's version. I read recently that Prince Charles shares this view.

The following evening at the Art Gallery of New South Wales my fellow directors and I were present at the opening of 'Fifteen Decades of Australian Paintings', sponsored by the *Herald*, with each decade since 1830 being represented by the major artist of that time. At lunch at the Hilton the next day, Friday 10th, Geoffrey Blainey, Professor of History at Melbourne University, launched Gavin Souter's history of the company, *A Company of Heralds*. This was an occasion of particular importance to me, as I had felt myself to be very much a part of the book's progress since its conception. Souter's total access to company records and his retention of final editorial responsibility were, as I said in the book's preface, quite revolutionary for the Fairfax company and would have had very few precedents in the genre of company histories. I was determined to support Souter to the hilt in this, with the backing of Falkingham, but I was doubtful of the attitude of the board and particularly Sir Warwick. The arrangement was that Falkingham and I should read the manuscript chapter by chapter as it was produced, while Farrell would check it for possible defamatory passages which would be referred to our legal advisers. Directors would read the manuscript on completion and would have the opportunity to suggest alterations which Souter would discuss with me, although the final decision would be his.

Souter agreed with me that the book should 'bend over backwards' to be fair to Sir Warwick, but the latter never felt it was. Souter had great difficulty in gaining access to him; he gave two fairly lengthy interviews but was unavailable after that. When he finally saw the manuscript, both he and Mary presented a long list of alterations and deletions, some of which Souter accepted, but nothing vital to the account was removed. I was always surprised that Sir Warwick never wrote his own account of his career — Mary told me many years later, when I was discussing my own book with her, that it was because he thought it would show me in too bad a light.

Looking back eight years later, I would reiterate the comment with which I ended both my speech at the launch and the book's preface: 'The resulting book is, I believe, a definitive history of considerable importance which will set new standards of truth and accuracy in its field'.

The evening after the launch, Prime Minister Malcolm Fraser came to our Broadway building to unveil the vast mural by Salvatore Zofrea, which covered the area above the lifts and two side walls in the entrance foyer. I had seen some of Zofrea's work at the Macquarie Galleries and had been impressed by his ability to handle figures and colour on a large scale in his paintings based on the psalms. I thought he had a natural feeling for composition, even if the draughtsmanship was not always strong. However, it was really Mervyn Horton who pressed Zofrea's claims. Horton was an old friend and editor of *Art and Australia*, the authoritative — and at that time the only — publication in Australia devoted to the visual arts. The artist, in gratitude, included Horton's short, neatly dressed, well-rounded figure with rubicund complexion and goatee beard, amongst the crowd at Circular Quay in one of the panels.

I paid a number of visits to Salvatore's studio in his house at Seaforth to discuss the mural and observe its progress, which I greatly enjoyed doing. I believe he succeeded extraordinarily well in his difficult assignment and produced a work that vividly depicts the major activities of the company, together with a reference to its history, in a manner that is both relevant and enduring.

When the Prime Minister arrived he was greeted by me and a group of

With artist Salvatore Zofrea, Prime Minister Malcolm Fraser and Tamie Fraser at the unveiling of the mural in the foyer of the Broadway building, 10 April 1981.

vociferous striking printers. It was a genuine pleasure for me to have Malcolm Fraser permanently associated with the company and building, through the plaque and mural he unveiled. It was, too, the first visit Tamie Fraser had paid to our offices. I remarked in my speech that comment in our publications had often not been kind to the PM, but in the heat of battle, personal relations between him and our board and editors had always been good. I said that Fraser had a particular capacity not to take even the most trenchant criticism personally — I might have added that this attribute has been shared by very few holders of the office of Prime Minister.

The Prime Minister had invited me and several executives and editors to dinner at Kirribilli House that evening, but it was to prove an eventful evening for both of us. Gardiner and Suich had to stay and deal with our increasingly serious industrial situation — for the first time ever we very nearly lost the next day's paper, in this case a Saturday, and it was Gardiner's skilful and cool handling of his first strike confrontation that saved the day. Suich afterwards said to me that events that night convinced him that we had the right man as chief executive.

When I arrived at Kirribilli House, Malcolm was on the phone to Andrew

Peacock, then Minister for Industrial Relations, who was threatening to resign over the issue of the 35-hour week, in particular in relation to ICI.[1] Malcolm motioned to me to sit down as I was about to leave the room, and I could not avoid hearing the conversation. During the course of the evening, as I received reports from Broadway, Malcolm was receiving calls from Peacock. An unusually jumpy John Howard was also present and I recall our host making not entirely successful attempts to be both jovial and roguish with Valerie Lawson (then the successful editor of the *Herald*'s Saturday Review section). Considering most of us were in a state of some anxiety, the evening was less bumpy than might have been expected and it rounded off a very busy week of sesquicentenary activities.

The Fraser and Fairfax families have been friendly for many years and over several generations — in fact, my parents and Malcolm's had been on the same boat to England on their respective honeymoons in 1928. I kept in touch with him while he was Minister of Education, then Defence, in the Gorton Government and sympathised with him when he resigned. I happened to see him in Canberra shortly after Sir Warwick had agreed to resign the chairmanship in September 1976, and he was the first to know I would be taking it over the following March.

Early in 1978 Malcolm Fraser contacted me regarding the Commonwealth Heads of Regional Governments Meeting which he was to host in Australia in March. Both for security reasons and to give the Prime Ministers and their spouses a breath of country air, he had decided to hold it at Berrida Manor, a private hotel cum health centre at Bowral, and was looking for suitable locals to provide some hospitality. Edwina Baillieu was having the ladies to lunch at Milton Park while their husbands were in conference, so I offered to have them all to dinner at Retford.

Following the bombing attack at the Hilton Hotel where they were staying in Sydney, which resulted in the death of a policeman and two garbage collectors, the preparations for the distinguished guests' arrival in Bowral on 15 February turned that quiet little town into an armed encampment. It seemed to the locals that the army was planning for an invasion. I had assembled my mother, Caroline and Philip, and invited Peter and Edwina Baillieu. With the help of the invaluable Geoffrey Smith, who had been seconded from the Victorian State Government where he was protocol officer and personal assistant to the Premier, Sir Henry Bolte, a seating plan had been drawn up.

The first arrivals were two enormous ambulance vehicles with enough equipment for a small hospital. They were followed by an attractive sari-clad Indian woman who was to prepare the meal of her Prime Minister, Mr Moraji Desai. Then came the Frasers, and my mother and I stood with them at the foot

With Lord Mayor Doug Sutherland and sculptor Stephen Walker at the opening of the Herald Square fountain, 16 April 1981.

of the portico steps as the prime-ministerial cavalcade swept up the drive according to Smith's perfect timing.

To break the ice, I took them on a brief tour of the garden to see the two kangaroos and flock of emus, the descendants of a pair kindly given to me as a birthday present by Sue Du Val (some years before the pair had descended on a surprised household in two boxes, with their heads sticking out of a hole in the middle). The Donald Friend mural in the dining room provided a further talking point and at my table were Tamie Fraser, Mr Desai and his daughter, the Prime Minister of Malaysia and the charming and sensitive Ziaur Rahman, President of Bangladesh, who looked too young to bear the burden of poverty and famine from which his country periodically suffered. He was sadly to lose his life during an uprising there in 1981.

At the other end of the scale, Mr Desai, a delightful, courtly character, seemed, at eighty, a little beyond the great problems of governing the sub-continent, and indeed our friend Mrs Gandhi was to replace him when she returned to power in 1980 (she had been Prime Minister from 1966–77). For his first course he had freshly chopped garlic in honey. My mother had to cope with the formidable Lee Kwan Yu from Singapore, together with the Jayawardenes from Sri Lanka. Dr Jayawardene complained to me in a very polite way at a later meeting in Sydney about the Australian media's 'obsession' with the Tamil situation, which he said was greatly exaggerated — a claim scarcely borne out in subsequent years up to the present. He was also a man of great charm and distinction, whom some would feel clung to power for too long.

Others who particularly stood out were the fine-looking Fijians: Ratu Sir Kamisese Mara and his wife, both well over six feet tall, and the bright and friendly Michael Somare of Papua New Guinea, whom I had met at the Mount Hagen show four years earlier. When I observed the friendliness and camaraderie between the prime ministers I could see some point in the existence of the Commonwealth as an entity, despite its points of dispute. A happy note on which to end is the sight of the comfortable form of Madam Dowiyogo, wife of the President of Nauru, reclining on a sofa with a beaming smile on her face and my three German shorthaired pointers draped over her.

At the 150th anniversary dinner, on 15 April, in the presence of the Governor-General and Lady Cowen, we had a good line-up of community leaders, both national and state, in a diversity of areas: the New South Wales Attorney General and Minister for Justice, Mr Frank Walker, representing the Premier, and Mrs Walker; the Federal Minister for Communications and Leader of the House of Representatives, Mr Ian Sinclair, and Mrs Sinclair; the Lord Mayor of

Sydney, Alderman Sutherland, and the Lady Mayoress, Miss Feodosiou; the Chief Justice of the Federal Court of Australia, Sir Nigel Bowen, and Lady Bowen; the President of the Australian Council of Trade Unions, Mr Cliff Dolan, and Mrs Dolan; the Chairman of the Advertising Federation of Australia, Mr Keith Cousins, and Mrs Cousins; the Leader of the New South Wales Opposition, Mr John Mason, and Mrs Mason; the Chairman of the Australian Broadcasting Commission, Sir Talbot Duckmanton, and Lady Duckmanton; the Chairman of Australian Consolidated Press, Mr Kerry Packer, and Mrs Packer; the Managing Director of News Ltd, Mr Ken Cowley, and Mrs Cowley; and Mrs E.H.B. Neill, representing the board of David Syme & Co. Ltd. The dinner also marked the last public appearance of Rupert Henderson, then aged eighty-five. I seated him next to Kerry Packer with whom, as with Frank, he had always got on well, and both men seemed to enjoy the evening.

The intrepid Mrs Neill, experienced in flying small aircraft with her late husband Colonel E. H. B. Neill, former chairman of David Syme Ltd, had chartered a plane from Melbourne and flown through an appalling storm to be present, as bad weather had grounded all flights.

In my speech (see Appendix VII), I discussed the meaning of the sesqui-centenary and its connection with the Fairfax tradition of editorial independence, how this tradition operated and how it was perceived by some of its more signif-icant readers, particularly politicians. One immediate result of these words — intended to be stirring and thought-provoking — was that the leader of the New South Wales Opposition, John Mason, came up to me and said it was a very good speech and that he did not believe a word of it. Therein lay the problem. However, the speech did evoke one of Sir Warwick's rare compliments and sitting afterwards with Kerry Packer and the Chief Justice, Sir Laurence Street, I was reassured by them on its impact. (David Bowman, referring to this speech in *The Captive Press*, said that I seemed unaware that Sir Warwick had tipped out two editors before their time because they had crossed him on editorial policy. In the case of Maude, he left by mutual agreement as it was felt he was not suitable for the job, but I would concede that I overlooked the reasons for Pringle's early departure by some months at the end of his second term.)

The last event of the sesquicentenary, which took place after Easter on Sunday 26 April, was the opening of the Fairfax Walking Track and Lookout at North Head by the New South Wales Premier, Neville Wran. I describe in chapter 12 the ups and downs of our relationship with Wran, but on this occasion it was sunshine and light — both literally and figuratively — and the Premier was in his best, witty and amusing form. We were kindly given lunch afterwards in the ballroom of the nearby School of Artillery, which was hosted by Brigadier Garland, Chief of Staff of Training Command and Lieutenant-Colonel Jansen, Officer-in-Command.

On this happy and friendly note, with a heightened awareness of the beauty of our city and its setting, our celebrations came to an end.

11

CURTAINS FOR CAPITAL

ATTEMPTS TO RAISE CAPITAL, 1981–85

A part from the problems of Sungravure and the Syme company, the first three years of Gardiner's regime were also concerned with two other ongoing issues from Falkingham's time: the arrangements for the sale of our H&WT holding to Queensland Press, and the vexed question of raising capital. The latter, which had its roots in our defence of the H&WT group, was to be an on-and-off preoccupation up to the time of Warwick's takeover bid. Murdoch's frustrated bid for the H&WT made a second bid inevitable unless he decided to withdraw from Australia. His successful takeover provided the growth conditions for the seed, already planted in Warwick's mind, that sprouted into his own takeover of John Fairfax.

Our capital problems following the H&WT purchase had continued. In February 1981 we had $100 million unsecured borrowings, with no share issue since 1964. It would take only one lender to drop out when they were rolled over to create an awkward situation. A company review was begun in October with a number of objectives: turning loss-making operations into a profit or selling them; acquiring another television station, radio stations, newspapers and magazines; reducing borrowings; strengthening the balance sheet and gearing; developing an adequate capital base to support a strong level of corporate growth; and ensuring that shareholders could meet financing requirements without a diminution in their percentage holdings. The company needed to take major initiatives to grow, with $90 million in shareholders' funds supporting $200 million in liabilities, and Gardiner favoured an ordinary share issue to raise a minimum of $5 million. The family was faced with the prospect of forking out just under half of this and we continued to examine alternatives.

At the September 1982 board, it was clear that most directors accepted the proposition that future expansion was essential, and that an improved capital base was equally essential to achieve this. Sir Warwick held back and began to develop the concept to which he was later to adhere strongly: that there was no point in raising extra capital unless there was a specific project for it. I should have led the board more forcefully, both then and a year later, in pushing for an ordinary share issue, as I could have got the support of Vincent and John. The hardening of Sir Warwick's attitude towards capital raising — an attitude which was increasingly influenced if not fundamentally inspired by his advisors, headed by Mary — was a major but not necessarily insuperable problem for the company over the next three years.

In July 1982, we sold our 14.9 per cent interest in the Melbourne *Herald* group to Queensland Press. By August 1983, this sale had reduced borrowings by $38 million, every company in the group was trading profitably and the change of bankers from the ANZ bank to Westpac and National had greatly improved borrowing facilities. By halfway through 1984, with the acquisition of BTQ, radio station 4AY Townsville and a number of country newspapers and national magazines, the company was well on the way to achieving the 1981 objectives in nearly all areas, although capital expenditure of close to $300 million would be required over the next three to five years for offset presses in Sydney and Melbourne.

Since 1964, expansion had been funded by internal cash flow, increased gearing, limiting growth of dividends and the use of 'off balance sheet' funding, such as leasing. Of course we could have gone on this way, or considered other options such as revaluing assets, deferring necessary capital expenditure and increasing leasing commitments, but in view of the dramatic improvement in profitability, the growth of the share price and the nature of the capital market, the time was ideal to raise capital.

At the June 1984 board, Gardiner presented the capital-raising options which ranged from an ordinary issue to various kinds of preference issues and unsecured loan notes. If one accepted the proposition that the best interests of the company lay in the major shareholders' retaining their equity, combined with an appropriate benefit to all shareholders and the raising of at least $40 million, there were disadvantages in all of them with the exception of the first option listed: a participating preference share issue (known as PIPS, the 'I' being for 'irredeemable', as it was first called). This scheme had been developed earlier that year by the company's advisers, investment bankers Dominguez Barry Samuel Montagu.

The terms of the proposal provided for an underwritten renounceable issue of 24 million cumulative participating preference shares on the basis of two PIPS for every five ordinary shares at a price of $3.50. There would be a dividend of 27 cents (6 per cent) per annum, participating *pari passu* with ordinary shares in any dividend in excess of 27 cents. The preferential dividend would rank for payment ahead of all other classes of shares and it would rank with ordinary shares for any bonus or rights issue. PIPS shares would have voting rights under the following conditions: if capital was reduced, if the company was wound up or sold, if the preferential dividend was more than six months in arrears, or if any proposal was put forward varying or abrogating the special rights and privileges attaching to PIPS. PIPS would be listed with renounceable rights.

The report described the significant features of the PIPS issue as follows:

It raises equity without existing shareholders having to subscribe new funds if they do not wish to and yet it does not dilute current voting rights and control.

It is a proposal similar to non-voting ordinary shares.

It is attractive to new shareholders because of the relatively high yield after tax.

It raises permanent capital at a cost of 6 per cent after tax until the ordinary dividend reaches say 27 cents per share and then costs no more than an ordinary share.

It recognises the unique Fairfax position and the fact that new and minority shareholders in John Fairfax Ltd buy shares in the knowledge of the existing major shareholding and family control position. They are buying for the expected future growth in the earnings of the company.

The scheme does not diminish the voting rights and percentage holding of current shareholders, but does dilute their equity interest in future profits once the dividend reaches the same level.

It reduces the gearing of the group at a time when interest rates are uncertain and the equity market is high. Thus it provides the company with full flexibility to grow in the future by taking advantage of opportunities as they arise or are planned.

Sir Warwick was intrigued by the scheme, but during the period between the meeting on 21 June and 4 August, when he sent to directors a twelve-page memo strongly critical of the proposed issue, his mind turned completely against it. He was to make clear that Mary was his chief adviser, and her letters to me at this time indicate that she was indeed his major influence. His other advisers were John Fletcher (formerly of the Rural Bank, he had worked for Sir Warwick since his retirement), Sir Rupert Clarke (one of his closest friends), Max Sandow (formerly chief general manager of the ANZ Bank in New South Wales), Carnegie Fieldhouse (his current solicitor, at Mary's suggestion) and John Barber of Morgan Stanley. All these people must bear some responsibility for turning Sir Warwick against a proposal that would have saved the company from its fate and that Murdoch is now endeavouring to adopt for the same reason we proposed it.

Sir Warwick's memo began by questioning the need for raising capital at all, arguing that Gardiner had failed to identify sufficient definite projects to which the incoming sum would be applied. He went on to say that ordinary shareholders would unnecessarily sacrifice their rights to potential future dividends by sharing them with PIPS, and he referred to the likelihood that the price of the ordinary shares would fall and the effect of the PIPS prior rights to dividends in the event of a major crisis such as war. He also questioned whether the PIPS funds replacing bank borrowings would necessarily generate a higher return. In relation to PIPS voting rights, he claimed that a predator could acquire sufficient of the publicly held ordinary shares and PIPS to outnumber the family on issues where PIPS could vote, particularly on any proposal to vary or abrogate the special rights and privileges attached to PIPS.

On re-reading the memo five years later, one factor stands out which did not seem to be particularly significant at the time. The first financial disadvantage put forward by Sir Warwick was that, as PIPS were irredeemable, it made privatisation impossible. Privatisation, he said, had been discussed as a possible if remote aim that would, firstly, place Fairfax control beyond the possibility of attack and, secondly, return to the Fairfaxes the full advantages of profits and capital gain which they had enjoyed before the company became public in 1956.

Gardiner's view, presented in a twenty-eight page memo on the 9th, was that a company should never approach the market when it needed the money — the money should be arranged well in advance of need to 'ensure that it can take full advantage of any opportunities available to it in the future'. The board strongly agreed with him, as did Ron Cotton, chief financial executive since 1981 (he was to serve Warwick in a similar position until his resignation in 1989). Gardiner pointed out further that there had been criticism levelled at the company by the financial press and business community from 1979 to 1982 because our borrowings were perceived as excessive in relation to our shareholders' funds.

Gardiner also said that, as with all shareholders, the proposal would enable Sir Warwick to increase his holding at no cost, depending on how many rights he sold. The tragedy is that had the issue gone through, the family could easily have built up their holding to over 50 per cent fairly quickly, regardless of predators in the market. In this event, Warwick's bid might never have happened and family cooperation might have ensured control in circumstances where talk of privatisation, and the outrageous campaign conducted against Gardiner by Sir Warwick and Mary, would have played no part.

Sir Warwick chose to ignore the enormous benefits flowing from PIPS and the fact that it was his refusal to agree to an ordinary equity issue in 1982, the preferred management route, that produced the PIPS proposal in the first place. He persisted in regarding the putative PIPS shareholders as a potentially hostile group, whereas it was open to the family to become substantial PIPS holders if they chose. While, as Gardiner conceded, the PIPS scheme made privatisation more difficult, it certainly did not rule it out. It was perfectly possible to make a commercially acceptable offer to the PIPS shareholders and use an arrangement to achieve complete acquisition — indeed, Packer had done something similar with his privatisation measure. Gardiner commented that, in his understanding, there was relatively little, if any, interest by the family in making such a move. This was not disputed.

Both the company's and Sir Warwick's legal advisers agreed that legislation to regulate so-called inequity to holders of non-voting shares — in other words to alter or substantially increase their voting rights — was extremely unlikely and there was no doubt in the minds of board members that Gardiner had effectively answered all the points raised by Sir Warwick. With the exception of Sir Warwick, Sir David Griffin spoke for all directors when he said he saw the issue as giving much added strength and enhanced financial flexibility to the company to enable the board to act quickly and not rashly in days of rapid corporate action. On 16 August, the resolution was adopted. Sir Warwick dissented but agreed to have his rights to the issue underwritten with those of the other major shareholders.

Between the August and 6 September board meetings, however, Sir Warwick continued his efforts against the issue, insisting, at the September meeting, that in the interests of the Fairfax family and shareholders as a whole, his support would not be forthcoming then or ever. He said the issue could be legally challenged, as could the board both individually and collectively, and that he would not subscribe to the underwriting. After Gardiner pointed out the disadvantageous effect this could have on his holding, Sir Warwick said he would reconsider the position. Several directors drew attention to Sir Warwick's refusal to abide by the majority decision. At the next meeting, on 11 September, Sir Warwick said he had signed the necessary underwriting papers and the issue was formally announced. The only outstanding matter was final confirmation from the Stock Exchange Committee.

Prior to the 11 September board, we had had two meetings with the Listing Manager at which all details were discussed. At the second of these the Listing Manager advised that, providing the securities were described as cumulative participating preference shares (PPS), there would be no difficulty in obtaining quotation. The next day (7 September) details were circulated to committeemen stating that it was proposed to announce on the 11th the issue of A shares, described as above, to raise $96 million. We were aware that the joint committee of the Sydney and Melbourne exchanges were also meeting on the 11th and, amongst other matters, were to give formal approval to calling the preference shares 'A' shares. There was no suggestion that we should not go ahead with our announcement of the proposed issue.

In spite of the dramas on the board, relations remained smooth outside and it appeared that Sir Warwick would reconcile himself to living with the decision. I even thought it might be a salutary experience for him.

I had arranged to fly to Los Angeles on 21 September, accompanied by John Hahir, to see our television program suppliers and then to meet Richard Walker in Kyoto. Before that, I went to Harrington Park for lunch and to stay the night. I was clearly developing a very bad cold, which was counterbalanced by a friendly, even warm, reception. Mary insisted on bringing up early morning tea to me herself.

On the 20th, I gave a large dinner party for Harry and Bridget Oppenheimer, who had been good friends for a number of years and with whom I had stayed in Johannesburg and Durban. Also present, brought by John and Angela Darling, were the Earl and Countess of Airlie, Ginnie Airlie being the daughter of my old friend Nin Ryan, from the International Council of the Museum of Modern Art (New York).

On Friday, just as I was leaving for the airport, a letter arrived from Mary, causing me some disquiet. She referred to an article in the *Financial Review* that suggested that PPS shareholders might be entitled to vote in the event of an attempted takeover, something we had already received advice on. She also suggested that the government could bring in legislation to make non-voting shares voting ones because of their dislike of the Fairfaxes — an absurd idea. She referred to the raising of ten-year bonds in Switzerland, as an alternative 'if the Stock Exchange gets tough'. She asked whether I could postpone my trip, questioning whether Gardiner had suggested that I take it, the implication being that he had manoeuvred to get me out of the way — hardly a compliment to either of us. These last two references made me think that she had not given up the battle, particularly as we had heard a few days earlier that the Stock Exchange Committee was delaying its final assent.

I took the plane for Los Angeles, swallowing Fisherman's Friends and hoping my now serious cold would not turn into flu. I had decided not to reply to Mary's insulting question, even though it seemed that she and Sir Warwick were regarding the PPS proposal as a sinister plot by Gardiner to further his own interests at the expense of the family. In view of the fact that the hold-up in Stock Exchange approval seemed only temporary, I saw no point in postponing my trip. As it was, I staggered through various meetings and meals with our television suppliers in Los Angeles and then set off with John Hahir to drive to San Francisco.

We stopped for a couple of nights at Santa Barbara to see Clyde and Kate Packer and then headed for W. R. Hearst's extraordinary castle of San Simeon containing, in its melee of Gothic and Renaissance rooms, some truly remarkable treasures. A fascinating feature was Hearst's home movies which showed, among his famous guests, Charlie Chaplin, Greta Garbo, Harpo Marx, Douglas Fairbanks, Mary Pickford, Jean Harlow, Gary Cooper, Talullah Bankhead and, of course, Marion Davies, frolicking around and swimming in the sumptuous pool. Staying near there for the night of the 27th, I received a call from Gardiner. He had sent a memo to directors dated the 28th in which he warned that difficulties being experienced with the Stock Exchange might jeopardise the future of the issue and that the AGM would have to be deferred. The Stock Exchange, he said, was arguing incorrectly that the preference shares were a form of quasi-ordinary capital and was seeking to impute to them a degree of voting protection unacceptable to the company and to the major shareholders.

There were no further developments until, in the *Sydney Morning Herald* of 4 October, Terry McCrann wrote, under the heading 'Exchange ignores own rule book', that the opposition by the Stock Exchange to the proposed $96 million share issue was disturbing. The Stock Exchange was concerned that the terms of the issue would set an unwelcome precedent by creating a de facto second class ordinary share, McCrann said. In his view, failure to grant listing would set a far more unfortunate precedent with wider ramifications. It would indicate a most extraordinary situation — that companies could no longer rely on a member exchange abiding by both the spirit and the letter of the Australian Associated Stock Exchanges' listing requirements. One member exchange had assumed, quite improperly, the role of telling a listed company how it should structure its capital, and in a way that positively undermined the Takeover Code.

On 5 October, the Melbourne *Herald* ran a piece by its finance editor, Barrie Dunstan, that appeared to be based on confidential documents submitted to the Fairfax board. How they obtained access to these documents was to be a subject of subsequent discussion by the board. It was titled 'Fairfax family fight over prefs' and repeated a number of arguments against the issue put forward by Sir Warwick.

Intense negotiations were under way between Gardiner and Jim Bain, the chairman of the Sydney Stock Exchange. On 10 October, in a long letter to Bain, Gardiner argued that all possible steps had been taken to ensure that the proposed shares would be suitable for quotation prior to our publicly announcing the issue. He said that the issue had been strongly and widely supported by institutional investors and that the company had already agreed to virtually all of the requests made by the Exchange. The only condition not agreed to related to a change in the voting rights for the shares in the event that anyone acquired more than 50 per cent of the ordinary shares and preference shares in total. Such a condition would be a fundamental change to the terms of the issue, possibly destabilising the company's share register.

Gardiner made further compromises but Bain, on behalf of the Stock Exchange, continued to insist that 'if any person becomes entitled . . . to in excess of 50 per cent of the total issued capital, cumulative preference shares shall become enfranchised'. Bain did not reply to a number of matters raised in Gardiner's letter. One of the conditions, setting a limit on the number of preference shares, contradicted an agreement previously made with the various committees, and directors asked that the original assent to the issue by the Exchange be honoured.

It was only then made clear to us that the real reason for the opposition of the Stock Exchange was a growing movement against the issue of shares with restricted voting rights. Bain finally replied to Gardiner's letter on 23 October, repeating that the committee regarded the shares as being very close to ordinary shares and for that reason should have voting rights equal to ordinary shares. The suggested compromise (including the '50 per cent' requirement) was designed to allow official quotation, while at the same time observing, as far as possible, the principle of one vote one share (a principle not observed by any of the world's stock exchanges, including Australia's, up to that time). Bain denied that the Stock Exchange had ever approved official quotation and alleged that we had announced the issue before this was settled. He said we 'may have formed the incorrect impression early in the proceedings that official quotation would be granted'.

Presenting the prize to John Cooper on Martin's Lad at the Sydney Morning Herald Three-Day Event, *Royal Easter Show, 1983.*

The argument on the characteristics of preference/ordinary shares and the question of official approval continued through a press statement from the Stock Exchange and in a letter from Gardiner on the 26th. He said it was inconceivable that the Stock Exchange could have written in the terms they had, just before the announcement, if it had had any doubt about the suitability of the issue. No suggestion had been made that they would not be suitable for quotation. On the same day, the board of John Fairfax announced 'with regret and disappointment' the withdrawal of the issue because of the Stock Exchange's refusal to grant listing.

There was no doubt in our minds that something had happened to change the Exchange's initially favourable reception of our proposal and replace it with suspicion and hostility. The question of formal approval seemed to be a convenient excuse for its discovery that the shares were 'quasi-ordinary'. Talking to me five years later, Bain said there was a generally held view on the Exchange committees that our capital raising proposal was a cynical move to maintain family control without putting money in. However, he admitted that the Exchange had not handled the matter well in giving us the impression, in the earlier stages, that there would be no problems, but said the intention had been to give 'an amber light rather than a green one'. He said there was a clear ideological move amongst various states' Stock Exchanges against the use of shares with limited voting rights and took up strongly Sir Warwick's point that we had not given sufficient indication of how we would employ the funds raised and the necessity of raising them. He told me Mary had indicated her approval of the Exchange's attitude and said she was in favour of one vote one share.

The withdrawal was a serious blow for the company, one that was to have a damaging affect on its remaining three years of operation as a public company. Indeed, it could be said that our capital problem hamstrung us over the following years to the point that it could have been a contributing factor in Warwick's takeover. With the PPS scheme in place, we would have had far more flexibility in dealing with the Murdoch takeover of the H&WT.

While some of the above events were taking place, I was on holiday in Japan (mainly Kyoto) and for the last four days was driving through the southernmost island of Kyushu. I was due back on 20 October and both John and Gardiner, while keeping me informed of the increasingly disturbing turn of events, urged me to complete my trip. In retrospect, the most comical incident occurred on 17 October, at the mountain resort of Unzen-Kanko. We were having dinner at the Japanese-Tudor style hotel when a telephone call came from Sir Warwick. Apart from a few Japanese, the only other occupants of the Elizabethan dining room were four Australian couples plus guide, all clad in kimonos and appropriate accessories provided by the hotel. They sat transfixed as I bellowed on a bad line my comments on the preference issue, and Sir Warwick's opposition to it, into the phone at the other end of the room. Whether it was a last-minute attempt to convert me, or whether he was anticipating facing difficulties at the board meeting the next day, I am not sure.

John contacted me at Nagasaki and told me he had said to the board that the leakage of documents and information, resulting in detrimental articles in the Melbourne *Herald* and the Bulletin, implicated each director and a degree of suspicion hung over all. He said it was being demonstrated publicly that the Fairfax family were in disagreement — indeed, the chairman of the Stock Exchange had commented on the dissension on the board. Arthur Lissenden said the matter should not be discussed at that meeting but should await a special meeting on my return. Bryan Frith wrote in the Australian on 27 October that 'elements' of the Fairfax family were believed to be exploring a privatisation scheme along Packer lines. There was a fear within the family, he said, that the proposed issue would destabilise the company and ultimately threaten family control.

On 20 October I was back in Sydney to preside over the obsequies and resolve, I hoped, the unpleasant situation on the board. I was greatly helped in this regard by Vincent who, on 12 November, circulated a memo on board confidentiality which stated plainly that there was evidence that Sir Warwick and Mary had talked freely about their opposition to the scheme. His main concern was that there should be no repetition and he said that there was no room on the board for directors who set out to frustrate the resolutions and defined policy of the board. He set out the evidence on the leakage and said further that if we could not regain some bond of loyalty, the chairman should change the structure of the board. If it were a question of not re-electing Sir Warwick, he said, it might achieve good accord if he (Vincent) were agreeable to dropping out at the same time. He ended by pointing out that opposition to the scheme by the Stock Exchange could have been encouraged by Sir Warwick's strenuous campaign in opposition to a resolution adopted by the board of which he was a director.

I thought this was too drastic because quite apart from the major upheaval — for the third time, in Sir Warwick's case — I had no wish to lose Vincent's services and support. In discussion with the other directors, we decided that I would make a statement at the board meeting to be held in Brisbane on 15 November, seeking assurances from all directors.

The board meeting had been arranged for Brisbane some months before, to enable directors to inspect the radio station 4MMM and the television station

BTQ, acquired at the time we sold our 14.9 per cent interest in the Melbourne *Herald* to Queensland Press. After the board meeting at BTQ's studios at Mt Coot-tha, we were to have lunch there with the Queensland Premier, Sir Joh Bjelke-Petersen, as our guest. We were also to see BTQ's new production facility at Mt Coot-tha and have a dinner at the Sheraton that night for the Brisbane directors and top management.

Sir Warwick had come to lunch at Lindsay Avenue on 8 November, partly for us to reassure ourselves that our relationship outside the office was still the same, despite the dispute on the capital raising. He only mentioned it briefly to say that I, unlike Gardiner, had accepted the decision and we should now get on with running the company. In that context, I felt it was not appropriate to bring up the statement I was to put to the board as I judged it to be more effective as a formal board matter. Also, I hoped that with the abandonment of the PPS issue, his and Mary's attacks against Gardiner would cease. The depth of their hostility to him, however, had yet to be revealed.

The last time I had been obliged to deliver a written statement to a board censuring one of its members had been after Ranald Macdonald's attack on us at the time of our purchase of the Melbourne *Herald* shares back in 1979. This time, the censure was by implication rather than direct reprimand, but I did not enjoy doing it any the more. When the meeting began, I said that I did not believe that a special meeting to consider the serious breach of confidentiality, as had been suggested, would accomplish anything constructive, but that I would ask for assurances that all directors were unanimous in their distress at what had happened and were resolved to ensure that such a thing would not happen again. I spelt out what I was seeking in more detail and commented that such a happening must even call to question, in the minds of the shareholders, the competence of the board in conducting the affairs of the company. After other directors supported the statement, Sir Warwick gave his assent with the one word, 'Yes'.

The curtain came down on our capital raising attempt at the postponed AGM on 23 November when, in outlining the sad saga, I pointed out that the proposed capital raising would have provided existing shareholders with a most attractive investment opportunity or, for those who did not wish to commit further funds to the company's growth, the opportunity of selling their rights for a handsome capital profit. The Stock Exchange, I said, had in our view put forward no cogent or logical reason in support of its changed attitude other than one which was novel and ignored its own listing requirements. I referred, too, to the widespread condemnation reported in the press that its change in attitude had evoked. Finally, as a sop, I announced a bonus issue of one for six and, rather

Facing the shareholders at the Annual General meeting on 23 November 1984. Photo: Sydney Morning Herald

to my surprise, there were no questions from the foregathered shareholders.

Gardiner returned once more to investigating capital raising schemes. In May 1985 he outlined a preliminary proposal whereby part of David Syme would be sold off and shares equal to its present capital be issued, bringing in $120 million. Syme would then invest this in shares similar to PIPS in Fairfax. Sir Warwick again expressed doubts on the need for capital raising and referred to the possibility of international crises such as global confrontation with the Soviet Union and a blowout in arms expenditure. However, at the June board, Sir Warwick said he fully agreed on the need for further capital after Gardiner outlined proposed expenditure of $345–$415 million on borrowings and leasings, updating of premises, installation of offset presses, commitments at ANM and the acquisition of holdings in the Adelaide *Advertiser* and Queensland Newspapers to offset danger from the two major predators — Murdoch and Holmes à Court.

Also at the June board, four possibilities were presented in a paper from Dominguez Barry Samuel Montagu. The first was a PIPS issue with listing to be sought only on the London Stock Exchange. The second was a more complex development of the one outlined in May while the third proposal involved incorporation of a new company called Fairfax Holdings, which would acquire the family interests in Fairfax in exchange for shares in the new company. It would then make an issue of shares to the public which would result in the family owning 66 per cent of the new company and the public 34 per cent, while the new company would own 50 per cent of Fairfax, the public 40 per cent and the various staff funds 10 per cent. The fourth proposal was simply an issue of redeemable preference shares.

The memo, which was very well prepared and excellently presented by Gardiner, went into exhaustive detail on the pros and cons of each proposal, and at the end of the day there was a clear preference for the second, setting up Syme Fairfax Holdings. Sir Warwick seemed more receptive, but any hopes that he might be on side were dashed when, on 5 August, he sent me an opinion from Lloyds International which he said he had sought on legal advice for the four family directors who together exercised control of the family holding. After we had considered it at a special meeting, it would go to the board and group general manager. I was not happy about the family caucus — the clear purpose of which was to attempt to get an agreement against the proposal and then present it to the board — but there was no way I could refuse to attend such a meeting. Vincent and John felt the same way.

The report retreated to Sir Warwick's 1984 position, saying that any share issue should be deferred until a specific and major need for funds had been identified. It then set out a number of alternative funding mechanisms that ignored our basic need for capital rather than debt. The report stated at the outset that it clearly could not be established that PIPS were without risk to family control and that it was not in the interests of the family for PIPS to be issued, or for any other fundamental change to be made in the capital structure of the group without a specific funding object. However it failed to produce any further evidence on the first point, and its argument on the second was based on the premise that it was wrong to raise capital unless an exact estimate could be obtained of the returns from ventures on which the capital might be spent. In the case of meeting or responding to a threat from the opposition, this was clearly impossible. It did acknowledge, however, that delay in raising capital could be a commercial disadvantage and correctly identified a possible objection by the Stock Exchange — the issue could be seen as an indirect means of obtaining listing for an investment in Fairfax PIPS.

The meeting of family directors was acrimonious, with Sir Warwick hostile, abrasive and intolerant of any view other than his own. Naturally there was no agreement.

Mary Fairfax had again been active in opposition, and had written in July to John and myself enclosing numerous press cuttings and suggestions for obtaining cheap finance overseas. I had written back pointing out to her that the purpose was to provide capital on a permanent basis, not temporary finance for a number of known objects. I said it was not easy to quantify expenditures to meet further challenges and opportunities, but timing was vital as there could be a downturn in the world economy.

The question became academic when, on 12 August, we received a joint letter from the Sydney and Melbourne Stock Exchanges stating that the proposal for listing Syme Fairfax Holdings was unacceptable. They reiterated their previous view that the PPS had nearly all the attributes of ordinary shares but had restricted voting rights which were neither appropriate nor equitable for the holder. They viewed SFH as a device to overcome the objection, previously expressed by the Sydney Exchange, to grant similar securities quotation. Gardiner admitted defeat at our board on the 15th, to our disappointment. He said it was time to let the issue slide and get back to his principal role as chief executive. Sir Warwick contented himself with saying that he was not pessimistic because of the very able administration of Mr Gardiner and that the suggestion that the company could not get ahead without capital raising was wrong.

Perhaps the last word belongs to Max Walsh, writing in the *Herald* on Australia's national debt on 26 June 1989, nearly four years later:

> *... the total level of debt carried by Australian corporations has reached unprecedented levels when compared with the level of equity. The advantage of equity over debt in economic downturns is that dividends paid on equity are optional while interest paid on borrowings is obligatory. And as the level of debt has increased, the coverage of interest by profits has fallen even though profits in recent years have been extremely buoyant.*

Two years after they were written, following many major corporate crashes, these words are even more valid. Also of interest is an indication that the Australian Stock Exchange seems likely to emerge from the dark ages and provide a service that has been available for some years on the international exchanges — namely, the issuing of non-voting shares or shares with restricted voting rights. Rupert Murdoch has prompted this move by his proposal to seek authority to issue non-voting or shares with limited voting rights even though he has stated that he does not have any specific plans to do so at this stage. I have emphasised as strongly as I can how important it would have been for the Fairfax company to have been permitted to issue such shares by way of the PIPS scheme in 1984 or 1985. I am inclined to agree with a recent comment by P. P. McGuinness in the Australian that the true story of how the Stock Exchanges 'nobbled' the PIPS issue has still to be written.

12

A WORD IN YOUR EYE

THE SYDNEY MORNING HERALD:
PERSONALITIES, PRINCIPLES,
PRACTICE AND POLITICIANS, 1977-87

The first board meeting at which I presided in March 1977 approved the appointment of David Bowman as editor-in-chief of the *Herald*. Ever since Pringle's second term, I had been convinced that the *Herald* should have an editor with responsibility for the whole paper. Of course, this depended on finding the right person. Harriott, who as editor now had responsibility for the Saturday magazine and book pages as well as the leader and facing feature pages, was a very competent editor with a vigorous, incisive style. His views coincided happily with those of the board, although I disagreed with his conservative views on social issues. Alan Dobbyn, who had succeeded Bowman as news editor, was very sound and reliable, and Bowman had considerable respect for his judgment. It seemed an ideal time to take action and I was convinced that Bowman, who had in fact suggested himself for the position in a report commissioned for the board the previous year, was the man.

He was then in what I regarded as one of our more impossible positions — executive editor in charge of other publications — and his job had been to try and impose, to some extent, the view of the board on such high flyers as Vic Carroll, Max Walsh, Max Suich and Evan Whitton. I thought he had carried out this difficult task with a considerable degree of success. There was no problem with his appointment as editor of the *Herald*, and in fact the board had quite a useful discussion about it.

Bob Johnson, the able news director of Channel Seven, was appointed executive editor in Bowman's place. He gamely accepted the post, but was never really happy in it. He lacked the necessary background in financial journalism, as well as Bowman's executive experience to mix it with the editors, and the appointment was a mistake on our part. Johnson subsequently became an outstandingly successful group general manager of Macquarie Broadcasting Holdings.

With the appointment of Bowman, I was finally able to apply my many years of training to the business of consultation with the *Herald*'s editor-in-chief. As far as the board was concerned, it took me several years to develop a completely satisfactory procedure. I asked the various editors to join us at board lunches at regular intervals, and I changed the time of the meetings from 2.30 pm to 10 am, which allowed three hours in the morning, with the option to resume after lunch if necessary. By the time Greg Gardiner became group general manager in November 1980, we had guests at every board lunch, drawn from senior executives from every section of the company. The boards and executives of all our subsidiaries also attended at intervals, and I restored the abandoned custom of inviting leading political figures from the Federal and State Governments and Oppositions.

I had already had a number of sessions with Harriott, but even though I got on well with him, they tended to be a little stiff and formal. Possibly he found the sudden transition from Sir Warwick to me a little hard to take. He also, quite understandably, found it hard to take the imposition of Bowman over his head; when I asked the latter, some days later, how things were going, he replied that the atmosphere was still glacial but beginning to melt a bit at the edges. (Many years later, Bowman told me he felt the board had passed over the problem of Harriott's position for him to deal with.) However, Harriott, who was a true professional, accepted the decision loyally and stayed on until his retirement at sixty-five, two years later.

I discussed the replanning of the *Herald* at length with Bowman, making sure that Falkingham was kept informed and encouraged to contribute. The outcome was the introduction of wider columns for the front page and editorial matter, and a rearrangement of material in the second section, which now began with finance instead of sport. Sport was shifted to the end, displacing the classified Births, Deaths and Marriages, which moved forward to follow finance. This change saw several hundred readers ringing to complain on the first day, but they soon became accustomed to the new positioning. Other changes included an upgrading of Letters to the Editor on a redesigned leader page, greater space for reviews of the arts (now permanently placed on the page following the leader and feature pages) and improved coverage of finance and sport.

Bowman was the first editor since Pringle to have a real interest in social issues. It was becoming a more permissive age, particularly for the young, and we gave these issues much more space. As a circulation booster and an additional service to readers, three sections were introduced — a 'Monday Job Market', a Tuesday 'Education' *Herald* and a Friday leisure feature called 'Getaway Extra' — around which Bowman proposed a promotional campaign involving expenditure of $267 000. Directors differed in their views whether any genuine gains in circulation had resulted from promotion, with McLachlan making the important but sometimes overlooked point that it was useless promoting sales unless the content was there. He said the major problem was the improvement of editorial content, rather than cosmetic changes.

The promotion of classifieds achieved good results and sometimes sales were increased by publicising a feature, such as the memoirs of a world figure, but the gains were usually temporary. As Souter puts it, the *Herald* was not the sort of paper that went in for dramatic disclosures, and there was no circulation advantage to be gained by telling people what they already knew — that the *Herald* was a good and serious paper. In short: do you promote the product itself or a feature of it? Do you urge people to 'Bank on the Wales', or draw attention to excellent lending facilities? The money was duly spent on promotion, but the circulation did not respond for several years.

The editorial changes made at this time were not, in fact, nearly as radical as those carried out by Suich and Carroll some years later. In terms of policy, I started off with a constitutional approach: the right of consultation, and the right to advise or warn. This was quite different from Sir Warwick's approach of outright direction after an often lengthy attempt to get the editor on side. I was aware that the time might come when I would have to give a direction, either on my own account or at the wish of the board, but until that happened, I was determined to develop gradually a philosophy of influence that could combine with a considerable measure of genuine editorial independence. Of course, I did not think this up overnight — it was nurtured in my relations with several editors and one executive in particular, Max Suich.

After I had resigned from the chairmanship, some press comment, I think flatteringly, described my later years as a 'golden age for editors', sometimes taken to mean that they had the freedom to do whatever they liked. Indeed this interpretation was occasionally fostered by Murdoch and Packer, neither of whom shared my concept of editorial independence or accepted what I was trying to do. It is, in fact, a complete misrepresentation. My views in this regard will develop of their own accord as the account continues.

I instituted a regular Wednesday afternoon meeting with Bowman and together we established an effective and profitable relationship. Sometimes the meetings were attended by Ross Gittins, the economics editor of the *Herald*, who in my view was one of the wittiest and most spirited writers on this subject. Until this time, the *Herald*, somewhat like a stern but kindly parent, had taken a conservative although understanding line on such issues as abortion, unmarried mothers and sexual matters generally, together with all the problems faced by youth and the young adult, married or single.

As the 1970s drew to a close, however, the use of drugs, and freedom in sexual behaviour, were issues coming increasingly to the fore. Bowman and I felt that the *Herald* should align itself with broad community feeling in such matters, while seeking to guide and point the way towards, or discuss the possibilities of, more liberal attitudes. I felt personally that there was a strong argument in favour of the legislation of marijuana but did not feel that the *Herald* should advocate it at that stage. On homosexuality, the *Herald* did support the legalisation of homosexual acts between consenting adults, which was a matter for state legislation, although the increasingly vocal Gay Lib movement felt that Harriott had been biased against fair treatment of their cause. On gambling Bowman took a sterner attitude than I did, and the legalisation of casinos was one of the few issues over which we disagreed.

On federal and state elections, I consulted directors informally. The *Herald* had strongly supported Malcolm Fraser in the 1975 election following the sacking of the Whitlam Government and, while quite vigorously critical of the Fraser Government on the economic front, it continued to prefer it in subsequent elections.

Malcolm Fraser used to ring me about media matters — more often in his earlier than later years as Prime Minister — and, in fact, a few days after his first election win he asked me what I thought about the reimposition of a licence fee for radio and television, payable to the Australian Broadcasting Commission (now Corporation). I said I thought he could easily get away with it at that stage and that it would be a very handy source of revenue if times got tough, quite apart from the fact that it was a totally justifiable impost, and had been until the Whitlam Government had abolished it.

One thing he did at my suggestion was to have regular dinners at the Lodge in Canberra for the editors of the major metropolitan and national newspapers. This reflected my concept of editorial independence and the need, which I emphasised to him, to convince our editors about the desirability of the policy Fraser might be proposing. I would play my part in discussing it with them, but it was more important for him to explain his policies through direct contact rather than through me. The Opposition press benefited too, although they were probably unaware of the initial reason for their invitations.

In the state sphere, I was clearly not as meticulous in discussing our policy in elections, as I recall Sir Warwick complaining about our failure to support the Liberal-National Opposition in the election of 1978. Unlike the Federal arena, the *Herald* had consistently supported the Coalition parties in the state, where Labor dominated from 1941 to 1965. With the advent of Sir Robert Askin, the Liberals finally found a strong and successful leader who headed a coalition government from 1965 until 1975. Considerable evidence of corruption under his regime was later uncovered and was included in a highly controversial *National Times* obituary, published with what I regarded as lack of proper judgment the day before his funeral, which took place on 14 September 1981.

Labor regained office in 1976 in spite of one of Harriott's more venomous leaders, published with Sir Warwick's approval, which described its recently elected leader, Neville Wran, as 'Whitlam writ small'. Unlike Rupert Henderson, who had managed to forgive Arthur Calwell for calling him 'that Quilp-like creature' in 1946,[1] Wran never forgave the Fairfax company for this description, continuing to blame us when the two people responsible for it had long since ceased to control the *Herald*'s editorial policy.

At this time, though, relations with Wran were generally good and it was the *Herald*'s very hedged support of his government in the 1978 election that occasioned Sir Warwick's complaint. (The leader of October 6th thought that Wran had got the better of the economic argument, but drew attention to the danger of a traditional socialist policy overwhelming his 'moderation and pragmatism'. It advocated a vote for the opposition in the Legislative Council, which was to be elected for the first time by popular vote.) In fact we continued to support his government, although not always with great enthusiasm, as the preferable alternative to several changes in Liberal leadership. He will doubtless be interested to know that his most consistent critic in our organisation was Sir Warwick. The point was, of course, that the Opposition coalition at that time simply did not measure up as a competent alternative government. (I was interested to read in the welter of comment that followed the appointment of a receiver to Warwick's company the suggestion that Wran and Hawke both cultivated Sir Warwick and Mary because if the latter two had been able to get control, editorial policy would change markedly in Labor's favour. It seems totally far-fetched to me.)

Despite the efforts made, the *Sydney Morning Herald* continued on a slow but relentless decline until the appointment of Max Suich as chief editorial executive in July 1980. In the first two years of my term as chairman, I had been somewhat defensive about the *Herald*, largely as a result of Sir Warwick's somewhat intemperate criticism, and I failed to see that the changes we were making to it were not going far enough, nor were they tackling some of the root causes of its decline. I defended Bowman to Suich as it was my earnest hope that under the latter's stimulus, Bowman would be the man to carry on the work — Suich and I started off from this assumption. If it were not to be Bowman, however, there were two overseas possibilities (Max McCrohon, managing editor of the *Chicago Times*, and Harry Evans of the *Sunday Times*) and four local contenders: Harry Gordon of Queensland Newspapers, John Allan of the Newcastle *Herald*, Carroll and Walsh. The overseas possibilities were not available, and the locals were soon reduced to Carroll and Walsh.

Carroll had left Sungravure when Fred Brenchley was appointed manager in January 1980 and was in a sort of limbo while fulfilling various editorial commissions, including a report on a proposed monthly business magazine. Walsh was still managing editor of the *Financial Review*, to which Paddy McGuinness had been appointed editor to replace Brenchley in July. After exhaustive discussions, in which Falkingham's view was also sought, Suich and I had decided that Carroll was our man and the proposal would be put to the September board in a lengthy submission by Suich.

The submission began by analysing Bowman's time as editor-in-chief, and the condition of the *Herald*. In it Suich said he realised what a serious proposal it was to remove a Fairfax editor, but the decline in the paper's quality presentation in recent times had been fairly obvious to many people, both inside the organisation and beyond it. He had reluctantly come to the conclusion that the present editor was not up to his job and had in fact gone stale. It was clear that the board agreed with this part of the submission.

Bowman was a rather solitary man, to some extent isolated from the paper, and he left a great deal of its running to the news editor. Looking back, I can see an obvious failure of communication between him and myself, for which we must both bear some responsibility. I was not sufficiently aware of what was going wrong with the paper and Bowman was not able to isolate the problems and carry through the necessary solutions. In his most interesting and significant book *The Captive Press*, Bowman discusses the obstacles he had to face, referring to Falkingham's 'narrow rectitude and accountant's discipline' which he says 'deprived him of all editorial vision'. He goes on to say that Falkingham 'used his authority and talents to guard the *Herald* from the world, the flesh and the devil'. I think this overstates the position, but I soon found that my own developing concept of how the *Herald* could adapt itself to a new age and how it could adapt itself to readers, or indeed gain more readers, also differed from Falkingham's. While not having fully formulated views and being somewhat uncertain as to the best way of putting them into effect, I felt the

Herald should be less conservative in covering social issues and much brighter generally. This view differed from the board's, too — I was in a minority, and not until the advent of Suich did the situation change. I suspect that if Falkingham had known how much the *Herald* would change, he would not have been so enthusiastic about Suich's appointment.

In *The Captive Press*, Bowman makes the interesting and honest comment: 'A bolder, braver editor-in-chief might have crashed through these barriers; I could not'. This was the major reason why Suich was to recommend Carroll for the job in place of Bowman. Bowman is right to suggest that he looked to me for encouragement in making changes but did not get sufficient support. Frankly, I did not have the necessary confidence or experience at that stage, nor indeed was I able to confide my problems and feelings to him. This may partly explain his comment that he was unable to come to grips with my personality.[2] In fact it took a bouncy street fighter of possible Yugoslav descent (Max Suich) to pursue the 'fugitive figure' down the corridor and force all this out.

Suich's submission to the board listed the possible candidates and dealt in detail with his two final contenders before coming to its conclusion. In many ways it was a very difficult decision, but what tipped the balance in Carroll's favour was the board's confidence in his capacity to rebuild the paper, and to attract and inspire the kind of top-level journalists essential to achieve this. Walsh could possibly bring greater brilliance and intellectual zest to the job and he had certainly built up an extremely talented journalistic staff at the *Financial Review*, but the particular problems facing a quality broadsheet daily were ones we felt Carroll's character, temperament and record were better able to handle.

While favouring Carroll's appointment, the board did not make a final decision and before the October board, John and I had lunch with Suich and Carroll to get the latter's views on the *Herald*. While we were not authorised to offer him the job, at that stage he would have been left with the clear impression that something major was in the offing. We reported to the October board our impression of Carroll's keen appreciation of the *Herald*'s problems and the enthusiasm with which he discussed possible remedies. It was agreed that in the interests of the company, the *Herald* and Bowman himself, the change should be made as soon as possible.

There was genuine regret at Bowman's departure and a real appreciation of his contribution in Canberra, in the difficult position of executive editor and in the various posts at the *Herald* culminating with editor-in-chief. In *The Captive Press*, Bowman apparently regards me as his ouster, especially as I did not convey the decision to him or discuss it with him before it was made. In fact it was thought that Suich, as Bowman's superior, and responsible to the board, should convey the decision; if Suich's position had not existed this would have been my responsibility.

I discussed these events with Bowman over lunch nine years later and I believe he appreciated my point of view. He told me he had never really hit it off with Suich and that this went back to the days when he was executive editor and Suich was editor of the *National Times*. During this period of growth and turmoil for the *National Times*, Bowman had to convey both instructions and rebukes from chairman and board to Suich. Suich was quite candid with me that their relationship had not been the happiest.

The *Sydney Morning Herald*'s sesquicentennial year, 1981, saw the new editor pressing forward with his program to win a broader and younger readership. It was the start of a period of rapid evolution, bringing a new forthrightness in analysis and comment, franker reporting of issues of concern to the young, added authority in politics and economics, vigorous investigative reporting, expanded space for news and features and the addition of regular lift-out sections each day to appeal to new middle class readers and to draw new retail advertising. Page layouts became cleaner and bolder, with greater use of explanatory artwork — diagrams, maps, sketches and graphs. The achievements of Carroll from late 1980 to early 1984, and their development by the young editors who succeeded him, brought a remarkable growth of the *Herald*'s stature through the 1980s.

Over the three years and four months he was in charge, Carroll's chief editorial collaborator was C. J. (Chris) Anderson. A former political correspondent of the *Sun-Herald*, he was editor of that paper when chosen to join Carroll at the *Herald* late in 1980. He became deputy editor of the *Herald* in January 1981, aged thirty-six, editor in February 1982 (when Carroll's post was restyled editor-in-chief) and editor-in-chief when Carroll chose to step down two years later at the age of fifty-nine. The pattern was set for young editors. Under Anderson, Eric Beecher became editor in July 1984 at thirty-two, and when Beecher left in February 1987, his successor was the thirty-five year old John Alexander, whom Warwick and his board retained.

The Fairfax directors were committed to change, as they had dramatically attested by their appointment of Gardiner and Suich to the top management posts in 1980, but when change touched the *Herald* there was often a worried response in the boardroom. Directors wanted a *Herald* of broader appeal, but did not always find it easy to consent to the steps taken by the editor to achieve it. Anxieties about the new direction of the *Herald* surfaced at the board meeting of 17 June 1982, leading to a rare board discussion of policy on editorial opinion. Doubts were expressed in particular about the move to a magazine approach and the increasingly cynical tone of the *Herald*. Sir David Griffin agreed with

Vincent that, in trying to find new readers, we were perhaps losing the old.

It was true, Suich said, that there had been a change of tone, but this was not unique to the *Herald*. The change was stronger in the *Age*, in the *New York Times* and in other United States newspapers. The *Herald* was not moving away from being a quality newspaper. He spoke of two intertwined strands in the paper: Carroll's contribution was intellectual, while Anderson was trying to put more appeal into the *Herald* through a youthful approach. He reminded directors they had seen a report on the demographic dangers to the *Herald* — most of the readers simply 'would not be about' in ten years. The problem was that the *Herald* was evolving more rapidly than it might have done because it had been neglected for so long.

Replying to further questions a month later, Suich said he had looked at issues going back two years, before Carroll took over, and had concluded that we now had a vastly better newspaper. Many of the changes were the result of Carroll's careful but determined policies to make the *Herald* more appealing to the 20–45 age group and the many well-to-do and middle class families in the western suburbs, where sales were weak. It was cleaner looking, its political and economic reporting much improved, its reporting of attitudes towards sex, alcohol and drugs had deliberately become more frank. On the question of market discontent, the paper's reputation and market acceptance were, if anything, greater than two years previously. There had been a noticeable sales growth in the first eighteen months, a decline coming only after the price rise from 25 cents to 30 cents on 8 June 1982.

A concern I shared with Suich and Carroll at the time was the youthfulness of the senior people under Carroll and Anderson. With the exception of a handful of thoroughly experienced writers and executives such as Harry Kippax, Alan Peterson, Peter Hastings and Ian Hicks, they seemed to be in their twenties or barely out of them. There was a generation gap at the *Herald*, Carroll would often say, and he and Anderson set about meeting the situation by pushing young, able people as section editors. Immaturity of staff on the *Herald* and our other papers, compounded by a new vigour in reporting, was contributing to our libel difficulties. Late in 1982, when we had to pay an expensive settlement to Senator Condor Laucke over a report in the *Sun-Herald*, Suich told the board that a relatively accurate story had been changed by editors and sub-editors to become highly defamatory. He was concerned about ignorance of staff about libel, and was instituting seminars and better basic training.

The direction of editorial opinion in the *Herald* again came before the board when, in July 1983, Sir David Griffin, took exception to a leader by Ross Gittins, the economics editor, on death duties. He complained that the *Herald* was now taking a stance that death duties and capital gains tax should be introduced. Had Suich or Carroll got guidance that this was truly the paper's view? Suich said he had discussed details of the leaders with the chairman but not the board. What Gittins had written was just a discussion. The style of leader starting to emerge was more like an essay rather than just an opinion. Carroll was hoping to adopt this style more and more.

It had been a tradition during Sir Warwick's time as chairman for him to discuss editorial opinion with the editor of the *Herald*, conveying when appropriate the broad views of the board. This I maintained. It had also been a tradition that points of editorial policy were not thrashed out in detail at board meetings. It was my custom as chairman to hold a meeting each Wednesday afternoon with Carroll, usually with Suich present. The custom continued with Anderson when he succeeded Carroll. Sometimes differences of opinion were discussed, but the purpose and tone of the meetings was an exchange of ideas, not the handing down of fiats from the board or myself, though of course the views of the board were reflected in my attitudes. Sometimes Carroll or Anderson would modify an editorial view as a result of our discussions. This happened, Carroll remembers, during the uproar over the shooting down of the Korean Airlines Boeing 747 by a Russian fighter on 1 September 1983. The *Herald*'s news coverage was vivid, detailed and well illustrated. The accompanying leader, however, was neutral in tone, 'sitting back', as Carroll put it, 'and asking why and how'. I thought this was wrong. The Russian action amounted to summary execution of innocent people and could not be excused. Carroll came around to my view and a leader taking a firmer line followed.

Questions by directors about editorial opinion in the *Herald*, their degree of accountability for this and other broad objectives of the paper, the tone and taste of some religious and sexual references, and the principles under which the chairman acted as the nexus between board and editor led to my arranging a directors' dinner at Lindsay Avenue, and during my chairmanship I continued this practice two or three times a year. For the first time for many years, directors were able to make a positive contribution to all aspects of editorial policy which they knew would be conveyed back to the chief editorial executive and editor-in-chief of the *Herald*. Dinnertime discussions sometimes included our other publications as well. Away from the pressure of usual board business, we had an opportunity here to discuss policies and our newspaper philosophy more deeply. The setting was less formal than the boardroom, the atmosphere more relaxed, but if the tone of discussion was conversational it was always purposeful and, I felt, usually productive. A concern among directors to be better informed on current interpretation of *Herald* editorial policy was expressed by Vincent in notes for our first informal discussions. They accepted, he wrote, that it was not their role to formulate editorial opinion from day to day, but believed they were 'accountable to the community for the effect of public expression made through the Fairfax media'. He was also concerned that, of late, leading articles appeared to lack direction and sometimes conviction 'despite the fact that they are well-informed'.

The most important of the meetings, on 16 January and 12 March 1984, led to the adoption of a statement of principles on the tradition and policy of the *Herald*, written by Sir Warwick and amended by him in the light of other directors' views. Directors felt that the memorandum was well timed, coinciding with the appointment of a new editor-in-chief of the *Herald*. It marked no significant departure from the principles and standards of the past, but it restated them in a form that would be helpful, in practice, to directors, executives and editors. It dealt specifically with the *Herald* — although it would be a touchstone also for other papers in the Fairfax group — and began with four principles:

1. *Belief in the Christian faith, sympathy with those of other religions, and belief that those of no religion are still under the care of God;*

2. *Loyalty to the Sovereign and support of the British monarchy as an institution;*

3. *Belief that newspapers, existing as a service to the public, must inform the public accurately and impartially and must ensure fairness in advertising;*

4. *Belief that commentary should have no other aim but the welfare of the community, but with respect for the rights of people of other nations.*

Dealing with policies, Sir Warwick said the *Herald* supported a free enterprise society because of its superiority over other forms of society in producing prosperity and welfare. It was watchful against the extension of government authority, government expenditure and taxation, but not dogmatic: 'The degree of socialism, government control or regulation is to be judged by its results. For this reason the *Herald* has never attached itself to any particular political party . . . The *Herald* supports whichever party it believes is acting in the national interest'. The *Herald* supported the concept of Federation and of the rights of the states; moderate tariff policy rather than high protection; and a strong foreign policy, as opposed to appeasement or pacifism, and therefore generous provision for defence.

The *Herald*, said Sir Warwick's paper, had always expressed its view firmly on any matter of public interest, in politics in particular. Some papers aimed at presenting the facts and leaving it to the citizen to decide how to vote, but the *Herald* 'would regard this as an abdication from its responsibilities. Votes must be cast one way or the other to select a government'. Here Sir Warwick was at odds with the recent history of *Herald* editorial advice at elections. In the 1983 Federal election that brought Hawke to power, the *Herald*'s final editorial would admit only the possibility of a fine balance in favour of the Fraser Government and assured readers that 'if Mr. Hawke wins we see no reason to take to the lifeboats'. In the state election which returned Wran to power in 1981, the *Herald* was mildly supportive of Wran, but so mildly that in the final editorial few readers would have detected a recommendation to vote one way or the other.

Directors expressed general support for Sir Warwick's paper, but it left Sir David troubled by the problem of ensuring that any guidelines adopted by the board would, in fact, be observed by editors. 'It seems', he wrote in March 1984, 'that we are probably trying to reassert an authority the board had once . . . in the early days of the absolute Fairfax ownership and more latterly during the Fairfax/Henderson axis.' Sir David found it ironical that the Premier, Neville Wran, at this time was accusing the Fairfax organisation of an orchestrated campaign against his government over corruption allegations arising from the recently published secret New South Wales police tapes. He wrote: 'It seems extraordinary that at the very time at which the board sees itself as having too little influence on editorial policy . . . the Government sees the board as having too much authority'.

Sir David thought it would be helpful for directors to 'go out of our way' to meet some of the new editorial cadets and let them have 'some idea of what we believe and what our role and responsibilities are'. This was an idea I was happy to take up, arranging for selections from new cadet intakes to meet directors over drinks in the thirteenth-floor sitting room.

Arthur Lissenden, acknowledging the practical difficulties, came down firmly in favour of the existing system, the system which I was to follow throughout the rest of my chairmanship. He wrote:

> *[The board] cannot edit the papers, therefore it chooses senior editorial executives in whom the directors have confidence, both as to their ability and the values and standards in which they believe . . . My firm view*

is that it should be left to the chairman to consult and convey to the chief editorial executive and the senior editorial staff the board's policy decisions and guidelines on editorial policy. These executives should then be given the maximum freedom to frame the paper's viewpoint within the general principles as determined by the board.

For Lissenden (and the rest of us) there was no questioning that the board had the last word: 'Should a situation ever arise where an editor — no matter how sincere or conscientious — felt unable, after the fullest consultation with the chairman, to accept the board's ruling, the board's view must prevail and the editor either accepts it or seeks the obvious alternative'.

Discussion of political policy at the 12 March meeting was dominated by the state elections, then less than a fortnight away. Most directors, including Sir Warwick, felt that the government's mishandling of corruption allegations was paramount and sufficient justification for voting the government out. John was with me in taking a more moderate view. We needed to weigh the policies of the two sides, he said, and consider whether the government deserved to be thrown out for corruption, and whether the Greiner Opposition was fit to govern.

I told the meeting I supported Chris Anderson's view that the *Herald* should offer no total endorsement to either side. Corruption — and perhaps style — apart, he believed it would be difficult to mount an intellectually responsible wholesale criticism of the Wran administration. At the same time, he believed it would not enhance the *Herald*'s reputation for consistency fully to endorse Greiner, who had admitted (before the campaign) that his party was not yet ready to govern. My own and Anderson's view prevailed, and was reflected in the *Herald*'s editorial on election eve.

Curiously, in spite of the *Herald*'s hedged verdict on the 1981 state and 1983 federal election contenders, Sir Warwick continued to assert that the *Herald* would regard it as an abdication to fail to give advice on how to vote. This had been the usual but not invariable *Herald* tradition, and it was applied in July 1987 when the board accepted that the *Herald* should support the case for a third term for the Hawke Government, despite certain doubts about personalities and policies.

The question of the degree to which a newspaper should advise or influence its readers to support a particular party in an election was one I often discussed with Carroll and Anderson. There can be quite a difference between indicating a preference and telling someone how to vote, and Anderson, while not going as far as Max Walsh, who maintained that his *Financial Review* readers were intelligent enough to make up their own minds after the issues had been analysed for them, was certainly in the former camp. My discussions with Anderson usually centred around the degree of preference to be indicated which, in the case of Fraser in 1983, was lukewarm — perhaps more so than I or the board intended. However, we never adopted the approach that Michael Davie did in the Federal election of 1980 when he was editor of the *Age*: two leaders on consecutive days before polling day summed up with scrupulous impartiality the position of each party. I always maintained to Davie that even his impartial summing up betrayed a preference — in this case to the Fraser Government. None of this would preclude a boots-and-all approach if the national interest demanded it.

During 1983 I had arranged a number of small lunches in the board dining room at Broadway to meet promising young people on Carroll's team, starting with talented C and B grade journalists and working upwards to the most senior echelons. On Monday 5 December, the guests were Eric Beecher, then assistant editor responsible for day-to-day news gathering and news presentation; Valerie Lawson, special sections editor responsible for the regular Monday-to-Friday liftouts; Alan Mitchell, editorial page editor; and Paul Kelly, political correspondent.

My impression of these four outstanding journalists — average age, thirty-five — as a strong team committed to the *Herald*'s future was fresh in my mind when the board, meeting in Hobart three days later, settled to a long discussion of candidates to succeed Carroll as editor-in-chief. Suich put it to us that the building of a talented senior team had been Carroll's significant contribution to the paper. Whoever succeeded him must be able to lead that team effectively.

We faced the choice of a new editor-in-chief because Carroll, to our regret, had decided to step down for family reasons. His wife, Valerie Lawson, had borne their first child that year. At fifty-nine, and with a distinguished record in newspapers behind him, Carroll was content to see his wife go on with her career, but foresaw that in continuing as editor-in-chief he would impose an unacceptable strain on his family and himself. As Suich explained it to the board, he believed his wife might be a widow in five years.

Suich favoured Anderson to succeed Carroll, but at the December meeting reported to the board on a range of other possibilities. He was anxious, he said, not to press the board towards a particular decision. I, too, saw Anderson as the outstanding candidate, but was intent that the directors should come to a consensus without haste or pressure.

Summing up Carroll's achievements, in addition to team-building, Suich said the *Herald*'s readership was now younger and included more women, changes that had stabilised circulation. The *Herald* was now in a strong position to recruit senior talent because 'the *Herald* is now the paper journalists want to work for'. As a successor, said Suich, we needed someone with high ability and staying power, preferably with youth on his side. We should be looking to a five- to seven-year appointment.

When the day ended I could detect a leaning towards Anderson, but no clear consensus. We broke up intending to have informal discussions in January 1984, with the aim of fixing our choice at the next board meeting in February. In his new submission Suich ranged over a dozen names, but came down firmly for Anderson: he had performed creditably when holding full control during Carroll's absence for three months in 1983; he was the leader in place; he had proved he could do the job; he had considerable potential to develop. The board agreed, and on 16 February Anderson's appointment was announced.

Innovation and expansion at the *Herald* continued under Anderson. A midweek 'Money' section completed the range of weekday liftouts, the *Good Weekend* colour magazine was added to the Saturday issue, and the *Northern Herald*, a weekly tabloid supplement of suburban news, was introduced in October 1984, to be followed eight months later by a matching *Eastern Herald*. Colour was tried as a promotional device on page one, not always with happy results, and I got frequent complaints at board meetings. The business pages, which I and other directors felt had lagged behind the rest of the paper in breadth and quality, developed under John Alexander to become, I believe, the best in the country.

Change, or proposed change, in the *Herald* continued to arouse concern among the directors. As late as the early 1960s, personal bylines were sparingly used in the *Herald*. Despite misgivings at board and senior management level, their use had grown steadily over more than twenty years until they had become the rule rather than the exception on staff-written material. But in July 1984 we were not ready to accept a personal byline on page one's Column 8. Suich told the board that Anderson, with his support, wanted to assign Joseph Glascott to the column as a diarist and give him a byline 'to give identity to the column'. Apart from the pseudonym 'Granny', with which the column began in January 1947 and which persisted until 1967, the column had never carried a byline. Sir Warwick, for one, could not agree that this should now change: 'it should be seen as the voice of the *Herald*'. I, too, had reservations about the concept of one person being connected to the column. It was difficult, Suich said, to persuade a senior journalist to do the column without a byline. He had in mind that in Glascott, a former foreign correspondent and then the *Herald*'s environment writer, we had a journalist who took it for granted that anything he wrote would carry his name. Suich said he would speak to Anderson and come back to the board, but the idea went no further and, as I write this, the column is still unsigned.

When the *Herald* itself became a news topic it was usually as a target for attack by state or federal governments who found the paper's reporting and analysis of their actions too intrusive. But it was by giving offence to the Indonesian government that the *Herald* pushed itself into the centre of one of the memorable news stories of 1986. On 10 April, under the heading 'After Marcos, now for the Soeharto billions', David Jenkins, foreign editor, wrote a long and detailed account of the business activities of President Soeharto, his family and friends, showing how they had amassed fortunes through financial favours and control of key monopolies.

The effect on Indonesian-Australian relations was stunning. A visit to Canberra by Indonesia's Minister for Research and Technology, Yusuf Habibie, due the following weekend, was called off abruptly by Indonesia. Visits by Australian journalists to Indonesia were barred and military cooperation programs and talks on the maritime boundary between Australia and Indonesia were put in jeopardy.

There had been a deliberate decision by the *Herald* to publish the article before, not during, Mr Habibie's visit (a decision that directors supported), and prior warning had been given to the Foreign Affairs Department. Suich's judgment was that the relationship with Indonesia had not been seriously flawed, though there would be reprisals by Indonesia against the Australian press for two or three years.

Five days later, however, without warning, Indonesia demanded visas for Australian visitors, turning away a planeload of tourists at Bali. The Indonesian action, to be reversed almost immediately, provoked a stern public reaction from Bob Hawke, then visiting Rome: 'I say, as Prime Minister of Australia, that Indonesia must understand that we do have a free media, uncontrolled by definition by the government, and that is the way it is going to remain'. The Indonesians were told that to confuse the remarks of the Australian press with the views of ordinary Australians, and to take retribution against ordinary Australians, was a foolish and serious overreaction.

The furore brought Bill Hayden, Minister for Foreign Affairs, twice to our Broadway office, not to complain but to discuss the latest events, although on his first visit he expressed the view that the article had been presented too bluntly and without enough explanation of the timing of its publication. As Suich reported to the May 1986 board meeting, the blocking of Australian tourists had changed the view of the Australian Government that the dispute would blow over fairly quickly. It decided then to seize the opportunity to set up some new, tougher ground rules for our relationship with Indonesia. Michael Byrnes, based in Jakarta as South-East Asia correspondent of the *Financial Review*, felt the consequences of the *Herald* article. He was allowed to remain for the time being, but when his visa ran out, renewal was refused and he was forced to leave Jakarta in November.

The *Herald*'s vigour in reporting corruption allegations and in its comment and analysis brought the paper the hostility of the state's Wran Labor Government for most of its term, and of much of the Labor Party's Federal leadership after Bob Hawke led the party back to power in 1983. The personal anger of ministers over certain issues could be understood, but there was, I felt, an irrationality, a lack of balance, in their repeated expressions of enmity. They seemed to take no account of the *Herald*'s reasoned support of many Labor policies in editorials and other commentaries, and the even-handed treatment of political parties in the news columns. There is little doubt the attacks harmed us unfairly among Labor supporters. There was a commercial penalty, too, for robust journalism. At different times we suffered a withdrawal of advertising by the New South Wales Government, the Bond Corporation and Ansett.

Many of the political attacks had a special intensity because the *Herald* was in the same corporate camp as the *Financial Review* and, more significantly, the *National Times*, that longstanding irritant to politicians for its dogged pursuit of corruption and other wrongdoing, and its talent for unearthing defence and security service documents embarrassing to governments. The editors had a jealous independence of one another and a competitiveness outsiders found hard to comprehend. As a result, they were commonly and wrongly lumped together as plotters. Sometimes, even the *Age* was cast as part of a Great Fairfax Conspiracy, particularly during the scandalous revelations arising from the telephone conversations secretly and illegally taped by members of the New South Wales police force. To anyone who knew Creighton Burns, the *Age*'s editor, and his spiky determination to preserve the independence and special identity of his paper, the suggestion of a Fairfax plot was laughable. The *National Times* earned particular Labor ire for its zeal to expose allegations against the former minister Lionel Murphy in his later role as judge of the High Court. The Murphy affair, with its consequent reflections on the administration of the law in New South Wales, was perhaps the most profound influence on Labor Party-Fairfax relations.

The ill-judged use of a picture of Wran in the *Sun* on 23 February 1982 led to a libel action in which I became personally involved. The unusual camera angle and the pose in which Wran was caught suggested a resemblance to Adolf Hitler, and the accompanying words referred to 'Neville Hitler' and 'Adolf Wran'. The Premier's original claim was widened late in 1982 to a claim for aggravated damages based on some two hundred separate articles in Fairfax newspapers since 1976. His claim also alleged he had been 'threatened' by me about March or April 1979, at the time his government awarded the state Lotto licence to a syndicate that included Rupert Murdoch's News Ltd and Kerry Packer's Australian Consolidated Press.

The Premier ascribed to me these words in a telephone discussion:

Murdoch, as you know, is our major competitor, the afternoon papers are only marginal, and to give Murdoch access to the cash flow from Lotto would give him an advantage with the Daily Mirror *that we could not match.*

And

Now, look here, we cannot tolerate Murdoch having this cash flow advantage and I want to warn you that if you go ahead and Murdoch gets the franchise you will pay the consequences.

I was ready to deny in court that I had used the words in the second sentence or had made any threat, implied or otherwise. I remembered the conversation well, and that it had taken place on 27 March 1979, my forty-sixth birthday. It came about because, at the board's request, I had sought to see the Premier and put our strong view that the government ought not to be entering an agreement with the effect of making media organisations the partner of the government in the gambling industry. Instead of seeing me in his office, the Premier came through on the telephone to my house at Darling Point early in the evening.

After the widening of the action by the Premier, Max Suich had a series of conversations with him, originally at the Premier's prompting. Suich made it clear that I was perfectly willing to go into the box to deny the allegation against me. Further, he told the Premier that the company was prepared, if necessary, to traverse in court the whole history and reputation of his government since 1976 — the inevitable effect of his citing so many articles.

Our lawyers felt that the claim for aggravated damages might assist us in our case, but Suich outlined to the board three problems it had thrown up. One was that we had previously agreed with Wran's barristers that the case would run for only three days. Tom Hughes, QC, could represent us only for that period and no other first-rate Sydney libel silk was available. Second, it was a rule of thumb in libel that the longer the case, the more advantage to the plaintiff, the sheer volume of evidence tending to influence the jury to some level of damages. Third, with the Premier giving his full commitment to the case, we would be in the difficult position of having to seek to question his reputation without aggravating any subsequent damages finding.

At their third meeting the Premier and Suich agreed to seek to settle with an apology to the Premier, payment of his costs and payment of a cash figure. Our lawyers advised that a settlement in the range of $75 000 to $100 000 in the circumstances would be a better deal for us than a court action, which would risk a loss, but even if we won would accrue costs of about $6000 a day for anything up to three weeks.

Some phone calls and a further meeting led to final agreement on an apology to be published in the *Sun* and the *Herald*, payment of the Premier's reasonable costs and a cash settlement of $100,000. In return, the Premier dropped not only this action but another troublesome action and agreed that in any future libel action he would not use material up to the date of settlement. He further undertook that he would not in any legal situation make further reference to the alleged conversation with me.

Directors accepted that the cash settlement was the right course, but none of us was happy about it, especially as other public figures had taken us on and lost. Suich said we had settled on the amount because we felt we might otherwise find ourselves haggling on the steps of the court and ultimately advised to pay more — had we gone to court we would have been damned if we won and damned if we lost. A peripheral consideration, he said, was the intimate association forged by the Premier with the new Labor Federal leader, Bob Hawke. This offered the possibility of a formidable enemy in Canberra if Labor won the following month's Federal election, which it did. Sir Warwick agreed that the company would have suffered much harm, particularly among Labor people, if we had gone to court. People would have thought we were persecuting Mr Wran.

Soon afterwards, more strain was placed on relations between the Premier and Fairfax during the Street Royal Commission of mid 1983. The Commission was announced on 10 May, ten days after a *Four Corners* program on ABC television concerning committal proceedings in 1977 against a former sporting official on charges of misappropriation. The Royal Commissioner, the Chief Justice of New South Wales, Sir Laurence Street, was asked to inquire whether the Chief Stipendiary Magistrate, Murray Farquhar, influenced or attempted to influence the outcome of the proceedings and, if so, whether Farquhar acted at the direction or request of the Premier. Sir Laurence exonerated the Premier, but found that Farquhar had influenced the outcome of the committal proceedings.

Day after day during the Commission's hearings, the *Herald* published penetrating commentaries by its chief reporter, Evan Whitton, suggesting new and broader lines of inquiry, raising Whitton's own awkward questions about the courts and the police, and filling gaps in the information before the Commission. Whitton's articles exhibited a freedom in discussing current proceedings before a judge which I believe has never been matched in an Australian newspaper. They were not welcomed by the Premier. On 28 July, the day of his vindication by the Chief Justice, he called his first press conference since his decision ten weeks earlier to stand aside for the period of the Commission. He was, in his own words, 'a little angry', and at the start had a question of his own: 'Evan Whitton not here?'

'Gone to London,' a reporter replied.

'What a shame,' said the Premier. Whitton had taken up appointment as the *Herald*'s European correspondent, having delayed his departure from Sydney until the Commission's hearings ended.

Reporting to the Fairfax board after the Commission's hearings, Suich said Fairfax had 'made no friends on Macquarie Street'. Presciently, Gardiner commented that the most damaging thing the Premier could do would be to instruct public instrumentalities not to use our publications for classified advertising. It was fifteen months later, in September 1984, that Wran did take state government classifieds out of our papers. It followed a further period of bad relations between the Premier and the Fairfax press, the Premier protesting angrily at the way the *Herald*, *National Times* and *Age* had dealt with corruption allegations. The *Herald*, he complained at one point, had conducted 'an absolute vendetta' against the government and against him personally. The main victim was the *Herald*, and the total revenue cost to the Fairfax company was $1.5 million a year. The Premier directed his ministers to put all classifieds in News group papers — the *Daily Telegraph* for advertisements within New South Wales and the *Australian* for those needing a national audience. His decision, he told his ministers in a memorandum, followed a detailed review and was in the interest of general efficiency and cost containment.

Publicly, Fred Brenchley said he found the withdrawal from the *Herald* 'a surprising commercial decision'. Although the *Herald* was the leading classifieds marketplace, it had not been told of the detailed review, so had no chance to participate. Privately, Brenchley told the Fairfax board the transfer was politically inspired and had nothing to do with cost efficiency. Two Cabinet ministers had said Cabinet was not consulted and the vendetta atmosphere in the government 'left them appalled'. But rather than continue open argument with the government, Brenchley, backed by Peter Gaunt, the *Herald* manager, and John Newnham, classifieds manager, turned to diplomacy at the senior bureaucrat level. Their discussions with the head of the Premier's Department, Gerry Gleeson, led to the calling of tenders for government advertising for a two-year period beginning in December 1985. As a result, government advertising was restored to the *Herald*, but with certain categories continuing in the *Daily Telegraph* as well.

At times we would have direct, private discussions with political leaders to listen to their complaints and to seek to persuade them that accusations of a Fairfax group conspiracy were unfounded, that the Fairfax 'hierarchy' was not directing an anti-Labor campaign. One of these meetings came about as a result of an extraordinary encounter between Neville Wran and Greg Gardiner in September 1983, not long after the Street Royal Commission. They fell into conversation at the Sunday night premiere of *Careful He Might Hear You*, the film made by Syme International Productions which was about to take eight of the major annual awards of the Australian Film Institute.

Gardiner asked the Premier how he thought our newspapers were performing. His smile unchanged, and maintaining a calm conversational tone, Wran roundly condemned the Fairfax newspapers and declared his wish to see them destroyed. Guests who were out of earshot would have seen only an amiable chat between the Premier and the chief executive of Fairfax, but Marilyn Gardiner, standing beside her husband, found it hard to believe the hostility of the Premier's words. Gardiner responded by suggesting that Wran should come to lunch.

Soon after, in the thirteenth-floor dining room at Broadway, Wran lunched with just three of us — Greg Gardiner, Max Suich and myself. We encouraged our guest to come out with every grievance he could think of. On the question of a conspiracy against him and his government, Gardiner put it to Wran that around the table he had the chairman of the Fairfax board, the chief executive and the chief editorial executive. If there was a conspiracy, these three must be responsible for it or must know about it and now was the time to thrash out the matter. I then encouraged the Premier to be as outspoken and forceful as he felt like in his comments — perhaps a rash invitation — but he proceeded to give in a measured way about a dozen fairly recent examples from all our publications of what he alleged was unfair treatment, which amounted to a campaign.

The three of us agreed with some of his complaints. We did not spend undue time on our major public confrontations, such as the *Age* tapes or the Street Royal Commission, and even though no punches were pulled, the atmosphere was reasonably amicable. At one stage I said to Wran that no matter how torrid our relations had been, I always felt that he and I could communicate. He told me that when he had talked to me at a reception at the Entertainment Centre some weeks before, a number of guests had expressed astonishment to him that he should do so. However at the end of the lunch he said that, regardless of his complaints, he accepted that there was no 'Fairfax Conspiracy' or conspiracy among the hierarchy against his government and that he would not use the term again. But in spite of our reassurances, I do not think he ever quite believed us, and it did not stop him dragging out the story once or twice in the remainder of his term.

Another private talk to try to clear away belief in an engineered bias against Labor followed Bob Hawke's denunciation of Fairfax newspapers at a caucus meeting in September 1986. The Prime Minister described the Fairfax press in general as the 'natural enemy' of Labor, but gave the *National Times on Sunday* special attention for its 'vicious' campaign against Paul Keating, the Treasurer. This was a reference to recent articles about Keating's friendship with the Sydney property developer Warren Anderson. Both the Prime Minister and Mrs Hawke had in fact spent part of a *Financial Review* Budget dinner in Melbourne assailing me about the *National Times*, one from my right and the other from my left. Hawke also attacked the *Herald* for its reporting of pressure for mining in Kakadu National Park. Interestingly enough, ten months after the Hawke denunciation, during the Federal election campaign in July 1987, the Leader of the Opposition, John Howard, at a lunch I attended at the Union Club, was extremely critical of the way the Fairfax publications, particularly the *Financial Review*, had dealt with his policy speech. The Murdoch press had been equally scathing about some faulty figures in his taxation proposals.

Max Suich consulted me and I agreed he should phone the Prime Minister's office and seek a meeting. As a result, he and Robert Haupt, editor of the *National Times on Sunday*, flew to Canberra to spend nearly three hours with the Prime Minister.

Suich reported back to the board that Hawke had made clear he had no commitment to the conspiracy theory. Indeed, he recognised the fair treatment of the government in the news columns of the *Herald* and the *Financial Review*, as well as the strong editorial support his government had received from both papers. Suich continued:

> *However, he declared in the strongest terms his distaste for the* National Times, *much of it founded on a curious belief that the* Times *has targeted Neville Wran, Paul Keating and himself, along with their friends, for political destruction. The business friends he named were Sir Peter Abeles, Warren Anderson and Kerry Packer. The Prime Minister got a lot off his chest and while Haupt and I listened there was little of his argument we could accept. However, the meeting ended in an amicable way with drinks and a discussion of broad Government policy and it was worth the trip.*

13

BITING THE BULLET

**RUPERT MURDOCH TAKES THE
HERALD & WEEKLY TIMES, 1986-87**

The evening of Wednesday, 3 December 1986, found me sitting in Tokyo's Narita airport with Richard Walker and John Hahir, about to return to Sydney after a short holiday in China and Japan. Around 7 pm, while waiting in Japan Airlines' first class lounge, I received a telephone call from Simon Holberton, the *Sydney Morning Herald*'s Tokyo correspondent, who told me that Rupert Murdoch had made a takeover bid for the Herald & Weekly Times group. He told me the bare essentials of the bid, which was $12 a share: $1.8 billion in cash with a scrip alternative. I had a lot to think about on the plane going home.

The situation at the H&WT had been simmering for some time, never completely going off the boil since the aborted Murdoch bid in 1979. It was also clear that the H&WT's assets — namely, 132 newspapers boasting a total circulation of 23 million (including the Melbourne *Herald* and *Sun-News Pictorial*), two television stations (HSV-7 Melbourne, ADS-7 Adelaide), extensive radio interests as well as 48.3 per cent of Queensland Press and 44 per cent of the Adelaide *Advertiser* — would not be left to ail much longer with the troubled company.

The early 1980s were peppered with frequent, widely publicised charges that mismanagement was to blame for the H&WT's drastic underperformance, of which declining circulation of the flagship *Herald,* and falling real profits, were embarrassing symptoms. These charges were given credence when John D'Arcy, a Queensland Press director who became chief executive of the H&WT in 1985, commissioned a consultant's report into the H&WT's management and prospects. The scathing verdict delivered in February 1986 precipitated the departure of H&WT chairman Sir Keith McPherson and financial director, Des Anderson, the following month.

During the course of 1986 we at John Fairfax Ltd were aware of various happenings at the H&WT. Some were conveyed by D'Arcy or others there, some we learned from outside information and some were mere rumours. But it was not until over a year after I had resigned from Fairfax that I received more detailed information on negotiations that had taken place.

In March, Murdoch had been in touch with the new management of the H&WT expressing concern at the possibility of Holmes à Court getting control of that company. The H&WT had in fact been concerned about a move from Holmes à Court ever since the sale of our shares to Queensland Press in July 1982 had ended the first stage of the saga. There is an indication that they would have liked us to stay permanently as shareholders but we made it clear we thought it was in both our interests for Fairfax to extricate itself in a manner suited to both of us.

In his March approach, Murdoch suggested that Queensland Press sell to News 20 per cent of its H&WT shares in exchange for his Chicago newspapers, which he was obliged to sell. The votes on those shares would be removed for a period before being restored to News. He was also interested in rationalisation opportunities between the two groups and questioned relations with Kerry Packer, who had recently sold his New South Wales country papers to the H&WT in exchange for a 5 per cent holding in that company. The view at the H&WT was that Murdoch saw the logic of a merger with Packer, suspected something was happening and wanted to get in first.

Murdoch's suspicions that discussions would eventuate with Packer were confirmed in July and he contacted the H&WT management again, stating that he would be interested in merging his Australian interests with those of the H&WT.

Packer, advised by Jim Wolfensohn, had approached the H&WT in June and the negotiations (the H&WT was called Galaxy and ACP Comet) took a sometimes bumpy ride through outer space until the expected galactic merger was abandoned. During negotiations, it was clear that Packer would move to acquire 51 per cent of the H&WT and that he would control the merged operation through his chairmanship of the executive committee. Gardiner repeated our earlier offer of assistance to D'Arcy, saying that we would give them a better deal than they would get from Packer although, if the Packer deal went ahead, Gardiner, John and I felt commonality of interests would ensure a reasonable degree of cooperation, despite our unfriendly relations — and it did settle the future ownership of the H&WT. But before we could take the matter further, the deal with Packer fell apart on the questions of control and price, the effect of the transaction on other members of the group and, finally, the doubtful agreement of shareholders. All in all, the H&WT felt the offer should be improved by around $100 million.

Following the failure of the Packer deal, the H&WT board discussed the possibility of a limited transaction with Murdoch, such as the H&WT acquiring the Ten Network in exchange for shares. Murdoch continued to push for a full-scale merger but the board was concerned about the Trade Practices implications and public acceptance of the reduction of the number of principal media proprietors from three to two. The board decided there were too many difficulties in a merger with any of the major media companies and to 'go it alone'. If there was a takeover offer and the price was good enough, they would accept rather than fight it. They refused further discussions with Murdoch and undertook to tell him if discussions with any other group ensued.

On 2 December, Holmes à Court approached the H&WT, proposing that their publishing interests be pooled, with Bell having 30 per cent and the H&WT 70 per cent. The H&WT would also have an option over Bell's 30 per cent of the new West Australian Newspaper Company and there was an arrangement whereby, in certain circumstances, Bell could acquire HSV-7 and the H&WT could acquire Holmes à Court's Queensland Press shareholding. The proposal was to be presented to the board on 3 December.

Some days before, Murdoch had been in touch with an H&WT director, Sir Laurence Muir, who had indicated to him that a price around $12 might be acceptable. He also proposed to make this offer at the 3 December board.

H&WT chairman John Dahlsen had been anxious to explain the Bell deal to Murdoch before the News offer was tabled, as he felt it would neutralise Holmes à Court's proposal. But when Murdoch was outside the H&WT boardroom, Dahlsen, who had just outlined the Bell proposal to the board, emerged with D'Arcy and asked Murdoch if he wanted any prior discussion before tabling the offer which the latter was carrying in an envelope. Murdoch refused, saying it was time the board 'bit the bullet' as they had been considering possibilities for too long. It would appear his impatience lost him a valuable tactical advantage in failing to learn of the proposed Bell deal and it also cost him the essentially conciliatory and open approach which the H&WT board had been adopting towards his bid. The board felt that $12 was a good price but questioned the 5pm deadline as possibly being contrary to the spirit of the Takeover Code.

After Potter Partners were called in for discussions on the valuation of assets,

Dahlsen telephoned Murdoch to ask for $13 which, if offered, they would accept by 5 pm. Murdoch declined, saying his offer was already too generous. Although he also declined Dahlsen's invitation to attend the next board meeting on 2 January, in fact he did turn up, saying, 'Surprise, surprise'. But this did not stop the H&WT from accepting an offer from Holmes à Court which had risen to $13.50. Dahlsen indicated to an annoyed Murdoch that he believed the H&WT would accept an offer from News which matched this figure.

Meanwhile at JFL, we had been discussing the situation, including the possibility of a Fairfax bid and potential contenders in an ownership joust. Gardiner posed two questions to the November board in the event of a bid: could we afford not to be involved, and would we be prepared to pay an exorbitant price? I had been thinking this over on the flight from Tokyo and called Gardiner as soon as I arrived on 4 December. It was clear from this conversation that Gardiner favoured an interventionist approach.

At the same time, I learned that Sir Warwick's health had deteriorated considerably while I had been away. Gardiner had briefed all the directors individually on the bid, but he had been unable to see Sir Warwick, as Mary had appeared to discourage a meeting on the ground that he was too ill to cope with it. We thought it most important that Gardiner see Sir Warwick as soon as possible. Accordingly I rang Sir Warwick and he agreed to see Gardiner that morning. When I spoke to Mary to suggest that she should be present too, I got the impression that she was shielding him from direct contact with Gardiner. At the meeting Gardiner found Sir Warwick perfectly able to follow the various options he presented, which ranged from doing nothing to a full bid for the H&WT. Mary intervened frequently, arguing strongly against devoting any funds towards a response to the Murdoch bid, mainly on the grounds that we would be spending too much money for too poor a return. Indeed, at one point Sir Warwick had to tell her to 'shut up and let Greg have his say'.

I arranged to go and see Sir Warwick the following Tuesday and drove up to Retford Park on Friday the 5th to spend the weekend thinking through the situation. I got a nasty shock that evening when Charles Fairfax arrived, having driven from Fairwater with Mary's chauffeur, conveying a handwritten note from her. This stated that Murdoch had called to see her on his way to visit Sir Peter Abeles, whom she described as 'our mutual friend'. Among other things, Murdoch had suggested that we work together to stop the proposed media cross-ownership legislation, announced by the Federal Government in November, which he said was disadvantageous to both of us.[1] In her note, Mary quoted Mudoch as agreeing to her suggestion that he refuse offers for HSV until this was resolved, allowing Fairfax first refusal at a marginally more attractive price.

She said further that he was willing to discuss anything of mutual interest, but only with me personally, and she gave me his country telephone number. I was appalled at the thought that she had been discussing the affairs of the company with our main opponent and at such a critical time. I also thought it was a very odd way for Murdoch to do business, whatever the merits of his suggestions (although, in a subsequent telephone call, he told me that, while the visit had taken place, he would never have regarded Mary as a suitable person to negotiate with or as representing the company).

I decided to sleep on it and the next morning rang Sir Warwick to discover that he knew nothing about it. He was most annoyed and told me I was quite right to have contacted him. He called me back half an hour later and a tearful Mary was put on the line with profuse apologies. Sir Warwick agreed that I would have to tell Gardiner and the board: I could imagine what their reaction would be, but said I would try and handle it in a way that would cause the least difficulty and embarrassment. When I spoke to Gardiner, we both wondered whether Mary had had the benefit of Abeles' advice on what our attitude should be to the takeover — she said it was he who had arranged her meeting with Murdoch.

When I saw Sir Warwick on Tuesday, I was shocked at both his appearance and manner. He was in his upstairs bedroom, opening onto the veranda, which a year before he had converted into a very comfortable bed-sitting room, surrounded with photographs and mementos of his career. Regarding the deterioration in his health, I was to learn from Caroline that the cancer of the prostate, for which he had been operated on some years earlier, had never cleared up, although I knew he had had subsequent ray treatment. He gave me his undivided attention for over an hour, with visible effort and minimal interruption from Mary, whom I had asked to be present. I described the damaging effect which Murdoch's ownership of the H&WT would have on our capacity to compete with him, and argued strongly that we must make some response. I did not believe that we would ever get anything significant through negotiation with him at this stage of the bid — we would simply be played off against Holmes à Court and other possible interested parties.

I recalled to him our interest in Queensland Press and reminded him that the permanent acquisition of HSV-7 would be dependent on how the proposed cross-ownership legislation turned out. Irrespective of whether Murdoch liked us or not, he had always respected us as forceful competitors and had frequently said a strongly competing press was in the national interest. I put it to Sir Warwick that it was indeed in the national interest, as well as our own, to make an effective response, and I believe that I had convinced him at the end of our talk, although I was by no means convinced that any move by us would be successful. Talking to Mary in the hall afterwards, I could tell she had been shaken by Sir Warwick's reaction to her meeting with Murdoch.

I could not help being moved by my meeting with my father, although I did not know that it was to be the last significant talk I was to have with him. I welcomed the gin and tonic I was offered by John Spalvins when I went on to a lunch at David Jones, where there was much speculation on the future of the H&WT.

The 10 December board was held in Melbourne. The board had agreed to the appointment of Sir Rupert Clarke as an alternative director to Sir Warwick and he called to see me the day before at the Regent. I filled him in on recent events before we went on to the Hilton, where the Fairfax board was entertaining the Victorian Premier, John Cain, to dinner. I had met Cain at the *Age* and found him extremely pleasant, easy to get on with and by no means possessing the somewhat wowserish image attributed to him. He was far less concerned with a change in ownership of the H&WT than he had been with our assuming control of the *Age* in 1984.

At the board the next day, which Sir Rupert unfortunately was not able to attend, I reported the circumstances of Mary's meeting with Murdoch. The directors, while deploring what had happened, chose not to place a record in the minutes. Gardiner then outlined three possible courses of action: we could do nothing, we could bid for part of the H&WT assets or we could put in a full bid for the H&WT.

The most desirable asset from our point of view was certainly Queensland Press: we had television and radio interests in Queensland and we believed it was the state with the greatest potential for growth. A bid for Queensland Press at $20 a share would cost about $890 million while one for the H&WT at $15 a share would cost $2.25 billion. There was a clear preference among directors for the Queensland bid for reasons of expedience, cost and likelihood of success. We were always reluctant starters in the race to achieve control of the H&WT: the financial risks were not negligible, the burden was considerable and the prospects of success were dubious, given that Murdoch could and probably would, top any offer we made.

There has been widespread misconception of the board's attitude on this point. In view of the 48.3 per cent holding by the H&WT in Queensland Press, success in the bid depended on acceptance of the offer by whoever controlled the H&WT. The board of the H&WT had recommended acceptance of Murdoch's bid in the absence of a higher one: a later bid from us could go to a board controlled either by the existing board, Murdoch, or a third party such as Holmes à Court. In Murdoch's case, the attitude of the Trade Practices Commission could be decisive in disposing of the H&WT assets and all of his bids were conditional on his obtaining all the H&WT assets. We also agreed to ask Macquarie Hill Samuel to give their assessment on the strategy to be followed in executing the bid.

Two days later, Gardiner outlined to Sir Warwick at Fairwater the board's discussion and obtained his provisional agreement to a course that might include a total bid, following one for Queensland Press. On the 18th I had lunch with Warwick, similarly to brief him about the meeting on the 9th, and to invite him to attend on the 23rd. He had returned to Sydney from the Harvard Business School, where he was completing his second year, for Christmas and in view of Sir Warwick's state of health I was anxious to involve him in the board discussions. He in no way disagreed with the course our board's discussion had taken.

The Macquarie Hill Samuel report was presented to the board on the 23rd. The Queensland option involved the existing Holmes à Court vehicle bidding for the H&WT at a higher price than Murdoch's, but expressly allowing the sale of its Queensland Press shares. This was necessary both to enable our bid to succeed and to remove the deterrent on the H&WT board which Murdoch's condition imposed. Fairfax would similarly agree to sell the H&WT shares held by Queensland Press. The report believed that the Trade Practices Commission would put pressure on Murdoch to accept the Fairfax bid for Queensland Press should he gain control, but noted that he could come to some other arrangement with the Commission. The report noted that the sale of Fairfax television interests to Holmes à Court could be a further inducement to him, as well as extinguishing our debt on the takeover. The $890 million cost (at $20 a share) would be reduced to $360 million by the sale to Holmes à Court of the H&WT shares, while estimated pre-tax earnings for JFL for 1987 were $121 million, including Queensland Press profit. After subtracting the $58 million interest cost, this would leave a pre-tax profit of $63 million, without selling any assets. Should the Holmes à Court bid fail, or be withdrawn by agreement with Murdoch, the alternative strategy was a full bid.

Here it should be emphasised that in our discussions with Holmes à Court, we were not acting as partners but communicating with each other on an area of mutual interest, which involved a simple undertaking from each if certain events came to pass. Holmes à Court made it clear from the start that there was always a strong possibility he would come to terms with Murdoch, and from our point of view he behaved impeccably throughout.

Under the second strategy — a full bid of $2.25 billion for the H&WT at $15 a share — Queensland Press and *Advertiser* would receive $532 million and

$266 million respectively from Fairfax for their H&WT shares. Fairfax would fund this with short-term debt and to reduce it would firstly sell David Syme and other assets, including Fairfax Magazines, the Macquarie Network, ATN-7 and BTQ-7 to Queensland Press and *Advertiser* for $1.2 billion, each taking 50 per cent. The two latter would continue to exist, controlled by Fairfax through the H&WT. The value of David Syme was estimated at $600 million and the other assets made up the remaining $600 million. Fairfax would then sell off certain H&WT assets, such as the Melbourne *Herald*, *Sun-Pictorial*, HSV-7 and ADS-7, Melbourne radio stations and the West Australian newspapers to raise $1.485 billion. Queensland Press and *Advertiser* would repay their $1.2 billion debt by repaying Fairfax the $798 million they received for their H&WT shares and by rights issues (Queensland Press $70 million and *Advertiser* $156 million) and borrowings (*Advertiser* $176 million). After subscribing $113 million to the rights issues and deducting Fairfax and H&WT borrowings of $211 million, Fairfax would be left with a cash surplus of $111 million.[2] At the end of the exercise Fairfax would control Queensland Press and *Advertiser* partly directly and partly through the H&WT; they in turn would each have 50 per cent of the new Syme company.

The estimated pre-tax profit for 1987 on a conservative but realistic assessment of the contribution of the assets was $104 million. In the event of a third party acquiring sufficient shares in Queensland Press and *Advertiser* to block resolutions at the meetings necessary to purchase the Syme assets, an alternative but less satisfactory funding arrangement was outlined, which would enable Fairfax to reduce its borrowings without the requirement of such meetings.

In relation to the family, Warwick's response to the bids was that there were arguments for following both routes and that it could be said that a full bid would have a greater chance of success, although he could not argue against the Queensland bid. He repeated this in a later phone conversation with Gardiner. It was a cautious statement — as has been every one he has ever made — and a far cry from his statement in the Tryart court case that he had urged a prompt full bid for the H&WT but his voice had been ignored.[3]

Sir Warwick fully supported our plans, although we still did not have Mary's total support. She had sent me a long letter, which I received on 8 December, in which she expressed legitimate concern on the extent of the borrowings needed, our ability to meet the interest and at the same time pay adequate dividends. With such debts, she asked, should we risk our whole lifestyle and that of our dependents on the assurances of any chief executive, no matter how talented? I recalled, somewhat wryly, how eager she had been to use debt rather than raise equity in our capital-raising proposals two years earlier. She suggested forming a consortium to share the risk and avoid selling any assets. It was a well argued letter, even though her calculations and conclusions were not accurate in all cases.

She wrote again on 24 December and thanked me for including her in our thinking and decisions about the company. This was the day Holmes à Court, through his bid vehicle J. N. Taylor, offered $13 a share for the H&WT, $1.9 billion in total, with a seven for four scrip alternative. Holmes à Court had met Dahlsen and D'Arcy on 5 December and the Bell board had in fact approved a takeover proposal on the 12th, the day Ron Brierly (chairman, Industrial Equity Ltd) sold his 12 per cent to Murdoch for $220 million. Murdoch, who was skiing at Aspen, Colorado, dismissed the bid as 'silly' and an attempt to 'punish' him for not agreeing to sell Holmes à Court some assets by private negotiation.

In her letter, Mary, who was coming round to the 'action' route, suggested we could avoid interest payments by obtaining underwriting and selling shares and notes to institutions. She said she had it on good authority — presumably Sir Peter Abeles — that Murdoch had done this and was virtually unexposed financially himself. Finally, in her letter of 31 December ('Dearest Chairman, Dearest James'), she expressed misgivings about Holmes à Court's role and urged our full ownership of the H&WT.

The dinner at Fairwater on 23 December was the last time I saw my father. He had turned eighty-five on the 19th and it had been the custom in the last few years to combine a Christmas and birthday celebration. He was not well enough to come downstairs, but as many as could of his own and Vincent's branches of the family trooped up to his bed-sitting room where he looked frail but elegant, sitting by the window in dark blue silk pyjamas with a white silk cravat. We sang Christmas carols to an accordion and each member of the family spent some time talking to him during the course of the evening. Although weak, he was completely lucid. Vincent and Nancy were there (John and his wife Libby being in Adelaide), the entire Simpson clan, Annalise and David Thomas, Warwick with an American girlfriend from Los Angeles, Charles and Anna, as well as Garth Symonds, Mary's son from her first marriage. Making up the numbers were our newest director, Eric Neal, with his wife Joan and their son, James, and a longstanding friend of my father and Mary, Enzo Oriolo. Perhaps we had to make a rather determined effort to be bright and jolly at dinner, but it certainly was not a sad occasion and the evening concluded with dancing on the veranda.

On New Year's Day Holmes à Court raised his offer to $13.50 a share ($2.05 billion) and after a four-hour meeting on 2 January, the H&WT board duly switched its recommendation to the Taylor offer. It was time for us to move on Queensland Press and, after a telephone round-up of directors, Gardiner launched the Fairfax bid at $20 a share ($890 million) at midnight on Sunday, January 4th. I left for Tahiti and Santiago at midday, having entertained H.H. the Aga Khan for drinks at Lindsay Avenue the evening before. Gardiner and I had agreed on the timing and last minute details of our bid just before the Aga's arrival. I decided to go ahead with an Antarctic trip I had planned as our most important decision had been made, but I was subsequently criticised both in the press and by Consolidated Press journalist Trevor Sykes for leaving the country at the time. It certainly did not make the slightest difference to the strategy we had determined to follow and Sir Warwick had urged me to go, if I judged it appropriate.

The day after our bid for Queensland Press, Holmes à Court indicated that he would accept for his 14 per cent holding, already having assured Gardiner of the H&WT's 48.3 per cent. On Friday, 9 January, the Queensland Press board met to consider Holmes à Court's $13.50 bid for the H&WT, particularly their 24 per cent shareholding, and our own $20 bid for Queensland Press. The week before, Holmes à Court had initiated legal action, based on Murdoch's 'foreign person' status under the Broadcasting and Television Act, which culminated in an injunction from the Victorian Supreme Court restraining Murdoch from acquiring more than 15 per cent of the H&WT.

After some subsequent legal skirmishing well documented elsewhere, Murdoch had obtained a Corporate Affairs Commission dispensation that enabled him to go to the meeting with an offer by Cruden Investments Pty Ltd (the family company) for Queensland Press at $23 a share, conditional on their accepting, by 5 pm, his revised offer of $15 for their H&WT shares. He had spent the previous three days in seclusion in New Zealand, having said publicly that he was returning to Los Angeles, agonising over the size of the two bids he was about to make. The board would not accept a suggestion by the chairman, Dahlsen, that Fairfax and Taylor be contacted to see if they would increase their respective offers, but Gardiner and Holmes à Court, aware of the meeting, managed to get through it and both said they were considering increased offers. The board decided to reject the Cruden bid for Queensland Press, but before it dispersed, directors of the H&WT who were not on the Queensland Press board were contacted by telephone and agreed to recommend acceptance of the Newscorp bid for the H&WT subject to the absence of a better offer and the resolution of legal proceedings.

Between the 9th and the 15th, Holmes à Court was unsuccessful in requisitioning an extraordinary general meeting of Queensland Press shareholders to consider the position of their vital 24 per cent in the H&WT — indeed, at no stage were the Queensland Press shareholders given the opportunity to express an opinion on the sale of one of their major assets. On the 14th, we raised our bid for Queensland Press to $24, while the Victorian Supreme Court lifted its injunction and the Federal Government (to no one's surprise) announced through the Foreign Investment Review Board that it had no objections to the Newscorp bid for the H&WT.

On the 15th, Murdoch and Holmes à Court reached an agreement: at 3.30 pm Perth time, Holmes à Court finally announced that he would drop his bid for the H&WT and all litigation. He would sell his 14 per cent Queensland Press stake, which he would have sold to Fairfax under the parallel bid scenario, to Murdoch in return for HSV-7 at $260 million and West Australian Newspapers for $200 million. Murdoch immediately relayed the news to Queensland Press with a renewed offer of $23 a share which, after a marathon telephone call to Queensland Press directors, was accepted in return for News convertible notes. The Queensland Press board also agreed to recommend his $23 bid to shareholders. With the 16 per cent he already held, he could now speak for 40 per cent of the H&WT.

Earlier in the day, Gardiner had heard about the deal from Bert Reuter, whom I was to meet in dramatic circumstances in my office eight months later, but that evening the Queensland Press board refused to accept his telephone call. He had indicated to them that morning that Fairfax could further increase its bid for Queensland Press and that a bid for the H&WT was possible. His laconic comment later was: 'They knew that the last time I had got through to them I had stopped them'. They certainly could have got a better price from us, freed as we were from any undertakings by Holmes à Court's withdrawal, and Murdoch would have had to beat it to retain the 24 per cent H&WT shareholding. Their shareholders were the losers.

We withdrew our existing offer on the 16th as one of the key conditions — that the directors of Queensland Press not sell their shares in the H&WT to anyone but Holmes à Court — was no longer capable of fulfilment. I received the news after a landing in a blizzard on Deception Island (off the Antarctic Peninsula) on the 15th. Gardiner's cable said: 'Sorry unable deliver success'. Our ship then passed through the Lemaire Channel to the (for me) inappropriately named Paradise Bay. The rashness of the Queensland Press board was demonstrated on the 20th when, in Sydney, the full Federal Court confirmed the authority of the Broadcasting Act to prevent foreign ownership or control of more than 15 per cent of a television licence. The judgment noted that if the H&WT bid went ahead, the restructuring proposed by Murdoch to overcome the problem (involving the creation of a new class of preference shares representing 85 per cent of the Ten Network to be held in a trust controlled by his family company) was a 'sham'. The News bid was now vulnerable to legal challenge and the door was open for JFL's last-ditch action. It was a long shot, but we decided it was worth it.

Armed with the Federal Court judgment, JFL issued a writ against News in the Victorian Supreme Court claiming the News bid for the H&WT was invalid and also sought, unsuccessfully, two injunctions. The first was to prevent the transfer of H&WT shares to News and the second, sought after the H&WT board's Part B statement supporting the News bid was sent to shareholders, was to prevent News' registration of H&WT shares. We then launched our long-awaited bid for the H&WT at $16 a share ($2.5 billion) which made it the largest ever cash bid in Australia's history. We also made a statement urging H&WT shareholders to wait for our Part A before accepting the News bid. However, the H&WT board rejected JFL's bid on the grounds that it was too late and that Murdoch already had control, although this was still under legal challenge. At this stage the action shifted from the market to the less predictable arena of the courts and regulatory bodies, with a full-scale Broadcasting Tribunal enquiry into the question of foreign ownership of News Ltd announced on 22 January.

However on 3 February, the Broadcasting Tribunal adjourned its hearing into News' ownership after only one day to allow the H&WT to consider the sale of its electronic media assets that would remove any breach of the Broadcasting and Television Act. The next day we bid $385 million for a parcel of assets including HSV-7 ($270 million) and ADS-7 and four radio stations in South Australia and Victoria ($115 million). This topped offers by Holmes à Court and Kerry Stokes (chairman of New Broadcasting Ltd and Australian Capital Television Pty Ltd) by $10 million and $5 million respectively.

On 4 February, the day our offer was received, the H&WT called for tenders for the 5th, thus setting up a one-day auction of its electronic assets with a deadline of 5pm. The following day the H&WT board meeting took eleven hours to divide the spoils. The day's negotiations saw a $50 million increase in our purchase price for HSV-7 to $320 million, coupled with an agreement to purchase all the H&WT's New South Wales regional newspaper interests, excluding Gosford, with a seven-year no-competition arrangement. We also had from the H&WT an agreement to equalise our AAP (Australian Associated Press) shareholdings and voting structure, which would be of particular benefit over time. News' *Tamworth Northern Daily Leader* was included for $5 million as added inducement to drop litigation over the bid. We agreed to do this, undertaking also to ask the Tribunal to end its enquiry into the takeover.

Stokes had won ADS-7 ($86.5 million) and the four radio stations for $130 million, taking him $20 million above his original bid price. Holmes à Court was widely regarded as being the loser, but when he threatened to sue Murdoch over the latter's failure to sell him HSV-7, Murdoch offered to sell him West Australian Newspapers for $100 million, half its original price. This bargain price, which Murdoch agreed to because of the increased price paid by JFL for HSV, enabled Holmes à Court to survive the stock exchange crash later that year by selling it on to Alan Bond with the Bell companies. Murdoch retained all the H&WT newspaper assets extending through four states. Three days later, Murdoch's Ten Network was sold to Northern Star Holdings and Frank Lowy's Westfield Capital Corporation for $842 million. This sum of $800 million was understood to represent $450 million for the Sydney station and $350 million for Melbourne. H&WT shares were delisted from the Melbourne Stock Exchange on 18 March, three and a half months after Murdoch's opening bid.

Although the results did not accord with the two objectives suggested in the Macquarie Hill Samuel document — to prevent Murdoch obtaining control of the H&WT and to secure print assets above electronic assets — we were satisfied. Gaining control of the Seven Network by the acquisition of HSV at a reasonable price — we would indeed have gone higher — was of immense importance in disposing of our television interests later in the year. We were strongly criticised both for the price we paid for HSV-7 and, later, for the price obtained in July from Christopher Skase (of Qintex Australia Ltd) for the network. Predictably, the Murdoch and Packer press were to keep this barrage going until well into Warwick's takeover.

The key to the HSV-7 acquisition was that Fairfax then had a full network either to hold and improve its profitability to more acceptable levels than in the past, or to sell to a third party. With HSV owned by Holmes à Court, he would have been the only logical and practical buyer for ATN and BTQ, and we doubted that he would be particularly generous! How many other potential buyers would have wanted to own part of a network (perhaps even as a minority partner) with Holmes à Court? There might have been some, but the sale would have been a disadvantaged one for us.

The acquisition of the profitable New South Wales regional newspapers was also of considerable importance as it stopped Murdoch from obtaining total country coverage throughout Australia, thus denying him the opportunity of applying across-the-board advertising discounts in both metropolitan and country areas which would have been very difficult for us to compete against. Our tactics had forced Murdoch to increase his bid for the H&WT from $12 to $15 and to make a separate bid for Queensland Press, which was not his original intention, and this bid we forced up from $20 to $23. He had been obliged to outlay $3.5 billion, $2.4 billion being for the H&WT and $1.1 billion for Queensland Press, as opposed to his initial bid of $1.8 billion. Also, by taking the 'Queensland Press route', we lifted the stakes by some $900 million, rather than the $100 million or so which a higher H&WT bid would imply.

Murdoch subsequently told me that his initial failure to take either our or Holmes à Court's bids sufficiently seriously had certainly added considerably to his cost burden. For Murdoch, the exercise was a form of capital raising. He desperately needed the cash flow to balance the considerable losses from his Australian empire; he had to get bigger or get out. JFL, on the other hand, had to be part of the action to pick up a plum — or at least a useful asset — and at the same time make things harder for him. This we succeeded in doing.

The criticism levelled by Trevor Sykes that 'the board members in the final analysis abdicated their powers to Gardiner, leaving him to conduct the defence up to and including a full takeover bid', is plainly nonsense. Gardiner was instructed to make a bid for Queensland Press and, the possible tactics having been thoroughly gone over, it was left to him to contact directors as soon as it became clear that the moment was right — this would most likely be the last week of December or the first week of January. This depended on a number of factors including Holmes à Court's bid and Murdoch's response.

Once we had elected to bid for Queensland Press we could not withdraw the bid until the essential conditions could not be met. The timing of our H&WT bid was not a factor, given our decision to go first for Queensland Press. In my view Sykes is not correct when he says the reason that we lost both bids, despite our higher cash offer in both cases, was that they were too late and too conditional. We lost Queensland Press because following Holmes à Court's withdrawal, its board succumbed to Murdoch's tactics and decided not to give its shareholders an opportunity to judge a potentially higher offer. The full bid was then our secondary tactic. Whether a full bid, made prior to our bid for Queensland Press on 4 January, would have ultimately succeeded must remain a matter of personal judgment. As I said earlier, I firmly believe we would have had to withdraw from the auction with Murdoch which would have ensued.

Our options were fatally limited by our failure to raise capital in 1984 and 1985, and by Murdoch's flexibility in this area. Our problem was that a strategy demanding total success was doomed to defeat. From the public relations point of view, we had to accept the fact that an outcome which we regarded as successful would be perceived by many as failure. Finally, our total borrowings were now some $450 million, which meant we would have to have another look at the vexed question of raising capital.

14

A PRODIGY AND OTHER OFFSPRING

THE NATIONAL TIMES, THE SUN AND OVERSEAS INTERESTS, 1981-87

Before recounting the final and most tragic acts in what I earlier described as a four act drama (Act 1: Retirement of Rupert. Act 2: Sir Warwick as Committee of One. Act 3: Deposition of Sir Warwick and my succession as chairman.), a tribute is owed to some of the company's publications and activities with which I was closely involved. No account would be complete without some reflection on the *National Times*, the *enfant terrible* that, during the 1980s, occupied my time and attention to a degree which was far out of proportion to its relative commercial importance among our newspapers. Apart from libel actions and the creation of influential enemies in politics and business, it had the abiding problems of soggy circulation figures, low advertising revenue and resulting unprofitability. Advertising difficulties flowed not just from a limited readership but also from the image of the paper as a muckraker. Whatever the public benefit of the raking (and I believe it was considerable), many companies simply felt that it created the wrong setting in which to show off their products or services.

Among the board members there was nagging unease over the paper's obsession with crime and corruption, the cynical thread in much of the writing, and at times a want of taste in dealing with sex. But we resisted any temptation to take the easy way and close it. We felt a pride in its reputation for disclosure, a pride that must have seemed perverse to those outsiders who clung to the notion of Fairfax as a company content to lean back on tradition, committed to the status quo.

When the *National Times* died in March 1988, Vic Carroll, who had been managing editor of both the *National Times* and the *Financial Review* when it began, described the paper as 'one of the products that distinguished Fairfax as a publisher, rather than just another manufacturer and marketeer of newspapers as advertising carriers'.

The *National Times* suffered badly when, in early 1981, its *Business Review Weekly* section was spun off to become a separate national magazine. The launching of the magazine, under the editorship of Robert Gottliebsen, was a bold and ultimately brilliantly successful move, laying the foundation for our strong Melbourne-based BRW Group of business and investment publications. But for the *National Times* it brought a circulation loss of 5000 to 7000 copies and contributed, I believe, to lack of balance in the paper's content, with too much emphasis on politics. It was a considerable burden to David Marr, the editor who had succeeded Evan Whitton when the paper reached its tenth anniversary in February 1981.

When Marr resigned as editor in March 1982, his place was taken by Brian Toohey whose taste for campaigning, disrespect for official secrecy and courage in the face of government and big business disapproval guaranteed a turbulent period.[1] In July 1984, a little over two years into his editorship, Max Suich raised with directors the idea of turning the *National Times* into a Sunday newspaper as the first step in a long campaign to cure its circulation and advertising woes. Suich said it had been a marketing mistake not to include a business section after the BRW spin-off. A further problem was that other Fairfax publications had taken ideas and formats from the *National Times*, luring the weekend readers away. He believed it was still a good newspaper, and he had great respect for Brian Toohey, but the paper had lost its strong sense of purpose. He thought it should be reconstructed to appeal to the middle-class reader and to women. Friday publication was difficult and he thought the paper possibly had potential as a national Sunday newspaper.

A month later Suich returned to the board with a case for appointing a managing editor over Toohey to bring the paper a broader vision and to apply marketing skills that Toohey agreed he lacked. While praising Toohey as a person of great integrity and personal honesty, he told of difficulties that had arisen between them. The first period of Toohey's editorship, which included the fall of Bill Hayden as Labor leader and the election victory of his successor, Bob Hawke, over Malcolm Fraser, had been very encouraging. But Toohey had then become more of a writer, particularly about corruption in New South Wales and in the federal sphere. As these issues became more important to him, his vision had narrowed. It had been agreed to strengthen the paper with improved reporting from Melbourne and on the arts, books and consumer affairs, but this had not happened. A request in June for preparation of a major promotional campaign had not been acted on.

The board of 16 August 1984 accepted Suich's recommendation to appoint Jefferson Penberthy, then editor of *Business Review Weekly*, as managing editor of the *National Times*, assuring directors that Penberthy would wish to keep investigative reporting as part of a broader approach. At the time of his arrival, various options for the *National Times* were being considered. The paper had lost $2.6 million in the previous year and in September 1985, with market research under way, Suich told the board that he and Brenchley were agreed something drastic had to be done. After long debate in December, surprisingly little of it devoted to the option of closure, the board resolved to relaunch the *National Times* as a serious, national Sunday newspaper in 1986, despite severe printing and distribution problems in Melbourne. The significance of the *National Times* to the company's editorial reputation was a major reason for our resolve to revitalise it. There was also a strategic consideration: if it was a success, and we printed it in Brisbane as well as Sydney and Melbourne, we would be cutting out an opportunity for the *Herald and Weekly Times*, and perhaps also frustrating the national paper Robert Holmes à Court had been talking about.

As editor for the venture we accepted Suich's recommendation of Robert Haupt, who had distinguished himself as political correspondent and US correspondent for the *Financial Review* and as associate editor of the *Age* before moving to television with the Nine Network. Penberthy, who was judged to have done good work in difficult times as managing editor of the *National Times*, was to move to the editorship of *Time Australia* under a new partnership formed by Fairfax and Time Incorporated of the United States.

The *National Times on Sunday*, as it was renamed, was launched on 10 August 1986, later than we had hoped and with the handicap of being printed in Sydney only. Melbourne printing had to wait a further six months until after the *Age* had found a favourable time to win union agreement to the operation.

Sales on the first day were 150 900 — at the bottom end of encouraging, Suich commented — then fell away at an alarming rate as readers failed to respond to the paper's deliberately relaxed magazine style of Sunday journalism. After fourteen weeks sales were down to 91 880, only 17 000 above the circulation of the old *National Times* six weeks before the relaunch. Improvements were clearly needed, including an early overhaul of the finance pages and magazine section and the appointment of a new advertising agency to promote sales. It was a measure of Suich's concern that Chris Anderson, editor-in-chief of the *Herald*, had his responsibility widened to cover the *Times on Sunday* as well.

In February 1987, the month that printing began in Melbourne, Suich told the board the paper had a long way to go to establish itself, but its strategic importance had increased with the Murdoch takeover of the Herald and Weekly Times group. A new editor, Valerie Lawson, took over in March and, amid the frustrations of a period of faulty national distribution, settled to what we intended to be the long haul of establishing the image of the *Times on Sunday*, and bringing it to editorial success and commercial viability in the 1990s. Printing in Perth began at the end of May and in Brisbane in July, just in time for the Federal election issue. This issue sold 100 000 copies, in a six-month audit period to 30 September in which average sales were only 86 000. It was the last circulation audit under the old Fairfax regime. Just before the next audit was due, the new management, lacking the resources for our planned long haul, and unable to find a buyer, closed the paper down.

The other notable newspaper death that took place in the wake of Warwick's takeover was the *Sun*, which had fought a long, costly and losing battle against Murdoch's *Daily Mirror* in the shrinking Sydney market for evening papers. Like the *Times on Sunday*, it was a loss-maker that nevertheless served a strategic purpose for the company. Against a trend of falling evening circulations around the world, the *Sun* and the *Daily Mirror* had enjoyed buoyant circulations through the 1970s, but the 1980s brought rapid decline for both.

Bingo, introduced from Britain by the *Mirror* in 1981 and quickly taken up by the *Sun*, staved off the worst for a time — at considerable expense — but buyers drawn by the offer of free gambling for big prizes stayed loyal only for as long as the games lasted. We were reluctant combatants in the bingo war, which was fought not only in the evening papers but on Sunday and in the morning, too. The *Sydney Morning Herald* did not use bingo, but its rival *Daily Telegraph* did, gaining temporary advantage from it. With other directors, Sir Warwick and I expressed a deeply held objection to the idea of bingo in the *Herald* when the board discussed the News group's tactics in October 1981. Max Suich's view was that we should not consider bingo for the *Herald* unless the *Telegraph* was able to use it to open up a circulation lead of 100 000 to 150 000 a day.

In 1987, when the *Sun*'s losses were running at about $5 million a year ($15 million if the share of the fixed overhead costs at Broadway which were allocated to it was included), our management estimated that the *Mirror*'s losses were between $3 million and $5 million. Both were victims of changes in the pattern of public transport usage, improvements in evening television's reporting of news and sport and, it seemed, a tendency of morning papers to be read later into the day.

As the losses by the *Sun* worsened, arguments for closing it down strengthened. But although we looked at that possibility a number of times down the years, we always found good reasons for holding back. To close the *Sun* would have meant to offer our chief rivals, the News group, a clear run in the afternoon. Further, by maintaining the *Sun* as a vigorous opponent of the *Mirror*, we were encouraging News to attend to the afternoon market while we took an increasing command in the morning with the *Herald*. Several times in the 1980s we considered ways of turning the *Sun* off its parallel track with the *Mirror*: making it a twenty-four hour paper, and making it more serious were two possible ways out of direct competition. But both carried risks and, according to Suich, any consequent further fall in circulation would be 'a mortal blow to advertising'.

In mid 1985, with the *Mirror* lead widened to 40 000 copies a day, Suich reported to the board that industrial problems in the production areas — stemming from the actions of a small group of tradesmen, the fitters — were hampering the *Sun*'s circulation efforts. This was to be a recurring problem as the *Sun*'s fortunes sank over the few years left to it. Ron Ford, the resourceful and energetic editor of the *Sun*, saw many of his editorial initiatives go to waste simply because there were too many days on which he could not get enough papers printed. At the end of 1985 he gave the board a list of 'devastating industrial action' during the year — seventeen days on which heavy shortfalls occurred in printing the first edition, the losses ranging up to 81 000 copies on the worst day. During this period the scale of the *Sun*'s losses forced us to decide to drop the paper's expensive liftout television magazine, which had been a major prop to Friday circulation.

In February 1987 our participation in dividing the spoils at the Herald and Weekly Times after Murdoch's takeover presented the opportunity to take a first step towards ending the *Sun* vs *Mirror* contest in a way profitable to both Fairfax and News and without placing Fairfax in the weak position of seeming to sue for peace.

Gardiner had been convinced for years that commercial logic would one day drive *Sun* and *Mirror* together, as had happened with London's *Evening Standard* and *Evening News* and in many North American cities. He was not hopeful that the day was yet near, even after he successfully opened negotiations. Fred Brenchley, however, formed a much more optimistic view as he and Bob Muscat, group general manager (newspapers) for News in Sydney, held discreet talks exploring ways of merging the two papers. Despite the stumbling blocks of location and redundancy costs, Brenchley felt negotiations were still alive and at a promising stage when Warwick's takeover bid changed the whole outlook for the Fairfax group.

Aware that Warwick's team was speaking to the News group about a number of matters in the lead-up to the takeover, Brenchley repeatedly tried to warn Warwick of the importance of carrying through the merger negotiations. He met the lack of response which was typical of the behaviour of Warwick's camp at that time — treatment that helped Brenchley make up his mind that he would resign as general manager, Broadway, before the arrival of the new guard.

Later, as the straitened circumstances of Fairfax under its new ownership became all too clear, there was of course not much inducement for the Murdoch people to continue negotiating on the merger. They could see that Warwick would be forced to close the *Sun* and all they needed to do was wait. The closure came in March 1988, when the *Sun*'s sales were barely 12 000 above the crucial 200 000 minimum feasible circulation that Suich had set in 1986. Like the *Times on Sunday*, it was a strategic asset that the new Fairfax regime could not afford.[2]

After a few unhappy years' experience of publishing and television in Hong Kong beginning in 1978, the Fairfax board made no venture into overseas publishing until early 1985 when it bought the *Spectator* for £815 000. This conservative political and literary weekly, published continuously in London since 1828, three years before the birth of the *Sydney Herald*, was a loss-maker, high in reputation but small in circulation. The purchase came about because the chief proprietor and chairman, J. G. (Algy) Cluff, on a visit to Australia late in 1984, let it be known that he wished to sell. Cluff, founder and head of Cluff Oil and associated companies, was an amateur publisher for whom, like earlier owners, the *Spectator* was an indulgence. He had now decided that it was an indulgence too costly to maintain. He was anxious, however, that the new owner should not only be able to give the magazine financial stability but should also have the will to maintain its traditions and standards.

Two cornerstones of the *Spectator* were good writing (perhaps the best to be found in any English periodical) and, in politics, a close attention to issues of concern within the Conservative Party. These were obvious attractions to the Fairfax directors, but with Hong Kong memories fresh, there was some heart-searching before we approved the purchase in January 1985.

Directors were concerned that, because of its distance from Australia, the *Spectator* would absorb much senior management time better spent on problems close at hand. While Sir David Griffin appreciated the argument of Brenchley, Gardiner and Suich that Fairfax should have a toe in the water in Britain to be ready for bigger opportunities, he felt we should move as soon as possible in a more substantial way. Suich argued that the *Spectator* offered a great opportunity to learn about English publishing and distribution and that, if we owned it, people might well come to us in England with newspapers for sale, as country proprietors now did in Australia. Gardiner saw possible advantages for capital raising, too: acquisition of the *Spectator* would allow us to operate through a London listing of the Fairfax company.

Looking at the prospective losses in the first years, Gardiner pointed out that we would be making the Tax Commissioner our partner in bearing these establishment costs. At the present company tax levels, 46 cents of every dollar of loss would in effect be paid by the Tax Office. With the present increasing profitability of John Fairfax Limited, this was an attractive proposition, a way to turn that profitability to our further advantage. It meant that the company's potential loss on the *Spectator* would be 'at very affordable levels'. This tax consideration did not, of course, apply only to the *Spectator* but to numbers of other ventures in which we faced early losses in building up to a soundly profitable base.

As predicted, the purchase drew British attention to Fairfax. It also generated goodwill for us among British press proprietors and executives and senior British journalists, who had feared the *Spectator* might fall into less responsible hands. This was reinforced as they recognised the professional way we set about rebuilding the *Spectator*, leaving in place the two able young men at the top — Charles Moore, the editor, and James Knox, the publisher — but giving them more resources. Although he had sold us all his shares, we were pleased to have Algy Cluff remain as chairman as a further sign of continuity and because it was in harmony with our Australian practice of having local chairmen of local boards.

When I called on Moore and Knox at the *Spectator* office I found it to be a narrow, four-storey terrace house in Doughty Street, on the Bloomsbury side of Clerkenwell. It was a few doors from number 48, where Charles Dickens lived in 1837–39 after his marriage to Kate Hogarth. Like the Dickens house it had been built in the eighteenth century, and while a modern office would have been more efficient, the address and the building were entirely appropriate to the Spectator's image. To walk the mile or so between the *Spectator* and the Fairfax London office, off Fetter Lane, and in the streets nearby was, for anyone with an imagination, to be cast back into the London of Dickens, and his Bleak House in particular: Staple Inn, Gray's Inn, Holborn, Chancery Lane, Cursitor Street, Lincoln's Inn were all close at hand.

The *Spectator*'s advertising revenue and circulation grew steadily under Fairfax ownership. In 1986, it overtook its rival left-wing weekly, *New Statesman*, in sales for the first time. The last audited circulation report before I left the chairmanship of Fairfax put sales at 34 142 — 70 per cent higher than when we bought the magazine. The *Spectator* was then still far from profit, though break even might have been less than two years away. It had, however, emphatically fulfilled the expectation that it would establish Fairfax's reputation in Britain for quality journalism and lead to offers of investment opportunities in British publishing.

The weightiest of these approaches came late in 1985 from Lord Hartwell, the 74-year-old chairman and editor-in-chief of the company that published the *Daily* and *Sunday Telegraphs*. His family, the Berrys, were in imminent danger of losing control of the company to the Canadian Conrad Black, whose extensive interests included newspapers in Canada and the United States.

The *Daily Telegraph* was the dominant quality newspaper in Britain, with a circulation of 1.2 million — more than that of the *Times* and the *Guardian* put together — but the *Telegraph* company, hampered by an ageing management and the overmanning and inefficient work practices endemic in Fleet Street, was in deep financial trouble. Pressed to meet a deadline set by the company's lenders, Lord Hartwell accepted equity participation by Conrad Black on terms which gave Black first option on any further issue of shares.

The capital raising left the *Telegraph* company still in trouble. When Lord Hartwell turned to us, his company had a commitment to repay £130 million in borrowings, but the annual cash flow to contribute to the commitment was £20 to £30 million short. The company was then 57 per cent owned by the Berrys, and 14 per cent by Black, with the balance of 29 per cent owned by institutions. What emerged, after a number of options for Fairfax involvement were discussed, was a scheme by which it was hoped Fairfax would be able to lend funds to the Berry family which in turn would lend them on to the cash-starved *Telegraph* company, thus staving off the need for a new offering of shares. In time, Fairfax would exchange the Berry family's debt for shares.

Gardiner and Suich were strongly in favour of the move, arguing that it would be hard to suggest a better opportunity for the first major Fairfax investment offshore. Although the current year's loss was £5 million, turnover was £120 million a year and significant reductions in costs were envisaged once the company settled down with new technology. It was, as Suich described it, 'a *Sydney Morning Herald* or *Age* opportunity in London'. A market leader editorially, the *Telegraph* was powerful in classified advertising and offered enormous scope for rejuvenation and wider readership.

Timing had become critical, however. Lord Hartwell, 'over a barrel', had only several weeks to get Fairfax or someone else to save him. He warned directors we had to be sure there was a respectable way through the legal maze, a reference not just to the Hartwell-Black agreement and the rules of the Berry family trust, but to the restrictions on foreigners buying British newspapers.

The board, proceeding cautiously despite the enthusiasm of Gardiner and Suich, authorised investigation of the possible acquisition. Before it next met, however, the outcome was plain: the Berry family, hamstrung by the bargain Lord Hartwell had struck with Conrad Black, were unable to find a way to bring Fairfax into their company. Black took control and, with a new chief executive and new editors, moved on to achieve the rejuvenation our Fairfax executives had been so eager to undertake.

Fairfax made one other purchase in Britain before the advent of Warwick's proprietorship ruled off such ventures. This was the acquisition early in 1987 of the monthly investment magazine *Money*, a lively, independent publication whose proprietors lacked the capital to do battle with a new rival, *Family Wealth*. The deal was negotiated by Bob Gottliebsen, head of our BRW Group, who sent in David Koch, editor of the group's successful *Personal Investment*, to reshape *Money* in the *Personal Investment* mould. Despite heavy spending on improving *Money*, and heavy spending to promote it, it was clear at the end of 1987 that the magazine faced a long, hard road. We had underestimated the difficulty of selling such a magazine without the cross-promotion and the distribution network that the large Fairfax group could give its business magazines in Australia. It was no surprise that both *Money* and the *Spectator* were sold off in the first half of 1988 by the new Fairfax regime — *Money* to the proprietors of *Family Wealth*, the *Spectator* to Conrad Black of the London *Daily Telegraph* for $AUD5.6 million.

Early in 1985, we moved into New Zealand, acquiring a half interest in Fourth Estate Holdings Limited, publishers of the weekly *National Business Review*, *New Zealand Business Who's Who* and *Capital Letter*. *National Business Review* was comparable to the *Australian Financial Review* of the 1950s, a weekly with potential to become a strong and eventually highly profitable daily. It would be the base, we intended, on which Fairfax would rise to dominance of finance and business publishing in New Zealand, as it had in Australia. The move was highly successful and, within two years of our original purchase, we announced in December 1986 that we had moved to full ownership. NBR achieved a circulation of 12 000 a day compared with 12 000 a week eighteen months earlier, and *Investor Magazine*, the rival monthly to *Personal Investment* which our *Business Review Weekly* group had established there, sold out to us three months later.

As in Britain, the takeover at Broadway at year's end put the company's New Zealand advance into reverse. For a time, Robert Holmes à Court was to be the new owner of *National Business Review* but when this agreement fell through Fairfax struck a deal, in mid 1988, to transfer half of Fourth Estate to the Auckland-based Liberty Publishing Ltd while retaining the rest.

When Fairfax moved into a third overseas country, the United States, the impetus came from Fairfax Magazines Pty Ltd, the general magazine group headed by *Woman's Day*. This company had strengthened dramatically since the painful decision to close its aged rotogravure printing plant at Rosebery in 1981, moving into profit in 1983–84 for the first time in five years. By the end of the 1983–84 year we calculated that, because of the plant closure, our results had since improved by $20 million.

Among the successes of Fairfax Magazines was *Dolly*, established in 1970, which had achieved a per capita sale in its teenage market unmatched by any magazine in the world. After many months of planning, including market research in the United States, John Hemming, general manager of Fairfax Magazines, and Sandra Yates, assistant general manager, were convinced early in 1987 that the American market was ripe for its own version of *Dolly*, although it would need to be more conservative and less sophisticated than the Australian version.

Sandra Yates, as president of Fairfax Publications (US) Limited, headed a New York team which set about preparations to launch *Sassy*, as the magazine would be known there, in February 1988 with a circulation target of 250 000. They were about six months from launch date when a very different opportunity appeared. It was the chance to buy *Ms*, the prominent national monthly which had been a mainstay of the women's movement since its establishment in 1972 by Gloria Steinem and Patricia Carbine. After years of losses it was now facing an acute cash flow crisis. The offer came to Fairfax in part because of the favourable publicity generated for us by the preparations for *Sassy* and because, as Greg Gardiner told the board in September, the owners of *Ms* were attracted by 'the rather feminist orientation' of both Sandra Yates and Anne Summers, who was also based in New York as North American editor of the Australian Fairfax publications.

Having served as head of the Office of the Status of Women in the Australian Prime Minister's office from 1983 to early 1986 and written *Damned Whores and God's Police*, a history of women in Australia, Anne Summers' credentials in the women's movement were outstanding. The owners of *Ms*, a tax-exempt non-profit foundation, were willing to sell to Fairfax on the basis that Summers would be editor-in-chief and Yates the business chief.

Summers and Hemming put a strong and enthusiastic case to the board. It was a rare opportunity, in Hemming's view, to acquire a nationally known title of high prestige for such a low price — $US10 million. He believed it could become profitable within three years, and within six years add nearly 200 000 to its then circulation of 481 000. It would give Fairfax instant presence in US publishing, as the *Spectator* had done in Britain, and serve as a springboard for future acquisitions or the launching of new publications. In the meantime there would be savings for *Sassy* in sharing managerial, marketing and circulation costs.

However, the proposition had come before the Fairfax directors at an awkward time, 17 September 1987, soon after Warwick's takeover bid was announced. At that stage there was no hint of the ultimate fate of the Fairfax Magazines titles — to be sold off, most of them, to Packer's Consolidated Press. Instead Warwick's camp had announced that they would be included with other interests in the floating of Syme as a public company. Some, including Gardiner and Vincent, thought that the timing of the venture was bad and there was concern that Warwick's idea of putting Fairfax Magazines into Syme envisaged the closure of unprofitable titles. The rest of the directors, though, expressed views in harmony with my own very positive feelings about it and in what was to be the last expansionary decision of the old Fairfax board, we authorised John Hemming to go ahead.

The financially devastating consequences of Warwick's takeover ensured that the Fairfax foray into the United States would be short-lived. By early May of the following year, both *Sassy* and *Ms* were sold off to Matilda Publications Incorporated, a company formed by Sandra Yates and Anne Summers with bank backing and equity participation by a US venture capital group.

15

ON THE AIR

As well as from its overseas interests, success and satisfaction had resulted from the company's involvement in electronic media. Looking back on my thirteen years as chairman of Channel Seven, and considering the parlous state in which the industry finds itself today, several aspects of what has always been a highly competitive field come to mind.

The first is that in my time, the three licensees always recognised that profitability was limited. The time available for commercial advertising was strictly regulated and the scope for rate increases was, of course, governed by market conditions. This meant that in order to maintain reasonable profitability, it was essential to keep program costs down — indeed, this was the only area where major cost savings could be made. This may all seem fairly obvious, but in their first flush of enthusiasm the new owners, Alan Bond, Christopher Skase and Frank Lowy apparently did not find it so.

In addition, there was the widespread belief in the industry that even in buoyant times the market could not sustain three commercial stations in all four major capital cities, so that the station occupying the third position in the ratings for any length of time would be making an annual loss. I still believe it is possible to run two successful and sensibly competing networks in this country, if their owners do not encumber them with heavy debt from their other companies and both government and Australian Broadcasting Tribunal policy do not encumber them with over-stringent regulatory demands. However, in its attempts to insist on the operation of three commercial networks, the Federal Government would appear to be flying in the face of economic reality. The logical approach now would be to permit the amalgamation of Channels Seven and Ten and provide a public television service along the lines of the UK Channel Four, as well as that provided by the ABC and SBS.

In the 1970s, competition for overseas programs was intense in America, prices paid were at the 'going rate' for series and feature films and annual increases were negotiated at the same rate by all three stations. This suited everyone as it provided a regular market for the American producers for material that they otherwise might not have been able to sell.

When I became chairman of ATN in 1975, I discovered how seriously the program purchasing arrangements between ATN and HSV had broken down, largely due to poor relations between Rupert and Sir Philip Jones, the chairman of the H&WT. Differences arose because of Rupert's personal negotiations with British and American suppliers on behalf of the partners, and because of Jones' preoccupation with the H&WT. These differences culminated in Jones refusing to pay the HSV share of the ATV (Lew Grade) contract. Grade, in his turn, was threatening legal action against HSV. This tricky situation was not alluded to when Rupert first took

Allan Tyson, the assistant general manager of ATN-7.

me to meet Jones, but I was determined to do something about it before meeting Grade in May 1975 to renegotiate the contract.

I was somewhat apprehensive as I drove from Bilgola to ATN at Epping in the second week of January for my first visit as Chairman. Even though I had been with the company for twenty years, this was the first time I had been given specific responsibility for one of our operations. I had met Ted Thomas, the newly appointed general manager, before Christmas. When he came to lunch a few days later he told me, with characteristic directness, firstly of his respect for Rupert and admiration for his contribution to the industry and, secondly, how he welcomed the new era he felt my chairmanship would bring. Thus began a thirteen year working relationship that has been one of the most satisfying and rewarding of my career.

At Epping I met Allan Tyson, the assistant general manager, Glen Kinging, the program manager, Mike Harrison, the advertising manager and Geoff Healy, the production manager. These five, to be joined a few years later by Robin Heeps as promotions manager, were the core executive of the station and remained so as long as I was chairman. I soon discovered what a highly talented bunch they were and realised how lucky I was to have them. At that stage they had not had much chance to display their potential, owing to the idiosyncratic regime of the former chairman, which had become rather oppressive towards the end of his time. I felt that morale could do with a boost, and similarly the new management were keen to refurbish the building and acquire badly needed new equipment. There was also a clear need to improve the ratings.

Glen Kinging, program manager of ATN-7.

The executives and I soon established a good working camaraderie, which was particularly evident at our lunches where individual senses of humour combined with diverse wit, and sometimes wisdom, to produce a very lively atmosphere. In addition to the above-mentioned five, the news director (for many years Bob Johnson), the creative talent in various areas and the managers of other divisions of the company swelled the numbers at different lunches over the years. In fact my visits to Epping, even when we might be facing a seemingly intractable problem, provided a welcome respite from tensions at Broadway.

The most immediate problem we faced then was the overseas program purchasing policy for the year. It was arranged that I should accompany the Seven Network executives to Los Angeles in April to see how the viewing and buying system worked. Our only link with the H&WT board, who were not television-minded, was Jones and in two major areas we had great difficulty in getting our views across. One of these was the investment in new equipment and the other was Australian content and local production. This latter problem was made more urgent by the introduction of full colour transmission on 1 March 1975, after six months of partial colour.

I was fortunate that my appointment as chairman coincided with this event. Profit after tax had deteriorated from $769 000 in 1972–73 to $175 000 in 1974–75, while in 1975–76 ATN's revenue increased by 62 per cent (compared with a national average of 33 per cent) to over $19 million, resulting in an after-tax profit of $2.2 million. In the first year of full colour we won seven out of eight surveys, having greatly improved our position in the second half of 1975, while local program costs increased from $2.8 million in 1974 to $3.6 million.

We secured rights to telecast the Sydney Rugby League competition Sunday games (the ABC had rights to the Saturday games and we shared the finals), which had caused a telephone call to me at Retford Park from Kerry Packer early in January 1975. Referring to former pooling agreements, he first by persuasion and then by bluster attempted to get me to agree to reopen the question, which I refused to do. Finally, we embarked on a long-term building and plant rejuvenation and expansion program, increasing depreciation from $345 000 in 1974 to $874 000.

One of Rupert's achievements as chairman of ATN was his encouragement of local production and talent. As Jim Oswin (then general manager) said, he had a streak of Goldwyn or Ziegfeld in him and he inspired such successes as *The Mavis Bramston Show* (with Gordon Chater, Carol Raye and Barry Creyton) and *My Name's McGooley* (with Gordon Chater and John Meillon). While not aspiring to those entrepreneurial accolades, I tried to persuade Jones that we should continue our pioneering role in this area. Thomas and Kinging worked on their counterparts at HSV in similar vein. However, they did not totally share our view of the need for creativity and were reluctant to come in on ventures until they were proven successful in the ratings — they were not risk takers. This was a continuing problem and it meant that if we wanted to get a new program concept going, we would have to bear the initial costs and financial risk at ATN.

In April I duly met Thomas, Kinging, Ron Casey (general manager of HSV) Gordon French (program manager of HSV), John McFerran of BTQ and Ian Woodward of ADS in Los Angeles at the Beverly Hills hotel where we were all staying. I had just attended the spring meeting of MOMA's (Museum of Modern Art, New York) International Council, which consisted of a whirlwind tour of Texas: Dallas, Fort Worth, Austin, San Antonio, Houston and Corpus Christi in nine days, so was sated with Texan hospitality and the visual splendour of its museums and art galleries. Something else again was the visual experience I was to undergo for the next nine days — roughly three-hour sessions morning and afternoon of the diverse comedies and dramas that made up the offerings for the American ratings season beginning in September. In spite of the long viewing hours it was an intriguing, often enjoyable and occasionally gripping experience.

We did the rounds, meeting Denis Stanfill, the chairman of 20th Century

Fox, in his elegant office with Oriental artworks, and visiting MCA-Universal, Columbia, Paramount, Warner Bros and MGM. Most of these studios had representatives in Australia whom I was to get to know and who were present in Los Angeles for their respective screenings. Among them were Pat Cleary (MCA), Peter Broome (Fox), George Morratoff (Paramount) and Bill Wells (MGM/UA).

However, one of the purposes of my visit was to meet studio chairmen or executives so that an overall contact could be maintained. Warners' Charles McGregor, President TV Distribution, used to give me an excellent and enjoyable lunch or dinner, usually at Chasens, but never deviated from his exclusive arrangement with the Ten Network, until Murdoch made an unwelcome bid for Warners. As I was not prepared to commit Seven to a contract of several million dollars over a dinner with McGregor at the Bel Air hotel without discussing it first with the Network, the contract went to Nine.

I also met Dr Jules Stein, founder and first chairman of MCA, and his wife Doris who were friends of Rupert, and saw his very fine art collection. Although I met the formidable chairman, Lew Wasserman, most of our dealings here were with Ralph Franklin, President TV Distribution. I always liked Franklin personally, but we all found he had a tendency to promise the same programs to too many people. His position was later filled by Bob Bramson, with whom we had an excellent relationship.

Another old friend was John Spiers at MGM, while Australian Bruce Gordon was TV representative for Paramount. Herb Lazarus of Columbia completed the group. After the viewings there were preliminary negotiations, often over breakfast — a curious American custom that has now unfortunately crossed both Pacific and Atlantic. These negotiations were not usually concluded until we returned to Australia. Competition for the programs likely to rate best on the three American networks (NBC, CBS and ABC) was intense, as overseas programs were considerably less expensive than Australian dramas and comedies; a long-running American rating success was a very valuable product.

In 1985, the Australian stations agreed not to buy until December so they would not be encumbered with product axed in America after a few episodes. This arrangement was broken by the Ten Network management under the ownership of Frank Lowy towards the end of 1987, with disastrous results in program expenditure, both for his own network and for the other two. Lowy agreed to buy all product produced by each individual studio, rather than those programs suitable for prime time in Australia, and this resulted in millions of dollars being spent by all networks on programs that were unlikely ever to be telecast in Australia.

Following our Los Angeles meetings, we flew to London for my first encounter with the flamboyant and irrepressible Lord Grade (created a life peer in 1976). I was feeling decidedly nervous when I arrived at ATV House, near Marble Arch, with Thomas, Kinging, Casey and Fenton, but I need not have been. It was 'Call me Lew', then 'Have a cigar' — about nine inches long, though surprisingly mild when I later smoked it — followed by an enormous tray with coffee things, including a silver coffee pot which he sent flying across the room while making an expansive gesture. In due course, after describing in detail the incredible value and quality of the product he was offering, he mentioned a sum for the privilege of having it for three years. It was so outrageous that we practically fell off our chairs. At another meeting, we were able to come to an arrangement satisfactory to both parties and the contract with ATV/ITC was still in place when we sold the network to Skase. It included the remarkable *Jesus of Nazareth* — he re-enacted for me in his office his meeting with Pope Paul VI when he 'sold' him the concept.

Other ITC programs included *Moses the Lawgiver*, *The Persuaders*, *The Julie Andrews Show* and *The Muppet Show*, together with such films as *On Golden Pond*, *Return of the Pink Panther*, *Boys from Brazil*, *The Eagle Has Landed* and *The Muppet Movie*. There were also a few failures, such as *Raise the Titanic* and *The Lone Ranger*.

I found Grade an endearing and always stimulating man, and enjoyed my meetings with him over the years, regretting his unhappy departure from ATV. The story of the Holmes à Court takeover is well known. Grade always regarded it as a betrayal and Holmes à Court as a legitimate business tactic. However Grade was certainly not helpful when, at a dinner at Fairwater in 1984, he used his own experience with Holmes à Court to warn Vincent and John against our PIPS capital raising proposal, which was an entirely different situation to the ATV one — a warning eagerly taken up by Sir Warwick and Mary.

Our other contract in England was with London Weekend Television and I was taken by Richard Price, whose firm was the agent for LWT, to meet the chairman, Lord Freeman. As John Freeman, he was renowned in his time as television's finest interviewer. At that time Murdoch was a major shareholder in LWT and when the contract was next up for renewal, not unnaturally he attempted to get it for the Ten Network. I recall putting a somewhat impassioned case to the LWT executives over lunch and a few days later successfully negotiated the renewal with Richard Price. Murdoch afterwards complimented me on what he had heard of my advocacy. Over the years I was to have many enjoyable and stimulating lunch sessions with Brian Tessler and his colleagues at the LWT building on the South Bank. We continued to get good value with such programs as *On The Buses* and *Doctor In The House*.

During Rupert Henderson's chairmanship of ATN, the concept of 'breaking into' the ABC's monopoly on BBC material had developed through the acquisition of re-runs of comedies already shown by the ABC. We were able to get ratings of 30 per cent of sets in use with third runs of *The Rag Trade*, *Hancock* and *Are You Being Served?* compared to 10 per cent of sets in use when they were first run on Channel Two. We were gradually able to extend the relationship by acquiring programs not taken up by the ABC, although the problem here was that the people who made such decisions at the ABC took an interminable time to make up their minds.

It became my practice to meet the BBC Overseas Division on my annual London visit. For many years it was headed by Brian Parkin, and he always gathered a galaxy of talent in various areas, such as Michael Checkland and Bill Cotton, whom I greatly enjoyed getting to know. I met a number of chairmen and directors-general of the BBC, either at Broadcasting House or Shepherds Bush. One of the most memorable chairmen was George Howard. I had first met him on a Nile cruise in 1980, where he used to encase his imposing figure each night for dinner in a caftan or gelabiya. He was the owner of the magnificent Castle Howard (so named for his Earls of Carlisle forebears who were kin of the Norfolk Howards) in Yorkshire, made even more famous by its use in the series *Brideshead Revisited*. Although an unlikely choice for chairman, he was no slouch in his brief time in the job. Together with Alasdair Milne (director-general), he withstood considerable onslaught from Mrs Thatcher's government for alleged bias in reporting the Falklands War.

The other relationship we established was with Thames Television, which produced some of the best programs in the country for the ITV companies. Bryan Cowgill was chief executive for many years and lunch at their Euston headquarters — or sometimes on board their boat, moored by their studios at Teddington — was a regular feature of our visits. I first met Jeremy Isaacs there. He moved on to establish Channel Four, providing its unique and valuable contribution to British television for its first three years, and is now chairman of Covent Garden. The Nine and Ten Networks began to follow our lead in buying British product, but our early links with Thames provided us with many successful programs such as *Father Dear Father*, *Widows* and *The Sweeney*.

My London and Los Angeles television rounds, which I have briefly described from their starting point in 1975, continued for thirteen years, although not always annually in each case. I found them both congenial and invigorating, but they were not all beer and skittles. There were inevitably occasional disputes on quality, price and making programs available to the opposition. While these usually took place on a management level, if they were unresolved, I was sometimes able to pour oil on troubled waters. They all, American and British, used to visit my Lindsay Avenue house for a meal or drink during their Australian trips. Some, indeed, were regular guests and all were most welcome.

Over the next eleven financial years (June 1977–June 1987), profits after tax averaged around $4–5 million and in the last five years they did not fall below $6 million. While this represented an adequate return on capital, it was no 'bonzana', to quote a Hendersonian malapropism. Two other areas over these eleven years require brief mention: government policy and regulation, and programming in general.

The Menzies Government's efforts to prevent the print media from dominating television were determined but unavailing. We gained control of Channel Seven, from a 33.3 per cent holding, simply because our partners were not prepared to risk putting in extra capital in those early, loss-making days. The ownership regulations went through a number of permutations over the years, but basically settled down to a restriction to a major shareholding in two metropolitan stations. Control was defined at the low level of 15 per cent, while a prescribed interest was 5 per cent. This remained unchanged until November 1986, when Keating announced the government's proposed changes to the Act which were to have such unintended and far-reaching consequences for Australian media ownership.

Regulation of programming has similarly been through a number of permutations, but the faulty concept that higher quality programs can be achieved through legislation and the amount spent on them still subsists, as does its corollary — that public taste can be educated and somehow 'uplifted' by the provision of such programs. At Channel Seven we were firm believers in the novel idea that the least amount of regulation would give the public the mix of local and overseas programs it wanted, in what was primarily a medium of entertainment which provided ancillary services such as news, current affairs and documentaries. When this is combined with the more specialised services provided by the ABC and more recently by SBS, television in Australia should, and often does, provide a greater variety of programming than anywhere else in the English-speaking world. The station that did not provide the public with the mix it wanted — and this has always revealed strong support for locally produced drama and series — would, of course, suffer an immediate loss of revenue. However at Seven we recognised that political reality dictated a degree of regulation, even though we never felt it could achieve the desired results.

During the 1970s we were winning the ratings with programming that included *Cop Shop* and *Willesee at Seven*, which our partners at HSV were finally prevailed upon to take. Australian investments included such feature films as *Sunday Too Far Away* and *Breaker Morant*, and on the sporting side, competition tennis, Rugby League and the Hardie Ferodo 1000 Motor Race at Bathurst. Our eighteen-foot yacht *Color Seven*, skippered by Iain Murray, won the World Championships for six years in a row, carrying our logo across Sydney Harbour.

We were not worried about our capacity to produce Australian drama, as this was an area where we had had considerable success, but by 1979 we needed to get some new shows going. We now had magnificent plant and equipment and urgently required an upsurge in local production to utilise the facilities. The comedy series *Kingswood Country* was a ratings success, as was the network produced program *This Fabulous Century* with Peter Luck, and the mini-series *A Town Like Alice. Skyways*, unfortunately, was not.

The problem in filling the 6 pm timeslot together with the perceived inadequacy of a half-hour news program finally led us to schedule an hour for news in 1984. Our decision, which I am quite sure was the correct one at the time, was ultimately to cause a significant disagreement on programming within the station. Thomas had been thinking of a long-term solution to the news position since 1979. As he put it, the global village was at our doorstep and the half-hour format, with a bare sixteen or seventeen minutes for the news itself after deducting commercial time, sport and weather, only allowed for a fairly superficial and inadequate treatment. In the light of the fate of all three of the one-hour news services, he recognises that he could have stayed with half an hour, but he still believes a winning hour of news is possible. Kinging, the program director, parted company with him in this belief, and as ratings fluctuated by up to 15 points behind Nine towards the end of 1987, Tyson and the other station executives joined Kinging in the view that we should return to the half-hour format. We stayed with the hour until after the sale to Skase and Thomas's retirement, and from the ratings point of view it could be argued that we hung on too long.

The comment is sometimes made that at a point in time — usually put at about halfway along television's thirty-five year life span in this country — Nine elected to go the way of news and current affairs ('real time, real world', in Bruce Gyngell's phrase) while Seven took the road to drama and Australian content. There was certainly no conscious decision at Seven to abandon current affairs, as our perseverance with *Willesee at 7,* followed by a renegotiated contract with him for thirty one-hour specials, would testify. When Mike Willesee went to Nine, his brother's show, *Terry Willesee Tonight,* was successful at 7 pm for four years, although the emphasis was on social and community affairs rather than politics.

However, it is perfectly true that we never succeeded in attracting our editors or journalists at Broadway over to Epping to any significant extent, or on terms and conditions acceptable to all parties. I have always regretted that discussions with Max Walsh never bore fruit. His subsequent career on television was very successful. Perhaps there is some truth in the suggestion that executives at both places had some difficulty in coming to terms with the idea that television and newspapers could be complementary rather than adversarial. At any rate, such problems did not seem to be so relevant in the personally run empires of both Sir Frank and Kerry Packer.

It must be emphasised that the 1980s were successful years for Seven. Our only poor year (1980–81) had been affected by loss of revenue on the Moscow Olympic Games. Following the Russian invasion of Afghanistan, Australia boycotted the Games, together with a number of Commonwealth, Western and Third World countries. The Seven Network held Australian rights and considerable pressure was put on both the station and myself to abandon coverage. We took the view that regardless of political implications, the public had the right to decide whether it wanted to watch them or not. However we lost two $3 million sponsorships. I recall that Malcolm Fraser spent most of the opening lunch for a *Financial Review*-Nihon Keizai Shimbun Seminar trying to persuade me that Seven should not telecast the Games results, almost ignoring the chairman of Nihon Keizai on his other side. Rather to my surprise, Kerry Packer had rung me to wish me a happy Christmas the previous December and as a result of this he came to lunch at Lindsay Avenue, during which he suggested going back to a pooling system for Olympic Games, where all stations shared the coverage.

In 1981 Howard Griffiths was appointed to start the Drama Unit. We had already contracted for two new dramas — *A Country Practice* (from James Davern) and *Sons and Daughters* (from Grundy), and Griffiths went on to develop *Kingswood Country* and two new pilots. One was for a movie, entitled *Soldiers,* and the other was for a drama serial. *A Country Practice*, still rating in the twenties after eight years, is one of the most successful television series made in Australia, while *Sons and Daughters* rated successfully for three years.

In 1984, Alan Bateman from the ABC took over the Unit. That same year we commissioned the mini-series *Melba, Land of Hope, Spearfield's Daughter, Nancy Wake* and *Sword of Honour*. I had some small personal involvement with the first of these as I thought it was essential to gain the cooperation of Dame Nellie Melba's granddaughter, Pamela, Lady Vestey. The family of her late husband (Lord Vestey) owned the vast, worldwide meat exporting and land-owning company. I had known Pam for some years and her parents George (Melba's only child) and Evie Armstrong, who had always lived in England, had been friends of my mother. It would be a great coup for the series if the director, Rodney Fisher, and the writer, Roger McDonald, could gain access to Coombe Cottage at Coldstream, outside Melbourne, to which Melba retired and where Pam lived surrounded by Melba memorabilia.

I had a lunch at the Florentino for Pam to meet the director, writer and the producers, Errol Sullivan and Pom Oliver. Pam, who had always been shy and was now leading a very quiet life, charmed all of them. But the lunch ended with her saying that although she liked them very much, she had the gravest misgivings about the series. She felt, with justification, that her grandmother's life had never been fairly or adequately presented before. The seed had been sown, however, and after some further encouragement from me, the desired visit to Coombe was made and she was extremely helpful. The resulting series, with Linda Cropper brilliant as Melba and Yvonne Kenny in glorious form as the 'voice', was a tremendous success artistically, dramatically and as a ratings scorer. Most importantly, Pam was very pleased with it.

Other network-produced rating successes during this period included *Kingswood Country*, *Wheel of Fortune* (the No.1 rated show on Australian daytime television), *Hey Dad*, *Beyond 2000* and the mini-series *Against the Wind* and *All the Rivers Run*. Bateman took over responsibility for *Rafferty's Rules*, a series built around the life and cases of a city magistrate, which had been suggested by Thomas and a pilot made. Production began in March 1985, financed by ATN

Lunch to celebrate Ray Beattie's twenty years of service with ATN, Epping, June 1986.
Left to right: *John Donovan, Gary Jackson, Michael Harrison, Phil Davis, Murray Stevenson, John Mathieson, Alan Bateman, James Fairfax, John Sturzaker, Ray Beattie, Geoff Healy, Jim Oswin, Chris Chapman, Royce Pedder, Ted Thomas and Gary Herring.*

without network support. The other network stations subsequently took it, but it must be acknowledged that it was not the success in other states that it was in Sydney, where it ran for two years. Before leaving Seven for Nine after the sale to Skase, Bateman got the Drama Unit to produce *Home and Away*, now running successfully on the network in the very difficult 6.30 pm weekday timeslot between the *News* and *Hinch at Seven*, and against A *Current Affair* on Nine. It is worth pointing out that until recently the Drama Unit has had two series concurrently in production at the Epping studios, which is a great credit to all concerned with the creative and production processes there.

I have referred several times to networking difficulties between ATN-7 and our partner HSV, owned by the Herald and Weekly Times. I do not believe it is appropriate here to go raking over the embers of old disputes, but there was a clear feeling in Sydney that over the years Melbourne had some reluctance to commit to new, live ventures and there was some heel-dragging in other areas, with ATN, occasionally, having to bear the initial financial risk. It is only fair to add that the former general manager of HSV, Ron Casey, whom I have always liked and respected, would dispute this in a number of instances. Perhaps the best way I can sum up the situation is to make the point that experience taught us that working with a network partner caused a number of disadvantages that ownership of the two most important stations in the network would obviate. This was the situation enjoyed by our competitors and it was, of course, a major reason for the acquisition of HSV.

During the last years of Fairfax ownership of ATN, we were leaders in the technical field. Mention should be made of Custom Video Australia, a state of the art videotape post-production centre managed for many years by Bill Nuttle, which I understand is still regarded as one of the best in the country. Also on the technical side, ATN were pioneers in camera technology in such events as motor and yacht races. Our coverage of the Americas Cup at Fremantle was shown throughout the USA and was greatly acclaimed, as was our coverage of the Indianapolis 500 which was used by the ABC (US) network.

An early official act of Prime Minister Hawke in April 1983 had been to inaugurate the Epping earth station for the Intelsat satellite, beaming direct telecasts from the United States. For two years we were the only Australian television station broadcasting material from CNN by direct satellite telecast (programs went to air live between midnight and 6 am and prerecorded items were used in news bulletins throughout the day). Channel Ten started taking parts of the CNN material from 1985 while Channel Seven terminated the arrangement in 1988 so was unable to take advantage of it during the Gulf War. I asked the Prime Minister afterwards if he was planning to maintain the Imperial

With Prime Minister Bob Hawke inaugurating the satellite link to Los Angeles at ATN, Epping, on 22 April 1983. Photo: Sydney Morning Herald

Honours system, with me as the first knight created by his government, as he twice referred to me as 'Sir James' in his speech.

As Fairfax reinforced its success in television and its reputation as the leader in quality print journalism through the 1980s, our Macquarie Broadcasting Holdings subsidiary underwent a renaissance which secured it the same high standing in radio. The flagship of the six Macquarie stations, 2GB Sydney, had lost its way in the mid-1970s. It had lurched uncertainly from one program format to another after losing touch with a solid audience of up-market, better educated listeners for whom the attraction had been a mixture of strong personalities, music and vigorous current affairs journalism. Although new, assertive and intelligent talkers such as Mike Carlton were in place, the successively deepening losses were not to be turned around until after the appointment of

R. A. (Bob) Johnson as Group General Manager at the start of 1981.

Johnson's appointment, like Carlton's, was a legacy of Max Suich's emergency, short-term executive directorship of 2GB in 1980 and, like Suich, Johnson brought a newsman's experience and instincts to its problems. He had been a news and feature writer for the *Sun-Herald,* news director of ATN, and executive editor at Broadway, responsible for the *Sun, Sun-Herald, Financial Review* and *National Times.* A 'period of agonising', as Johnson was to express it later, led to an idea from Nigel Milan, the man he appointed as 2GB manager, for a format that had never been tried in Sydney before: news and talk only, no music. It appealed to Johnson since it offered a way to build on two of 2GB's strengths — in the newsroom, able journalists, and at the microphone able talkers with a taste for controversy combined, in Carlton, with a talent for funny, at times risky, mimicry of public figures. Macquarie won the backing of the Fairfax board for the switch, and 2GB embarked on a course which steadily led it back to its old place among the top-raters.

Outright leadership did not come, however, until after John Laws left 2UE for 2GB in 1985. Sir Warwick had been keen to bring him on board as early as October 1981 but, the Macquarie board and Gardiner argued, as he cost more than ten times as much as Mike Carlton, the station could not yet afford him. Both Johnson and John Fairfax agreed with Gardiner that the time to draw Laws into a contract — to 'get the king', as Johnson put it — would be when 2GB became comfortably profitable.

That time came in 1985, when the successful negotiations to take him from 2UE were perhaps helped by his concern at signs of a decline at 2UE. Laws took over from 9 am to noon in place of John Tingle, Carlton having moved to the breakfast session, and Tingle moved from morning to afternoon. These three, together with the strongest commercial radio news service in Australia, were the keys to the dominance then secured by 2GB.

For Laws, the switch to 2GB was comfortable. A friend of Sir Warwick and Mary Fairfax as well as myself, he admired the standards of Fairfax journalism, both in print and on the air, but had never worked in the Fairfax group. Johnson felt that Laws, in joining us in his fiftieth year, saw himself rounding out a career in which he had achieved all else.

There was a curious omen in 1987 when, after two years, it was time for a new contract. Laws insisted on a provision that he should be free to break the contract if ownership of Macquarie changed. Did he have an inkling of the upheaval Warwick would bring before the year was out? Had he picked up some hint from Martin Dougherty, Warwick's adviser and collaborator? Dougherty, after all, was a friend and financial adviser to Laws. Certainly those whom Laws dealt with at Macquarie saw no prospect that the escape clause would ever be invoked. Our lawyers looked at it closely, and so did John Fairfax and Greg Gardiner. All agreed that it hardly mattered. But when Macquarie moved to new hands after Warwick's takeover, Laws was free to go — and he did.

After the success of news/talk at 2GB we used it at 3AW Melbourne and grafted it to an existing news format at 5DN Adelaide to bring both these stations to the top of their markets. With 4BH Brisbane continuing to exploit its traditionally successful music, Macquarie found itself for a time with the top station in each of the four capitals. The network grew in numbers, adding 4AY Townsville (later renamed 4RR — Reef Radio) and an interest in 6PR Perth to the original six in Sydney, Melbourne, Brisbane, Adelaide, Canberra and Wollongong. From losses of more than $1.5 million a year as the 1980s began, Macquarie moved up to be earning at the rate of $5 million a year in the final period of Fairfax ownership.

Technical innovation, particularly in news, marked this time of growth. Newsrooms at all network stations were linked by a twenty-four-hour leased channel so that editors from one side of Australia to the other could confer instantly at the touch of a button. A computerised system for writing and editing followed. Apart from the efficiency gained within each newsroom, the system gave editors around the network the capacity to scan one another's news files and to extract and edit elements of them for their own bulletins. The Macquarie news service, the biggest commercial radio news operation in Australia, was extended to fifty stations in addition to the eight in the network.

With other Fairfax directors, I shared Macquarie's pride in a pioneering venture named Macsat. Launched in 1986, it delivered packaged Macquarie programs to regional stations, using the Aussat satellite system in place of the more expensive landlines of the past. Client stations were able to take news, current affairs, sport and personality-based programs through receiver dishes financed by Macquarie on a leaseback plan. With client stations totalling nearly forty, Macsat was moving towards a profitable base by the end of 1987.

To round off this stage of the Fairfax company's development it is worth pointing out that the prudent ploughing-in of a high proportion of earnings through the 1980s secured for the Fairfaxes and for all shareholders an increase in assets unmatched in any other period of the company's history. In the face of this fact I found it grotesque that when Warwick ambushed other members of the family with his secret takeover plan it was offered as a justification that he saw an urgent need to save the company from mismanagement.

At the Annual General Meeting in 1985, I noted in my address to shareholders that their funds had increased from $112 million in 1980 to $342 million at 30 June 1985, an increase of more than 200 per cent. A year later the shareholders' funds stood at $443 million, up 295 per cent on 1980, and at 30 June 1987 (two months before the takeover bid was announced) $1 103 million, up 884 per cent.

In market capitalisation, the first five years of the 1980s saw a rise from just over $70 million to more than $700 million, an increase of 850 per cent. At the 1986 AGM I was able to quote from a letter from the Sydney Stock Exchange which dramatically illustrated the rising fortunes of shareholders. The Exchange said it had calculated that an investment of $1000 in John Fairfax Limited on 30 June 1981 would have appreciated to be worth $9469 at 30 June 1986 if all dividends and proceeds from the sale of rights had been reinvested in the company. This was a total return on investment over the period of 56.77 per cent a year, which, I commented mildly, 'compares more than favourably with the 16.1 per cent per annum return on the Australian Stock Exchange All Ordinaries Accumulation Index'.

By 30 June 1987 market capitalisation had risen to $1350 million, but this figure was dwarfed before the year was out. The offer by which Warwick achieved ownership put a valuation on the company of $2550 million, thirty-six times the market value of 1980.

16

CUCKOO IN THE NEST

SIR WARWICK DIES, WARWICK MAKES HIS
FIRST MOVE, JANUARY–AUGUST 1987

My father died at 2.25 pm on Wednesday 14 January 1987. I was summoned to the communications room next to the bridge of *Society Explorer* at 1.30 am Antarctic time to take a call from Caroline, who had just come from Fairwater. Mary had two guests for lunch that day: Susan Renouf and Mrs Diana Price, from England, and Caroline was asked to join them. Not unnaturally she did not feel like doing this. I was to get fairly used to taking early morning calls in that room over the next ten days, on both funeral arrangements and questions concerning the H&WT takeover.

With me forever will be the memory of sitting by the ship's radio-telephone looking at an enormous pale blue iceberg glide past, glistening in the eerie light of an Antarctic summer night, while I took in the fact of my father's death. We had experienced an extremely rough crossing of the Drake Passage that day and Dorothy Edwards and myself, both being good sailors, were among the very few who had appeared for dinner amidst crashing crockery and broken glasses. On the return crossing, the entire complement of the captain's table, which did not include our party that night, was precipitated quite gently onto the floor like a long row of falling dominos. I remember thinking how amused my father would have been.

Indeed, I thought a lot about him during the rest of the voyage and the office struggles and breaches seemed to slip away. I returned in my mind to happy school holidays at Harrington Park where, wearing an antique straw hat, he would be reading the paper on a rickety chaise longue on the lawn, with four or five dogs draped over him. He was a singularly unpretentious man and his true nature placed little importance on the possession of wealth or power. This may sound an odd and unlikely comment to make but, until he became obsessed with the idea of controlling the company himself, I believe it to be true.

It was not long before the problems of the funeral arose in a series of calls from Mary, Caroline, Warwick (at Harvard) and Annalise. It was agreed to delay the funeral until Warwick had completed his term in the last week of January and I had arrived back from Buenos Aires on the 28th. After consultation with Archbishop Loane and the appropriate church authorities, it was decided that St Andrew's Cathedral would be the appropriate church. It was clear, though, that Mary visualised a far more elaborate ceremony than the rest of us had in mind — or indeed thought that our father would have wanted. One of her ideas was a procession representing all the world's religions. Caroline and Annalise had to bear the brunt of this, with Warwick bringing some pressure to bear on his mother by telephone. I was quite relieved not to be involved.

On the day of the funeral, Friday 30 January, I went to Fairwater at 10.15 am to find Mary in the drawing room with Warwick, Charles and Anna, and a

*Sir Warwick Fairfax's funeral at St. Andrew's Cathedral, Sydney, 30 January 1987. James Fairfax with Warwick, Mary, Anna Bella and Charles. **Rear:** Caroline, Annalise (partly obscured) and Philip. Photo:* Sydney Morning Herald

large coffee tray complete with a bottle of brandy. Mary and I decided a slug of brandy in our coffee would help us through the day. Earlier in the month, the papers had been full of tributes from federal and state government and opposition leaders, the media industry, including Richard Searby for News Ltd and Kerry Packer and other business and community figures. In a curious way I was quite surprised, as I had never thought of him as being a national figure until the tributes came rolling in. There was a crowd outside the cathedral in the blinding January heat and inside a host of family, including my mother and Hanne. The 'dignitaries' were headed by the Governor, Sir James Rowland, and Sir Roden Cutler, who gave one of the addresses (the other being given by the Assistant Bishop of Canberra and Goulburn, the Right Reverend B.W. Wilson).

The lessons were read by Warwick and myself, while Annalise read from my father's recently completed and final work on philosophy and religion, *Purpose,* which is to be published. It was one time when I felt I was of some help to Mary, as she was clearly struggling to control her emotions. There was no division of purpose here and on a number of occasions afterwards, she expressed her gratitude for my support. I was too preoccupied with the role I had to play to think much about the service itself. After the service, I think I spoke to nearly everyone who had been in the cathedral and we finally headed the long procession to the South Head cemetery.

Most of the family from great-grandfather James Reading Fairfax onwards had been buried in the family grave there (John and Sarah were buried at Rookwood) and looking at the inscription on a large stone memorial plinth which recorded my grandmother's burial, I realised for the first time that she had consistently been putting her age back three years and had died in her ninety-fourth year.

After the burial, family and friends gathered at Fairwater for a buffet lunch and for the first time I realised, looking round the room, that the family — whatever its divisions — had lost its patriarch and that here was an opportunity for a renewed unity. I felt this even more after lunch, with the family sitting around on the veranda in the still intense heat, and while I puffed away at my cigar, I was aware of the relative youth of its members.

Vincent was the senior member and, with cousin Mick, their wives Nancy and Sue, and cousin Margaret Morrow, represented the older generation, as indeed did Mary. But most of the cousinhood fell into the middle-aged or 'approaching it' category, while their children were either grown-up or of school age. I was very much aware of my own responsibility, both as chairman of the company and head of our branch of the family. Here, indeed, was a chance for John, Warwick and myself, together with our different families, and the children of Mick, Margaret and my late cousin John, with their children, to come together in a way the older generation had not been able to achieve since the days of Auntie Mary at Ginahgulla. However, this dream was to have a rude awakening.

As events following the H&WT takeover settled down, issues related to the newly acquired HSV-7 were of major concern. At the Fairfax board meeting in February 1987, Gardiner was critical of both management and accounting procedures at HSV, arguing that costs would have to be substantially reduced. For an interest outlay of $50 million on the $320 million debt, it was earning only $5 million profit. The two main areas where costs could be cut were a move away from VFL football and a move towards a networking operation with Sydney. Both these actions would be strongly resisted at the station and there would be a public reaction, even though ratings for VFL had fallen.

It must be recorded that the HSV management under the leadership of Gerry Carrington handled the very difficult ensuing strike with skill and determination. Pickets surrounded the HSV building for several weeks following the cancellation of the VFL and the telecast of the news from Sydney with Victorian inserts. Channels Nine and Ten had long since ceased to have any particular Melbourne identity, but HSV's concentration on local sport, particularly the VFL, had given it a different image. Even though we in Sydney were greatly criticised for the decidedly unpopular action we took at HSV, our view was that the nettle had to be grasped, and the ensuing pain withstood.

The long-awaited cross-media legislation could well force us to sell HSV, and John suggested that we should seriously consider selling the network, especially as the company might have a chance to buy back in later if it were sold into friendly hands. As Sir David Griffin pointed out, a sale would create a cash-rich company. In John's view, holding the television assets and raising capital would necessarily restrict avenues of other expansion such as overseas and through Brisbane or Adelaide newspapers. I had not yet come round to this view, despite misgivings about the future of television, and believed that there were other options, such as floating it off to friendly partners and retaining a minority holding. Gardiner favoured raising additional capital rather than selling an asset to make us cash rich. Opportunities for media expansion were now limited in Australia and he thought we should look overseas. John and Vincent remained keen on getting out of television, but it was agreed that we should look at a further scheme of capital raising which Dominguez Barry Samuel Montagu were currently working on at Gardiner's request.

The scheme proposed to raise $400 million in a convertible note issue for John Fairfax Ltd, and simultaneously float a new listed investment company,

Newco, initially to house the television assets. Under the scheme, Newco would raise $215 million from the public, of which $200 million would be used to purchase the Fairfax notes. The family would sell 13.3 per cent of Fairfax into Newco (26.6 per cent of its total holdings) in return for shares in Newco, while Newco would acquire the family's entitlement to the note issue. The end result would be that the family retained 29 per cent of JFL and 50 per cent of Newco, while the public would have 50 per cent of Newco and 50 per cent of JFL, and Newco would hold (post-conversion) 21 per cent of JFL.

It is hard to know whether Warwick had begun his takeover discussions with anyone other than Dougherty or Mary when Newco was put to him. Certainly Warwick and Mary would have been suspicious of anything Gardiner put up. The plan won qualified support at board level and was particularly favoured by Gardiner, who said it was the 'best and most viable available', and carried 'enormous scope for later growth and diversification'. Late in February, Warwick called in Baring Brothers Halkerston (BBH) to advise him on the proposal, and their report, prepared by Mark Burrows, concluded that it was not in the best interests of the family: 'It potentially imposes taxation penalties, impacts on the market value of the family's investment in John Fairfax Ltd and puts at greater risk . . . the independence of the company'.

Burrows predicted that the share price would fall as people took account of conversion rights on the notes, and institutions interested in the higher return swapped shares for notes. Meanwhile, the family would have to exchange assets exempt from capital gains tax for those that would incur the tax and there was a high risk of shortfall in the necessary underwritings, he said. Moreover, Newco shares were unlikely to command the same loyalty and respect as JFL shares, raising the risk that the family might sell Newco shares should they need to raise cash.

I subsequently learned from Mark Burrows that while the Newco scheme was still under discussion, Warwick had commissioned BBH to prepare a feasibility study into whether he could take over the company. This explains the hostility of Warwick and Mary to the scheme, of which we were unaware at the time, and also made clear the double game Warwick and Mary played during my attempts to get Warwick to join the Fairfax board. I told the March board about a telephone conference I had arranged with Warwick at Harvard, attended in my office by Vincent, John, Halstead (as my advisor), Barry Taplin of Touche Ross (as Vincent and John's) and Keith Halkerston (of BBH) for Warwick in Sydney. I hoped that this conference would either bring Warwick around or at any rate elicit some opinion from him that we could work on.

Far from having burned the telephone lines to the three family members and Gardiner — another example of Warwick's disinformation, apparently accepted by Trevor Sykes — during the course of the conference, it was extremely difficult to get a firm opinion from him about Newco at all. He said he supported a capital raising but queried whether it was the right way to go. Further, he accepted, more readily than I thought he would, that the board would have to make a decision even if he disagreed with it. Every concern raised by BBH had been considered by the board but Vincent, with memories of PIPS and Sir Warwick, said it was essential that Warwick accept the board's decision. Before putting the resolution I said I thought he would, even if he were not totally convinced, and that Mary would go along with him.

I was clearly quite wrong in this belief (as Warwick later said at the Tryart court case: 'I thought to myself at the time: how many of these proposed reconstruction proposals can I defeat?'[1]) and even though I had some worries about Mary's attitude, from the telephone conversation with Warwick, I thought I had a clear undertaking that he would go along with the majority decision — an assurance which, as it turned out, did not have to be tested. At all events, the board did not accept the assessment of BBH and resolved to proceed with Newco subject to further detailed checking.

In the end, the Newco proposal was withdrawn by Gardiner as he had some doubts about the total efficacy of the chain of control, although the manager of the Stock Exchange listing committee said he thought they would be 'quite relaxed' about it. At the April board Gardiner said he had never been completely satisfied with the scheme, but he had to put it to the board as a possible and viable option, and as a reminder that there was still a 'very real problem'. The problem was, of course, the same as it always had been — how to raise capital without putting at risk at least part of the family's holding. Gardiner was the victim of the family's inability to agree on a form of capital raising, which went right back to Sir Warwick's refusal to consider an equity issue five years earlier.

In the early stages of the Newco proposal, a most significant event was Warwick's February purchase of 1.5 per cent of the company's capital at prices around the $20 mark. Warwick had called me several times from Harvard expressing concern at fluctuations in the share price and he finally suggested that he, John and I should jointly buy another 1.5 per cent. I considered this but decided against it, telling him that I thought the family holding of 48.51 per cent was adequate protection, although I conceded the desirability of achieving 50 per cent. John and Vincent agreed to participate but were asking Warwick to consider a guarantee against a fall in the share price.

Before this issue was resolved, Warwick went ahead and bought the 1.5 per cent on his own, which gave rise to some friction between him and John. I endeavoured to smooth this over, as I was working towards his entry into the company and early acceptance of a seat on the board. John's account of his own negotiations with Warwick on the proposed purchase is contained in a letter he wrote to Trevor Sykes, which I quote in part:

On the weekend of 14 February, 1987 Warwick rang me from Boston while I was trout fishing near Queanbeyan. He rang several times in relation to the need to purchase 1.5 per cent of the company's capital.

[A family meeting] considered Warwick's request to meet half the proposed amount, which would have represented $15 million. We also considered a contribution of $10 million which would have been our one-third participation had James also agreed to participate. James, as you correctly point out [in Operation Dynasty], did not wish to do so.

Our advisers worked over the numbers and we found that the absolute maximum we could contribute was $6 million, and this would leave us financially strapped for quite a number of years. However, we felt that in the interests of our own family, of John Fairfax Limited, and of the desired harmony of working with Warwick in future years, we would like to help him on this occasion.

The substantial borrowings that would have been required to make a family contribution of $6 million would have resulted in potential financial uncertainty to some, if not all, members of our family. It was in this context, therefore, that we collectively agreed to suggest to Warwick that he be prepared to buy the shares from us at the same price we were now paying should there be adverse economic factors (it was not a condition of us contributing the $6 million, and I made this perfectly clear to him).

Warwick made very little comment on the offer, said he would consider it and ring me back. He returned the call the next day and said that he had given further consideration to the whole question and had decided to purchase the entire 1.5 per cent himself.

The negative response to our proposal was totally unexpected and quite shattering, considering the urgency of it all over the previous few days, and the great trouble we had taken to go out of our way to commit $6 million.

John also pointed out that he was more than happy to assist Warwick to settle into JFL when he returned from Harvard, even though he was uneasy about the latter's ultimate motives and mindful that his mother was playing a significant background part at that time. How Warwick could have regarded the actions of either John or myself on this matter as evidence of lack of determination to protect family control, if it came under threat, defeats the imagination. It is also surprising that he evidently had not bothered to obtain a detailed list of family holdings, as Sykes describes him as being furious when he discovered from Catherine Foley, formerly Sir Warwick's secretary, that it was under 50 per cent.

Gardiner, John and I speculated on how Warwick could finance the $34 million debt, secured on Rockwood shares.[2] Sykes is undoubtedly correct when he says that the purchase was 'a critical folly because it now forced Warwick to act in some way or other to resolve his position. In other words, one of his reasons for making the bid may be to solve his own financial problems.'

In correspondence in the Sydney press regarding her role in the takeover, Mary Fairfax recounted how she was 'regrettably' persuaded by Warwick to guarantee half the $34 million debt when he decided to go ahead on his own without giving John and Vincent a further opportunity to participate. Warwick's initial approach to us and his subsequent decision to buy the 1.5 per cent in no way invalidates his clear determination to gain control of the company, as Mary Fairfax suggests. Whatever the truth of the disputed conversation with Dougherty in December, the course had clearly been set then.

Other things were happening as well, particularly in relation to our Hunter Street property and possible further development at Broadway. For several years discussions had been held about moving management and all administrative departments, together with some editorial staff (such as finance and possibly all the *Financial Review* staff), back to a building in the central business district. Increasing traffic problems were making Broadway more isolated and the board favoured the idea of a city 'presence'.

At the same time proposals were being examined to establish a media centre on the Broadway site which would accommodate Macquarie/2GB, Channel Seven city office and Fairfax Magazines. We considered several available buildings in the city and finally decided on a development plan for our block bounded by Hunter and Hamilton Streets, and Curtin Place and Little Hunter Street, part of which housed our city offices in two knocked-together buildings.

I encouraged the board to offer the project to Harry Seidler, because I thought his talents would provide the most imaginative architectural solution for the site and his fine Australia Square Tower complex stood on the other side of Curtin Lane. He might have been surprised to be offered the job, as we had been involved in an acrimonious libel action over a *National Times* article, which he had finally lost on appeal. Also, his father-in-law, Clive Evatt, QC,[3] had been a frequent antagonist in libel and defamation actions against both our own newspaper group and others in the state. If he was surprised, he did not show it and took up the task with enthusiasm. I had known Harry and his wife Penelope for some time; she and I had been on the International Council of the Museum of Modern Art in New York for many years and had met in various countries for the spring meetings.

I looked forward to working with Harry in this enterprise but it was not to be. After much negotiation, the Heritage Council decided in its wisdom that it was more important to preserve the façade of an undistinguished late Victorian building which they thought vital for the jumble of old and new which the streetscape of Hunter Street presents. It was a good example of the mania for preserving everything old regardless of quality, stifling an original creation which would have blended perfectly with its neighbour and been an ornament to the city. While we were considering an appeal, Lend Lease offered $22 million (later raised to $25.3 million) to buy the block for a development to adjoin their Australia Square Tower. We decided with many regrets to put the site up for tender and the best offer received was from Citisite Developments at $35 million. Warwick's bid interrupted events at this point and doubtless he would have abandoned the Seidler plan even if it had been approved, but it was another opportunity lost for the city. The façade, so prized by the Heritage Council, collapsed of its own accord on 8 August 1990, fortunately causing only minor injuries — a final comment on the futility of 'façadism'.

Warwick had returned to Sydney from Harvard on 14 May and, apart from a brief trip back to take his degree in June, was able to devote himself to his takeover plans. I was able with some difficulty to persuade Vincent and John that it would be appropriate and beneficial for Warwick to represent his branch of the family's interest on the board. I was particularly anxious too, that John, who had a natural concern about his own position, should be involved with Gardiner in the circumstances of Warwick's joining the company and the position he was to hold.

When John joined the Fairfax board in 1979, he had resigned as manager of Federal Capital Press, as it was felt that a situation where a director held an executive position with the company could lead to a conflict of interests. Seven years later, I argued that it was sufficiently important to get Warwick on the board, to represent his own and his mother's interests, for us to take the risk. In other words, Warwick would become a director and pursue an executive career at the same time — an advantage that had not been open to John.

Somewhat to my surprise, I found a curious reluctance on Warwick's part to take up that responsibility. He said he preferred to wait until he had established himself in an executive position in the company. I enlisted Mary's aid in urging him to accept, but the reason she gave for his reluctance was curious — he was so fond of me that he did not want to be in a position of disagreement with me at board level! In less emotional moments, she described him as not wishing to damage our relationship through possible disagreement on the board. To my mind, however well-meaning, this was neither a satisfactory nor a mature position. Mary plugged what I can only describe as the 'fondness angle' to an excessive degree until her departure for Europe in August. Of course, I remained blissfully unaware both of her motives and Warwick's, thinking Mary's response was an emotional reaction following my father's death. In fact, as a director of the company, he would not have been able to launch his takeover bid.

Following discussions with John and Gardiner, Warwick started work — at an appropriate salary and with a company car — as assistant to Peter Gaunt, publisher of the *Herald*, *Sun* and *Sun-Herald*. He filled this position and absorbed a certain amount of critical comment about the management until the end of August. He continued to draw his salary until the day he took over the company, even though from 31 August he moved into Rothwell's Sydney office.[4]

Between May and July our main concern was, of course, the sale of the Seven Network. In the critical comment this sale aroused, a number of aspects have consistently been ignored. Firstly, we had for some time been considering our commitment to television and what future form this might take in the light of the anticipated government legislation and a possible downturn in the industry. Secondly, the prices obtained by Packer and Murdoch for the Nine and Ten networks tended to be regarded as a benchmark, whereas they were grossly excessive. Thirdly, calculations as to whether we would have been better off financially by selling ATN and BTQ without acquiring HSV are purely speculative, and conclusions cannot be drawn from the price we got for the network. Finally, the decision to sell was partly prompted by our failure to achieve a capital raising, for reasons I have described at some length.

Gardiner believed that a prompt sale of HSV could realise the purchase price, while if ATN and BTQ were sold as well, $650 million to $800 million could be raised, leaving the company debt-free with money in the bank. Paul Keating's statement in the *Herald* that we had refused an offer 'in the vicinity of $900 million' for the Seven Network was totally untrue. His statement in a subsequent letter in the *Herald* that 'It was widely known at the time (of the purchase of HSV) that a number of substantial purchasers were interested, a number beyond those cited (Skase and Stokes) in their (Gardiner, Suich and Brenchley) letter' cannot be substantiated because such purchasers referred to did not exist.

Keating's persistent denigration of the Fairfax management prior to the takeover could be related to the journalistic activities of the *National Times*.

Gardiner's initial work drew approaches from Holmes à Court, Sir Roderick Carnegie (representing a group of Melbourne interests) and Kerry Stokes, who in June was considered the prime prospective purchaser. Just as Gardiner had decided to recommend the Stokes proposal, which would have made Fairfax and Stokes holders of the largest television network in the country, Christopher Skase approached the board on 1 July with a plan for $780 million in payments staggered over three years. This, as Gardiner pointed out in his letter to the *Herald*, was the only serious cash offer.

At the board meeting on 16 July, which Warwick attended, Gardiner was equally prepared to deal with Skase or Stokes, and said he believed the man who got his scheme past the post first would be the winner. However, apart from providing us with a lesser sum of money, the Stokes deal would have involved us in a further financial commitment in an industry we had decided to get out of and whose future profitability was under some doubt. We would also have had to remain, as Gardiner described it, 'merely a member of a cooperative rather than of a true television network'. We had had that arrangement with the Herald and Weekly Times, and it did not work satisfactorily. The Skase deal, on the other hand, enabled us to retain a sustainable 15 per cent stake in his flagship

*The September 1987 meeting of the John Fairfax board, included a lunch in honour of former managing director Angus McLachlan. **Left to right:** Bruce Taplin, senior partner of Touche Ross and Co.; Max Suich, chief editorial executive; Barry Moore, group chief accountant; Fred Brenchley, general manager Broadway; John Fairfax, deputy chairman; Sir David Griffin, director; Angus McLachlan; Ian Cumming, group company secretary; James Fairfax, chairman; Sir Vincent Fairfax, director; Sir Eric Neal, director; Greg Gardiner, group general manager. Photo: John Fairfax Ltd.*

Qintex and possibly re-enter the industry at a later stage.

After Warwick's takeover, Tryart expressed some self-righteous shock about some elements of the deal. In fact Tryart could have learned of them much sooner — as indeed it could have in respect of a number of other areas — had Warwick and his advisers taken up our offer to provide information at the 3 September meeting, instead of keeping us all at arm's length for the next two months. Warwick could equally well have passed on to Dougherty and Connell both the preliminary details of the Skase deal presented to our July board and its final form which came to the August board meeting. He passed on everything else, breaking board confidentiality in the process, and it is a mystery why he neglected to do so on this issue. Other than expressing a preference for maintaining a greater interest in television (such as through the Stokes deal), Warwick specifically approved of the Skase deal in its final form.

It is somewhat academic to speculate on the fate of this investment had Warwick's takeover not emerged and the proposed 'close developmental and promotional relationship' been forged. But it is at least possible that our experience in the industry might have enabled Skase to avoid some of the actions, such as the bid for MGM/UA, which contributed to his downfall. What is certain, however, is that the renegotiation of the deal, which became essential for Warwick when the Skase debt became a crucial asset in the Fairfax post-takeover crisis of early 1988, deprived it of a great deal of its value. In fact, a fair price was reduced to a bargain, estimated at only $467 million by Sykes, for Skase. By this calculation of value, it was fallaciously claimed that we would have been better off if we had simply sold ATN and BTQ. The reality is that both the Bond and Lowy deals for Nine and Ten were based on Sydney and Melbourne being part of the network acquired, while Sydney and Brisbane, with Melbourne owned by a highly independent partner such as Holmes à Court, would not be nearly such a valuable acquisition.

There is no doubt in my mind that our decisions both to buy HSV and sell the Seven Network were correct at the time and have been amply justified by subsequent events. While we could not have foreseen that the management and general financial policies of the new owners would send two networks into receivership and virtually hand back the third to its former owner, we felt strongly it was time to get out and turn our attention to other areas of expansion with greater potential.

In the aftermath of the H&WT takeover, the issue of the control of the Fairfax company reappeared. Holmes à Court and Abeles were buying shares but, although Holmes à Court's stake had reached 3.1 per cent by August, I later learned that he had told two separate sources that he had only ever intended to build up a tactical stake in Fairfax, which he might use to advantage if there were a family falling out and that he had never planned a takeover bid. I also thought the 50.1 per cent now controlled by the branches of the family was reasonably secure.

17

THE BUTCHERING OF BROADWAY

THE THIRTEENTH FAIRFAX BREAKS A
DYNASTY, AUGUST-DECEMBER 1987

On Saturday 29 August, I was at Retford Park for the weekend when, at about 3 pm, I received a telephone call from Warwick asking when I would be back in Sydney. I told him Sunday afternoon and he indicated, without conveying any particular urgency, that he would like to see me then. Accordingly, I arranged for him to come to my house at Lindsay Avenue around 5.15 pm. I heard the same day from Gardiner that he had received a similar call seeking a Sunday meeting — neither of us had any idea what it could be about, although Gardiner referred to the takeover rumour of the previous week. I took my house guests, who included my mother, Patricia Guest from Melbourne and Ian McLachlan from Adelaide, to drinks at the Griffins' property at Mittagong later on Sunday morning. David and I were later to recall that it was our last 'normal' day.

On arrival at Lindsay Avenue Warwick began by saying that he was still very worried by takeover threats to the company: there had been increased activity the previous week with Robert Holmes à Court building up a shareholding of nearly 4 per cent and the market closing on Friday at $7, having risen during August from around $5.50. I said, as I frequently had in the preceding six months, that, with the combined family holdings now at 50.1 per cent, and providing the three family groups stuck together to make sure that the odd 2 per cent of smaller holdings included in this figure sold only to the family groups, we had nothing to worry about beyond a nuisance holding of up to 20 per cent being built up by Holmes à Court, Kerry Packer or possibly Sir Peter Abeles, the latter having built up a holding of 3.2 per cent over the last few months.

Warwick said he thought the time had come to take action and that he was proposing to make an offer for the company. He verbally outlined the offer before handing me a press release which, to my consternation, was to be made public at 9 am the following day. In essence, the offer, made through the shelf company Tryart Pty Ltd, was $7.50 cash per share, or three David Syme shares plus $4.50 cash, or fifteen Syme shares for every two Fairfax shares. The second part of the offer proposed to sell the *Financial Review*, the *Business Review Weekly* group and Fairfax Magazines to David Syme which would be refloated as a public company with Fairfax retaining a 45 per cent interest. The bid, which valued the company at $2.25 billion, was to be financed by the ANZ banking group and was conditional on Tryart winning control of John Fairfax and then being able to issue the David Syme shares.

It took a few minutes for me even to begin to realise the implications of the proposal. Warwick's action was putting the company into 'play' and establishing a market value for its assets based on a share price which any potential aggressor could overbid.

Warwick went on to outline a fairly complex arrangement whereby the three family groups would remain as shareholders in the reconstructed Fairfax company, or possibly another company owned by it, or they could take up shares in Tryart. It seemed that Warwick, through Tryart, would be in a position to control the company, but he did not make clear to me the final composition of Tryart. He said he wanted me to remain as chairman. He clearly wanted Vincent, John and myself to remain in the company rather than accept the cash or cash-plus-Syme shares offer, although the details and consequences of this arrangement were not at all clear. Most astonishing of all, he sought — evidently anticipating success without any family discussion — agreement to the press release, which contained the statement that the family supported the offer!

Having ascertained that he was determined to go ahead, I concentrated on trying to persuade him to delay the announcement for twenty-four hours, so that both the family and the Fairfax board could discuss it. He refused, and although his reason was to become only too evident later on, I was unable to obtain any satisfactory explanation that night. Consequently, I gave no undertaking to him that I would not sell my shares. He then left to see Gardiner, accompanied by former Holmes à Court executive Bert Reuter. Later, on his own, he also visited John.

I spoke to both Gardiner and John towards the end of the evening and their reactions had been pretty much the same as mine: they had both tried to persuade him to delay the announcement for twenty-four hours. We were all stunned and found it impossible to believe that either Warwick or his advisers — Bert Reuter,

Laurie Connell and Martin Dougherty — had seriously expected the three family members to support the bid under those conditions.

According to John, Warwick (who appeared particularly nervous throughout their discussion) said he was very concerned that there were predators wanting to take over John Fairfax Limited and this was reflected in the very sharp increase in the share prices. He felt something was about to happen and that it was only on Friday that he had been able to get agreement with his bankers to put together a privatisation scheme for the family. He said he had a vehicle, Tryart Pty Ltd, that would buy the family shares in John Fairfax. When John asked him whether he saw John and myself being part of that new company, he said 'no', it was something he was doing himself in the interest of the whole family — although again he left a confused impression about ultimate control. John told him that it was not privatising but simply a takeover bid by one member of the family. He refused to give Warwick any commitment and said that the press statement was totally unacceptable.

A lot of people first heard the news on John Laws' top-rating talkback program on station 2GB at nine on Monday morning, although there is evidence that he, as well as Murdoch, Abeles, Packer and two eminent figures in the government had prior knowledge. Certainly, the announcement provided the only information Fairfax management had, other than the somewhat opaque vision the three of us had been given by Warwick. But we were unable to discuss it all together until we met for our usual Monday lunch, attended by Max Suich and Fred Brenchley as well as John, Gardiner and myself.

At this very early stage our discussion centred around three main points. Firstly, what were the chances of the bid succeeding? At $7.50, it was not high enough and did not represent the true value of the company — predators would be attracted to carve it up, take what they wanted and sell the rest. Even if Warwick raised the price, which he must have anticipated having to do, he would still have to neutralise Holmes à Court (nearly 4 per cent) and Packer remained a threat. Secondly, there was Warwick himself — his purpose, motivation, method of proceeding and choice of advisers.

The third issue we had to consider was the position of the family. If, as seemed probable, he wished to control the company himself, would we want to stay on as minority shareholders in the reconstructed company? My own inclination was very much opposed to this, although later developments caused me reluctantly to state that I would remain as chairman. Two options were to emerge here: we could stay on as directors and shareholders, or as directors of a company totally owned by Warwick. The latter course was the one we adopted when negotiations were completed at the end of September, but a lot of water was to flow under the bridge before that happened and a most surprising and in some ways inexplicable situation was to come about, which resulted in quite a different resolution.

At the end of lunch on Monday the 31st, the one thing we were all agreed on was that things would never be the same again. By the end of the day, after appropriate consultation with the other directors — Vincent, Sir David Griffin and Sir Eric Neal — we had issued a statement acknowledging receipt of Tryart's letter. We stated that we had no additional information other than that contained in Tryart's letter to the Stock Exchange and that we awaited further information in the Part A statement. We advised shareholders not to sell until we had had an opportunity to evaluate the information.

Following the opening of the Stock Exchange that morning, the share price had soared to $8.10, reaching a peak of $9.06 and closing at $9 with a turnover around 1.5 million units. The diverse reaction in the press on Tuesday is indicated by some of the headlines: 'Market tips fresh bid for Fairfax', 'Fairfax: test of a family's cohesion', 'Fairfax heir shores the family defences', 'High risk strategy to buy back the jewels', 'Unlikely alliance to save the family jewels'. Most media commentators felt the bid would attract a counter-offer, probably from Holmes à Court. There was speculation about the board's obligation to recommend the highest bid, and much interest in the proposed sale to David Syme of $1.2 billion of Fairfax assets which, according to one estimate, valued the *Age* at $700 million, the *Financial Review* at $300 million and the magazines at $250 million. They took the view that once the main board had initially recommended a bid, the company would be up for auction as it would have to recommend a higher one. Albert Smith in the *Financial Review* made the interesting point that shareholders were being asked to accept shares in 55 per cent of less than half of what they already owned — even if they were some of the best money-spinners freed from the drag of less successful earners.

Most of the interest, however, centred on Warwick and his advisers. Warwick's education and career — Cranbrook School, Oxford University, J. Walter Thompson in Sydney, Boston Investment Banker Gordon Berg, the Chase Manhattan Bank for two years where he was a loans officer in the media acquisitions area and finally the MBA (Business Adminstration) course at Harvard — were all examined. Amongst other things, it was noted that, the night before he broke the news to us, he had attended the twenty-first birthday party of Kerry Packer's daughter Gretel.

Bryan Frith in the *Australian* gave three reasons for Warwick's action: to give permanency to the family's outright control of the group through majority ownership; dissatisfaction with recent Fairfax management decisions, including what Warwick described as the 'disastrous $320 million purchase early this year of Melbourne television station HSV-7', and, finally, that it was time to change the guard. Warwick, Frith felt, had demonstrated greater leadership qualities than John or myself — an interesting comment in view of what was to follow. Basically, Warwick received a good press. He was shown as acting decisively, albeit at some considerable risk, to make the family inheritance permanently secure. Not much attention was paid to the question of whether it was in any danger, beyond unsubstantiated threats from people who had been wheeling and dealing in the industry for years. Rupert Murdoch congratulated Warwick and said he thought it was a very courageous move and the right one for him and his family. He said he thought it would succeed but 'maybe not at this price'.

The colourful careers of the three advisers were also described and there was some surprise that Warwick had not turned to more traditional if not conventional sources. All three expressed confidence that the family would support Tryart, although they had no evidence for this belief. This, of course, was the crucial point: without family support the bid could not succeed in its present form. John Durie in the *Financial Review* noted this as did Frith, who observed that, providing the family maintained a united front, it would still retain control in the face of a higher bid. Interestingly, he was the only one to refer to Warwick's lack of confidence in the management — a situation which, if true, had not been conveyed to any of us privately, or at board meetings, or indeed on that Sunday night. The full significance of family support, which both Tryart (publicly at any rate) and most commentators assumed would be forthcoming, would become much clearer following a meeting between ourselves and Tryart three days after the announcement.

On Thursday 3 September, Warwick arrived at our Broadway building at 10 am with Connell, Reuter and the Tryart solicitor, Aleco Vrisakis of Dawson, Waldron. Awaiting them in my office were John, Gardiner, Rod Halstead and myself. Connell, Reuter and Vrisakis sat in a row on my sofa and I suddenly had an absurd wish to photograph the line-up. I opened the proceedings by saying it was not an appropriate time for recriminations about what had happened or how it had happened, the purpose of the meeting was for us at Fairfax to get more information about the bid and how it would work.

Reuter, as consultant to Rothwells — Connell's merchant bank which was advising Tryart — had been credited with the development of the scheme, although there was press speculation that it had been conceived at Harvard during visits made by Dougherty. So it was Reuter, with some intervention by Warwick and Vrisakis, who outlined the bid and responded to questions. Gardiner, in particular, questioned them closely on the financing by the ANZ bank and whether the $1.2 billion, which it transpired was the line of credit, would be adequate. This was designed, we were told, to cover any situation from a share and cash mixed response by shareholders to a complete cash payout to all shareholders other than family.

The third possibility of fifteen Syme shares for every two Fairfax shares had been withdrawn the previous day, as they had discovered that if enough shareholders took this option, Syme would not have sufficient capital to provide the shares. In the event of the family's staying in and partially accepting either the Syme share and cash or cash only offer, the bank would provide further credit, but if the family elected to get out completely on the cash offer they would, as Warwick put it, force the sale of assets to provide the necessary finance.

Halstead took him up on this point and I saw for the first time the stubborn persistence, for which our legal adviser is well known, at work. He finally got Warwick to admit that it was his action in making the bid that had put the assets on the line, not the family responding to a situation which was not of their making. At this stage we moved from my office to a conference room and Reuter, with a number of elaborate flourishes which he ascribed to his part-Italian ancestry, used a whiteboard to illustrate the shifts of assets and their funding between the different companies and the structure of the new Fairfax company. We saw straightaway what we had suspected from the start: Warwick would control the new company through Tryart's 51 per cent interest and his remarks indicated he wanted to keep it that way. This was confirmed to John when he was later negotiating a possible shareholding in Tryart and Warwick said he was determined to retain 51 per cent of that company. For the family, that was a key point in the lengthy negotiations that followed.

The other proposal which emerged as part of the deal — the sweetener for the family — was a special one-off dividend of $200 million to be paid by John Fairfax Limited to the remaining shareholders when the takeover had been completed and this, they said, would be tax-free. To emphasise the point, Reuter made rough calculations of how much cash each of us would get, including my mother and sister. At this stage we did not comment further and the meeting broke up amicably with the company offering to provide any further information to Tryart we felt we could, with legality and propriety, provide.

So there it was — Tryart had made a takeover offer. Its initial success and financing depended on the family's accepting a minority position in the new company and yielding control to Warwick, although the family had never been consulted about the proposal, nor even made aware of it until the last minute when it was too late to do anything about it. At the end of the week Peter Robinson said in the *Financial Review* 'Perhaps nothing could more vividly suggest that a new "Fairfax era" is in the offing and the changes will almost certainly be deeper and more widespread if the other members of the Fairfax family decide to downgrade their active participation in the new companies. This will inevitably be a situation more unpredictable than any which has surrounded the Fairfax company since it went public.' How right he was.

On Thursday 3rd, TNT confirmed that their 3.4 per cent holding had been bought by Packer, by way of a right of first refusal he was believed to have had from Abeles. There was speculation as to whether his shareholding could be regarded as 'friendly' — friendly to Warwick, that is, as he certainly harboured no friendly feelings towards the current board and management of Fairfax. It is significant that Murdoch, Packer and their journalists were the only people I am aware of to have words of praise for Warwick's bid. In what was to become its disastrous progress some, notably Trevor Sykes in *Australian Business*, even managed to argue at its conclusion that Warwick had emerged a winner. I thought at the time, and still think, that Packer's motive was simply to get a slice of the action and use whatever spoiling tactic he could towards the board and management, including helping Warwick achieve his aim. In one sense his action did not affect the outcome of the bid, but it enabled him to end up with the *Canberra Times* and the magazine division.

On Tuesday 8 September, two important events took place: the first meeting of the Fairfax board since the bid had been announced, and what was to be the second and last discussion I had with Warwick. I little suspected that this would be the case at the time. Apart from the five directors, the board meeting was attended as usual by Gardiner, Suich, Ian Cumming (the group company secretary) and Halstead.

In outlining the steps Tryart would have to take to achieve the new structure, Gardiner regarded the $1.2 billion borrowings as a minimal figure. Of this, $450 million would be lent to David Syme to enable that company to purchase assets in John Fairfax Limited. The repayment of the loan would be satisfied by the allotment of 900 million shares of 50 cents each in David Syme to John Fairfax shareholders. John Fairfax, in turn, would subscribe for preference shares in Tryart to the value of $1.2 billion. There was also to be a special dividend of $200 million for Fairfax shareholders after the completion of the takeover.

According to the information then given to the board, it appeared that the profits generated by the new company would be insufficient to meet interest repayments, with a possible shortfall of some $40 million. We felt there was something relating to the offer we had not been made aware of, such as a further reconstruction or the involvement of a third party.

We then discussed, at length, the provision of information that Tryart required for its Part A statement, including an indication of the family's intentions. The statement also included confidential information about the assets going to Syme and the 1987 Fairfax results which were not yet available for release and were due to be considered by the board the following week. Tryart, which was not yet a shareholder, was asking the board to agree to sell assets to Syme in order to make the bid possible. The interests of our shareholders were paramount, as was the obligation to keep them informed, and it seemed likely that the Part A might not be out for a month. Clearly the board could not give any immediate indication of its reaction until it was in possession of all the facts. The bid was fraught with legal complications and we decided not to make any further statement at that stage, either as a board or family, particularly in relation to Dougherty's claims that the family were 'behind' the bid. Indeed, we maintained that approach until we were in a position to indicate the family acceptance of the bid and to recommend it to shareholders.

After hearing Halstead's advice, we agreed to provide most of the information sought and also decided to appoint Murray Gleason, QC as adviser to the board. The family were considering negotiations with Warwick, but a firm decision to set them in motion had still to be made.

I had asked Warwick to come and see me at Darling Point on the evening of the eighth as I was most anxious to find out how he saw the bid progressing and, assuming it was ultimately successful, how he visualised the role of the family and the future management; the background and events leading up to the bid I hoped to leave for another occasion.

He arrived at 5.30 looking a little apprehensive and left at 7 pm, and I must confess that at the end of the exercise I found myself very little the wiser. I suggested at the outset that the reason he had not consulted the family in advance was that they might have been able to stop him; this was the way someone would act if their prime motive was to gain control of the company. The only explanation he had given previously was that approval of finance from the ANZ bank had only come through on the Friday and it was essential to act immediately. He did not respond to my suggestion and I took silence to signify assent. He repeated that he wanted me to stay on as chairman, and John and Vincent as directors, but would give no commitment of any kind regarding Gardiner, Suich and Brenchley beyond saying it was all still 'under consideration'. Indeed he did not volunteer an opinion, critical or otherwise, about them. I could find out nothing, either, about his concept of his own role or that of his advisers, although I later learned that on 3 September he had said to Gaunt that after the takeover he would stay in marketing. When Gaunt replied, 'You can't after this', he said, 'I've always been a little unusual'.

I told him that, as well as having their responsibilities as directors of a public company, the family members had to consider their personal positions inside and outside the new company. This would involve intensive negotiations with Tryart, the outcome of which could affect the whole future of the bid. My staying on as chairman would depend on the future composition of both board and management and at that stage, I told him, I was very much in two minds about it. This did not seem to worry him too much. I believe I also made clear my disinclination to become a minority shareholder in the new company, a point I emphasised when negotiations began.

The meeting was perfectly amicable, apart from some initial tension when I delivered some sharp views on the bid, but it was the last time I was to see Warwick, despite my best endeavours, until 8 December. Later in the week I contacted his secretary at Rothwells' Sydney office, to which he had moved from Broadway on 31 August, to see whether we could meet for lunch the following week. Apparently he had gone to America, although still employed as assistant publisher of the *Herald* and drawing a salary. On two other occasions, equally unsuccessful, I tried to arrange lunch and was finally reduced to writing to him as I was unable to get him on the telephone either. There was no response. Something had obviously happened to change his attitude towards us — possibly the final realisation that we would not come in as minority shareholders.

On 10 September there was a bombshell in the *Financial Review* in the form of a document circulated by stockbroker Rene Rivkin, who was to underwrite the proposed Syme issue, detailing the rationalisation and closures planned by Tryart for the group after the takeover. There had been no consultation with Fairfax executives, although it became clear the next day that some of the material had come straight from board minutes through Warwick to his advisers. As Max Suich commented, if the bidder had been anyone but Warwick, one of our defences would probably have been to take legal action over inside knowledge and insider trading.

The effect of this disclosure on the staff of the whole organisation can well be imagined, and our misgivings on the way Tryart was conducting the bid were correspondingly increased. Warwick rang Brenchley in New Zealand to give reassurances following the leak and, in reply to Brenchley's comment that John and I were put between a rock and a hard place by the bid, he said he knew some of the family saw it that way, but at the end of the day they would do what was in the best interests of the company and its employees. The bid, he said, telegraphed some decisions that had to be made then rather than in another ten or fifteen years, and to work out something equitable required sensible and rational negotiation. In Brenchley's view, Warwick had little regard for the importance many staff placed on working for the Fairfax family and was only paying lip service to family unity.

At an 8 am board meeting at Lindsay Avenue on 11 September, Halstead reiterated the three issues facing the board: firstly, what price to place on the assets to be sold, how it was to be determined and whether the board was satisfied it was correct. Secondly, there were two weaknesses in the bid: there was no mechanism to increase the price from $7.50 and, as far as we could gauge, insufficient funds to purchase the family's shares. Further cash would have to come from the sale of assets and this would involve restructuring the bid. Thirdly, the company would be put into a continuing loss situation and the board would have to look at the transaction in this light and the effect it would have on future profitability.

On Wednesday the 16th, the board met to consider the annual accounts. A major agenda item was the extremely disturbing effect the *Financial Review* article had had on key executives, particularly editors. We had to provide some security in relation to their positions and continuity of employment. Halstead advised that we were entitled to enter into contracts with staff members at the time of a possible takeover, if we believed we were acting in the best interests of the company. We all required assurances on this point and after discussion on the propriety of taking this step, I summed up by saying that our aim was to secure our existing executives and we agreed to take reasonable action to make certain that they would not be disadvantaged by staying with the company.

The rest of the meeting was taken up with the annual accounts. Basically the company had had a good year in achieving an increased pre-tax profit in excess of $90 million, and we had virtually eliminated its debt. Preliminary discussion about the dividend revealed a general feeling that we would be justified in making a gesture to shareholders, perhaps going to two or two and a half times the cover.

By the fourth week of the bid Warwick had become, as far as we were concerned, virtually incommunicado. In our negotiations with him, John and I, through our separate lawyers, were proceeding on the basis that a satisfactory agreement could be reached. We were in a strong position because of Warwick's need to get us on side. Similar terms in any such agreement would have to be offered to all shareholders — a point we had to insist on — and it would finally be the Fairfax board's decision whether to recommend acceptance of such terms.

At the same time, Vincent, John and I had to consider which course we would ultimately adopt. We had four options: we could sell our shares to a higher bidder who, even though Tryart was negotiating concurrently with Holmes à Court and Packer, could still emerge; we could make a takeover bid ourselves; we could remain as minority shareholders in a company controlled by Warwick; or, we could sell to him.

We dismissed at an early stage any thought of being minority shareholders but the possibility of making a counter offer was always there. We had to consider, though, the 50 per cent of public shareholders. Were we entitled to deprive them of the certainty of getting a good price for their shares — at that stage we were close to reaching agreement on $8.50 — by making an offer that would have had to improve on that figure in some way, but that would almost certainly have attracted another bidder even if Tryart itself did not respond? In the resulting auction, with its possible legal complications, they might or might not be better off in the end. There was the possibility, later confirmed in the Tryart court case, that Warwick would sell out himself, which would not have been in the interest either of the company or its shareholders.

Gardiner and Suich, although disappointed with our ultimate decision, did not try to apply any pressure on us to oppose the bid, although two former chief executives, Angus McLachlan and Bob Falkingham, had expressed the opinion to Gardiner that we should be urged to fight. At lunch with me on the 24th, Charles Lloyd Jones offered to place whatever resources he could assemble at my disposal to fight the bid.

Further, we had to consider our own families. I had a responsibility to my mother and sister and her family, while John had his own family, as did his two sisters and brother (Sally White, Ruth Armitage and Tim Fairfax). All were married with children. In making a counter bid we could well be putting ourselves in the position of not being able to finance the borrowings — the very position in which Warwick was to end up. If we didn't make a counter bid, we had to consider whether ownership by Warwick which, whatever we thought of him, still kept the company in the family, was preferable to ownership by one of the opposition whose higher bid we might eventually have to recommend to shareholders. Would the interests of the company as a continuing entity and its employees be best served by coming to an agreement with Warwick or by throwing them into an auction?

We still had no idea of the future composition of the company although rumours were circulating that Gardiner and Suich would definitely be out; Brenchley's position was less clear, but he could have been prevailed upon to stay. All three had been putting pressure on me to stay on as chairman in the event that I sold my shares to Warwick. They argued that I could protect the editorial independence of the publications and the position of each editor. Also, Chris Anderson, editor-in-chief of the *Herald*, said he would stay on if I did. As a last resort, I had the weapon of resignation with the attendant uproar that, hopefully, it would cause.

On the morning of Thursday the 24th, I heard that the *Financial Review* would have to go, and by Friday we had the details of the deals with Holmes à Court and Packer. Holmes à Court would get the *Financial Review*, the *Times on Sunday*, the Macquarie radio network and the New Zealand *National Business Review* for $475 million, while Packer took the magazine division, the *Canberra Times* and the *Canberra Chronicle* for $250 million. Warwick was left with the *Herald*, *Sun*, *Sun-Herald*, the Newcastle and Wollongong papers, some twenty-four suburban and regional publications and some trade magazines in New South Wales, the *Age* in Victoria, the *Business Review Weekly* group and shareholdings in Australian Associated Press and Australian Newsprint Mills.

On the 25th I went to Retford Park where, for the first time for many years, I was opening my garden for the ten days of the Tulip Festival. With thousands of people tramping round the grounds below, I sat on an upstairs veranda going over the appalling dismemberment of the company which I could hardly believe was happening. Vincent and John were going through the same process and, independently of each other, we came to the same sad conclusion — to sell to Warwick at $8.50, in the absence of a higher offer, with great regrets about the consequent sale of assets.

I also allowed myself, with great reluctance, to be persuaded to remain as chairman. Although I was convinced my position would be an impossible one and could not last, I was prepared to give it a go. John, I think, had similar feelings but was to indicate his willingness to stay on the board, and that of David Syme, something I had decided against doing as I thought it better to concentrate on the possible future struggles in Sydney. John and I announced our decision in a statement released to the press on 28 September and the contracts were signed on 5 November.

Executives and employees throughout the group were disappointed, although I believe the majority had an understanding of the position in which we were placed. The directors of Tryart appeared not to share this understanding: several were to say publicly that the drastic sale of assets was necessitated by the family's forcing the price up by a dollar to get more for their own shares, a criticism repeated by Mary Fairfax in a letter to me just before Christmas. However, none showed much awareness of the faulty premise on which the bid was based (the family remaining as shareholders) or on our obligations to all shareholders as directors of a public company. As major shareholders, acceptance of the bid would indeed bring large sums of money to us, and this was something we had to come to terms with. I do not believe, though, that it was a significant motivation for any of us in concluding the negotiations.

In reply to Daphne Guinness' question (in a *Bulletin* interview, 23 May 1989) as to whether I was 'having some fun with this lovely lolly' or whether it was weighing heavily on me, I said, 'I don't think of it that way. I've got more than I used to have but I don't know that it's an excitement or interest either. I don't regard it in any way except I've got a bit more and it is no longer invested in Fairfax shares, so something else has to be done with it. It's not a burden. Neither is it an excitement'.

On Monday 27 September, the first to leak the news of the Fairfax empire's dismemberment was Terry McCrann, one of the most astute financial commentators in the country and a great loss when he was poached from the *Age* to work on the Melbourne *Herald* by ex-*Sydney Morning Herald* editor Eric Beecher. His was some of the most perceptive comment, although I did not agree with his conclusion about the inevitability of a takeover and that the 51 per cent family holding was an 'illusion' of control. His comment about the low profit generated in relation to the assets — now valued at $2550 million under Warwick's revised bid — has to be considered in relation to the failure of our attempts to raise capital and the unfortunate necessity of financing development through earnings.

McCrann pointed out that Warwick, in setting out to claim an inheritance, very nearly lost it and that he had largely destroyed the institution built by his late father and long-time manager 'Rags' Henderson (as the staff usually called Rupert). He said that the reality that the rest of the family were sellers left Warwick and his bid perilously exposed and made inevitable the sort of deals Tryart was proposing (of which the *Financial Review* was crucial to a solution for Warwick) which, in crude terms, dismembered the Fairfax media empire. 'Warwick's camp found they would have to bid — and pay — for 74 per cent of Fairfax's capital and not the originally expected 49 per cent. That extra $600 or so million was bad enough, but Robert Holmes à Court and Kerry Packer had also to be faced and faced down.'

There is no doubt that Warwick's deals with Holmes à Court and Packer were put together in haste and confusion and were later to reveal inconsistencies and ambiguities which were to bring Tryart considerable difficulties and much delay in concluding the takeover. They were caused by Tryart's ignorance of the nature and structure of many of the assets they were selling. Although we could have enlightened them, we were not consulted, nor had we been asked for any further information since the early stages of the bid. Indeed, because of this Tryart did not learn essential details until our penultimate board meeting in November, to which they sent two representatives. As Brenchley later commented in a note to me:

Warwick's deals were done in extreme haste, and showed it. [Max Suich's] comment that the Holmes à Court and Packer deals were done by 'bull market children' was very astute, but both deals also displayed a desperate haste to do a deal almost at any price. The sellers did not know what they were selling.

The Packer deal was signed by Marty Dougherty, and was agreed in one and a half pages only. It did not even specify whether Warwick (or Marty) was selling the company as a whole, or just its assets. The real estate was negotiated later. The deal did not specify exactly what magazines Packer had bought. You will recall the confusion over whether Packer had bought Homes Pictorial. Rob Henty from ACP rang Audrey DeGraff at Homes Pictorial and wanted to come down and inspect his new magazine. Audrey was horrified, and rang us. At that last board meeting I asked Marty whether Homes Pictorial had been sold or not, as nobody seemed to know. Marty gave it some thought, and said that if it wasn't one of the Fairfax Magazine stable, it wasn't sold. In New York, Murdoch told the Editor-in-Chief of Time that Packer had bought Time Australia from Fairfax. Time were shocked, as any such deal was completely barred by our joint agreement.

The Holmes à Court deal to acquire AFR/TOS/NBR (Australian Financial Review, Times on Sunday, NZ National Business Review) and Macquarie was signed by Laurie Connell, who was in such a hurry he forgot to ask for a deposit. Dawson, Waldron, Warwick's legal advisers, reviewed the Connell document, and commented: 'The initial agreement made no reference to payment of a deposit, but payment of a 10 per cent deposit is a common term in sale transactions'. They said such a deposit clause should be included in the detailed agreement.

Warwick's deals showed a distinct lack of concern for staff. You will recall that the Tryart statement as proposed to announce the increase in its bid price and the sales to Packer and Holmes à Court made no mention of the superannuation rights of Fairfax staff transferred to these new owners. I told Greg that the statement in that form was totally unacceptable, and we simply had to force Warwick/Tryart to build in such guarantees. Greg phoned you and Warwick/Tryart were told that you, as Chairman, insisted that such an assurance to transferred staff be included. It was. For a company and a family that had taken great pride in staff welfare, this was an amazing lapse.

If Warwick had not broken up and sold the Fairfax Group, the Sun and Mirror would have merged and Murdoch would not have gained a monopoly of the Sydney afternoon market.

The sale to Packer gave him complete dominance in the women's, young professional, youth and general interest magazine areas, which must have been some consolation to him for having failed to crack, with *Australian Business*, the hold that Fairfax's BRW group had on the vital and expanding business magazine market. The *Canberra Times* was an unlikely journal for his interests, but it would appear to have been a pay-off by Tryart for not delivering to him either the *Financial Review* or the BRW group, both of which he particularly wanted. Two headlines alone sum up the unhappy result: 'Media moguls carve up the cake' and 'A broken dynasty'.

Back at Broadway, part of the broken dynasty spent the next few days trying to cope with a very depressing situation indeed. John and I had to explain to sceptical, if not actually hostile, executives and editors the reasons for our decision — for abandoning them to the enemy, as some of them saw it. In this difficult task we were loyally and actively assisted by Gardiner, Suich and Brenchley.

My first task was to see the editors of the *Financial Review* and the *Times on Sunday*. The *Review*'s Alan Kohler was on holiday in Italy and thus heard the news that his paper had been sold from a call-box in a north Italian village. At an emotional meeting that day Suich had announced the sale to the *Financial Review* staff. The acting editor, Glenda Korporaal, rose to the occasion and made a rallying speech. She had spoken to Holmes à Court by telephone on the Saturday and he had promised no reduction in staff. In terms of editorial independence, he said he had a very clear idea of the relationship between the proprietor and the editor and that the *Financial Review* was the flagship. I saw her the following day and reassured her as much as I could.

As far as the *Times on Sunday* was concerned, selling it to Holmes à Court was the best guarantee of its survival. I had total confidence in its editor, Valerie Lawson, and we were all reasonably confident that, with a year or two of support, the paper would continue to pursue its vital role in investigative journalism which, in spite of disagreements, no one had supported more strongly than Sir Warwick. I saw Lawson on Wednesday and, as I had with Korporaal, explained the situation to her and gave as much encouragement about the future as I felt was justified.

Even though there was a feeling among journalists that Holmes à Court was on trial, generally speaking his assurances were accepted and there was relief that the two publications had not fallen into Packer's hands. Another who, of course, was relieved at the outcome was Bob Gottliebsen, managing editor of the *Business Review Weekly* group, and his staff. He had come from Melbourne to see me the previous week, in an anxious state as it had been rumoured his charges would go to Packer. Max Walsh, a former editor of the *Financial Review*, put it this way: 'It depends very much on the editor. If he appointed an editor who second-guessed him, he could end up with a crappy paper. If you impair the credibility of a paper like the *Financial Review* you impair the value of the assets'. A great part of the assets were the journalists who worked for it.

John, as chairman of Fairfax Magazines, Macquarie Broadcasting and senior Fairfax representative of Federal Capital Press, had the equally difficult task of explaining our decision to their chief executives: John Hemming, Bob Johnson and Graham Wilkinson, respectively. It was the end of thirty years' intensive competition in the magazine field, primarily with the Packer group and later Murdoch as well, and most of our major magazines were performing very well. Similarly, 2GB and most of the radio stations in the Macquarie Network had recovered from low- to high-rating positions. Both divisions were success stories: previously the major loss-makers, they were now effective profit contributors. For everyone at the *Canberra Times* the sell-out to Packer was even more traumatic after its honourable history with the Fairfax group, and the general manager Graham Wilkinson, an old *Herald* man of some years standing, felt this as much as any. All three divisions were evidence of the strength of the group at the time of Warwick's takeover.

Government comment was restrained but Treasurer Paul Keating, not surprisingly, welcomed the changes in media ownership that his government's legislation late in 1986 had done much to set in motion. Greater diversification had resulted from the divorcing of newspaper and television interests, he said. The results of this legislation have been much disputed, particularly in correspondence in the *Financial Review* (April 1988) between Keating and Ian McPhee, Opposition spokesman on the media until sacked by John Howard for strongly condemning Murdoch's takeover of the H&WT.

In my view Keating never really answered McPhee's point that the effect of the legislation was to assist the creation of an unacceptably high ownership of the print media by Murdoch and an unacceptable duopoly of print media ownership throughout the country. Ownership of a television station does not, except in the most marginal way, confer opportunities for exerting political influence or indeed influencing voters on any particular issue. Television stations do not, of course, have an editorial policy and the conditions of the licence enforce a scrupulously even-handed approach both in news and current affairs, as is evident when there are claims that this even-handedness has been breached. I believe Keating, together with Prime Minister Bob Hawke, welcomed the proposed change in the ownership of Fairfax to one that they felt, rightly or wrongly, would be more compliant and less likely to probe embarrassing areas.

Brian Toohey commented in the *Eye* (a publication he had left the company to start) on the reasons why Messrs Hawke and Keating, as well as some prominent public figures, might welcome a change in ownership at Fairfax:

The Fairfax record may have its imperfections, but can anyone seriously believe that Laurie Connell, Rene Rivkin or any of the parvenu media barons entangled in a dozen different deals with governments will ever have the 'bottle', let alone moral commitment, to publish material that they know in advance will cost them millions in lost advertising and millions more in changes to the rules by vindictive governments?

A year later, in October, I was walking down a street in Paris on my way back to the Bristol Hotel when I passed an antique shop from which I had recently bought a pair of Louis XV *fauteuils*. It appeared to be closed but as I peered through the window, the door was suddenly opened by a familiar-looking figure and I was admitted by Paul Keating. We had a chat about recent media events as well as French decorative arts. During it he expressed regret at the change in ownership at Fairfax — perhaps by then he had had second thoughts. Following the receivership, I shall comment again briefly on the above aspects in the final chapter.

On 1 October, the Fairfax board met to consider three matters, two relating to the release of information and the other, Tryart's timetable for the takeover. For its Part A, Tryart was seeking details of the trading results of certain assets, particularly the BRW group. Public release of such details could be prejudicial to the company, but after discussion it was decided, with the advice of Halstead and Johnson, to authorise the accountants, Touche Ross, to release the information. A request from Consolidated Press for information on the magazines was turned down until such time as Tryart controlled 75 per cent of Fairfax and the deal with Packer came into being.

Tryart was also pressing for the release of our Part B to shareholders at the same time as the Part A, which we decided was neither practicable nor necessary. The question of the transfer of AAP and ANM shares as part of the Holmes à Court deal also arose. This was another example of lack of consultation by Tryart as this proposal was in breach of an agreement with Murdoch regarding pre-emptive buying rights in both cases. The eventual sale of both these important and valuable assets — in the case of AAP the potential was tremendous — to Murdoch caused a political furore. Finally, we continued to consider the terms of contracts for key executives to encourage them to stay and protect them if they found themselves unable to work with the new ownership.

On 5 October, Martin Peers speculated in the *Financial Review* about who would run the new company. Its diminished state meant that the roles of Gardiner, Suich and Brenchley would be considerably reduced even if Warwick wanted them to stay. How would a twenty-six-year old with no direct executive management experience run a medium-sized company with a debt of at least $500 million after the asset sales? The new chief executive would have to decide on a cost reduction progam, as well as whether further sales of assets were necessary, and all attempts to ascertain the future of the three present top executives drew a blank.

Peers pointed out that Warwick's profile in the bid was unusually low. He had not spoken to anyone from the press and was not involved in any of the negotiations with either Holmes à Court or Packer. He had not made any effort to outline what the post-bid company would look like and, unlike Holmes à Court, he refused to answer questions put by the *Financial Review* about plans for the company, the role of his advisers and his view of editorial independence and the role of the editor and proprietor.

The state of morale in the organisation can well be imagined. Reuter, however, dismissed any suggestion that Warwick's role was largely symbolic and said he had been involved fourteen hours a day in talking tactics and making final decisions. When asked about their own roles, the Tryart representatives simply said that 'all of those things have not yet been considered'. There was much speculation, but little evidence, that Mary Fairfax was the power behind the bid. Most people who had known Warwick at various stages of his career dismissed suggestions that he was a puppet — he was 'determinedly independent and his own man'.

The world stock market crash on 19 October, followed by the failure of Connell's Rothwells bank, received worldwide publicity. The board's normal October meeting was held on the 22nd, in the middle of these dramatic events, although we were not to know the full details of the Rothwells debacle until the rescue operation, mounted by Bond with the cooperation of the Western Australian government, was announced the following Monday. The Macquarie Bank's report on the Part A, which had been received from Tryart on 9 October, was tabled together with a timetable for the preparation and dispatch of the Part B. It would be an advantage to have the Part B in the shareholders' hands before the Annual Meeting so that I could mention it in the chairman's speech.

A number of executives had expressed appreciation for the service contracts and said this action had settled them down to continuing service. Long-mooted improvements to our superannuation funds, including a reduction in the early retiring age to fifty-five years, were also discussed and implemented at the October board. Suich reported to the board on his talks with Tryart on AAP and what he had been able to ascertain about Tryart's talks with Ken Cowley, managing director of News Ltd. Tryart had negotiated with News Ltd without any consultations with Suich (as the senior Fairfax representative on AAP) or any other Fairfax representative. I concluded by saying that there was no doubt Tryart had not acted in the best interests of the Fairfax company.

Over the weekend Gardiner rang me several times at Retford Park to discuss Rothwells' problems in Perth. It seemed a real probability that the bid would have to be withdrawn and we discussed briefly what the situation would be for us if that happened and whether the company could return to a 'status quo ante bellum'.

At the board meeting on Monday the 26th, given the uncertain situation, I asked Michael Johnson of the Macquarie Bank for his views on the share price. He said that prior to the stock market fall, they might have arrived at a higher figure, but he believed $8.50 to be fair and reasonable. The cash and share offer was also fair and reasonable and could be seen as more attractive by some shareholders. After some discussion each director indicated his support for the Part B Statement.

During this meeting we learned — from the National Companies and Securities Commission, who had agreed to keep us informed, followed by a confirmation from Vrisakis — that Tryart was withdrawing the share component of the offer, altering it to cash only. Vrisakis said the ANZ Bank had agreed to the funding and that the Part A would be dispatched the following day with an addendum. As we were recommending acceptance of the $8.50 cash offer in our Part B there was no problem in agreeing to a full cash bid. Also, we were told that our consent to the withdrawal was not necessary for NCSC agreement — they were merely seeking our comment.

In subsequent discussion it was clear that directors believed the withdrawal of the *Age* float, which was part of the original offer, would necessitate the sale of further assets including, possibly, the *Age* itself. A debt of between $500–700 million could not be matched by income and the new company could well go to the wall in quite a short time. It was resolved that Sir David Griffin and I should sign the Part B recommendation on the cash offer. It was also agreed that directors would accept the Tryart offer for all their shareholding and ask Halstead to suggest to Tryart that shares be made available to the directors they wished to retain on the board of the new company. It was still assumed that Vincent, John and I came into this category and I believe Sir David would have stayed on if asked.

On Tuesday 27th, the NCSC approved the Tryart application to 'abandon' the *Age* float. Warwick said the decision to 'defer for the foreseeable future' the Syme float was based on market conditions and Syme's strong cash flow.

Dougherty said he believed the debt would be much more manageable with 100 per cent control of Syme and that cancellation of the sale had 'nothing at all' to do with the troubles faced by Rothwells.

At the eleventh and final AGM I chaired, I delivered what the *Herald*'s CBD column described as a wistful eulogy on the importance of an independent press: 'Australia needs an independent press — a press that is prepared to stand aloof from Government and vested interests. With the privatised John Fairfax Ltd, that need not change and indeed I hope and trust that it does not'. My speech might have had a touch of wistfulness in it, but it was intended as a very direct message to the new owners and their readers. At the end of the speech I sat down for a full thirty seconds awaiting questions; in a silent room, this is a longer time than you imagine. There were none, although had Ernie Fairbrother — former father of the chapel and a regular and useful contributor on these occasions — been present it might have been a different story.[1] After I had closed the meeting and thanked shareholders for their attendance, we were given a round of applause led by media analyst George Sutton, which was most gratifying to us all. Neither Warwick nor any of the Tryart representatives were present.

The resignations of Gardiner, Suich and Brenchley were a major consideration at the 4 November board meeting. I had discussed Gardiner's position with him a number of times over the past month, both of us agreeing that with the assets sales, his position as group general manager had ceased to exist even if Tryart had wanted him to stay, which they clearly did not. Dougherty and Vrisakis agreed that the three should be dealt with in accordance with their contracts and the company's customary procedure. The board arranged to give Gardiner the entitlements he would have received had he continued his employment until his contract expired in December 1988. In the case of Suich and Brenchley, we approved payment of their full entitlements, together with an additional sum. All three resignations would take effect when the Tryart offer reached 75 per cent acceptance and became unconditional. None of us disputed the right of Tryart to instal its own management, but as all three men had offered to stay on temporarily and give whatever help they could to the incoming management, we felt Warwick and his representatives could have handled the matter a little more graciously. We had, as Peter Robinson was later to write in the *Financial Review*, lost some remarkable executives. Finally I expressed my own and the board's great appreciation of the efforts all three had put into the company and said they had all made a tremendous contribution. Gardiner, replying for all, said Fairfax had been a magnificent company to work for.

By 5 November Tryart had received 84 per cent acceptances of the ordinary shares and had declared the bid unconditional, a remarkable endorsement by the shareholders of the offer we had negotiated. Press comment began to focus on the financial problems of the new Fairfax company. When Tryart began to negotiate the sale of the shares in AAP and ANM, attention returned to the assets sales reducing the debt. The *Financial Review* pointed out that the $275 million that Tryart would receive for the two sales was considerably less than the estimated pre-crash $500 million value. Murdoch would certainly get a bargain, but what else could Tryart do?

John Durie in the *Financial Review* described the sales as the equivalent of the New Zealand cricket team giving its champion strike bowler, Richard Hadlee, to Allan Border for the coming Test series. Warwick was handing over complete control of two of the key inputs to his business, news copy and newsprint, to his main competitor. It was lucky he had no shareholders to answer to, said Durie, because there was no doubt that he would not be re-elected to the board on recent moves. But what else could he do now? The sales had remorselessly to proceed. Nevertheless at this stage it was still felt he would be able to get his interest bill down to an acceptable level and that the sale of profitable assets would be balanced by the removal of losing ones. Our own figures told a different story.

We invited Tryart to send two representatives to the penultimate meeting of the old Fairfax board, held on Thursday 19 November, as we felt they should be present to discuss the management transition which we wanted to be as smooth as possible. Dougherty and Vrisakis attended and, as guests of the board, were told they should feel free to make any comments they wished. At this meeting, Vrisakis confirmed to me that Tryart would be settling within the required thirty day period after the offer had been declared unconditional which was, in fact, 5 November.

Gardiner referred to the need for the new management to make contact with the staff to settle them down, the company having been badly destabilised as a result of the bid. Dougherty indicated that they had begun this process at certain levels and the Australian Journalists' Association had been given certain assurances. In summing up Gardiner referred to the excellent condition and the major growth potential of the company. He pointed out that it had shown one of the highest rates of growth of any company on the Stock Exchange over the last few years. In concluding, he thanked me for the very productive relationship we had had as chairman and chief executive and said it had been an honour and privilege to work for John Fairfax Ltd. Sir David said that Gardiner's contribution had been outstanding over the years he had been on the board.

After covering his own area, Brenchley referred to a number of asset sales where it was not at all clear which individual publications had been included.

He also referred to the transfer of publications to Bell. The agreement needed to be clarified particularly in relation to the SII system and business computer which could be completely disrupted. He left for Tryart a draft report on the production of the *Herald* and *Financial Review* after the latter's transfer. He concluded by saying the Broadway production system would take the company into the next century and that the plant was one of the most modern in existence.

Suich tabled an extensive manual to assist the spinning off of the *Financial Review* and *Times on Sunday* from the group. He referred to a letter circulated to staff about the changes to the superannuation arrangements which had allayed many genuine and justified fears. He said he would help in any way to establish good relations between the editorial area and Tryart. There followed a discussion on the executive's contracts, one or two aspects of which gave concern to the Tryart representatives. These were finally left for Halstead and Vrisakis to iron out and over the next week this was done. Suich raised again the question of a possible breach of the AAP Articles and offered to assist in any way he could. In conclusion he paid tribute to Gardiner and thanked myself and the board for their support during his period as chief editorial executive.

One of the most extraordinary aspects of the takeover bid was our total lack of success in making any kind of contact with Warwick. Various writers had, from the early days of the bid, commented on his inaccessibility to the media and, later, his lack of contact with the staff he was about to take over. This was regarded as unusual for the principal in a takeover bid. Negotiations with the family had been conducted by his representatives as had those with Holmes à Court and Packer. More recently the company's sole links with him had been through Halstead contacting Dougherty and Vrisakis. I had neither seen nor spoken to him since 8 September and the situation was similar for Vincent and John. On 15 October I wrote the following letter to Warwick as I was very worried about the situation at Broadway regarding both executives and staff.

Dear Warwick,

I wanted to tell you that I believe it is essential for the future wellbeing of the company that you talk to Fred Brenchley and Chris Anderson as soon as possible.

Any further delay in doing this would, I think, prolong the existing dissension unecessarily and could also result in industrial unrest.

I understand that they have both been in touch with you to seek discussion on a number of important matters.

I received no reply but Warwick did see Anderson and gave him some assurances about his future and his own confidence in him.

In spite of all this, the three family directors had intended to remain on the board, an intention held at least until the AGM. From then on, two facts became increasingly clear: the first was that Warwick did not want us to stay on and the second that our positions, if we did, would be intolerable. We would bear full responsibility for the increasingly precarious financial situation of the new company but would be powerless to do anything about it. By the time of the November board meeting the three of us had decided not to stay on.

Quite apart from the financial responsibility, I felt Warwick's attitude had nullified any possible force I could bring to bear editorially and I still did not know the future composition of the board or management in spite of press speculation — which included the possible appointment of Peter King[2] as chief executive, and the return of Ron Cotton.[3] I had told Warwick on 8 September that I would need to know about both of these areas if I was to remain as chairman and I had been told nothing. In the discussions leading up to the 19 November board meeting, Halstead indicated that the three of us would be resigning and summarised our reasons. Looking back I can only feel Warwick did not know how to tell us personally that we were not wanted. Vrisakis accepted our decision without much comment, and as though it had been anticipated.

On Monday 23rd, I flew to Europe for ten days with Richard Walker, to see a major exhibition of Dutch landscapes of the seventeenth century at the Rijksmuseum in Amsterdam, and outline events to my mother in London. Two months before, I had read a review by Giles Auty in the *Spectator* under the heading 'Give yourself the break you deserve'. I did not expect to be able to take his advice but have been grateful ever since that I did.

On Friday 4 December, the day I returned, John announced the resignations of Gardiner, Suich and Brenchley and the stage was set for the final meeting on the 7th. Tryart was to begin the settlement process that day. Vincent, John and I met in my office before the meeting. It was a sad occasion. I do not think John and I had really come to terms with the fact that our careers with the Fairfax company of twenty-seven and thirty-two years respectively had come to an end, and Vincent had been completely shattered by the whole experience.

Warwick attended himself this time, together with Connell, Dougherty, Cotton and Vrisakis, while Sir David and Sir Eric had sent apologies. After I had welcomed them and the minutes were confirmed, I asked Warwick to nominate two people to fill the two vacancies existing on the board. He indicated himself and Connell, whom we duly elected. I then tabled letters of resignation from the five 'old' directors together with a statement for release to the Stock Exchange. Following several other formal matters the meeting resolved to accept the resignations and I asked Warwick to assume the chair. Messrs Dougherty and Cotton were then appointed directors as was Peter King in absentia. After Dougherty congratulated me on the dignified manner in which we had handled the transfer of control, Vincent, in an audible aside to me on Warwick's failure to undertake this simple task, said, 'Wouldn't you think the little ponce could have said it himself?' It was all over. I ended by extending my best wishes to Warwick, the new management team and all employees.

Warwick, for the first time, briefly outlined in a statement to the press his editorial and management philosophy. The *Times on Sunday* had correctly predicted the new team on 29 November: Warwick would be proprietor, the first to hold this title since his great-grandfather, Sir James Reading Fairfax, died in 1919, although how active a role he planned to play was not clear. Dougherty was managing director (editorial) and Cotton was managing director (finance) under King as chief executive.

Warwick also wrote to the staff saying that the takeover period had been difficult for everyone. He continued:

> *The foundation upon which this company was built and upon which it continues is the skill and dedication of its employees. I will continue to call upon that skill and dedication . . . The Fairfax family has a long and honourable tradition of producing great newspapers. So does the Fairfax staff. We are going to continue that tradition to the mutual benefit of staff, management and the community.*

Dougherty said that Syme would remain a separate company and that new directors would be appointed. He also said the new board had total confidence in Greg Taylor and Creighton Burns.

Around lunchtime on Wednesday 9 December, after a few farewells, I drove away from the Broadway building for the last time.

18

INTERLUDE: KOSHIHATA

In May 1988, I started writing this book at a small mountain village of some two hundred inhabitants an hour's drive west of Kyoto in Japan. Following my traumatic final departure from Broadway in December and the shattering events of the previous three months, I had felt I could never get the book started in Australia and I hoped that this would provide the necessary tranquility in a totally different environment. It was to prove the perfect place. Two and a half years later, in November 1990, I returned there to complete my task and this I did, apart from a few later additions and alterations in the light of subsequent significant events in December.

My first sight of the village of Koshihata was at six in the evening on Friday 22 April 1988. I had just spent two weeks in Japan's old capital seeing some of the most spectacular cherry blossom for many years (according to my friend Harold Stewart, the distinguished Australian writer and poet, the best in his twenty-seven years of residence there).

The Manor House at Koshihata, which translates as 'the rice-fields over the mountain', was to be my home for the next nine and a half weeks. It, together with most of the surrounding neighbourhood, has been owned by the Kawahara family for the past 370 years and is at present leased by a Canadian friend, John McGee, Tea Master and Lecturer at the Urasenke Foundation in Kyoto. The Kawaharas were samurai supporters of the Toyotomi rulers of Japan in the sixteenth century. After the fall of Osaka Castle in 1615 to Tokagawa Ieyasu, who established the Tokagawa Shogunate which was to rule Japan for some 260 years until the Meiji Restoration in 1867, the Kawaharas retreated to Koshihata, where they appear gradually to have taken over the whole district and have been there ever since.

The approach to the house is now from the side of the fortified entrance gate with its moss-covered thatch roof and the whole enclosure was once surrounded by a wall of which traces still remain. On one side of the gate there is a vast gingko and just inside to the left, in a bamboo-enclosed garden, a large maple with an ancient, twisted pine, camellias, rhododendrons and azaleas. The maple and pine are at least 200 years old and in one corner a magnificent 300 year-old National Treasure camellia spreads its vast umbrella from a richly gnarled trunk nearly a metre in diameter at its widest point. The path leads to the samurai entrance with the noble entrance on the left, the thatched roof above has the typical gable and on the right stands the rice house. On the west side there is a Zen garden with another old maple on a landscaped hummock of moss, around which stretches the sea of white pebbles and across the small country road, mercifully almost free from traffic, a stand of cryptomerias, pines and bamboo frames the Western mountains. Finally at the back on the North side is the treasure house.

Before describing the village of Koshihata, I must say a word about the interior of the manor house, the oldest secular building in the Kyoto Prefecture. The samurai entrance with its beaten earth floor, sliding wooden *amado* (door) and traditional gong leads through another pair of slatted *amado* to the old kitchen, where the curving wooden-stepped stove with five circular ovens and

The manor house, Koshihata, in 1988. To the left, the high-gabled thatched roof of the main house. To the right, the gingko.

James Fairfax in his room at Koshihata, November 1990.

cauldrons stretches across the recently installed floorboards. Two sofas provide some Western comfort, the bar is now on the stove and a bamboo partition, on which hangs an Indonesian *kilim*, separates it from the new kitchen.

From the noble entrance which is barred by a screen and vase, the *tatami* leads to more slatted *amado* beyond which is the central hall with its *ryorii* and, in an alcove at the end, a Western dining room table and chairs which look back on the whole length of the house. On a left wall is a painted silk collage by talented Australian artist Carolina de Waart, now working in Kyoto. To the left of the noble entrance is the long front room with veranda overlooking the enclosed garden, which serves me as bedroom, sitting room and sometimes dining room — alone, with guests or with the household.

At the end, behind a pair of *fusuma* (painted sliding screens), is my writing room where the word processor is set up. Its view is towards the Western mountains. Overlooking the Zen garden is the *kotatsu* room, which serves as another room for meals or a second bedroom — the *kotatsu* being a stove for heating in an alcove below the central table and very necessary when we first arrived. Beyond this is another bedroom and at the end a staff room with access from the veranda, occupied by Shotaro, a bright young Japanese who helps in the house.

Throughout the house the partitions are either *shoji* (sliding paper doors) or *fusuma*, most of which have been painted with traditional Japanese scenes and inscriptions by Clifton Karhu. The rest of the delightful and extremely competent household assembled for me by John McGee are Lynn Sterling from Toronto, Canada — a superb cook, in both Japanese and Western styles — and Tanya Clark from Vancouver, B.C., our calm and assured driver, maid of all works, and a prize-winning engraver of wood block prints. They occupy the Koura house. The genial and very knowledgeable owner, who at almost two metres towers over his pupils and Tea Ceremony guests, ascends to the mountains from his Kyoto house in the Ginkakuji district just down the road from the famous 'Silver Temple', with its unique Muromachi garden, and visits us from time to time. It is always an interesting and entertaining experience.

Our 'main' road leads southwards up hill to the village with its single shop and vast old cherry tree, beneath whose blossoms the entire village population, including our household, celebrated the planting of the rice crop with much sake and local delicacies the night after our arrival.

Just down the road live Jun and Noriko Tomita — weaver and journalist respectively — in whose house, to my surprise, I was to meet Lord Rothermere for lunch. We had quite a lot to talk about as he was most interested in the recent developments in the Australian newspaper world. Another friend of the Tomitas turned out to be South Australian journalist Peter Ward, who had recently interviewed me about my art collection for the *Australian*.

There are two or three narrow winding roads circling the hillside which make up the rest of the village. The houses are generally prosperous-looking with Kouras and beautifully kept gardens, although a number have replaced their thatched roofs with dark curved tiles — many have the circular *mon* in the gable indicating descent from different samurai families. Every inch of land is terraced into rice fields or vegetable crops, but always scattered around them are clumps of dwarf maple, azalea and iris. The wild azalea and camellia are everywhere in the mountains and a little further down, carpets of wild wisteria hang over pines and anywhere else they can spread their tentacles.

Walking every day along these little back roads and paths, acknowledged by the inhabitants with a bow and a *Konichiwa*, I do not think I have ever been more conscious of the change of seasons — from late winter through spring to early summer — as cherry blossom gave way to bright pink and red azaleas, which were then joined by purple, blue, white and yellow stands of iris. Perched in its hillside site and commanding sweeping views in every direction across to distant mountains, Koshihata is truly an idyllic place, and I often think how lucky I have been to live there and absorb its atmosphere and way of life.

My return visit in 1991 was notable for two events, the first being the coronation of the Emperor Akihito which our group (Dorothy Edwards, Harold Stewart, Billy McCann, Richard Walker, John Hahir and our excellent and charming cook-housekeeper, Atsuko Tanaka) watched on television at John McGee's house near the Ginkaku-ji temple.

As a historical preview for this, I had arrived in Kyoto just in time for the Jidai Matsuri or Festival of the Ages, held annually since the nineteenth century to commemorate the transfer of the capital from Kamakura on 22 October 794. The procession from the old Imperial Palace to the Heian shrine is virtually a panoply of history, beginning with the Patriots and Royal Army of the Meiji Restoration in the 1860s and culminating with the palanquin of Emperor Kammu, the city's founder. In between, on foot, horseback and decorated ox carts, there passed by a marvellous array of shoguns, samurai and famous court ladies of both intellectual and martial achievement (including the redoubtable Murasaki Shikibu, author of the great tenth-century classic poem *The Tale of Genji*), attendants and bearers spanning the 1100 years, and suppliers of necessities to the court. All were dressed in contemporary costume, many of which were originals lent from museum collections and, in some cases, the shoguns and dignitaries were portrayed by their lineal descendants.

The main secular Enthronement Ceremony, the Sokui-no-Rei, took place at the Imperial Palace at Tokyo on Monday, 12 November. The Daijosai, the Great Food Offering rite, in which the Emperor reports the Enthronement to his Imperial ancestors as well as heavenly and earthly deities, was to take place later in November. The procession of the six Imperial Princes, the Crown Prince clad in red ceremonial court robes, representing the rising sun, and the others in black and white, marked the start of the ceremony. They were followed by the eight Imperial Princesses, a breathtaking sight encased in twelve layers of kimonos and huge heart-shaped wigs as they glided one after the other in stately file to the Seiden (state room). Their robes weighed around forty kilos, in most cases probably the weight of the ladies themselves, and the design of all the court ceremonial robes dates back 1000 years to the Heian period. They were followed by the Empress Michiko, similarly encased, and finally by the Emperor in the red of the rising sun and towering black lacquer headdress. The latter two disappeared to be dramatically unveiled when the curtains of their elaborate lacquer thrones were pulled aside.

It was from here that the Emperor read the proclamation of his Enthronement to the 2500 distinguished guests facing him across the court in another hall, while below him were numerous officials of the Imperial Household in their ceremonial court dress bearing banners and various forms of symbolic weaponry. During the course of this spectacular and, indeed, moving ceremony, the princes and princesses stood stock still for nearly one and a half hours, not moving so much as a facial muscle.

Later in the day, having changed into less formal attire, the Imperial couple drove in an open car through the streets of Tokyo, where large crowds politely waved flags and whose interest and respect was in no way deterred by the somewhat massive police presence.

The other event, which was no less moving, took place in slightly different surroundings, namely the old kitchen, converted into a sitting room, of our house at Koshihata. Here Harold Stewart (Harold has published several volumes of poetry from 1940 to the present, as well as *By the Old Walls of Kyoto*, a comprehensive history and guide to Kyoto; he is also known as the perpetrator, with James McAuley, of the famous Ern Malley hoax) read the proem of his latest work, an epic poem appropriately entitled 'Autumn Landscape — Roll' and based on a Chinese Tang dynasty legend. The proem in four cantos describes the arranging of a painting contest by the sixth Tang Emperor, Ming Huang — a great patron of the arts — between Li Ssü-Hsün and Wu Tao-tzu, two of the most famous artists during the period of the dynasty. Before the contest there is highly amusing and subtle dialogue between the artists. Following Ming Huang's decision that the honours are even, Wu disappears over the mountainous

Dorothy Edwards, Tanya Clark and Harold Stewart at lunch in a Kyoto riyokan.

horizon of his own painting. The poem proper describes his subsequent adventures, including encounters with deities and demons.

Harold's powers of recitation and acting (he used to run his own radio program — 'Library Review' for the ABC) applied to his beautiful and superbly descriptive language, made the whole legend come to life and he reminded me of Emlyn Williams' recitals of the works of Charles Dickens. We sat spellbound for thirty-five minutes and eagerly look forward to learning what happened to Wu.

19
POST MORTEM

THE WHY AND HOW OF WARWICK'S TAKEOVER
OF JOHN FAIRFAX LTD, 1 9 8 0 s

I t is now time to consider three basic questions: why the bid was made, when the concept first emerged and how it proceeded until that Sunday evening. I had not seen a great deal of Warwick during his years overseas but I had always maintained regular contact with him. Since his early Cranbrook days I used to have him to lunch each school holiday and take him to a movie, and this continued over the years of estrangement with Sir Warwick. On any visit to England or America, I made a point of seeing him and I felt I was gradually building up a relationship and gaining his confidence. Curiously enough, I felt we almost became close in the two years before the bid, when we increasingly discussed his future entry into the company. In April 1986 I took him to stay with Henry McIlhenny in his magnificent eighteenth century house in Philadelphia's Rittenhouse Square. Henry's hospitality, both here and at Glenveagh, his 30 000 acre estate in County Donegal, Ireland, with its nineteenth-century castle brooding over the lake and its fine garden, was legendary as was his generosity. His death in 1986, shortly after our stay, was a great loss to Philadelphia and his magnificent collection of paintings now hangs in the Philadelphia Art Museum of which he was a former chairman and his family major benefactors.

Warwick had all of the Fairfax reticence, but there was also a deeper quality I could not quite define, which made me wonder sometimes if I ever knew what he was really thinking. There were times when I felt that there was some desperate spark of feeling deep within him which was struggling to escape or appealing for help. I felt this particularly at times he was relaxed and enjoying

The State in Schuylkill lunch for James and Warwick Fairfax, given outside Philadelphia by the Schuylkill Fishing Company in April 1986. **Left front:** *Henry McIlhenny and president Harry R. Nielsen.*

himself, such as at Henry's house or staying with Frank McDonald and Tony and Sandra McGrath at their beautiful property Bundanon on the Shoalhaven River (it is now owned by Arthur Boyd). But it was more than I could do to release this small flame.

Warwick was in Sydney for part of the second Participating Irredeemable Preference Shares proposal in 1985 and was particularly careful not to commit himself either way. When we had lunch at the Bangkok restaurant on 20 August, ten days before he proposed the takeover, we discussed office matters, including how he was settling in and the recent Seven Network sale. Everything appeared totally normal and not a hint was given of what was to come. So, why?

Four basic reasons emerge, gleaned partly from his own comments, partly from those his mother made to me early in 1988, partly from others close to him and partly from evidence in the Tryart court case (see Appendix VI). The first was revenge for my role, and that of Vincent, in the departure of Sir Warwick from the chairmanship in March 1977. I have already related that in one of the more unpleasant meetings I had with him at the time, my father had said he would make quite sure Warwick knew what sort of a man his brother was. It certainly had a great impact on Mary, in spite of the reconciliation, as she referred to it with particular emphasis several times in correspondence with me at the end of 1987 and early 1988. His parents' violent reaction undoubtedly had a permanent effect on the impressionable boy of sixteen, even though I am sure my father's wish for reconciliation was genuine and lasting.

In the letters to the press mentioned in Chapter 16, Mary Fairfax has denied that she harboured any thoughts of revenge. In her letter to the *Herald* of 22 December 1990 she ascribes what she called the 'vendetta myth' to Rupert Henderson, motivated by a desire to 'take the spotlight off himself' because of the *Mirror* deal with Murdoch which had taken place sixteen years before Sir Warwick's deposition from the chairmanship. She makes the astonishing and untrue assertion that she only met Henderson once. Apart from the Rome meeting (Chapter 6), there were a number of occasions when she asked him to see her at Barford, which he recounted to me back at the office, at which she suggested to him that they could run the company together. It is hard to accept, in view of the bitterness and hostility she displayed both in 1961 and 1976-80, that both these events did not influence her future actions to some extent.

The second reason which emerged was dissatisfaction with the management, although I must again emphasise it was never an explanation Warwick gave to me. According to his court evidence, though, it applied in several areas: the handling of the bid for the H&WT group and the acquisition of HSV and the sale of the Seven Network. In fact, Warwick was present at board meetings which discussed all three proposals, but gave no indication of any disagreement inside or outside the boardroom, even when his views were canvassed.

It became clear, during the course of his own bid, that Warwick had only the sketchiest idea of how the company operated and what, under my chairmanship, the board and management were endeavouring to accomplish. Dougherty's statement in court alleged that Warwick had told him Gardiner was a bigger threat to the family than Rupert Henderson, and was 'in league with Holmes à Court and will do whatever he can to help Holmes à Court to split the family and take over the company . . . Gardiner constantly opposed my father's proposals, James and John do what he wants. I might have to make a takeover before these fools lose it'. Sir Warwick might have held this view of Gardiner, myself and John, but if he did, with the exception of the capital-raising question, he never made complaints along these lines and he certainly supported me as chairman. Warwick denied making these statements — whether his or Dougherty's is the more believable version is for the reader to decide.

Paranoia such as this has all the hallmarks of brainwashing by Mary, but it is interesting to recall my summons by Sir Warwick to Shand QC's office in 1984 to hear the idiotic accusation of Gardiner's 'plotting' with Holmes à Court.

Unfortunately Warwick appears to have accepted without question Sir Warwick and Mary's criticism of Gardiner as general manager and the antidote to this view, provided by me, was not effective, although I was not to realise this until much later. In those two vital years (1985–86 when he was at Harvard), we might have been able to wean him from his preconceived prejudices had we been in regular contact with him in Sydney.

Failure to join with him in the February purchase of 1.5 per cent of Fairfax capital was clearly a third major reason. I certainly underestimated his strength of feeling on this matter, but had John, Vincent and I been face to face with him instead of on a telephone to Harvard, there might have been a better chance of resolving it. In his evidence Warwick did not deny that he was 'moved to tears' when telling Dougherty of this episode. According to Dougherty, he said it was 'typical of the way the family have been doing business for too long' and that 'it was time to do something drastic'. It is interesting that his only admitted emotion (other than the 'hole in the heart' letter, reproduced later in this chapter) over the entire affair should have been concerned with the family's achieving a 50 per cent shareholding. I still do not understand how he could have regarded a reasonable and logical decision on my part as evidence of lack of commitment to family ownership, when my whole career argued the exact opposite.

Warwick's fourth reason — his perception of a takeover threat — is linked to his attitude to his family following the share purchase question, the only explanation he was able or prepared to offer on 30 August. I have always regarded it as phoney: even if he genuinely feared a possible Holmes à Court or Packer takeover, it would only have been in the context of frustrating his own plans.

The motives of revenge and dissatisfaction with the way the company was being run were the key factors. My decision not to participate in Warwick's 1.5 per cent share purchase, together with Warwick's own decision to go ahead before he had achieved agreement with Vincent and John, gave a final impetus to a process already in motion. This $34 million purchase also made necessary an urgent and practical rearrangement of his finances, as there was no way he could meet the interest bill to the Midland Bank. He chose a drastic way of solving this problem. While his parents must bear the major responsibility for his attitude and motivation, his father would have been horrified at the thought of revenge, nurtured over the years, as a reason for action of this kind. Regrettably, I believe his mother kept the flame alive. Unfortunately, after the failure of our attempts at capital raising, Sir Warwick's confidence in the management did not return and as his health declined, the influence of Mary was predominant.

The 'when' and 'how' of Warwick's actions perhaps date back to 1975, when the issue of privatisation first arose. That was the year that Vincent, John and

I attended the meeting with Sir Warwick, Philip Munz and Willi Perndt of Price Waterhouse & Co referred to in Chapter 7. The issue lay dormant for many years until revived by Sir Warwick in 1982 when capital requirements were increasingly coming under discussion. Gardiner had prepared a report showing that profits would have to be maintained at a reasonably high level for the family to meet its interest commitments on the borrowings. The risk involved and the commitment for the family were considered too great and the proposal did not get further than informal discussion.

Mention was made earlier that Sir Warwick's opposition to the PIPS scheme in 1984–85 might have been partly because its implementation would have made privatisation more difficult at a future date. This would have presupposed that he never lost sight of it as an ultimate aim. Certainly, his opposition to the PIPS scheme and to the acquisition of the London *Daily Telegraph* in 1985, together with his pressure to alter the Kinghaven Settlement[1], were consistent with planning towards, and agreement with, an eventual takeover by his younger son. Sir Warwick would naturally be opposed to a capital issue, or a reconstruction following a major acquisition, if this was his aim.

It also suggests he might have had some knowledge of Warwick's plans before his death or indeed, together with Mary, have been involved in them. Dougherty quoted him as agreeing with this general approach on occasion during 1985 and 1986 and finally there is the remark made by Warwick on Sunday 30 August and overheard by the hire-car driver, which the latter later repeated to a Fairfax executive: 'My father said they would react that way'. The same driver recalled Warwick's clear elation after the meetings with myself, John and Gardiner.

It does not appear to me that any of this is enough evidence to link Sir Warwick with an ongoing plan, even if he did express general support of an eventual privatisation. I have already said that Sir Warwick must bear his share of the responsibility for proselytising Warwick with the belief that, regardless of my own competence as chairman, or indeed John's, he was the sole person with the competence to run the company in the future and that this should be sooner rather than later. But for me to believe that my father was capable, even in old age and illness, of the kind of deception that involvement in the above-mentioned plan would indicate, would make a mockery of our relationship in those last years — not to mention the reconciliation in 1980. I find this hard to credit and do not think, given the relationship established between us at the end of his life, that he could have concealed such a stratagem from me, even if he had wanted to.

Further, Warwick remarked to John that he could never have made the bid in his father's lifetime. There is certainly enough evidence that Sir Warwick and Mary were sufficiently opposed to and suspicious of the Fairfax management after 1984 for them to constitute a 'Fairwater faction'against both board and management. Vic Carroll kindly described to me in advance some of the themes his book[2] would pursue and the activities of the 'Fairwater Fairfaxes' certainly played a considerable part. However, in spite of Sir Warwick's supposed views on privatisation and on Warwick's own role, I do not believe there is enough evidence to justify belief in a consistent policy followed by Fairwater up to Sir Warwick's death and continued after it.

According to Dougherty, it was Warwick who first raised the possibility of a takeover in 1984. From my impression of him at the age of twenty-three, on visits from Harvard, I think this is most unlikely. I think it is far more likely that Mary and Dougherty discussed the possibility of a takeover in 1985–86, during Warwick's absence at Harvard and while his father's health was declining. This could go some way to explaining the contradiction between Warwick and Dougherty's evidence on this point, in that each would be inclined to believe that the other was initiating a takeover discussion. It is impossible to tell to what degree Mary indoctrinated Warwick during those two years but clearly, at the Warwick/Dougherty lunch in December 1986, whoever first mentioned the word 'takeover', neither was surprised to be discussing it with the other.

It is not my intention to canvass the issues raised by the Tryart court case. This has been done exhaustively elsewhere, particularly in Gavin Souter's *Heralds and Angels*. (Once again I ensured that he was given access to all material and was given complete editorial authority. It is only fair to add that he received total cooperation from the management of the company under Warwick's control.) Regarding the conflict of evidence between Warwick and Dougherty, the latter's counsel, Palmer QC, said that one of the two had to be lying. The settlement of the case answered few of the basic questions and an examination of the evidence leads to the conclusion that, in different areas of disagreement, the 'honours' — if one can call them that — between Warwick and Dougherty are even. They both had motives for concealing the truth and it is up to any interested individual to make his or her own judgment in these areas.

It is possible that Mary encouraged Warwick to think specifically of a takeover between 1984 and the end of 1986, but it is unlikely that she could have done so without Sir Warwick's knowledge. Sir Rupert Clarke, who was one of Sir Warwick's closest friends and a director of his family companies, told me he thought it impossible that Sir Warwick could have had any involvement in takeover discussions without his knowledge. He also said that, as Warwick's guardian for many years, he had been hurt that Warwick had not confided in him in any way concerning his takeover plans. I believe that Sir Warwick had no knowledge of the takeover plans but I find it hard to believe that Warwick never thought of making a takeover bid until Dougherty allegedly suggested it.

Certainly Mary has been credited in various circles as being the mastermind behind the bid, but it is important to note that she categorically denies this. In a letter to me dated 22 December 1987 she says:

The simple fact is I was not consulted by Warwick concerning his decision so how can I tell whether I would have agreed with it or not. I was informed a little earlier than you either Friday or Saturday at Salzburg where I was with Tony and Suelyn Grey for the Festival.

Later in the same letter she claims that Vincent and John had always been hostile to Warwick, and goes on to say:

I'm sorry the family chose the money. I'm not surprised the family did not want to be 49 per cent against Warwick's 51 per cent. I think it was naive to expect it. Finding money for the family necessitated the huge asset sale. So no matter how angry I get with Warwick and I do get angry, very angry, I feel he is not a victim of greed, not a conspirator but imbued with a sense of mission & protection & determination to build up what circumstances compelled him to sell to win.

She made a similar denial when I called on her at Fairwater on 17 March 1988 before my departure for Japan. She had complained to me several times since Sir Warwick's death that Warwick did not consult her or keep her informed, as well as emphasising how fond he was of me. It was during this visit that she suggested I should devote a substantial part of the funds I had received for my shares to assisting Warwick with the financial problems of the new company. I was so taken aback by this preposterous suggestion that I could scarcely reply. When she farewelled me at the front door, calls of 'Remember baby James!' pursued me up the drive — a reference, presumably, to a future heir of Warwick, who would be my beneficiary.

In a letter dated 23 January I told her I accepted her assurance that she had not influenced Warwick with the bid, or indeed known anything about it. I was still at that time inclined to give her the benefit of the doubt:

. . . However in view of comments supposedly made by you about the control of the company in the past, I don't think you can be altogether

*surprised that some of the family have this belief [that she was behind
the takeover]. When you talk of keeping the family together I must refer
to the divisive and damaging tactics employed during the PIPS scheme
period.*

*I tried to explain to you in December that once the bid was made the
family directors could either oppose with all means in their power —
and this was seriously considered — or negotiate in the interests of all
shareholders in accordance with their duties as directors of a public
company. The latter is of course what we did. Quite frankly W's reasons
for not consulting the family until the last minute are not convincing
regardless of whether he considered the enemy to be John, HAC or Packer
— and if J was the enemy logic would have to put me in the same
category! My own belief is that W and his advisers saw it as the best
way of getting control of the company and once it was clear that the
family would not accept a minority position and would support the
existing management, we were disposable.*

The commissioning by Mary and Warwick of the Newco feasibility study from
Baring Brothers Halkerston in February 1987 represents the first concrete move
towards achieving their aim, and despite her disclaimers to me, it is clear that
at that point Mary was totally involved. Mark Burrows delivered their takeover
report to Mary and Fieldhouse in March and it was the latter, not Burrows, who,
with a rather surprising disregard for security, sent it to Warwick on the Harvard
facsimile machine, available for anyone to see.

The conclusion was by no means what the young predator had hoped for:
on current and future profit estimates and with the existing debt level (including
the HSV purchase), it was doubtful whether the company would be able to
produce a sufficient cash flow to cover the increased borrowings incurred by a
bid. Gearing of liabilities to assets would be dangerously high and the report
felt the balance sheet could not sustain the maximum level of new debt.

As an alternative, the report suggested including an equity partner friendly
to Warwick and Mary in the bid vehicle. This would require a belief on their
part that such a partner could protect the family heritage more effectively than
Vincent, John or myself. In proposing a partner, Burrows would have had in
mind someone of high standing and reputation in the community. The final
sentence of the report was: 'We believe that it is more appropriate for Warwick
and Lady Fairfax to wait for an opportunity to put forward proposals which would
be in the best interests of the family and shareholders'.

The conflict within the family concerning the management of the company

— a conflict of which two branches were unaware — would have been difficult to resolve. But who knows what might have emerged from frank and open discussions? We certainly had no opportunity to find out. As far as another partner was concerned, events were to show that Warwick and Mary did indeed believe an outsider could better protect the heritage than their own family. The person suggested for this role by Martin Dougherty and accepted by Warwick and Mary was, of course, Laurie Connell — before Warwick decided he wanted to be sole owner and offered Connell the $100 million fee for his services.

After receiving the report, Warwick wanted to retain the services of Burrows to work with the prospective partner, but when Dougherty proposed Kevin Parry, followed by Connell, Burrows refused. In fact his response to the suggestion of Connell was 'You must be joking!' There was already some tension between Burrows and Dougherty: several times when Mary and Dougherty arrived for conferences with Burrows, he refused to discuss matters relating to BBH's advice in Dougherty's presence. Mary seems to have recognised the value of keeping Burrows involved, but the evidence points to Dougherty being the driving force in urging Warwick to act.

Dougherty described the Newco proposal as an attempt by John and myself to sustain our control and used it as a trigger to propel Warwick into action, encouraging at the same time the implication that the company was in danger of takeover by Holmes à Court. Similarly, he seems to have been the main force in pushing the joint venture proposal with Connell. As far as the history of the takeover planning is concerned, Dougherty asserted, in the Tryart court case, that it had been under discussion at Fairwater since 1984. Warwick, however, was endeavouring to demonstrate that he never considered making a takeover bid until Dougherty suggested it at lunch at Pancakes, Bondi, in December 1986 before his departure for Harvard early in January. According to Dougherty, Warwick said:

> *Vincent, James and John have very little business ability. The company has some very good assets but there is no leadership and no direction. I cannot accept a life where I am tucked away in a minority position watching the business being mishandled. I am going to see if I can make a bid as soon as possible. I simply have to try and take over the company. I could not forgive myself if I did not try. The management is totally incompetent.*

Looking back on the negotiations from mid-May to August, several questions arise. The first is, where was Mary? After Warwick's return to Sydney in May, she seems to have played little part in the negotiations over the next few months. She left for Europe in August, well before the Tryart agreement was signed on Friday the 28th, I believe at Warwick's urging as he did not want her in contact with the media when the bid was announced. Clearly, she would have been kept informed as the negotiations proceeded and a meeting in Perth, when Connell agreed to withdraw from the original joint venture in return for the $100 million fee, took place on 22 July.

Alan Anderson, invited to play tennis at Fairwater by Warwick in July, described to me the arrival of Dougherty and Rivkin for a conference that clearly included Mary, although she looked me straight in the eye at Fairwater the following March and said the first she knew of the takeover plan was when Warwick rang her at Salzburg on 28 or 29 August. My reaction then was to believe her, partly because I thought she would have spotted the risks in the plan if she had known about it, and not given her agreement. I can only conclude now that she was being disingenuous, if not economical with the truth. Clearly the news imparted to her at Salzburg was firstly that the Tryart agreement had been signed and secondly that the bid would be announced on Monday the 31st following Warwick's Sunday visits to John, Gardiner and myself. I have been told that she in fact received vast numbers of faxes there in the days prior to the call which she says gave her the news on the 28th or 29th. One can only speculate on the degree to which she was kept informed during August. The logical conclusion is that she was actively involved until the introduction of Connell, after which she appears to have been pushed into the background to the point that she could claim to me her lack of knowledge of the takeover itself.

The second question is how Warwick and Mary could have accepted the Tryart agreement. Warwick was not necessarily the innocent abroad, exploited by self-seeking adventurers, as he argued in the Tryart case, but nor was Dougherty a disinterested party when the agreement was finalised on 28 August. It was in his and Connell's interest to push the agreement through and Dougherty's role as negotiator for Warwick and ally of Connell was indeed ambiguous. On the other hand, Warwick totally misled Connell, through his own lack of judgment, on the reaction of the family to the bid, a key issue in the legal battle to determine whether Connell and Rothwells had fulfilled the requirements of the Tryart Agreement.

Here, Warwick's argument that he should have been alerted by an outside adviser as to the characters and possible reactions of the three main members of his family outside his parents, whom he had known and been involved with since childhood, seems pathetically weak. It is an indication of character that Warwick was apparently unable to draw such conclusions himself. It is also astonishing that Mary, if she was given the opportunity, was unable to demonstrate to him that the family's hostility to the bid could result in their getting out completely. In fact Connell and Dougherty argued that they had drawn Warwick's attention to the possible pitfalls in this regard. Certainly Dougherty's own knowledge of the family through his relationship with Sir Warwick and Mary should have given Warwick insight into the family's likely reaction.

The three main participants later gave differing accounts as to the degree of pressure applied to Warwick at the meeting on 28 August, with Connell allegedly telling him to put up or shut up and Dougherty emphasising that Connell would withdraw unless Warwick made concessions on the Rothwells fee.

An assessment depends on whether one accepts Warwick's view of Connell and Dougherty, or thinks that Warwick, as expressed on behalf of Rothwells and Bond Media in court, was a conniving and ruthless young upstart prepared to do anything to gain control of what he regarded as his birthright. Was Warwick's demeanour and response to the intensive three-week cross examination clever stone-walling or the dissembling of a devious mind? Most of us have the capacity to be devious in some circumstances if we are backed into a corner, so perhaps the wisest decision on his undoubtedly impressive performance is that it was a mixture of both.

At this stage Mary still had total confidence in Dougherty although, at the time of their bitter estrangement in October/November, she was to blame him for, as she regarded it, leading Warwick astray. She told me she only met Connell twice, yet she entrusted him, albeit on Dougherty's advice, with such a vital enterprise. In her letter to the *Telegraph-Mirror* of 27 December 1990, Mary asserts that 'she had never heard of Mr Connell before the privatisation was finished' and that the 'victory' or 'success' dinner on 8 December was to 'find out some facts about the privatisation'. She says she asked Warwick to invite his advisers as she had never met Connell and wanted to meet him.

In the same letter containing these astonishing statements, she refers to an eleven-hour negotiation with Warwick's lawyers on the commitment of her shares to the takeover in exchange for the $2.9 million annuity. One wonders what they were discussing during the eleven hours. It remains baffling to contemplate how mother and son — the one experienced in business and finance and married to his father for twenty-nine years, the other with a total of eight years working for a bank and at the Harvard Business School — could have let themselves into such a situation, unless their determination to gain control of the company had blinded their sense of reality.

Perhaps Warwick can best be judged by his actions. Nancy Carter, secretary to Sir Warwick for many years, has several revealing stories about Warwick giving her instructions when he was around ten years old. On one occasion, when he asked her to obtain some books on a project he was doing and said he would send the chauffeur and car in to collect them, she questioned some aspects of the project in an endeavour to be helpful. She got the reply: 'I've asked for the books I want, just get them, that's all'. Robert Haines has told me that during a visit he made to Fairwater when Warwick was around ten years old, he asked Warwick what he was going to do in the company. The reply was, 'I am going to be chairman'. When Robert asked 'What about James?', the reply was, 'I'll fix him'. His determination to prevent his mother joining either the Tryart or the John Fairfax Group boards was a major cause in the former case of her rupture with Dougherty, as well as being a source of dissension between mother and son. Indeed, he felt the need towards the end of 1987 to write her a letter explaining his attitude and assuring her of his affection.

Warwick's actions from December 1986 show an obsession with secrecy, a fear of betrayal and a belief that revealing himself would give somebody else an advantage over him, that must have deep psychological roots. I have no idea whether or not he was aware of Mary's use of the 'fondness' ploy in relation to his joining the Fairfax board and other areas mentioned. He has denied making most of the critical comments about me that Dougherty alleged he made.

At the end of the day I really do not know what he has felt about me either on a personal or company level. He must have had powerful inner feelings to take the risks and mount the challenge — his religious commitment gives evidence of this, as does his letter to John in September 1987:

> . . . I know that you feel very hurt now. You had a vision of another Fairfax who cared about the business coming home . . .
>
> Yet, no sooner does he come home, than he stabs you in the back and tramples on you. John, I understand how you feel . . .
>
> I have a vision that has been burning a hole in my heart for some time now. It has grown during the time that I have been away. It has come from reading many cases over the last two years about successful companies. It has come from working at Chase Manhattan Bank, where I felt like a very small unimportant cog in a big machine. It has come from working at the Los Angeles Times last year, where there was a tremendous feeling of loyalty and team spirit.
>
> I want John Fairfax to be a company where there is a real sense of leadership and vision. I want people to be able to say that they know where the company is going for the next 10 years. I want them to know what our long-term strategy and mission is . . .

In the three months since I have been back, I have found that the
employees are very loyal to the company and that they would much prefer
to work for us rather than Murdoch. But I want more than that . . .
      Your vision for the company is probably not that different. However,
I am afraid that I have not taken the time to learn about your vision.

One would think he must have been deeply scarred by the experience and its
disastrous result, although there is little outward evidence of this, and I find it
hard to have any sympathy for him.

   In the final analysis of the events of 1987 and the preceding few years, one
can only conclude that Warwick had formed a particular view of the company
which, combined with his concept of family control and the other reasons
canvassed earlier, was solidifying into a determination to act at the right time
and that was to be after the death of his father. Following the family dispute
over the purchase of the extra 1.5 per cent of Fairfax capital and the financial
burden it placed on him, together with the disappointing response by BBH in
the feasibility study into takeover possibilities, it would not have needed much
encouragement to stir Warwick into action. Did Dougherty sow a seed or nurture
one that was already there? I think the latter.

20

'WHO ARE HER PEOPLE?'

LIFE AND SOME PARTICIPANTS, IN SYDNEY
AND BEYOND, 1950s–1980s

W as there a world beyond Broadway? Indeed, and in Chapters 2 and 3 I did describe something of my life in Sydney before going to Oxford in 1952. However, several readers of the first draft of this book all pointed out that I had said almost nothing about it from the time of my return from Glasgow in 1957 to the present day. How about writing something on 'Sydney Society'? they all asked.

I was wondering how to begin this daunting task when, fortuitously, an article by Daphne Guinness appeared in the *Bulletin* entitled 'The decline of high society', while the puff on the front page proclaimed, 'High Society goes down market'. Two of the three photographs on the opening page were of those two golden girls Sonia McMahon and Susan Renouf, and if being constantly photographed at parties for visiting celebrities, charitable causes, or the launching of a product is one of the criteria, they must surely constitute a major ingredient in what now passes for Sydney society. But as they do not, to the extent of my knowledge, entertain on the scale of some claimants to the position, I suppose they can hardly be described as 'society hostesses'.

On the other hand, my stepmother, Mary Fairfax, who was the subject of the third photograph, has entertained a great deal on a large scale, often for her main cause, the Metropolitan Opera Awards. This sort of occasion could comprise 600–700 paying guests, as did her party to thank Melbourne for being so marvellous, or to launch the Sydney Swans. Her smaller dinners for forty or so would always have included leading politicians, federal and state, along with some of our top business tycoons, but not 'old society' — although the two are not always mutually exclusive. I shall return to this later, but the theme of the *Bulletin* article is that every party now has to have a reason, such as the three which I have given, and that no one entertains on a large scale for the sake of entertaining. Paying guests contribute to the cause and 'can see themselves as mixing it with the upper crust', while the PR person 'doesn't care that the social pages have gone commercial. To get her clients mentioned is all that matters.'

It is a time-honoured fact that the charitable cause has provided the entree into British, European and American society for 100 years or so. It is equally true that some of Sydney's best known post-war hostesses, who were little known before the war, employed this means, which perhaps reflects two universal adages which I hope I can be forgiven for hauling out again. Firstly, from the immortal Latin bard Publius Vergilius Maro, *Tempora mutant et nos mutamus in illis* (times change and we change with them); and the other, anonymous, *Plus ça change, plus que reste la même chose* (the more things change, the more they stay the same). This, of course, is very true of 'society', of which two of the definitions my dictionary provides are: 'a group of people bound together by a common interest or relationship' and 'the wealthy fashionable social class and their life' (happily it does not employ that unfortunately now acceptable piece of jargon 'lifestyle').

The one constant factor of society anywhere in the world is that it is always

James Fairfax with Juliet Powell, Liza Eaton, Ingrid Osborne, Leslie Walford and Dick Keep at Chequers, in the mid 1960s.

changing. There is the biological need for new blood and the material one for more money. This applies to even the most cast-bound of aristocracies, as anyone who has read Simon Schama's magnificent work on the French Revolution, *Citizens,* will readily appreciate. The pre-revolutionary French aristocracy was in a ferment of new ideas and philosophies. They had studied their Voltaire, Rousseau and Diderot and were far more receptive to additions to their ranks from wealthy professional or merchant classes than their confraternity across the channel. The storming of the Bastille owes more to the salons of Mesdames de Sévigné, d'Epinay and du Deffand than is often realised. That well-known genealogical expert, Queen Victoria, was no snob and was constantly urging her innumerable European relations to look further afield for their marriage partners, quite apart from those she arranged for her own family. One of her daughters and several of her grandchildren married outside royalty. Today's royal families help ensure their survival by marrying commoners, whether rich or of more modest means.

When I was a child, Sydney society was much more clearly delineated and even as children we were aware of who the old and the not-so-old families were, partly from seeing who our parents invited to dinner. Our godparents were drawn largely from the Stephen family, who my mother had known since her childhood move from Strathfield to Yandooyah in Bellevue Hill. My Fairwater grandparents were close friends of the Knox-Stephen cousinhood and Helen Rutledge recalls her father, Sir Colin Stephen, saying to her mother, 'Do we have to have the Geoffs and the Jims again?' as Lady Stephen was trying to fill her dinner table. This would appear to indicate a dearth of acceptable people in the years following World War I. I have described the Red Cross ball given by my parents at Barford in 1939 and it is clear that by then the guidelines could be stretched a bit. World War II, of course, stretched them much further, as the various women's committees for the services and other wartime activities recruited members from wider social circles. The end of the war brought the golden age of charity committees which, in differing forms, has been with us ever since.

In her book *Connie Sweetheart,* Valerie Lawson uses the final and most important part of Connie Robertson's career, her twenty-six years as social editress and editor of the women's pages of the *Sydney Morning Herald,* to give a fascinating picture of the Sydney social scene from the late 1930s to the mid 1960s. To illustrate who was who, she draws largely on those two former bastions of social prominence — Prince's and Romano's — whose lifetime coincided with Connie's time at the *Herald.* In 1951 they were still at their height and I often used to take parties of six or eight to dinner at Prince's, always going to see Pierre Henri first to arrange the menu and which of the banquettes (floor tables) we would occupy. By that time Romano's was regarded as more of a lunch place, a different crowd going there at night.

By 1955, as Lawson writes, life had begun to move to the suburbs. After my three years at Oxford, the longest time by far I ever had or still have spent out of Australia, I was naturally far more conscious of the changes to our hidebound little society. There were two major factors: one of the many civilising influences of European immigration was the introduction of its cuisine and the opening of restaurants of many different nationalities in the inner suburbs; the second was the introduction in New South Wales of sensible liquor licensing hours and of 10 pm closing for pubs. The first of these, in particular, was to sound the death knell for Romano's and Prince's in 1965 and 1968 respectively.

By the time I returned from Glasgow in mid 1957, we were on the threshhold of the swinging sixties. Our relatively sedate circulation round the dance floor of Prince's and the bridge parties at home were superseded by noisy dinners in Italian bistros and raucous visits to pubs. The Macquarie Arms in Woolloomooloo, with its skiffle group, almost became fashionable, rather to the resentment of the locals. There were still times of formality with the Black and White Ball, then at the Trocadero, headed by the dynamic Nola Dekyvere, and the Peter Pan Ball at Prince's, and later at the Wentworth Hotel, by the equally dynamic Joan Hill. My long-suffering stepmother, Hanne, put up with reports of wild parties at Barford over the weekend while she and my father were at Harrington Park, quite rightly conveyed to her by our only live-in staff: Mrs Goetel, the Czech cook, who was a great character.

However, during my Barford days Hanne and I did organise two very good dances. There were some tussles over the guest list, however, as I wanted to include a number of my friends from the older generation, who were not so well-known to Hanne, or indeed to my father, who at that stage, in spite of her urgings, still led a somewhat reclusive social life. This resulted in some of the guests mistaking him, as he stood at the entrance in his white tie and tails, for the major-domo to announce their arrival.

As well as the friends I have mentioned in Chapter 3, others from the older group who 'encouraged' my group by asking us to their cocktail parties or to weekend lunches were Ruth Inglis, Joan Bode, Nola Dekyvere, Mary Hordern, Joan Hill, Elsa Albert and Helen Blaxland. This suited me down to the ground, as from an early age I have always enjoyed the company of older people, a preference that occasionally got me into trouble, such as at one charity ball when I abandoned my partner, Diana Horn (Mrs Simon Heath — she soon kindly forgave me), for Rada Penfold Hyland.

I was on Christian-name terms with all my older friends, but never with

Harold Hertzberg, Sue Du Val, James Fairfax, Valerie Carswell, Morson Clift, Malcolm Carswell at the Chevron Hilton, 1963.

Mary Hordern's sister, Gretel Packer, who, with Frank, took a much more formal attitude to the young and was gracious but a little distant. I can still see her glamorous figure in a snow-white dress at a New Year's Eve dance they gave at Victoria Road in 1960, not long before she died. It was not until his second marriage to Florence Vincent that Sir Frank asked me to call him Frank. He may have found this difficult to avoid, as Florence and I used to cook dinners for each other at her flat in the T&G and mine at Retford Hall. Sir Frank was always most kind and encouraging to me during my early days as a director of the Fairfax company. He took the trouble to discuss newspaper matters when we met and tend some useful information.

Hannah Lloyd Jones, or 'Aunt' as Caroline, Philip (on his marriage to my sister) and I called her, was in a slightly different category. Valerie Lawson refers to the business and social links between our two families and how Connie Robertson felt obliged to keep Hannah 'under surveillance' and regarded herself as sealing the relationship between John Fairfax and David Jones. While it is true that Mary Hordern (who was fashion editor of the *Women's Weekly*) and Gretel Packer were always much closer friends of Hannah Lloyd Jones than my mother was — for many years after her departure for China in early 1946, she only returned on short visits — there were contacts between the two families and firms on many levels.

My father always had a real liking and respect for Sir Charles, and while

Rupert and McLachlan may have 'looked after the Joneses' (as Rupert put it), the most important factor, which Lawson acknowledges, was the firm view of the David Jones advertising manager, Eleanor Donaldson, that only the *Herald* could give them the results they required. Lawson describes the various rifts between the Lloyd Jones and Packer families that this attitude caused.

I always thought Hannah's involvement on the business side added a bit of spice and amusement to our affairs, particularly in the case of Rupert, who had a genuine affection for the whole family. When McLachlan and I went into his office once, he said: 'I've just had the Jones woman on the phone. She asked how her boy Angus was. I didn't know who the hell she was talking about.' Quite apart from the Fairfax company, 'Aunt' was indeed a loyal and devoted friend to Caroline and me until the day of her death. It may be true that uncertain status following Sir Charles's Reno divorce caused early social problems and that she and Connie had a mutual assistance pact, but in later years she certainly was regarded as Sydney's leading hostess. Her friendship with Bob and Pattie Menzies doubtless helped in some spheres, but as long as she entertained at Rosemont, international celebrities — whether political, commercial or artistic — mingled with old families and more recent arrivals at her parties.

Mary Fairfax has been regarded as an aspirant to Hannah's crown — something she has not achieved to date in this country, but perhaps it will be a different story in New York. Her efforts should not be belittled, however. Other writers have suggested she never really made the grade with what was regarded as Sydney society from the mid-1960s on, be it old families, or pre- and post-war successes in the business world (again I must emphasise that they are not mutually exclusive) and that her interests were primarily with the rich, powerful and famous. However, the latter observation could be attributed to many hostesses throughout the world, so perhaps she should not be overly criticised on this point.

Hannah Lloyd Jones always paid as much attention to old friends as to any visiting fireman; this was not the case with Mary. Where she has succeeded, to quite a degree, is where she mainly wanted to succeed. She has also been well-received by much, but by no means all, of Melbourne society, thanks largely to the exuberant welcomes she has received from her friend Kath Clarke, whose husband, Sir Rupert, was one of my father's closest friends in his later years.

Rupert, being a baronet, bears one of Australia's few hereditary titles (the Baillieu family's baronage is another, and some interesting inheritances such as the Earl of Stradbroke have emerged more recently). Generally, most visiting members of the British nobility are greatly sought after by all hostesses worthy of the name. Some have close friends in Australia and stick to them, but most succumb to determined pursuit. There is less enthusiasm for European nobility, whose titles have to be much more carefully checked. The *Almanach de Gotha* does not figure in many libraries in Australia.

Mary's dinner parties are well done: Fairwater lends itself to such occasions, with its long hall, its drawing room modelled after an early eighteenth century English one but panelled in pale Queensland maple, and its dining room, with square leadlight window panes, just holding forty. All three rooms open onto the wide stone veranda where dancing takes place after dinner. Some find her custom of making a speech about the guest of honour disconcerting — including, sometimes, the recipient of her remarks, who has to reply to them — but there is no doubt she has the knack of getting her high-powered guests to enjoy themselves. One guest of honour who certainly did not mind replying was the Federal Treasurer, Paul Keating, at the last dinner I attended. He was surprisingly warm in his words about the Fairfax organisation. As it was in March 1987, presumably neither Warwick nor Mary had confided any takeover plans to him, although he was later to make a number of comments that suggested that he had indeed played a role in the Murdoch takeover and all the events which followed on from it. I shall return to this in the concluding chapter.

His charming Dutch wife, Anita, was sitting next to me and she complained strongly about the attention their house in Elizabeth Bay was getting from the 'Stay in Touch' column of the *Herald*. Public figures have to expect a degree of interest from the populace in their domestic lives, but I felt the 'Stay in Touch' section had devoted enough attention to the Keatings' house and I sympathised with the security aspect. I passed this on to Chris Anderson, but tried to make clear to the Keatings that it was his decision whether to issue an instruction not to mention it again, not mine.

Others I can recall at that dinner were Michael Duffy, then Minister for Communications, the Victor Smorgons, Kevin Parry and Bruce Judge. I recall, also, trade union executive John McBean calling out after his hostess's description of her guests as being some with old money and some with new money, 'and some with no money at all.' However, it was clearly felt she would retain some influence with the Fairfax organisation following her husband's death in January. My father usually appeared at Mary's dinners until his last year and often enjoyed them, but in spite of the new social life his third marriage had brought him, his capacity to tolerate people had not greatly changed and he could equally look thoroughly bored.

In a changing society, attitudes towards appearing in the social columns would change. For many it was unthinkable in the 1930s, while the younger generation, my mother and her friends, accepted it as an occupational hazard without being particularly concerned about it. As Connie Robertson's activities after the war have shown, for those wishing to gain admittance into society it was essential. While the Thursday women's sections carried photographs of those who were there, as well as those who were trying to get there, many still resisted. When Connie enlisted my aid, at several parties held to promote some aspect of *Woman's Day*, in persuading suitable guests who were friends of mine to be photographed, a number of the more conservative still did not like the idea.

It was not a problem I had to face myself as the opposition press had no reason or desire to publicise my social activities unless I did something particularly foolish, which happily I usually managed to avoid. I did appear on the front page of the *Mirror*, for the first and only time, when I bought my Darling Point house, under the heading: 'Bachelor's Dream Home'. Of course after I became chairman there was greater interest, which was fair enough. Though some rather curious interpretations of my job and my attitude to it were made, I have basically had no objection to anything that has been written about me. In fact some, such as the occasional mention by my old chum David McNicoll, I have really rather enjoyed and he has, as a true professional, always been scrupulous in clearing up any small misunderstandings that might have arisen.

I referred earlier to the longstanding rule in our own organisation of not mentioning the family unless it was a genuinely newsworthy event — this could include marriage, divorce, business activities and occasionally, good works — and to the problems caused by Mary's interpretation of this rule, and her attempts to enforce her interpretation. However, succeeding chief executives, with my support as a director or as chairman, have managed to deal with the situation and the rule has generally been observed. It was most in danger of being ignored during the 'Committee of One' period, but Falkingham was there to wield a blue pencil.

One often hears complaints that the only people one can read about in the social pages are the professional party-goers, or the people who are trying to join that category. I was reflecting that in the last two years I attended three major social events about which, as far as I am aware, not one line appeared in the papers. Indeed, the respective hosts and hostesses may not thank me for referring to them now. Just after Easter 1989, Rachel, daughter of Pat and Sally Osborne of Currandooley, married George Vestey of the previously mentioned English clan. Gathered at the house for the reception, and the next day at Turalla (owned by Bill and Dimity Davy) for a lunch given by the ladies of Bungendore, were a great array of country families together with a sprinkling from Sydney, Melbourne, Adelaide and Tasmania.

Earlier in 1990 in Sydney, Caroline and David Parker gave a farewell party at Rona, home of the Knox family and its descendants for 120 years until its sale that year, and while there were not many survivors of the current older generation, there was a goodly gathering of the middle-aged descendants of prominent families of earlier generations, together with their offspring. Both these events would certainly have been 'picked up' in the 1920s and 1930s and probably the 1950s, but *tempora mutant* . . .

The third occasion was in the Western District of Victoria, given by David and Fleur Gibbs at their property, Toolang, near Hamilton, to celebrate their thirtieth wedding anniversary. There has been too much written about the squattocracy of the 'WD' for me to want to add to it, except to say that it was all there, as was *le tout* Melbourne and contingents from other States.

I mention these three occasions to demonstrate how possible it is to keep them relatively quiet, so that social editors and reporters tend not to hear about them, quite apart from the fact that their attention has been successfully diverted in other directions by assiduous publicists. It is, perhaps, unfair to blame social editors and writers for this situation, which changing circumstances have created. They, after all, are expected to know what their readers want, but I cannot help feeling that a little more research would enable them to give both a more interesting and better balanced coverage. It can be done, as writers such as Daphne Guinness and Claudia Wright in Melbourne have demonstrated.

In Melbourne the social boundaries have continued to be more clearly defined, with country and city families contained within the borders of Toorak, as well as their country estates. But in spite of this I have always felt that, over the years I have been writing about, Melbourne hostesses made a greater effort to include interesting people from different backgrounds, be they the groves of academe, various legislatures or the world of the arts. It is perhaps a truism not so applicable today, but it used to be said that at Sydney dinner parties the conversation was about people, while in Melbourne it was about issues.

The best illustration of Melbourne mounting a social operation can be found by examining some of the events surrounding the Melbourne Cup during a period of around twenty-five years from the 1950s to the late 1970s. On the Thursday before Cup Day, Colonel and Mrs E. H. B. Neill (Nancy Syme) would give a cocktail party at their Amesbury House apartment in Domain Road, which was followed, on Friday, by Dame Hilda (Rudd) Stephenson's party at her St Georges Road house. The line-up of official cars in Dame Hilda's drive — Governor-General, state Governors, Prime Minister, Premier and ambassadors — proclaimed the guest list. The Derby Eve Ball was also on Friday and we used to race from Rudd's to one or other of the smaller pre-ball cocktail parties, then to the ball itself which was sometimes held in a private house.

After the Derby, with its numerous picnics in the members' car park overlooking the course, we would squeeze into Louis Nelkin's flat, trying to obtain a drink from his long-suffering butler, and then go down the road to the British High Commissioner's. For a number of these years, it was the very popular Sir Charles and Natasha Johnston. Natasha was a daughter of the Georgian Prince Bagration and her mother was a Romanov. Her description of the family's flight from their palace of Pavlovsk (today perfectly restored and open to the public), outside Leningrad, during the Russian Revolution makes a fascinating story. It ended in Bucharest where her relative (Aunt) Queen Marie of Romania, in heavy flowing black, swooped down to embrace the startled child who cried out in alarm, 'It's the Angel of Death!'

On one of those Saturdays I gave a cocktail party in the penthouse suite of the Southern Cross, to return hospitality, and the next morning was covered in little red spots. The hotel doctor thought I had scarlet fever and wanted to send me straight to the infectious diseases hospital, but a second opinion showed it was not the case, fortunately, as otherwise festivities could have been seriously decimated and a number of prominent guests affected. To be on the safe side, I decided to return to Sydney and was driven overnight by a kind Terry Clune.

On Sunday, Rupert and Kath Clarke would have a lunch for about a hundred at their property, Bolinda Vale, near Sunbury, where we munched Santa Gertrudis steaks and participated in the Clarke Cup sweep. On Sunday evening Sir Norman and Dame Mabel Brookes would give a large dinner party at Elm Tree House in Domain Road where they lived for many years. Monday was for recovering, apart from the cocktail party at Government House, while the last event of Cup Week was the Livingston brothers' (Frank and John) ball at Menzies Hotel on Tuesday evening after the running of the Cup. Both brothers appeared in full Highland rig playing the bagpipes and in the course of the evening we worked off earlier indulgence in particularly strenuous Eightsome Reels, Gay Gordons, Dashing White Sergeants and Strip the Willows. Each of these parties was an institution. Younger hosts and hostesses have naturally taken over and entertain differently, the Clarkes' Sunday lunch being the only survivor of that old round.

The David Syme board meeting, of course, no longer takes me to Melbourne once a month, but I continue a longstanding custom of going for about a week each spring and autumn, usually staying with Guilford Bell and Denis Kelynack but sometimes with Claudia Creswick, whose welcoming aviary of parrots, magpie geese and assorted wildfowl maintain an intermittent chorus. The ranks are sadly but inevitably depleted. Most of the Cup party-givers I have mentioned are no longer with us, nor is the elegant and wise Ginty Grimwade. Who could forget her dinner parties at St Georges Road, or weekend lunches at Marathon, both

James Fairfax and Pie Grimwade at the Melbourne Cup in the 1960s.

of which sometimes featured, on the piano, her exuberant and zestful husband John who was also renowned for telling all his guests at Marathon that they had parked in the wrong place?

The sparkling Pie (Mrs Geoffrey Grimwade, who was christened Lavender) was my companion at both Derby and Cup for many years and brave as a lion during her last painful illness. She was my real introduction to Melbourne and often entertained the 'young' at her Irving Road house. I recall one hilarious evening there when for some reason we all ended up wearing carpets, which put me in bed for several days with severe pharyngitis, a condition which curiously has recurred spasmodically ever since. Chester Guest has gone, but Patricia continues to preside over one of Melbourne's most scintillating dinner tables with a vivacity and wit that some of her distinguished guests have found particularly memorable. Reflecting on good times past in Melbourne draws me further south to one of my favourite parts of Australia: northern Tasmania. I had visited the Australian Newsprint Mills plant at New Norfolk along the Derwent from Hobart twice, when I returned in February 1973 for the opening of the Wrestpoint Hotel and Casino. The next day, Rod O'Connor drove three fairly hungover people — the other two were his wife Ros and myself — to their property, Connorville, which occupies a sizable chunk of the central part of the state. Rod was a great character, and a great host, who lived life to the full. Most sadly, he died at the age of fifty-five in 1982. Evenings at Connorville usually lasted until the small hours of the morning and I returned there several times, also seeing other friends such as Nigel and Sandra Campbell at Saundridge and Ken and Berta Von Bibra at Beaufront.

It was in 1968, however, that I had one of my most interesting trips to Tasmania with Mervyn Horton. The main purpose was to see its magnificent heritage of Georgian-Colonial architecture, scattered in the north and centre around such towns as Campbelltown, Ross, Longford, Perth, Cressy and Fingal. Our tour was arranged by Milo Talbot (eighth Lord Talbot of Malahide whose family occupied Malahide Castle in Ireland for 700 years) and Liz Turnbull, the remarkable wife of the Senator, Dr 'Spot' Turnbull, a well-known and controversial figure in Tasmania's often Byzantine politics. They were friends who could not have been more unalike, but between them they opened every door.

Our journey began with the Willoughby Norries and their Aide, Jimmy Zouche (eighteenth Baron), at Hobart's smallish, Gothic Government House and from there we went to Malahide, at Fingal in the north-east, to stay with Milo. A forebear who obtained the land grant in 1824 had built the classic two-storey Colonial house of Fingal stone in the 1830s, but from 1900 until Milo decided to pay it a visit in the mid 1960s, it had been managed by trustee companies. Milo, a rather brooding man with an unexpectedly quirky sense of humour who had worked during the war for both Secret Services (he knew Philby, Burgess and Maclean about whom he had many anecdotes), had completely restored the homestead, coach house (now an art gallery) and stables. However his great contribution was commissioning the six volume *The Endemic Flora of Tasmania* with illustrations by Victorian artist Margaret Stones. It was a graceful and enlightened act of patronage which his sister, Rose, completed with the sixth volume after his death. Rose now lives at Malahide and it was in the castle outside Dublin with its great botanical collection that the Boswell papers were found in an attic.

Mervyn and I must have visited about fifteen houses of this fascinating collection, each with its distinctive architectural style, and in each we were warmly welcomed. I particularly remember drinking Madeira with the Archer family at Woolmers while sitting at the Duke of Edinburgh's table (he was there in 1868), sloe gin with the Fitzpatrick sisters after lunch at the Fitzpatrick Inn, the Mills family at Panshanger and Margaret Ransom at Killymoon. Alan and Edmée Cameron, Ros O'Connor's father and stepmother, had us to lunch at Mona Vale, built in 1865–68. The archetypal Italianate Revival mansion of three storeys and tower, it supposedly had 365 rooms and inspired many similar edifices on the mainland including, possibly, Retford Park. The timing of our visit was fortunate as the Camerons were just about to move to a house they had built on the property.

To end in Launceston on a family note, the well-known Tasmanian historian, Dr Craig, invited us to dinner to meet my cousin Dr Lachlan Wilson and his wife Nan — my architect great-uncle Hardy was his father. In 1979 we returned to stay with Rose and the O'Connors and were once again overwhelmed with hospitality in this marvellous corner of Australia.

With Edward and Marie-Heléne Gilly at the French consulate, New York, after their wedding on 31 May 1972. On the right, Jacqueline Onassis.

Going over what I have written about the circles in which I have moved, it is interesting, but perhaps not altogether surprising, that I have been drawn to the earlier years, when I was more conscious of 'personalities'. Of course I was at an impressionable age and one probably takes the personalities of one's own generation more for granted, so beyond using one or two events to make a point, I have not said much about the 1980s. Apart from making a few obvious comments about the background of myself and many of my friends, I have, for the most part, let my thoughts dwell on people whom I was fond of and entertained by, and whom I admired for a host of different reasons. Were they 'society'?

I suppose I would have to answer that they were then, but they, or in many cases their children, may not be now because they do not necessarily fill the criterion of 'fashionable', to the extent that they do not want their social life publicised. We reflect the times we live in and as barriers of all kinds are continually being broken down — here I make no moral judgements — our interests become more eclectic. This is reflected in the search for intellectual stimulus, as well as diversion and merriment, from much broader circles and backgrounds. The process is of mutual benefit and, to me, epitomises true 'society' much more now than giving or going to large parties, charitable or private, or the pursuit of fashionable or social goals through the media or other methods. I do not mean to disparage the latter. There is, of course, room for both: to each his own.

I hope that parts of what I have written do not sound too much like a certain social journal. Old families bound by ties over several generations like to preserve them through various gatherings, and there is nothing snobbish about this. It simply fulfils the first of the two dictionary definitions. Alongside this there are the changes in attitude and composition I have noted.

I shall refer in conclusion to two Sydney people who to me represented different aspects of Sydney 'life' — I would urge the use of this word rather than 'society'. They came from quite different backgrounds but neither would be totally surprised at being bracketed with the other.

Mary Allen, a New Zealander, lived in a small brick house in Bellevue Road, with her husband Dundas — of the old legal family and author of *Early Georgian*, a history of his family's days at Toxteth in Glebe from the 1830s. She was one of the wittiest and most well-read people I have known and gave dinner parties of about twenty assorted relatives and friends, scattered around three small rooms.

Mervyn Horton's career in the art world is now well-known but, after studying law, his father had wanted him to follow on in his own profession of running coal mines. In the 1960s, Mervyn moved from St Ives to a house in Victoria Street, Potts Point, bought from my stepmother Hanne. His parties certainly covered a much wider circle than Mary Allen's did, but both comprised a multitude of talents and provided many exceptional evenings. For me they

Dundas Allen, M. E. Fairfax, Mary Allen at Bilgola in the early 1960s.

are two people who most readily come to mind when an amusing incident, bizarre situation, or major experience in art, theatre, literature, travel or life in general occurs and one says 'Wouldn't so-and-so have loved that?'

I end this chapter with a party. As I write, it happens to be the last one I went to, but it is also one of the ones I have enjoyed most in the last year or so. It was a lunch for about a hundred given by film producer Margaret Fink for retired couturier Frank Mitchell's seventieth birthday, at her Wallaroy Road house in Bellevue Hill, formerly owned by Gregory and Helen (Dame Helen) Blaxland. The guests included artists, writers, journalists, actors, fashion designers and people from the business and legal world, current and retired. It lasted from 1 pm until the early evening, and was Sydney life at its best.

21

TRAVELS WITH MY ART

FROM MADONNA TO MOLDAVIA AND THE ART OF COLLECTING, 1960s–80s

I referred in Chapter Three to the art master at Cranbrook, Eric Wilson, and to my first real art purchase at the age of twelve, of one of his Paris street scenes, from the Macquarie Galleries. My second acquisition two years later was a David Strachan still life of fruit and flowers in rather sombre yellows and greens, and these two paintings remain in my possession. At Geelong, Ludwig Hirschfeld-Mack introduced me to the bright colours of the Bauhaus. Although abstraction was a little beyond me, clearly something sank in.

In my Oxford days I met Harry Tatlock Miller, a partner in the Redfern Galleries in Cork Street, and Loudon Sainthill, by then established in England as a leading stage and costume designer. Both had been members of that remarkable creative coterie resident at Merioola just after the war, and I was aware of Loudon as a designer of ballet sets and costumes from childhood visits to the Kirsova Ballet. On a different note, Merioola's days as the main Sydney residence of the Allen family are evocatively recalled in Margaret Gifford's book *I Can Hear the Horses*.

At the Redfern I added to my embryonic collection with Rouault and Chagall lithographs and, through spending part of each vacation in Paris and later London, I was gradually expanding my artistic horizons. My first major acquisition came during my Glasgow time when, egged on by Harry, I bought a Henry Moore silk-screen print for £120. One of an edition of thirty, and the only time he used this process, it was to become the centrepiece of my flat in Retford Hall.

Formerly the major residence of the Hordern family and designed by

My mother, M. E. Fairfax and family at Retford Park, September 1979. **Left to right:** *Alice Simpson, Caroline Simpson, Alexander Gilly, Oliver Gilly, Edward Gilly, Aurelieanne Gilly, Emily Simpson, Philip Simpson. M. E. Fairfax, Louise Simpson, Edward Simpson, Marie Heléne Gilly, James Fairfax . The balustrade comes from my former flat in Retford Hall.*

Edmund Blackett in 1865, I bought the Retford Hall flat on my return from Glasgow in 1957. I had been to children's parties there when it was owned by Tony and Mary Hordern, given for their daughters Edwina and Romaine, little thinking that one day I would live there, or that Edwina and I would be neighbours at Bowral for over twenty years.

I had no plans to acquire a country house, but chatting to Peter Baillieu, Edwina's husband, at a cocktail party in December 1963, I learned that Retford Park and ten acres of land were to be sold, having been passed in at auction with seventy acres. As Peter put it: 'We're trying to flog it for £20 000.' I said at that price I might be interested, and a few days later flew up to see it with Terry Clune, who had also been at the party. Its owner for many years had been Sam Hordern who, two years earlier, had been tragically killed while driving in a taxi to Sydney. His widow June sold it to King Ranch (Australia) of which her cousin Peter Baillieu was managing director. King Ranch had already bought Milton Park from Tony Hordern, so Edwina found herself living in her old home by virtue of Peter's position with King Ranch. The Baillieus were later to buy back Milton Park and some of its land from King Ranch, which they finally sold in 1985. It is now a hotel/condominium with two golf courses under construction.

With Donald Friend at Bilgola in 1981. Photo: Richard Walker

Our first sight on a wet and windy day was after forcing our way up a very overgrown drive which had not been used for a number of years, the back drive to the stable buildings having been thought more convenient. Walking through the dark and gloomy rooms, denuded of furniture, I tried to remember what it had looked like when June had been the chatelaine and to imagine how it could be given a new lease of life. I was encouraged in this by Terry and by the time we joined Edwina and Peter for lunch at Milton Park, I had pretty well decided to make an offer. When my offer of £15 000 for the house and ten acres with an option to buy another ten within three years was accepted, I went through the usual 'What on earth have I taken on?' syndrome, but soon recovered as I got involved in the redecoration which was being done by Leslie Walford.

Some six months later, in the winter of 1964, I commissioned Donald Friend to paint a mural in the dining room. I had met Donald a few years earlier when he was contemplating leaving Ceylon, where he had been living and painting for some years, to return to his native land for a while. He would come round to my Retford Hall flat, spread squares of masonite, on which were painted studies for the larger of the two murals, on the floor and proceed with much gesticulation and laughter to develop its theme, which was the four Elements. Fire has the city of Sydney spreading out between his legs, while Water encloses a dinner party in his arms with the identities of the guests indicated by their thought balloons. Above them are Air and Earth, the female figure, with a multitude of depictions and allusions — classical, mythological and contemporary — swirling about them.

The smaller mural over the fireplace contains some family history with Ginahgulla, my beach house at Bilgola and Retford Park set on swags of turf supported by caryatids and centaurs. There are three Muse-like creatures with attributes altered from classical tradition: Prosperity has her arm round a printing press, Literature caresses a kangaroo while Philosophy crowns my father with a laurel wreath. Nearby, Pan is piping to a Fauntleroy figure while a determined lady with a butterfly net is chasing a symbolic butterfly. These have been identified as young Warwick and Mary, but it was the artist's interpretation, not mine.

Donald took two months to complete the murals, working in two-week stretches in a virtually unfurnished house, with me appearing with baskets of goodies at the weekend. He was interrupted from time to time by curious locals, who had heard stories of pornographic paintings, trooping up the long drive. The dining room, which contains works only by Donald — other than the Russell Drysdale wartime portrait — is now a memorial to him as he died in 1989.

I stayed a number of times at his extraordinary and beautiful Balinese retreat,

Batu Jimber, on the coast near Sanur and, on my first visit, was housed in a small pavilion formerly occupied by a Rajah's fighting cocks. As Donald's establishment grew, so did the standard of my accommodation, and the last building he erected was designed after the judgment hall at Klungkung, with a broad outside stairway leading to an open pavilion on the roof.

Here, seated in oriental splendour and dressed in the local sarong, we were served gin and fresh lime juice by one of the boys forming his household. I was present when the local Buddhist priest blessed the building in an elaborate ceremony which was followed by a superb performance of parts of the Ramayana legend by some of Bali's best dancers.

Donald left a series of diaries, started during the war, of which I was the custodian for some years. They form a brilliant social document of the times, written with all the wit, animation, vitality, powers of description, humour and, in places, wickedness that were part of his personality. They should be published as fully as possible, in spite of potential problems with the laws of defamation. John McDonald's assessment of him in the *Herald* was headed 'Minor Major Life, Major Minor Art' and the view was expressed by several commentators that he would eventually be more renowned for his diaries than his paintings. As a draughtsman, Donald had few equals and in an often dull and conformist age, he was a larger-than-life character who will be greatly missed. Before leaving Bali he established all the boys who worked for him, together with their families, on income-producing farms. A ninety-minute film entitled *The Prodigal Australian* and produced by Don Bennetts has been released on ABC television and for a short commercial run to general acclaim.

To return to the beginnings of my art collecting, when I had settled into Retford Hall at the end of 1957, I began to look round the local scene. My interest in cubist and non-figurative painting had been aroused by a large retrospective exhibition of Georges Braque at the 1956 Edinburgh Festival. This was a real eye-opener for me, and greatly influenced my early collecting.

Hanne had introduced me to the works of John Passmore before I went to Glasgow and the *Herald* art critic at the time, Wallace Thornton, provided a further impetus towards the works of Ian Fairweather, John Olsen and Godfrey Miller. I acquired paintings by these four and at the same time became interested in William Dobell, Russell Drysdale, Sidney Nolan and Rupert Bunny.

As well as buying their paintings, I came to know a number of the artists. Through the Clune family, I became friends with Bill Dobell and Tas and Bonnie Drysdale who, together with Passmore, Miller and Olsen, were all periodic visitors to my flat. Frank Hodgkinson, Carl Plate, Stan Rapotec and Leonard Hessing were soon added as weighty representatives of abstract expressionism, while Sali Herman (his wife Paulette had given me French lessons when I was about nine), Charles Blackman and Leonard French joined the figurative side of the collection. James Gleeson, writing in *Art and Australia* in 1965, makes the point that although my collection covered a broad segment of Australian artistic activities, it was still only a segment and the exclusions as much as the inclusions reflected the personal taste of the collector. He describes my only concession to pop-assemblage, Colin Lanceley's *Atlas*, as standing awkwardly like a guest uncertain of his welcome. Nearly twenty-five years later, Atlas found a companion, a Lanceley painting, *James' Garden — Autumn, Winter, Spring*, with sculpted collages inspired by my Bowral garden.

Gleeson notes the absence of any paintings from the colonial period, but these were to come later when an increasing interest in European art of the seventeenth and eighteenth centuries drew me to examine the Europeans painting here in the middle years of the nineteenth century. Such painters included Conrad Martens, Eugene Von Guérard and Louis Buvelot. Here, the contribution of Frank McDonald must be acknowledged. He firmly steered public interest back to the colonial era with an opening exhibition devoted to Martens in his new Clune Galleries, appropriately sited in Macquarie Street. Frank rescued Von Guérard from obscurity in a Vermeer-like operation after considerable research by him and his staff.

These works naturally led on to my acquiring, during the 1970s, examples of the Heidelberg quartet: Arthur Streeton, Tom Roberts, Fred McCubbin and Charles Conder. These were the first truly Australian artists who painted the country as it really was, rather than through European eyes with, in some cases, eucalypts resembling conifers. They have been given the rather misleading description of Australian 'Impressionists'.

Gleeson quotes me as saying that in order to collect contemporary painting intelligently and well, one must live in the country in which it is produced and have an intimate knowledge of what is going on. This explains the direction my collecting of paintings took up to the mid 1960s, but I had been expanding in other directions with some European sculpture (Rodin and Epstein), as well as Thai and Khmer bronzes and stone and terracotta statues, encouraged by Robert Haines who maintained a standard of excellence at the David Jones Gallery, specialising in these areas as well as furniture and the decorative arts of the seventeenth and eighteenth centuries.

I visited Bangkok quite often in those days as I used to stay with an English friend, Lionel Thompson, who ran a school there. He lived for a time in the former abbot's house of a monastery on the Bangkok river, which had a spectacular view as well as authentic early Thai furnishings. Since those early days in Bangkok, the Oriental side of my collecting has expanded to include my interest in Japan, with emphasis on paintings and screens of the Muramachi, Momoyama and Edo periods and sculpted wooden figures of the two earlier periods.

Two people in particular started me thinking about collecting European art works: the first was Gladys Penfold-Hyland, who had succeeded her late husband Frank as chairman of Penfolds Wines. I have mentioned that Gladys' daughter, Rada Russell (later Collins), together with her husband Paddy, who was a marvellous character and a good friend, had been very kind to me in my Oxford days. Gladys, as well as being a very astute businesswoman, had a fine collection of English and Dutch paintings of the seventeenth and eighteenth centuries, together with important English silver, porcelain and furniture of the eighteenth century. Apart from the Felton Bequest at the National Gallery of Victoria and the Haywood Collection in South Australia, it was the only significant collection in this field in the country. Appropriately, it is now in the South Australian Gallery, in which state Dr Rawson Penfold planted his first grape vines in the 1840s.

During my Retford Hall days, I used to dine with Gladys about once a month at Toftmonks, her beautiful old house at the end of Elizabeth Bay Square. She was a bouncy little lady of great wit, with a highly individual sense of humour as well as considerable knowledge in the area of her collection, and many enjoyable evenings were spent by me absorbing all of these aspects.

My second influence was John McDonnell, a Queenslander who had early left his native State for greener intellectual and artistic pastures and became the European adviser for the Felton Bequest. A man of enormous knowledge, and quiet charm with a quirky sense of humour, he was highly respected in the British and European art worlds and was one of my mother's oldest friends. She always said that some of the great experiences of her life were the trips she took with him to all sorts of places of cultural and historic interest, from Portugal to Mexico. In my Oxford days he used to take me to lunch or dinner at the Ritz or the Marlborough and Wyndham Club, and there another seed was planted. In the 1960s it germinated firmly in two directions: Old Master drawings and French eighteenth-century furniture. But if the interest and desire to possess were there, the process was gradual.

In 1964 I went with John Russell, the art critic of the *Sunday Times*, to an exhibition of Master drawings at Agnews in Bond Street. There my eye lit upon the Hon. Frederick North, drawn by Ingres in Rome in 1815. The son of Lord North, who 'lost' the North American colonies, he was a delightful eccentric, clearly evident from his face. One of his activities was to found an English university at Corfu where, having designed sumptuous robes for himself as Chancellor which he continued to wear around Europe, he lost interest in the project. This was my first venture into the Old Master field. It was to be followed initially by other drawings, French and Italian of the eighteenth century, and, when I felt I could afford them, paintings of the seventeenth century as well, including several of the Dutch school. More recently, fifteenth-century Germany has been added to the list, but the emphasis now is on French and Italian paintings of the eighteenth century — both landscapes and portraits.

I have bought primarily from Agnew and Colnaghi, and once or twice from Heim, as I think it is important to stick to the same dealers once a relationship of mutual trust and confidence has been established. I say 'mutual' because in my view the best art dealers prefer their finest works to go where they will be most appreciated and this requires knowledge and discrimination on the part of the purchaser. One of the most satisfying aspects of collecting is the acquisition of these two qualities which, over the years, enable one to build up confidence in one's own judgment. This is the mark of collectors like Baron Thyssen and Paul Mellon; it is an educational process which does not stop as long as one remains a collector. By all means take advice but the final decision should be one's own alone: having someone else to do the job is not what forming a collection is about.

Like the Japanese, art dealers sometimes hide away their best things until they have sized one up — I recall talking to Eugene Thaw in New York for about twenty minutes before he would show me anything. Getting to know the people one deals with over the years is one of the pleasant sides of collecting.

Julian Agnew and his late father, Sir Geoffrey; Richard Knight and Nicholas Hall at Colnaghi (and Edmondo di Robillant, formerly of Colnaghi and now with his own business), have played an important part as my collection has grown. So indeed has John Partridge, through whose doors I was steered many years ago by John McDonnell and from whom I have bought most of my French furniture, with occasional forays to Malletts, from whom I have recently bought some important English pieces.

Learning from other collectors is also part of the educational process. While staying with Hienie Thyssen at La Favorita in Lugano, I spent a whole day looking at his great collection and talking to his curators and conservators, which was a fascinating and valuable experience. Interestingly, I read not long ago that the collection was to be moved to Spain and housed in the former Villahermosa family palace, next to the Palace Hotel in Madrid.

My interest in art was to a great degree both stimulated and fostered by the many trips I made over the years, especially in seeking out the art treasures

Prague in April 1974. Guilford Bell, Denis Kelynack, Elizabeth (their city guide) and Billy McCann.

of Europe. The following account, which brings together the experiences of several such trips mainly in Eastern Europe, is a good example of this stimulus, derived from the people I met as well as the treasures themselves.

They say it is worth going to Dresden just to see Raphael's *Sistine Madonna* and they are right, although many treasures that escaped the appalling British fire-bombing raid on 13–14 February 1945 are still to be seen there. 'They', in my case, was Sir Steven Runciman, famous historian of the Crusades, Constantinople and the Ottoman Empire. Steven weaves his spells from a Scottish border castle in Ayrshire dating variously from the twelfth to the fifteenth century and equipped with several ghosts. He is gifted with psychic powers and, by reading my palm around 1960, gave a largely accurate forecast of my career — unfortunately, I did not entirely believe it. However, talking to him before travelling in Europe is a wise precaution, particularly eastern Europe where he spent much of his career.

One of my early childhood memories was seeing Charlie Chaplin's *The Great Dictator* (1938). An early scene with a simple, farming family having a peaceful meal outside their cottage in an idyllic countryside, only to be brutally interrupted by invading planes and soldiers, imprinted itself indelibly on my five-year-old mind. From then on, the countries of eastern Europe became

Richard Walker, Mervyn Horton and James Fairfax in Leningrad, looking across the Neva to the Winter Palace, June 1979.

enveloped for me in a romantic haze: whether it was a case of Bohemian knights, Transylvanian castles, or simply humble peasants ploughing their fields by the Danube, there they all were, waiting to be rescued like Andromeda chained to the rock waiting for Perseus to save her from the sea-monster. Perseus, as we know, turned out to be a fat Russian thug with a bristling moustache, only later seen in his true guise. My feelings were made stronger in my prep-school days at Edgecliff, when a belligerent Miss Van examined the various front lines at our morning wartime sessions.

My desire to visit these places was not to be satisfied until 1979 when the *Viking Star*, with Mervyn Horton, Richard Walker and myself aboard, stopped at the Polish port of Danzig, an appropriate place as the existence of the 'Polish Corridor' was a contributory cause of World War II. In spite of war damage, the restored centre of the old city, with its high-gabled sixteenth- and seventeenth-century houses, narrow crooked streets, canals, gothic churches and squares with fountains, was just what I had expected. Our visit ended with a recital on the beautiful baroque organ in one of the churches. Our party, joined by Billy McCann, then went on to Berlin.

The city induced in me a singular depression. Neither the magnificent collection in the Dahlem Museum, that in the palace of Charlottenburg, nor even Nefertiti, could compensate for the flashy vulgarity of the Kurfurstendamm, the desolation of the Tiergarten district and ultimately the horror of the Wall itself. To me it was as though Sydney was cut in half at the foot of William Street, with the beleaguered residents of the eastern and southern suburbs only having access to a couple of museums.

We shot through Checkpoint Charlie in a large Daimler in about ten minutes — our driver knew all the guards on both sides — and my mood changed immediately. Here was historic Berlin, albeit grey and depressed with the population the same, but driving down the Unter den Linden with its fine nineteenth century buildings either intact or restored, there was a sense of history. Most of the museums, including the Berlin State Museum containing the wonderful Altar from Pergamon, are situated on the Spree island which is, unfortunately, dominated by the hideous Marx-Engels-Platz, where the royal palace of the Hohenzollerns stood until demolished by the East German government after the war. One sad little central portico remains from which Karl Liebknecht proclaimed the founding of the German Republic in 1919.

The main purpose of our visit was to see the palaces at Potsdam, which were a two-hour drive from East Berlin (or a fifteen-minute one from West Berlin, if a different border crossing had been permitted). Their location had saved them from the Russian tanks, even if it was to place them firmly in the German

Democratic Republic. Potsdam still has a pleasant village atmosphere, dominated by Frederick the Great's enchanting Sans Souci which has some of the finest surviving Rococo interiors in Europe. Both here, where we had a picnic lunch in the palace gardens, and at the vast Neues Palais, we were greatly assisted by Nancy Mitford's scholarly and entertaining life of Frederick the Great, one of the most interesting monarchs that any dynasty had produced. An incongruous note is struck by the mock-Tudor Cecilienhof, given to the last Crown Prince as a wedding present by his father. He certainly had not inherited the taste of his eighteenth-century predecessor. The Potsdam conference was held there in 1945 and around the conference room there are life-sized cut-out photographs of the main participants in various poses.

In 1983, leaving our somewhat depressing hotel (there is now an Intercontinental) in Dresden, Richard and I walked through the broad Altmarkt towards the River Elbe, and were immediately conscious of a different atmosphere to that of East Berlin. Even though most of the surrounding buildings were destroyed, the people — the young wearing jeans (with many toting guitars) — looked cheerful and relatively brightly dressed. At night we were to find the bierkellers crowded with the guitar players.

Turning hurriedly to the left past the ugly Kulturpalast one comes to the Zwinger, the glory of Dresden Baroque architecture, built by Poppelmann between 1711 and 1732 for Augustus the Strong of Saxony and now completely restored. The pavilions forming the square have housed the bulk of the Saxon Royal collections since Augustus, the most famous being the porcelain collection with its magnificent Meissen, including the remarkable white glaze animals by Kaendler and Kirchner. The rhinoceros is the size of a real baby rhinoceros.

Here, too, is the collection of Old Masters, amongst which we found the object of our pilgrimage, the superb *Sistine Madonna* which must be one of the less well-known of the world's masterpieces. This wonderful painting with Virgin and Christ-child soaring in heroic fashion to the top of the clouds is described by Professor Otto Stelzer as expressing the Classic spirit of the High Renaissance at its purest and achieving a synthesis of the human and the Divine. One aspect of this synthesis is two singularly bored cherubs, leaning in a world-weary way on a parapet at the feet of Pope Sixtus II and Saint Barbara, who flank the figure of the virgin.

From the Zwinger one passes the now reopened opera house, built to the designs of Semper in 1871, to reach the important Baroque cathedral built by Chiaveri between 1739 and 1754 with its altarpiece *Ascension of Christ* by Mengs. The cathedral has also been restored but the worst casualty was the Schloss or Residenz next door. A gutted facade is all that remains of what was an architectural and decorative history of Saxony and its electors and kings from the fifteenth to the nineteenth centuries. The Government of the GDR was planning to rebuild it (and hopefully this will still be done under the new, united government), but of course its priceless interiors are lost for ever.

The paintings of Bernardo Bellotto (sometimes confusingly called Canaletto after his more famous uncle Antonio) give an exact depiction of Dresden's historic centre by the Elbe, and there has been enough restoration to give some idea of what it was like. There are still palaces along the Bruhl Terrace overlooking the river and one of them, the Renaissance Albertinum, contains another chunk of the Royal collections. The miraculous survival of what was virtually five hundred years of collecting in one of the richest and most civilised, but by no means the most powerful, courts of Europe is something for which we should be eternally thankful. The wealth came largely from Saxony's silver and semi-precious stone mines and, apart from the paintings and porcelain, the collections include jewellery, bronzes, armour, prints and drawings and decorated gold, silver and jewelled Baroque and Rococco objects, functional and ornamental.

The scope of the collections makes them unique and a large selection went on tour in the United States in 1978–79 under the title of 'The Splendor of Dresden'. Included was the most precious of all the treasures, those of the Grunes Gewolbe or Green Vault, named after the rooms, decorated in the colours of Saxony, where they were housed in the Schloss.

Dresden is a perfect centre from which to explore other parts of this fascinating and little-visited corner of Europe. Forty-five minutes by boat upstream at Pillnitz there are a group of palaces — two by Poppelmann, built in 1720 — set in an early nineteenth century garden and this is the most popular excursion from Dresden. Leipzig is half an hour away by car, and much of the old town here survives, including the church of St Thomas where J. S. Bach composed some of his greatest works: the *Mass in B Minor*, the *St Matthew Passion* and the major organ preludes and fugues.

It is interesting in view of my earlier remarks on the free and happy atmosphere of Dresden that the East German President as I write, Hans Modrow, was for many years mayor of that city and obviously played a leading role in its way of life. I was intrigued, too, to read an article in the *Australian* written from Leipzig in December by Nicholas Rothwell, after my own visit there. Leipzig, he says, with its enormous demonstrations burns with political ardour as the 'capital of the revolution of 1989' and West Germans are asking: 'Why Leipzig?' Rothwell answers the question:

For the people of the city it is no mystery; their history provides the answer. One student protester looked upwards to the skyscraper housing the Karl Marx University: 'They thought they were teaching us Marxism, but there is the master we listen to,' and he points to the statue of Johann Sebastian Bach beside St Thomas's Church.

Rothwell says that more than other East German cities, Leipzig retains an overwhelming nostalgic awareness of its pan-German heritage.

Luther preached in these austere churches, Leibnitz taught, Mozart, Beethoven and Wagner all followed in Bach's footsteps, while Goethe set the climactic scene of his version of the Faust story here, in the Auerbach Keller, which survives to this day with a smart bar, aptly named Mephisto, placed temptingly next door.

Two of the most attractive old towns further west in Thuringia are Erfurt and Weimar, both also associated with Bach and the latter also with Goethe and Schiller. As a centre of learning and culture, it was chosen to found the ill-fated Weimar Republic in 1919. The cathedral of Erfurt preserves intact its early fourteenth-century stained glass windows, some of the finest I have seen in Europe, while the Schloss museum at Weimar has a remarkable collection of southern German religious art of the fifteenth and sixteenth centuries. Both towns are delightful to walk through, particularly Erfurt with its mediaeval houses jostling each other on the bridge.

So ended a trip which began with the somewhat cramped luxury (although the dining cars were beautiful and the food excellent) of the Simplon-Orient Express to Venice where the Cipriani, before dispatching me to an attic room, told me I could not afford a larger one. Ever since I have stayed happily at the Gritti — and who wants a swimming pool in Venice? There was scarcely time to use it. With us in various parts of the city were the Simpsons and my niece Emily, Jeffrey Smart, Ermes Dazan, Harold Hertzberg, Morson Clift, John and Caroline Laws, and Peter Stafford, who introduced us to some of the Foscari and Franchetti families over lunch at his Giudecca apartment.

The Cipriani at Asolo partly made up for our disastrous reception in Venice, and from there we visited our American friend, Evelyn Lambert, at her Palladian villa at Longa near Vicenza. We had lunch at long tables under the pine trees where her staff, in local peasant costume, spent as much time spraying our ankles against insects as they did serving us.

At Sona near Verona we called on friends, Count Justo Giusti del Giardino and his wife Mats, whom I had last seen in Tokyo where Justo was Italian Ambassador. Their villa at Sona is what I would call 'understated' Palladian, with a double flight of steps leading up to a single-columned arcade beneath the central pediment. Elegant, slightly rundown offices and farm buildings form the other three sides of the square. The 'giardino' from the title is a magnificent seventeenth-century formal garden next to their former palazzo in Verona, which they presented to the city.

Justo was Ambassador to India before Japan and I remember him relating to me, with great gusto, Mrs Gandhi describing to him the various kinds of contraceptives available to her populace, with appropriate gestures for each. 'A very down-to-earth woman,' he said.

This 1983 trip was clearly one of my longer ones as after returning to London for some television rounds, I had a few days at the Brenners Park hotel at Baden Baden before ending up at Bayreuth for my second visit to the Wagner festival. Unlike Wieland Wagner's triumph in the early 1950s, the new Peter Hall production of the *Ring* was trounced by the critics and at several points booed vociferously by the audience. The temperature in the Festspielhaus was well into the hundreds but we returned each night to the comfortable rural atmosphere of Plaum's Posthotel at Pegnitz.

Before departing from Frankfurt for Sydney we had supper with Princess Margaret of Hesse and the Rhine at Wolfsgarten, originally a hunting lodge outside Darmstadt and now one of the few properties remaining to the Hesse family. The history of this ultimately ill-starred family is related in a number of recent books: *Louis and Victoria* by Richard Hough, *Mountbatten* by Philip Ziegler and, in a more revealing way, by Lord Lambton in the first volume of his Mountbatten biography — as I write the second has still to appear. Most of the Hesse family were killed in a plane crash over France in 1937 on their way to England for the wedding of Margaret Geddes to Prince Louis of Hesse. The prospective bride and her fiance were at the airport awaiting their arrival. I had first met Princess Margaret about ten years before when she came to lunch at Retford Park with Sid and Cynthia Nolan, Benjamin Britten and Peter Pears, all of whom had been at the Adelaide Festival. The main thing I recall about the lunch was that Cynthia, whom I liked and admired, refused to utter one word to Mervyn Horton, whom I had placed next to her and whose magazine, *Art and Australia*, had carried an unflattering review of one of her books.

In the Land of Hesse, and particularly around Darmstadt, Princess Margaret is greatly respected and plays an important role in many civic activities. She showed us over Wolfsgarten: the children's house in the garden where Louis Mountbatten and his sisters played with their royal German and Russian cousins, the first private swimming pool in Europe (circular in shape, it had been installed in the late nineteenth century), and the window pane in the drawing room where generations of European royalty had scratched their names with a diamond. Not far from Nicky and Alix were Charles and Diana.

My thoughts on this 1983 trip began with the *Sistine Madonna*, but it is ironic that the very day I am writing this, twenty thousand East Germans are in Budapest awaiting permission to leave Hungary for West Germany. The changes that Mr Gorbachev's glasnost and perestroika are beginning to create in Eastern Europe recall to me the repression existing in the countries I visited. It was worst in Prague, the greatest surviving Baroque city and once the cultural centre of Europe. In 1974, when I went to visit a chillingly Stalinist deputy foreign minister in the Czernin palace, I saw the window from which Jan Masaryk committed suicide — or by other accounts was thrown to his death — in 1948. I thought that little had changed.

Guilford, Denis, Billy and I got the lowdown from our country guide, a remarkable woman and a real maverick, who took us to Carlsbad, Marienbad and Pilsen (to use their German names). Near Marienbad we saw the Metternich Konigswart palace with its famous library. I later met its former owner, Prince Paul Metternich, and his wife, Tatiana, in Madrid. (Recently I heard that following the liberation of Czechoslovakia, the Metternichs were planning to revisit Konigswart.)

Tatiana tells her fascinating story in *Tatiana: Five Passports in a Shifting Europe*, culminating with their escape from the advancing Russians at Konigswart, assisted by the French prisoners of war interned there. With her husband and parents she travelled the 600 kilometres by horse and cart from Konigswart to Johannisberg on the Moselle, where they owned the famous vineyard and castle. It was in ruins when they arrived but has now been restored and the vineyards were intact. Tatiana now illustrates her own books while Paul's great interest, apart from his vineyards, is motor racing.

Tatiana's late sister, Missie, wrote an equally fascinating account of her wartime years in Berlin with the German Broadcasting Service and later the Foreign Office, *The Berlin Diaries 1940–1945 of Marie Vassiltchikov*. She and a number of her friends (including Adam von Trott) formed one of the cores of opposition to Hitler, which many feel were both mistakenly and unjustly ignored by Churchill and Roosevelt. Her description of the Allied bombing raids and life in the ruined city is remarkable. She knew in advance about the July 1944 plot on Hitler's life and many of her friends were executed.

An interesting comparison to that book is the English Christobel Bielenberg's account of her own war years in Germany, *The Past Is Myself*. The latest addition to the accounts of these three remarkable ladies of their wartime experiences, *A Mother's War* by Fey von Hassell, is perhaps the most moving of all. It culminates in the almost miraculous recovery of her two young sons, snatched from her by the Gestapo in 1944, while she, together with some very well-known fellow prisoners, was being shunted from concentration camp to concentration camp. Her father, General Ulrich von Hassell, was executed for his part in the July plot against Hitler.

After the visit to Prague — ice cold in April 1974 — I flew to Bucharest with Richard to see the painted churches of Suceava in Moldavia. Mr Ceaucescu was then regarded as a useful ally, to a degree independent of Moscow, and he had not yet begun his megalomaniacal efforts to tear down everything of historic or architectural value. Little did I think I would see his corpse on television sixteen years later.

The city retained something of its nineteenth-century French flavour and we even saw the Orthodox Patriarch, an imposing figure almost two metres in height and accompanied by his bishops, all in full canonicals, leave his palace and sweep off in a cavalcade of black limousines. Bucharest, however, with apparently jolly gypsies playing and singing in taverns, certainly had a happier atmosphere than Prague.

There are six monasteries, dating from the fifteenth and sixteenth centuries, set in the rolling hills of Bukovina in northern Moldavia. They have a curved apse at the east end and jutting wings or a colonnade at the west, and the exteriors are covered on all four sides with the most incredible frescoes displaying the great events of Christianity from the Old and New Testaments.

There is a particularly vivid day of judgment covering a whole wall, with the righteous ascending to Heaven on a long ladder to receive their reward from a head-magisterial God. On the side, row upon row of angels applaud enthusiastically with the expressions of doting parents. On the other side of the ladder the sinners, repenting too late, are desperately and vainly trying to hang on to it in every imaginable position, like incompetent acrobats. This really gives Michelangelo a run for his money. There is a gentle white-haired saint hanging upside down over a fire, another rolling down a mountain attached to a large wheel and, closer to our times, a dramatic panorama of the fall of Constantinople.

The most important monastery, built by King Stephen the Great in 1488, is Voronet, and the Meridiane publishing house of Bucharest brought out a book on it in 1971. In 1974, all the monasteries were in extremely good condition except on the northern 'weather' side. The Romanian consul, then residing in Caerleon, my great-uncle's former house next door to Ginahgulla, where he gave me Romanian brandy in its elaborately carved dining room, had been very helpful in providing information for my trip. These monasteries could become one of Europe's major tourist attractions and it is to be hoped that the new regime will turn its mind to this in due course.

A final note on my own collection: one beneficial result of Warwick's takeover is that increased resources have enabled me to expand it more rapidly, and in areas which previously I could not have afforded. This applies to the eighteenth century French and Venetian artists — and in one case to post-revolutionary France. I am at present contemplating plans to pass over both my Old Master collection and some of the best of the Australian paintings to public collections.

22

FROM GRANDEES TO
THE YANGTSE GORGES

TRAVELS AND PEOPLE IN SPAIN,
FRANCE AND CHINA 1968–82

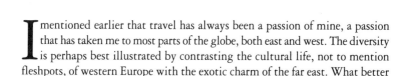

I mentioned earlier that travel has always been a passion of mine, a passion that has taken me to most parts of the globe, both east and west. The diversity is perhaps best illustrated by contrasting the cultural life, not to mention fleshpots, of western Europe with the exotic charm of the far east. What better place to begin than Spain, to me the most fascinatingly diverse country in Europe.

The unique assimilation of the Moorish civilisation with the Roman and Visigothic roots, and that brought by the conquering Catholic monarchs, Ferdinand and Isabella, created a remarkable cultural and social mixture. As a result of this, the Spanish character developed in a totally different way from the rest of Europe. My mother and I came to know the country well through an introduction provided by our friend Billy McCann. Billy was born in Adelaide, brought up in Argentina and later in England (where his father was South Australian agent-general) and worked for many years as a personal assistant to John Loudon, the managing director of Shell. Before the war, however, he was with the British Information Service in Spain, in a capacity involving intelligence work, and was able to come to the aid of many of the friends he made among the old aristocracy, whose lives and property were endangered by the Republican forces.

This is no place to discuss the horrors of the Spanish Civil War, but most of the people I met were basically monarchists, nearly all of whom had lost members of their families in the fighting, who were grateful that Franco (with considerable skill) had kept their country out of World War II. Some were suspicious of 'La Democracia'; indeed the Caudillo was no supporter of it, but it is clear that almost the whole population enthusiastically support his chosen successor, King Juan Carlos, who has wrought such a remarkable transformation in Spain. Franco knew more about his native race than he has been given credit for.

Billy introduced us to his closest friends, the Santa Cruz family. Billy's sister Mollie correctly observed that if one is introduced to certain circles in Spain, it is very difficult to avoid making any account sound like a monumental exercise in name-dropping. I make no excuse for this; the two hundred or so grandees are officially recognised as part of the Spanish state, as are their rank, titles and privileges. The privileges have never taken a legislative form, but from their number the monarch chose his advisors and commanders. These privileges consist of such things as the right to fly flags on their cars (which none of them do) and once included diplomatic status which the socialist government has removed from them. Indeed, they lead quiet and unobtrusive lives but are regarded as being very much part of the history and tradition of Spain. An occasional event, such as the recent marriage of the Duchess of Alba's son, the Duke of Huescar to Matilde Solis, may attract vast crowds — in this case outside the Cathedral of Seville.

Casilda Santa Cruz uses the title of her ancestor, the first Marqués, who commanded the Spanish fleet at the battle of Lepanto in 1571, a great victory for the Christian forces over the Turks and decisive for the future of Europe. However, she could have used quite a few other titles both older and more senior, but while her mother, the Duquesa de Santo Mauro, was still alive she chose not to. Following her mother's death two years ago, she still does not, although recently — with royal approval — she conferred another family title, Duque de San Carlos, on her eldest son, the Marqués de Viso. Her late husband Pepe, whose name was Villaverde, took the more senior title of his wife, as is the custom, and as happened with the Albas. All this may seem a quaint survival in a democracy but, as I have emphasised, the Spanish sense of their history is very strong.

The sixteenth century Santa Cruz palace, one of the last in Madrid both to survive and be inhabited by the family, occupies a block in the Calle San Bernadino in the old part of the city. It was the custom of the old Duquesa to receive family and close friends nearly every evening between 6 pm and 9 pm, seated in a gallery-like sitting room under Sir Philip Laszlo's portrait of Queen Victoria Eugenie, whose lady-in-waiting she had been for many years. Here my mother and I were bidden with Billy at 7 pm, normally afternoon tea-time but Casilda, with innate Spanish courtesy, had placed in one corner a very small chromium cocktail trolley laden with drinks, which looked somewhat incongruous in the grand room. This was the start of our friendship and, under Queen Ena's regal gaze, we were to meet over several visits all of Casilda and Pepe's family and many of their friends.

Among the first was the Duquesa's sister. Called by all, and eventually us, 'Tia Lily', she was (she died in 1990) the Condesa de San Martin de Hoyos and after years at the San Bernardino evenings, she finally established them in her own fine house in the Via Almagro. The other was Paul Metternich's ninety-year-old mother, who had reverted to the title of Condesa de Castillejo and lived in another wing with her companion, the Polish Countess Marysia Borkovska. She lived to be ninety-nine and was delighted when I told her I had visited Konigswart in Czechoslovakia, where she had lived with her first husband. Here, in Madrid, I also first met Paul and Tatiana Metternich.

Pepe and Casilda's three sons and daughters-in-law, their daughter who works for Christies, and Pepe's sister the Condesa Isabel Orizaba, were all in and out during our visits. After her mother's and husband's deaths, Casilda is now doing up part of the San Bernardino for herself, while her eldest son Alvaro and his family are also moving in — so the family tradition continues. The Santa Cruz family owns a farm just outside Toledo and a large country house, Las

M.E. Fairfax and the ladies of Spain at the San Bernardino palace, 1979. Condesa de San Martin de Hoyos, Condesa de Orizaba, Marquesa de Santa Cruz, Duquesa de Santo Mauro.

Fraguas, designed by an English architect (most likely a follower of Sir Edward Lutyens), near Santander in the north. They also owned palaces at Viso del Marques near Ciudad Real south of Madrid, and at Trujillo near the Portuguese border. On our biennial trips to Spain, which began early in the 1970s, we went to all these places.

We drove to Viso from Toledo, where Casilda and Pepe had lent us their delightful farmhouse, surrounded by olive groves, with a nice couple who spoke no English (fortunately we had Billy) in attendance and a labrador called Paloma, whose name I took for my Rhodesian Ridgeback. We were visited there by Rupert and Anna Murdoch, who were in Madrid for a conference. Anna did a 'dry run' of Toledo's main treasures the previous day before taking Rupert, who is not noted for being a sightseer. I have never known him more relaxed, so it is a pity he does not seem able to do it more often.

We found Viso a vast Renaissance pile in the middle of totally bare countryside, a strange place for Casilda's distinguished naval ancestor to choose. In spite of his advanced age, the admiral had been appointed by Philip II to command the Spanish Armada in 1588, but died before the fleet sailed and was replaced by the much less competent Duke of Medina Sidonia. As was shown in the magnificent exhibition at the Royal Naval College at Greenwich in 1988, had he lived, the course of European history might have been different. Viso is now owned by the Spanish Navy, but Casilda retains the use of an apartment designed as a replica of the captain's cabin of a sixteenth century galleon. She also has, in the San Bernardino, the pair of two metre lanterns from her ancestor's cabin and two he removed from the cabin of the Sultan's commander at Lepanto.

At Trujillo, where we stayed with decorator Duarte Pinto Coelho, the fourteenth-century castle had been given to an order of nuns who were delighted to see their benefactress again. Casilda keeps an apartment here, too, where she occasionally goes into retreat with the nuns. Las Fraguas, where the family spends the summer, has been unchanged since it was first built for the Duquesa and her husband at the request of King Alfonso XIII, who had a summer palace at Santander and wanted his close friends nearby. The interior is the epitome of an English gentleman's house of the Edwardian era. Alfonso's palace, resembling a wedding cake (it was in fact a wedding present from the Spanish government and people), is now a hotel cum golf club, but the Duquesa's Edwardian pile continues its family life in comfortable somnolence surrounded by chestnut trees in the Spanish summer sun.

It was actually early autumn in 1976 when my mother, Billy and I first stayed there. The architect must have been slightly influenced by his Spanish surroundings as the garden front, with two very Cotswold-looking, shallow,

Las Fraguas, the Santo Mauro summer house near Santander in 1976.

high-gabled wings, has between them, on the ground floor, a colonnaded veranda which could come from Seville. Country mealtimes were happily earlier than Madrid, lunch being at 2 pm and dinner at 9 pm with the staff drawn from the local villages. The younger ones were sent on to the San Bernardino where the bright lights tended to lure them away from 'service'.

A number of interesting guests passed through during our stay, including the Archduchess Margarita of Austria who had spent the war in a Japanese prison camp in Shanghai. She lived for part of the year nearby in Santillana del Mar. When she arrived for lunch she had difficulty in preventing the Duquesa, then well into her eighties, from dropping the curtsey she thought appropriate to a descendant of the Emperor Charles V. I later called on her in Rome where she lived under her married name of Marchesa Taliani in a secluded villa with a wonderful view on the top of the Aventine hill. She was an intelligent, strong-minded and delightful woman. Another visitor at Las Fraguas was the 'Bunker Duchess', widow of the Prime Minister General Castello Branco, who had been blown up in his car while leaving mass in Madrid.

Also at Santillana, living in a sixteenth-century tower, was Casilda's cousin the mayor, the Marquesa de Torralisa, who also turned out to be the active owner of a number of local newspapers. Near Santillana del Mar are the wonderful painted caves of Altamira which have been dated to the mid-Magdalenian period, between 15 000 and 14 000 BC. The prehistoric artists have in some cases used the rock formations to give a three-dimensional effect to their red-ochred representations of charging or fighting bison, their heads and bodies clearly and forcefully delineated in black. Then there are horses and deer delicately depicted with skill and grace. The caves are now only open to scholars and researchers of the period.

We drove on to Santiago de Compostella by way of Leon and arrived at the Hospice de los Reyes Catolicos a day before the Feast of St James, so the place was jumping with pilgrims and sightseers. It is the only time of the year when the monks swing the cathedral's six-foot high censer of cast silver the entire length of the two transepts from ceiling to ceiling. It was a breathtaking if slightly alarming experience, as one had visions of it sailing through one of the stained glass windows at each end.

Armed by Casilda with a letter to the Duquesa de Medinacelli, we visited her at one of the family estates at Oca outside Santiago. We got there on a Sunday, just in time to see her, with her son and the priest, processing along a balustraded walkway leading from the first floor of the castello to an elaborate seventeenth century Baroque chapel. She waved gaily to us and told us to walk round the gardens — she was not to know that two of the three of us were Catholics. The superb water gardens descended in a series of terraces with stone statues and bridges topped with large blue and white urns trailing white geraniums. *Pace* the mass, it was almost a religious experience and we finally joined our hostess, her son and the priest in the house for several glasses of *jerez*.

Through Mimi Medinacelli, we were received two years later by her husband at their famous Casa de Pilato in Seville, the design of which was traditionally inspired by the palace of Pontius Pilate at Jerusalem. Seville, with its Moorish architecture and atmosphere, has always been one of my favourite Spanish cities, but the two repositories of some of Spain's finest paintings are sometimes neglected by visitors.

The Hospital Santa Caridad contains, in my view, Murillo's best works. In *Moses Bringing Water from the Rock* and *The Miracle of the Loaves and Fishes*, the people of Israel are shown as earthy Spanish peasants with none of the sentimentality he shows in his later work. There, too, are the grim paintings of Valdes Leal, with their vivid symbols of death and the beckoning grave. *Triumph of Death*, in which death has a coffin tucked under his skeletal left arm as he clambers over some visible emblems of the vanities and pomps of this life, is particularly vivid.

Peace and tranquillity are restored by a visit to the miraculous Zubarans at the Museo de Bellas Artes. This is housed in the magnificent convent of the Casa Grande de la Merced dating back to 1612 — surely one of the world's finest museum buildings. This is where the greatest Zubarans, Murillos and Valdes

Leals are found.

Our Spanish trip ended that time with a drive to the Domecq Bodegas at Jerez, where we stayed at the magnificent Domecq guesthouse, formerly the family palace. Manolo and Jose Domecq gave us a fascinating tour of the Bodegas, which included a luncheon table groaning with the best of Spanish food and wine, especially their own products. After inscribing my name on a vast barrel of *jerez*, we made one last call at the fourteenth century castillo of Arcos de la Frontera, whose owner, the Marquesa de Tamaron, we had met at Jerez. Gazing from its battlements down to the river crawling hundreds of metres below seems an appropriate way to leave Spain, to which I have devoted far more space than I intended.

Before leaving Europe I shall return briefly to France, a country with which I have always felt a bond because of our French 'in-laws' and my mother's six-year residence in Paris.

I was to get to know a slightly different aspect of French life through a remarkable woman, Claire Clémence, Comtesse de Maille, known to her friends as Clé Clé. She was an anthropologist who turned up in Sydney in the 1960s, having spent some time studying various native tribes in the jungles of New Guinea. I went to see her in Paris, where she lived in a large house near the Boulevarde St Germain with her mother, the Marquise, and immediately found myself swept up into a whirl of glamorous parties with some well-known names. She took me to a grand ball given by the Guy de Rothschilds at Ferrières, their sumptuous house outside Paris, which seemed to be floating in the air as enormous transparent silk panels wafted up and down its facade. There I met the Duke and Duchess of Windsor, who were later to invite me to their house, the small chateau at 4 Route de Champ d'Entraînement in the Bois de Boulogne, leased from the city of Paris for a nominal sum. I found both of them charming and interesting and always enjoyed seeing them. As I write, the Windsors' reputation seems to have sunk to an all-time low, with recent books not maintaining the admirable balance of Francis Donaldson's account in *King Edward VIII*. By all means let us have the former Prince of Wales warts and all, but let us still have some sympathy with the terrible predicament faced by them both — even if it was largely of their own making. He is not the first person to prove unequal to an inheritance, indeed he was sensible enough to get out of it before he could make a botch of it.

Once, sitting next to the Duchess at a dinner given by Princess Lubomirski at Maxim's (it included several of the former Bourbon royal family whom, I was interested to note, were addressed by their full titles), we had quite a talk about

Australia, which she said she longed to visit as the Duke had enjoyed his visit so much as Prince of Wales. Unfortunately it never came about (there would have been some interesting questions of protocol), but one reason for the then Prince's enjoyment was undoubtedly Mollie Sargood. I can still see his jaunty little figure with silver-gold hair and cigarette holder stuck up in the air, reminiscing about 'Maarlie' in his American accent.

There was a totally unfounded story that Mollie's son, Tony Chisholm, who was the Duke's godson, was in fact his own illegitimate son. When Tony, who bore a resemblance to the Prince, was astonished to be questioned by people in London about this story, he asked his Aunt Sheila Milbanke for an explanation. Lady Milbanke replied that if he were the Prince's son his mother must have been an elephant, as it took three years for him to be produced. Tony Chisholm was born in October 1923, while the Prince of Wales was in Sydney on the *Renown* for ten days in 1920. The Prince was certainly very smitten with Mollie Little, but it was understood that she was shortly to marry Roy Chisholm. She and the Prince went out several times with her closest friend Ursula Caterell (mother of my brother-in-law Philip Simpson) and Lord Louis Mountbatten. Indeed, Lord Mountbatten invited Ursula Simpson to dinner at Admiralty House on his last visit to Sydney, but, as she did not then go out at night, she suggested tea would be more appropriate.

Clé Clé took me to visit the magnificent Louis XIII palace on the Ile St Louis, part of which was then leased by Arturo López-Wilshaw. This wonderful and rare example of a seventeenth century 'hotel particuliere' has had over the years of this century a number of distinguished tenants, including the Rothschild and Polish Czartoryski families, Charles de Bestigui and Baron Alexis de Redé. I can still picture Clé Clé lying full-length in the back of her car en route to a 'headdress' party given by Helene Rochas at the Pré-Catalan in the Bois, her head with a sixty-centimetre bejewelled Marie-Antoinette wig and hair-do protruding from the window.

I cannot leave Paris without a mention of two of my closest 'international' friends, Ian and Nicole Bedford, who have a *pied-à-terre* there at the Quai d'Orléans. I first met them when they brought the 'Treasures of Woburn Abbey' exhibition to David Jones Fine Arts Gallery in Sydney, when Robert Haines was its extremely talented director, having come there after a term as director of the Queensland National Gallery.

Then, as now, English dukes and duchesses were hotly pursued. They did not mind this as they regarded it as part of the job, but to enable them to get away from everyone I lent them my small beach cottage at Bilgola. This established a bond of friendship that has persisted over the years and their now

James Fairfax with Ian and Nicole, the Duke and Duchess of Bedford, at Santa Fé.

peripatetic existence — since handing Woburn over to his son the Marquis of Tavistock — has meant that we have caught up with each other all over the world. Perhaps the best experience was staying at their beautiful ranch near Santa Fé in New Mexico, where they spend about three months of the year. This practice is followed by a number of cultivated Americans from the East who like the pleasant climate, the friendly and unpretentious style of living and the various cultural pursuits, including the deservedly well-known opera. It is a remarkable little corner of the vast American continent and one to which I would always return with great pleasure.

If anyone had asked me during my two trips to China in 1982 and 1986 whether a widespread student protest movement would be brutally put down by the People's Army with considerable loss of life, I think my answer would have been that one only needed to look at events in Tibet to see how the Chinese government of Deng Zhao-Ping dealt with dissent. This is not being wise after the event, but at the time I could not help being aware of the contrast between what we were shown in China and the ruthless suppression, often with loss of life, of various attempts at protest in Lhasa. This was heightened by the sight of a richly caparisoned 'official' Tibetan delegation, which we saw at the recently reopened Temple of Confucius in Beijing in 1986 — an irony indeed. But in 1982 there was still great relief at the ousting of the 'Gang of Four', which four years later, under the apparently benevolent rule of Deng, had solidified into a belief that society would continue to become more open and the economy continue to improve. It should be noted that by then the 'Freedom Wall' had been removed after its brief period as a protest point in Beijing, student riots, however, seemed far away.

Inspired by my mother's stories of her life in China with Pierre Gilly in 1946, getting to China was my other great travel dream, and I can still recall the feeling of excitement I experienced when Richard Walker, John Hahir and I landed at Shanghai on 17 September 1982. After being taken to the exotically grand western suburbs guesthouse, we pushed our way through the milling crowds on the Bund for the obligatory visit to the former Cathay Hotel to see where Noel Coward had written *Private Lives*.

Before taking the train to Souzhou, there was an equally obligatory visit to a spotless commune under the control of a deceptively grandmotherly figure. Souzhou offered our first sight of elegant pavilions in beautiful gardens with their lakes and bridges; along the canals near our hotel were whitewashed houses with overhanging wooden balconies. We also saw at the circus, after some breathtaking acrobats, an unfortunate giant panda riding a bicycle that pulled a cart with some dogs in it.

The four-hour boat trip to Wuxi, on Lake Tai, was via the Grand Canal, constructed from Beijing to Hangzhou by the Tang emperors. It afforded a fascinating glimpse of Chinese life, a river version of the Trunk Road in Kipling's India. The vast number of barges, together with their cheerfully waving human component, contained every imaginable form of produce and livestock, even pet dogs seldom seen elsewhere. In Wuxi, only surpassed by Hangzhou in the magnificence of its setting, we also had the pleasure of seeing part of a surgical operation carried out under acupuncture at its glisteningly clean hospital.

Our train to Zhenjiang, where our group of thirty-five were to board MS

Kun Lun, had a large portrait of Zhou En-Lai on the front of the engine and, as on our first train trip, we were extremely comfortable in heavily stuffed armchair banquettes with tea and cakes. The Zhenjiang Hotel, to the amusement of our American and Canadian travelling companions, had been entirely decorated by an Australian firm and we were surrounded by a full range of Aussie flora and fauna on walls, curtains, bedcovers and even on padded bar chairs — possums for Dame Edna.

We were also surrounded by some extremely fine and ancient temples and pagodas. One of the temples, the Ding Whei, was surprisingly Taoist — one of the very few in China — and parties of schoolchildren were being taken around by very elderly monks. Our final sight was the beautiful Jin Shan, or Golden Hill temple which, as its name indicates, is the colour of gold. With its six-storey red pagoda, it dominates the city.

In the evening we boarded the MS *Kun Lun*, then chartered by Lindblad. It had been used previously by Chairman Mao to entertain visiting heads of state and his cabin, allocated to me following an earlier request, turned out to be monumental in size. There were three of the obligatory 'Mao' armchairs and a vast desk, but while the bathroom had a large marble sunken bath, it was unfortunately impossible to fill it higher than five or six centimetres. The portholes were bullet-proof windows. The decor throughout was comfortable 1930s and the Chinese food, as well as the service, was excellent. Those rash enough to ask for Western cooking were given something inedible at small segregated tables. Many of us had not often travelled in groups before, but this one was by general consent a singularly happy lot and we had some uproarious evenings when the Mai Tais were flying around at the end of dinner. Our trip was perfectly organised by expedition leader Bill Hurst and escort Mikel Edwards, while Dr Peter Van Ness was our knowledgeable Sinologist.

I shall not attempt to describe everything we saw on this fascinating trip, which ended eleven days later in the smoke-blackened city of Chongquing, crawling higgledy-piggledy up the steep hill from the Yangtse. The great engineering feat of the Nanjing-Yangtse Bridge is worthy of mention, as are the Southern Tang and early Ming tombs in that city. The large avenue of guardian deities and animals were more solid and less sophisticated than those at Beijing, and I found them more impressive. A day or so later, we were at Juijiang to visit the little town of Guling in the Lu mountains where two of our company, whose parents had been missionaries here in the 1930s, started talking to a tourist in another group. He turned out to have been a childhood friend, whose parents had also been missionaries in Guling at the same time. They had not seen each other for fifty years. If either party had arrived a day, if not hours, later, they would have missed each other completely.

After Wuhan, with its curious mix of modern industrial city and ancient China so often seen on the Yangtse, we arrived at Shashi on 1 October, China's national day. There the entire population was milling round the central square, all in their best clothes, the children being particularly beautifully dressed. It was certainly a contrast to the grim grandmothers of the communes, who strictly enforced the rule of one child to a family to the point of ordering abortions. Even here, though, few families had more than one child. The previous evening, the captain of the Kun Lun had given a banquet reception with innumerable toasts, so we were still in rather a daze. At the old city of Jingzhou, outside Shashi, we were given the best food we had in China in honour of their national day. Those of us who got up at six am every morning for the Tai Chi classes, rain or shine, on the stern deck, had reason to be grateful we had made the effort.

Just before entering the Gorges we came to China's other great engineering project, the Gezhouba Dam, which was begun in 1970 and completed in 1986. It is a truly amazing sight. One of the largest low-water dams in the world, with the fourth largest hydro-electric power capacity, it seemed an appropriate gateway to the towering majesty and mystery of the Yangtse Gorges, which recalled every painting one had seen of ancient China. We were the first boat through the Gorges after recent floods and we were presented with every kind of wonder: tiny villages clinging to the mountainside, distant temples swathed in mist, hopping goats often pursued by hopping children and junks loaded to the gunwales with the usual cheerfully waving crowd and complement of livestock. We emerged at the Shibao Block after an all-too-short twenty-four hours passing through the three main gorges — the Silhouette, which is the narrowest part with limestone cliffs soaring over us to a height of 500 metres; the Cow Liver and Horse Lung with its strange yellow rock formations; and the Wrongly Opened gorge, where a divine thunderbolt aimed at a dragon created a chaos of wrong directions. The extraordinary stone chop of Shibao had a village at its foot with narrow, winding streets paved with stone blocks. The wooden balconies leaning towards each other were almost Tudor in style. It was our only chance to see an unchanged rural community. Crawling unsteadily up the Block was an eleven-storey temple cum pagoda, each floor containing wooden or stone statues of local deities, which was certainly worth the climb.

We were all sad to leave the *Kun Lun* after ten wonderful days on the Yangtse. The most memorable thing about Chongqing was seeing three voracious giant pandas breakfasting on bamboo shoots at the zoo and the most unmemorable things were our gaudy hotel where nothing worked, and a duck abattoir adjoining the 'restaurant' where we were attempting to eat lunch. Our group flew back to Beijing and tours of the Forbidden City, the Summer Palace and the Great Wall. En route to the last, the ladies had their first experience of army-style lavatories with no partitions where they were able to enjoy a chat with the locals. Some found it disconcerting.

In Beijing I had a particularly interesting lunch with Mr Han Xu and some of his colleagues. He was then Vice-Minister for Foreign Affairs (US and Pacific) and subsequently Ambassador to the United States. He was clearly an extremely able man and I soon learned that one had to be very careful in choosing one's words, as questions and answers are taken absolutely literally. The Chinese meal in a private room at the Beijing Hotel, to which Mr Han helped me himself, was almost the equal of Jingzhou.

We returned to China in November 1986, following an 'S' shaped route from south to north which took in Guilin, Hangzhou, Xi'an and Tai Yuan. Guilin is famous for its Li River, where pinnacles and grotesque little mountains rise sharply from the plains and fields along the bank. It is more intimate than

John Habir on the Li River near Guelin, November 1986.

the splendour of the Yangtse Gorges, but the eighty-kilometre boat trip gives a fascinating impression of a landscape that is uniquely Chinese.

I had always wanted to go to Hangzhou since acquiring an Ian Fairweather painting of it dating to the late 1930s. I was determined to find the great arched bridge with its crowd of townsfolk, peasants and animals passing over it and mountains dotted with temples in the distance. I certainly found it — in fact, I found ten of them, stretching over various parts of the magnificent West Lake, any of which could have been mine. The West Lake, fifteen kilometres in circumference, provides the most perfect example of a traditional and unchanged Chinese vista one could wish for. It is bisected by six of the linking hump-backed bridges and there are several islands, large and small, with their own temples, pavilions and gardens. Even the modern hotels seem to sink back into the hills, while the mountains extend for miles into the distance, until their temple roofs become little red and orange blobs.

It was in this delightful city that I was cured within twenty-four hours of the virulent Beijing flu. When I asked the hotel for a doctor, a Chinese man and woman were at the door of my suite exactly at the appointed time, clad in surgical white from head to toe and wearing masks. I was given a thorough examination with the assistance of interpretation by the hotel manager and they then prescribed a variety of remedies: animal extracts including snake bile, herbal preparations and an antibiotic added at the last minute. Who is to say which was most effective?

So much has been written about Xi'an's famous Qin warriors with the horses and chariots, and examples of them have been exhibited in many parts of the world; all I shall add to this is to say that the great thing in going there is seeing them all together. Walking amongst them and becoming aware of their individuality and the extraordinary range of their expressions is a breathtaking experience, unlike any I have had before. The old city has preserved its walls and gates, with a number of interesting pagodas towering nearby. Xi'an is also noted for Chiang Kai-Shek's imposing residence in the hills. It is from here that he escaped from Mao's soldiers in his pyjamas — our guide gave a highly amusing and certainly libellous account of the whole undignified episode.

We departed for the ancient city of Tai Yuan in what seemed to be an equally ancient Russian plane, furnished and decorated in Chinese Louis Sieze. We were seated at the back on an elegant sofa that did not appear to be attached to the superstructure and were served with tea and Mai Tais. The main attraction of Tai Yuan is the beautiful monastery of Shuanglin, situated about one hundred kilometres from the city and dating back fifteen hundred years to the northern Wei dynasty. It contains some of the finest Soong dynasty Buddhas and other deities in China. Inside its old wooden buildings, wall follows wall of these superb carved figures ranging from delicate Kuan Yins to the massive two-metre high Immortals seated on their thrones. On the way back we had lunch at the old walled town of Ping Yao, which is a wonderful mediaeval survival. The closest approximation to its towering walls that I could think of is Avila in Spain. One got the same sense of startled awe when, rounding a bend in the road, one suddenly came upon them. Inside the walls was a marvellous melee of citizenry, horses and carts, oxen and donkeys, chickens, ducks and geese, and children who clearly had seldom seen 'waiguoren' before — and no cars. Saint Theresa, well used to carting her nuns around the scorching hills and plains of Old Castile in a ramshackle carriage with leather blinds, would indeed have felt at home here. This is the China I want to remember.

23
REPRISE

M y concluding chapter must begin with a final reference to my father and Mary. An assessment of Sir Warwick's life and career must await a knowledgeable and unbiased biographer. However, I think he would regard as the two most significant events in it since the war, his assumption of executive power in the form of the Committee of One in 1969, and his deposition as chairman in 1976. In a recent conversation with me, John Pringle compared the first to Gorbachev taking presidential power in the Soviet Union and the second to the advent of perestroika and the loss of power by the Soviet Communist Party (although he was not, of course, equating the competence of the then management with that of Brezhnev).

I am conscious that the account I have given of the years when Sir Warwick and I were both involved with the company has inevitably concentrated on the more negative areas where either he and I, or he and the management, were in disagreement. The undoubtedly great contribution he made both to the *Sydney Morning Herald* and to the later public company in over sixty years of association must be for someone other than myself to appraise. Although Gavin Souter has certainly performed this task ably in his two books, my father deserves a book to himself. I have said in the preface that our relationship ended in a basic mutual affection and trust. I do not think I shall be proven wrong on this point, but the many ups and downs we experienced in our relationship, both inside and outside the office, certainly affected our careers and lives. It might even have affected the ultimate fate of the company.

The role played by Mary following her emergence on the scene in 1957–58 has been described earlier, but a brief re-examination of her motives is necessary. From the time of their marriage, she worked successfully to change Sir Warwick's concept of his own role in the company, and at first she must have genuinely thought him capable of assuming the command. Henderson was still powerful, but whatever he had contributed in the past, he had had his day. McLachlan was an enemy and whatever his competence, he must be got rid of. James, she considered, did not play a significant part (she was appalled when she discovered the size of my shareholding and the Kinghaven arrangement).

There is no doubt that she held these views and propagated them — she saw herself as restoring her husband to his rightful position, rather than obtaining power herself. She clearly wished to be able to influence him, but it must be said that her support transformed him into a far more formidable figure than hitherto, as anyone who had close experience of him before and after the marriage would accept. As for my own position, I think she recognised her initial impression was incorrect and, after the four years' silence, felt — initially, at any rate — that I was doing a good job as chairman. She stated this specifically in several letters, the last being in late 1986, only months before the takeover plan began to be formulated. I have said that personal relations between us were usually good.

From the mid-1980s, when she began to concentrate on her son's succession, she indoctrinated him with her views about the management and this, combined with the already instilled belief in his own ability, sent him on his way. She said to me at Fairwater in May 1990 that Warwick had never been able to make a decision on his own and clearly she did not allow for his capacity to be influenced by others. This was said in bitterness at a time when the value of her own 50 per cent stake in the privatised company was in danger of being decimated, and she told me she was contemplating taking legal action against him. She was clearly most unhappy about Warwick's attitude to the financing of the John Fairfax Group at this time and what she regarded as his manipulation of her through the various private companies. Relations between mother and son were not then warm.

In November 1990, the John Fairfax Group still owed $1.7 billion to the ANZ, Citibank and the junk bond holders, and looked likely, the following month, to be in breach of the borrowing covenants that stipulated that cash flow be 1.2 times rolling interest cover. So far, Warwick had been unable to obtain a valuation of more than around $1.2 billion for the assets, which was the amount due to the banks alone. He had not been able to attract new equity, even on a basis that would leave him and Mary with a token 5 per cent holding, which the Kelman board were endeavouring to achieve in August. Receivership was in the offing and — irony of ironies — Mark Burrows was advising the banks and Keith Halkerston (from residence in England) had taken the chairmanship in place of the pushed-out Bryan Kelman.

Two weeks later, on Monday 10 December 1990, the John Fairfax Group went into receivership. This was the day for the rollover of $850 million in bank facilities and the two banks had refused a request by the directors to change the terms and roll over the funds for fourteen days. Halkerston and Bill Beerworth[1] felt unable to sign the ninety-day certificate stating that the company could meet its debts as and when they fell due and the receiver, Des Nicholl of Deloitte Ross Tohmatsu, duly moved in. It was believed that Warwick and Mary were about to do a deal with the $450 million junk bond holders, which the banks felt would weaken their position.

I have referred in Chapters 16 and 19 to letters Mary wrote to various newspapers in the welter of publicity — in which I was happy to make my own modest contribution — which followed the appointment of the receiver. There were also interviews with her on television and radio and the whole effect has been rather baffling when one considers the message she may be trying to get across. In defending Warwick or explaining his actions, Mary's problem is that both he and she have a credibility gap. Few people believe that she was not a major force behind the takeover and few people believe that the seed planted by Dougherty late in 1986 fell on virgin soil — some companions were already germinating there.

Her public comments have been somewhat inconsistent and I have noted a clear misstatement of fact and a self-contradiction in her letters (Chapter 19) — in mounting a defence she seems undecided in which role to cast herself and her son. There is that of a doting mother, who would agree to anything for the sake of her son. This involved her casting aside her belief — only now publicly proclaimed and in contrast to her statements on debt during the PIPS proposals — in conservative financing and sacrificing herself to take on risks such as the purchase of the 1.5 per cent shareholding, the basic Tryart agreement and, finally, the committing of her shares in November 1987, after the stock exchange crash, in exchange for the $2.9 million annuity.

It has been pointed out that by refusing to pledge her shares, or indeed by simply accepting Warwick's offer, she could have stopped the takeover as it could not have borne the cost of the payment. To answer this, she has portrayed herself (in an interview in the February 1991 issue of *HQ* magazine) as a victim of her son's determination to succeed at all costs, in spite of her growing distrust of Warwick's advisers.

In order to preserve some shreds of her much-prized reputation as a shrewd commercial operator, she has to veer from this image of the macho Warwick who refused to involve her in the details of the privatisation, to a wimpish one under the control of Dougherty ('He had no idea what he was doing' — *Herald*, 15 December 1990), ironically echoing her son's dilemma in the Tryart case.

Her description of him as being in a desperately vulnerable state through grief over his father's death and worry over his Harvard exams are contradicted by his attitude and demeanour in the lead up to and the course of the bid. Grief I am sure there was, but it did not stop the almost indecent haste with which he moved. Dougherty's own comments throughout — whatever self-interest he may have had in making them — have always supported the concept of Warwick being his own man and, indeed, his arrogant belief in his truly appalling business judgment lends weight to this.

Final judgments are difficult until Warwick chooses to give his own account, but there is no doubt about Mary's desperate attempts to distance herself from all aspects of the takeover. She must certainly be devastated that all the efforts of her son and herself have resulted in the loss of 150 years of family control of one of the world's oldest and most important newspaper empires and the disposal of some of its vital assets. These efforts have also resulted in the decimation of their joint shareholding, which was assessed at around $500 million at the time of the takeover.

As my godmother, Helen Rutledge, wrote to me in September 1987: 'It is always frightening when a child can lay its hand on firearms, and Warwick seems to have lost control before he ever had it.' Whatever Mary's personal conviction in the rightness of her cause, ambition and bad judgment have brought a sad end to her and Warwick. The former proprietor has not even expressed any regrets. It is a melancholy commentary that he did not feel he could send a message of thanks or goodwill to his staff, who have laboured so tirelessly on his behalf for the last three years. One result of his action has been the increased power it has given the Murdoch organisation through the weakening of its only major opposition in this country. It might be appropriate to say at this point that I have never been a Murdoch knocker, regardless of the differences his company and Fairfax have had over the years. He has built a great international media empire from very small local beginnings and was one of the first to realise and achieve the global concept of communications, something for which I do not think he has been given due credit in this country. In the last few months he has been having considerable problems with his level of debt and has been having discussions with his various bankers in an attempt to convert nearly $3 billion of short-term debt out of a total debt of $10.4 billion into long-term debt, having sold a number of non-core assets.

In a filing with the Security and Exchange Commission in January 1991, News Corporation said that it would not have enough money to meet its debts beyond the 30 June balance date and could not generate sufficient funds internally, or borrow further funds. However, after a nerve-wracking round of negotiations, which caused News Corporation shares at one stage to fall to a low of $3.19, the 150 banks in the negotiating syndicate have finally agreed to new arrangements regarding the $10.4 billion debt, although on stringent terms. Our tactics during the H&WT takeover in December 1986-January 1987 forced him to commit his family company, Cruden Investments, to the purchase of Queensland Press and his AGM on 23 October 1990 authorised News Corporation to issue non-voting shares and, if necessary, to arrange for de-listing by the Australian Stock Exchange.

While it appears that Murdoch has surmounted his debt problem, it will indeed be ironic if the only way for him to maintain his controlling share of his company — and this control is regarded as a priceless asset for the company — is recourse to a device that was forbidden the Fairfax company six years ago. I have already stated my belief that had the Stock Exchange and its Listing Committee not been so narrow and obtuse, Warwick might well have been unable to achieve his takeover bid and this country would still have two strong and highly competitive print media companies, although under new ownership this can still be achieved.

A recent article in the *Economist*, surprisingly reprinted in the *Australian*, entitled 'News Corp too big to be a one-man show' quotes Murdoch as making two significant concessions. He said he is willing to issue new voting equity, even if it meant diluting his control — and this following his moves to issue stock with restricted voting rights. Secondly, he would appoint a chief operating officer to whom he would delegate day-to-day management. Alan Kohler in the *Financial Review*, commenting on the importance of these changes: 'Rupert Murdoch has survived his brush with bankruptcy but it was oh, so close', says that the experience must have permanently changed News Corporation and Murdoch's management of it. It is, of course, too early to pass judgment on Murdoch's career while he is still at the helm and likely to be so for some time, but he certainly will take his place among the great media entrepreneurs of this century — I trust it is still possible to use this expression in a non-pejorative sense.

It is true the die was cast by the failure of the Trade Practices Commission to do anything when Murdoch bought the H&WT, but that is water under the bridge and I certainly would never have favoured government intervention then any more than I do now. I cannot see any possible reason why Robert Maxwell should not acquire newspapers in this country, or indeed why overseas interests should not acquire television stations here. Both will have to give the Australian public what it wants — something no government or administrative body can tell it. Murdoch is quite right to describe as 'baloney' Kim Beazley's suggestion that overseas ownership of television stations is somehow going to deprive them of their Australian character.

I can understand the dismay of the people of Victoria in the event of the *Age* passing into overseas ownership — and during the lifetime of the Syme partnership agreement, we in Sydney scrupulously left editorial control in Melbourne — but if no local group is prepared to raise the finance for an adequate bid, I do not see any other alternative. What would Paul Keating have done, I wonder, if Warwick had decided to live mainly in America and take American citizenship? Perhaps the Murdoch example would have given him the necessary protection.

In my public comments since the receivership was announced, I have said the most important consideration is the future of the newspapers themselves. Whether their strength and independence can best be preserved by local groups such as that of Dr Tony O'Reilly[2], Chris Corrigan's Jamison Equity, Melbourne group Jim Leslie's Australian Independent Newspapers or Janet Holmes à Court, or whether the English Pearson Group (*Financial Times*) or the dire Maxwell would ensure greater competition despite the alleged disadvantages of overseas ownership, has been much debated.

Present indications are that both the Federal Government and the receiver, Mr Des Nicholl, would prefer to keep the group intact. Under the latest amendments to the Broadcasting and Television Act, overseas ownership for both individuals and companies is restricted to 20 per cent. While this naturally does not apply to print media without electronic interests, it could be taken as a guideline, although some government figures have spoken of 15 per cent as the maximum overseas interest desirable for the Fairfax Group. This is in line with the Foreign Takeovers Act which restricts overseas interest in Australian companies to 14.9 per cent to an individual interest and 40 per cent in aggregate. Beyond this, it is necessary to obtain the federal treasurer's permission. Clearly, the best result would be a public company which keeps the group intact, attracts investment from local institutions and, if necessary, from overseas media interests and comes to an arrangement with the bond holders. It is, of course, greatly desirable that such a group would include people with proven newspaper experience — and in such a way that there was not a further concentration of ownership in the media.

However, the overseas media owners, either individually or as a consortium, may well not be attracted by such limitations on their holdings. I do not believe percentages of control are important in the case of overseas buyers, but would concede the emotional attachment to the concept of a 49 per cent limit. Nor do I believe it is in the interests of any buyer to tamper with the chief assets and qualities of their purchases — three great newspapers, two with the 'rivers of gold' classifieds. Changing the rules may be unfair retrospectively to Warwick, but it may be best for the future of the papers.

The name of Paul Keating returns to my narrative at an appropriate time. I have never been a strong believer in conspiracy theories, whether the Fairfax company has been the supposed conspirator (which both Hawke and Wran have maintained from time to time, if not believed) or whether a government figure has been the conspirator, in which role some would cast Keating. Vic Carroll develops this theme in his book, while discussing Labor's relations with Fairfax, which he described to me as a 'neo-Seven Year's War'. (The Seven Year's War (1756–63) involved Britain, France, Russia, Prussia, Austria and Spain; Britain did best out of it, gaining Canada, Florida and several Caribbean islands.) Souter has also given it due attention in *Heralds and Angels*.

It is known that Keating gave Murdoch and Packer prior knowledge of the proposed broadcasting and television legislation in 1986 because of the government's hostility to ourselves and the H&WT, and there is evidence from a reliable source that there was contact between Tryart and the Government on 30 August. This allegedly took the form of a telephone call from Connell to Hawke, arranged by an intermediary, in which the future management of Fairfax was discussed. Hawke supposedly said that Gardiner was a Liberal and had to go, while Suich had done terrible things to the Labor Party through the *National Times* and was out of control. Brenchley was part of the Gardiner team, but he expressed no view on Anderson. Hawke, as the account goes, consulted Keating. He agreed in general, but did not knock Suich and was vigorously in favour of Anderson, who he said was a friend and should stay.

The theme of Fairfax managers and editors being 'out of control' during the mid to late 1980s is one it has suited our own opposition, in the shape of Murdoch and Packer as well as the Hawke federal and Wran/Unsworth state governments, to propagate. I can best answer this ridiculous assertion by referring the reader back to the chapters dealing with management and editorial policy during this period, which marks the second part of my chairmanship. It was a period of unprecedented expansion in regard to both profits and products and the very success of our major newspapers was indeed a cause for envy and irritation. The end result may well be: 'if you can't beat them, buy them', and at the time of writing, Packer would appear to be in the running at least for the *Financial Review*, despite much equivocation from his executives. There is also talk of him joining an overseas interest, such as Conrad Black of the London *Daily Telegraph*. The media cross-ownership rules would of course restrict his share-holding unless he disposed of the Nine TV Network.

During the course of the H&WT takeover, Keating made several comments which indicated that he did not mind receiving the credit for putting it into 'play'. In a memo to the board of March 1987, following a long meeting with Keating some weeks after the completion of the H&WT takeover, Suich related how Keating persuaded Murdoch to treat Holmes à Court's bid seriously and do a deal with him, thereby depriving us of Queensland Press.

> *Keating says his motives for getting involved in the H&WT takeover were a desire to see the H&WT broken up and a desire to hurt Fairfax. The reasons for wanting to hurt Fairfax fundamentally come back to two matters. The first, and as far as can be judged, the less important, was the publication in the* Times *on Sunday in the middle of last year of a two-part series concerning Warren Anderson and Anderson's relationship with Keating.*
>
> *Keating, however, says that while the article made him angry at the time it did him no harm and he is more upset about a series of references to his Elizabeth Bay house in the* Sydney Morning Herald *over a period of two or three years, mainly in the 'Stay In Touch' column. These references, he said, made clear that the house was empty which left it open to being occupied by squatters.*
>
> *When it is put to him that his anger about the* Times *on Sunday and the* Sydney Morning Herald *reporting played a significant part in putting the H&WT into play and then assisting Murdoch to gain 60 per cent of Australian newspaper circulation, he agrees. He also acknowledges the considerable editorial support for the economic policies of the government and the fair reporting of the government's activities in all the Fairfax papers. He says that is irrelevant. If the Fairfax papers are going to attack him personally he will do his best to damage the family and the company and even dismember it. He also acknowledges that ultimately the Labor Party may regret the assistance it has given Murdoch.*
>
> *My conclusion at the end of a five-hour interview with the Treasurer was that his feelings of dislike were passionately held.*

But whatever the comments conveyed to Connell during Warwick's takeover, I have no reason to believe that Keating was not genuine when he told me in Paris that he regretted what had happened to the Fairfax company. In spite of the comments in Suich's memo, I believe Keating is too sensible a politician to let himself be corroded by the destructive effects of a vendetta. Hawke, of course, is more emotional and less capable of giving up an obsession. However, before I left the company, he conceded to our editorial executives several times that we had treated the government fairly and that there was no Fairfax conspiracy, but it seems that the albatross of what he regards have been the sins of the *National Times* would not fall from his neck.

I do not think that any impartial observer could possibly agree that Keating's cross-media legislation has resulted in a greater diversity of media ownership and it is astonishing that he continues to claim that it has. For a period he succeeded in divorcing the major print and electronic media and, as a result, the latter passed to inexperienced owners who saddled them with impossible burdens of debt and, in some cases, spent recklessly on programs. As Fred Brenchley recently commented, the 'massive increase' claimed by Keating from cross-ownership has come in concentration of print ownership and in the number of receiverships. Keating could not have foreseen that Warwick's stupidities would so reduce the financial effectiveness of Murdoch's only competition. But it is worth reiterating that had our bid for Queensland Newspapers succeeded (or, indeed, our admittedly less achievable bid for the H&WT group), this country would still have three competing newspaper groups.

It is interesting that evidently Hawke and Keating knew Warwick's plans before we did and that the Tryart directors felt an obligation to consult them, but there is no evidence that the advice greatly influenced them. The management and Suich were clearly due for the boot, regardless of Warwick's offers to Gardiner on his own position, while even the Tryart directors realised they would be crazy not to make every effort to keep Anderson. He was the one person capable of putting the company back on the rails, and indeed he and Greg Taylor in Melbourne were the only executives in the group with knowledge of running newspapers.

Now, more than three years after leaving my Broadway office for the last time on 9 December 1987, it might be appropriate for me to reflect on some aspects of my career.

I think my greatest failure was not being able to unite the family behind an effective capital raising proposal. This inhibited both our growth and competitive capacity in the 1980s in ways I have described. Going back to earlier times, I have often wondered whether I could have played a more forceful role in the disputes between my father and the management about the control of the company, which developed through the 1960s up to the mid-1970s. While supporting the management point of view, I was at first unwilling to face up to the fact that it would have to culminate in drastic action, as it did in 1976. My efforts to reconcile both sides were doomed to failure.

Returning to my own years as chairman, there was a general feeling among the business community and financial writers that we failed to deal adequately with the Murdoch takeover of the H&WT and that the acquisition of HSV and subsequent sale of the Seven Network was a financial disaster. I totally reject the criticism on these matters and believe I have given a satisfactory explanation of our actions. While the results emanating from the Murdoch takeover were not as much of a plus as we had hoped, I regard the sale of the Network as a very definite plus.

Where I feel I was able to make my best contribution was in effecting the change in the company from the paternalistic regimes of Rupert and Sir Warwick — and the paternalism applied at both management and editorial levels — to one where chairman, board and chief executive operated successfully in their separate spheres. I was fortunate in having two exceptionally able general managers in Bob Falkingham and Greg Gardiner, and I worked very happily with both of them. On the editorial side I believe my support, and the support board and management gave me, for the (editorial) independence of editors has had a beneficial effect on the industry as a whole throughout the country. Indeed, one or two commentators have been kind enough to write to this effect.

It was my intention to retire from the chairmanship in February 1991 on the sesquicentenary of Fairfax ownership of the *Herald*. It would have taken my service with the company from thirty-two to thirty-five years, which I would have liked to have completed. Also I believe I could have been of some use in helping John assume the chairmanship and encouraging Warwick towards what I hoped would be his assumption of the position of chief executive, which would lead to his own chairmanship. This was Gardiner's intention, too, and it would have happened as soon as Warwick had demonstrated to the board his capacity to take the job on.

By the time this book is published I will have passed my fifty-eighth birthday. Feelings of anger, frustration and sadness have lessened with the passing of time, and I enjoy the kind of life I am living now. It enables me to spend more time at Retford Park and overseas, and I have no worries about occupying myself in the future.

There is one last and inevitable question — could we have foreseen Warwick's action? Clearly we underestimated him, and I must bear my share of responsibility for not reading his character and attitudes correctly. He has to live with what he has done, but the newspapers are another matter.

On 7 December 1987, at the end of the last board meeting, I wished him and his company every success — and I meant it. Now the hope must be that under new ownership all the publications remaining in the group go from strength to strength. My thoughts are with all the employees of the *Sydney Morning Herald*, the *Sun-Herald*, the *Financial Review*, the *Age*, the *Illawarra Mercury*, the *Newcastle Herald* and the BRW magazines. I wish every good fortune to them and their publications — after all it was my life's work too.

POSTSCRIPT

It has been suggested that for this edition of my book I say a few words on the new ownership of the Fairfax company. I can best do this by referring to the answers I gave to interviewers during the pre-launch promotions for the book in October 1991. It will be recalled that potential bidders for the company began to emerge immediately upon the appointment of the receiver, Mr Des Nicholl, of Deloitte Ross Tohmatsu, on 10 December 1990.

By mid 1991 there were four leading contenders: Mr Conrad Black's Tourang, of which Mr Black's London Daily Telegraph company held 20 per cent, Mr Kerry Packer 14.9 per cent, and the US investment group Hellman and Friedman 10 per cent; Independent Newspapers, led by the Irish businessman Dr Tony O'Reilly, whose children's trust controls Australian Provincial Newspapers; Mr Jim Leslie's Australian Independent Newspapers, Melbourne-based and backed by institutional investors; and Mr Chris Corrigan's Jamison Equity Limited (which dropped out of the running in August after the AMP Society and National Mutual Life swung behind AIN rather than Jamison).

In addition, the merchant bank CS First Boston, while not a bidder, proposed a $1.5 billion float of 100 per cent of the company with limits on shareholdings to preserve independence. In response to questions I said I maintained a strict neutrality regarding the bidders and that all were feasible. I was concerned to make this point because both the O'Reilly and Tourang bids were being attacked on the question of overseas ownership, while Tourang was also being attacked on the question of local concentration of ownership through the Packer shareholding.

It would take another book to do justice to the controversy which raged over several months before Tourang came out the winner, following the withdrawal of Packer on 28 November — almost at the eleventh hour — and an even later trimming back of foreign equity to satisfy Canberra. Indeed, I have heard that such a book is being written by Fairfax journalists Glen Burge and Colleen Ryan.

John Kerin, on his last day as Federal Treasurer on 6 December, had blocked the Tourang bid as contrary to the national interest under the Government's foreign investment policy. Tourang swiftly recast its $1.45 billion bid: the share to be taken by Mr Black's Daily Telegraph plc was reduced from 20 per cent to 15 per cent and Hellman and Friedman's 10 per cent was reduced to a 5 per cent non-voting stake, leaving 80 per cent for institutions and, later, small shareholders through a projected float early in 1992. Tourang thus produced an equity structure matching that of Dr O'Reilly's group, which already had Canberra's approval. In the last months of the contest for Fairfax the two issues of overseas ownership and concentration of ownership became hopelessly confused in what amounted to a campaign against the Tourang bid from a number of different quarters. Two former prime ministers — Malcolm Fraser and Gough Whitlam — jumped hand in hand onto the hustings in an unlikely alliance to protect the purity of the Australian media from the supposed evils of non-Australian ownership and the depredations of Kerry Packer. Here again there was confusion between the part Packer played in the setting up of the Tourang bid and the influence he was likely to exert on the company if its bid succeeded. This latter perception extended to Trevor Kennedy, who had resigned as managing director of Kerry Packer's Consolidated Press Holdings to take up a similar position with Tourang. Mr Kennedy withdrew on 15 October amid allegations that he was still 'Packer's man'. Replies he later gave in response to questions from the Australian Broadcasting Tribunal are now the subject of litigation. Tourang is seeking to be released from any obligation to pay Mr Kennedy $250,000, the balance of a $500,000 severance payment, on the basis that Mr Kennedy breached his obligations to Tourang by giving the ABT information that went beyond the questions the ABT asked him. Tourang is also seeking damages from Mr Kennedy, alleging that the information he gave caused the ABT to announce an inquiry into Tourang's bid, leading to Tourang requesting Mr Packer to withdraw from the consortium and arranging to pay Mr Packer compensation.

As the Black-Packer bid for Fairfax gained momentum there was alarm, despondency and anger among Fairfax employees — the journalists particularly

— which expressed itself in public demonstrations arranged by the Friends of Fairfax and The Age Independence Committee. Packer, while acknowledging a role in the setting-up of Tourang, vehemently denied any intention of controlling it and ridiculed the possibility of doing so with a 14.9 per cent shareholding. In a remarkable session with the House of Representatives Select Committee on the Print Media, which did not show our legislators in their most glorious light (one longed for some rough and tough debaters from both sides — Wilson Tuckey, say, or Graeme Campbell), Packer reiterated these points and made the further, perhaps obvious, one that if he wanted to control Fairfax, all he had to do was sell the Nine TV Network and no-one could stop him. His slaughter of the Committee members, with the exception of Ian Sinclair, only served to confirm in many people's minds the dominating role he would play in any undertaking. I shall return briefly to the inquiry into the print media later.

In the political arena there were conflicting loyalties within the Hawke Government. The left wing were particularly anxious not to extend Packer's influence in the media, but Packer was a friend of the Prime Minister who felt he had some obligation to him. Black and O'Reilly both put their respective cases to Kim Beazley, the Minister for Communications. It soon became clear that O'Reilly was the Government's favoured candidate. Jim Leslie's AIN did not suffer from the disadvantages pertaining to the two bids with overseas shareholdings; however it was perceived in Government circles to be allied to the much disliked Melbourne establishment.

The extent of the Government's dilemma was made clear in a recent *Four Corners* program when Mark Burrows, adviser to the banks on the sale of Fairfax, said Hawke and Treasurer John Kerin were "amazed and somewhat perplexed" by Packer's withdrawal. The same program threw light on some of the strains and conflict within the Tourang group as it travelled on its bumpy road to success. Malcolm Turnbull, who had represented Mr Packer in court and acted as his financial adviser, and who had delivered to Tourang a crucial agreement by the US holders of Fairfax junk bonds to settle their claims against the company, revealed that his seventeen-year friendship with Packer was at an end because of his having been dumped in November as a Tourang director and as a prospective director of Fairfax. (At an earlier stage of the Fairfax drama his firm, then Whitlam Turnbull, with Neville Wran chairman, collected a $10 million fee for advice to Warwick.) Strong feelings were also expressed by Conrad Black in his contribution to this televised postmortem. Even though he emerged the winner, he trenchantly criticised the Federal Government's conduct, particularly its initial rejection of his bid. He was also extremely critical of the way the Fairfax press had reported the saga and Packer's participation.

As originally intended, the board of the new John Fairfax Holdings Limited has former Governor-General, Sir Zelman Cowen, as chairman. The other members are Mr Black (deputy chairman); The Hon Sir Laurence Street, former NSW Chief Justice; Mr Daniel Colson, representing Mr Black's *Daily Telegraph* company; Mr Brian Powers, from Hellman and Friedman; the industrialist Sir Roderick Carnegie; the advertising executive Mr John Singleton; and Mr Gary Pemberton, chief of Brambles Industries Limited.

In the final chapter of my book, entitled 'Reprise', I said I could not see any objection to overseas interests acquiring newspapers or television stations in this country while conceding the emotional attachment to a 49 per cent limit. I returned to this theme in my speech at the book's launching by Sir James Darling which took place on 4 November 1991, appropriately at the height of the Fairfax ownership drama.

Some weeks ago, an interview I gave appeared in the Australian *under the headline: 'Any owner will do, says ex-chairman of Fairfax' — as though I would welcome a consortium formed by Saddam Hussein, Fidel Castro and Colonel Gadaffi. Speaking in the context of the then current three bidders, I was endeavouring to make the point that an element of overseas ownership was not necessarily a disadvantage and that it was in the interests of any prospective owner to preserve the standards and traditions of the publications. The new owner will have to give the Australian public what it wants — something no government or administrative body can tell it. It is all very well to support — as most of us do — both the concepts of local ownership and diversity of ownership, but if governments start making value judgements on the desirability of different proprietors quite outside the rules they lay down they are treading on dangerous ground. I shall return to this point later. Foreign ownership with limits imposed is not in itself an evil. It can bring a much needed diversity of opinion and independence of outlook, quite apart from contributing to management and editorial skills. Favouring a bidding group over others which may be equally or more competent, because it does not contain an overseas interest is not judging each group on the merits of its bid and the contribution it can make to the good-running of the Fairfax newspapers. I would refer to Mr Conrad Black's own comment here: shouldn't we at least hold up and espouse a goal of a fair adjudication of the competitive merits of [these] bids?*

Regarding concentration of ownership the pass was sold early in 1987 and there were very few voices on either side of parliament raised in protest at the reduction to two major groups. In fact the Opposition sacked one of its front-bench spokesmen Ian McPhee for daring to do so, while the government smugly observed the break-up of the hated H&WT and the supposed discomfiture of the Fairfax group as the former passed to Murdoch. It is also ironic that so many members of parliament from both sides of the House have signed a petition calling on the Prime Minister to oppose any sale of Fairfax newspapers that would result in a greater concentration of media ownership — in view of their deafening silence on this point early in 1987. Better late than never — I suppose. But with great respect to the eminent signatories of the recent letter from former political leaders on the ownership of Fairfax, I do not believe that the Australian print media or the public that reads their products — even if there are only two major owners left — needs the total umbrella of legislative protection they advocate. They urge government intervention on both the grounds of overseas ownership and media concentration. I find it hard to see that a voting overseas shareholding of 20 per cent laid down by the government as legitimate, even if in the case of two of the bidders it constitutes control — and this has been disputed — is unacceptably high.

However it is the area of concentration or dominance by an individual where most emotion has been aroused. In 1979 the then general manager said to the Fairfax board: 'Control of the Herald & Weekly Times by Mr Murdoch would create political and public disquiet. This would lead to repressive legislation and press controls which would make it difficult for us to perform the role we see for ourselves in the community.'

Perhaps it was inevitable from this event that the print media would be removed from their traditional free-market setting and their destinies placed firmly under government control — albeit for the highest of motives. I view the precedent which the action by the government suggested by the eminent persons would create — and which would supersede its own established rules — with some disquiet and am not convinced by the arguments put for it. It is perfectly true that if the group, which we are told by some is controlled from overseas by Mr Conrad Black and has Mr Kerry Packer as a 14.9 per cent shareholder, should acquire Fairfax, it indirectly increases the latter's ownership and capacity to influence the media as a whole because of his television and magazine interests. But as I have said, all groups are entitled to be evaluated according to the rules and by the bodies set up to administer them: the recently strengthened cross-media ownership legislation, the Australian Broadcasting Tribunal and the Trade Practices Commission. Over and above these is the power of the Federal Treasurer to decide on the permissible degree of foreign ownership in an Australian company in the national interest. This is the ultimate safeguard.

Emotion in a cause one passionately believes in and ways of expressing it are part of our democratic society and no-one could fail to be impressed by the support given to the demonstrations by the Friends of Fairfax and the Age Independence Committee against further concentration of media ownership. There has been similar public support at the Sydney and Melbourne meetings addressed by Mr Fraser and Mr Whitlam. The appropriate authorities will certainly be very aware of the feelings expressed. Perhaps it was inevitable that the demonstrations should take on the personal note they did but I think it was regrettable.

I have since stated that I did not regard Mr Packer's 14.9 per cent shareholding as an insuperable objection to the Tourang bid, nor have I doubted the sincerity of those who did, however, I have to agree with Mr Black's criticism. I think that there were times when the Fairfax publications lost sight of the principles of fair reporting and comment in their handling of this matter. Since then the Fairfax board has agreed with the journalists to adopt the Fairfax Charter, guaranteeing editorial independence of the newspapers from proprietorial interference. The charter embraces the principles set down by the Australian Press Council and those of the Code of Ethics of the Australian Journalists Association. This is encouraging, but I hope that my constitutional concept of the board and management's right to be consulted, to advise and to warn in editorial matters will be preserved. My own view for what it is worth — and I have not met either Conrad Black or Tony O'Reilly — is that the best bid won. As I wrote to Mr Black, who has a proven record as the owner of quality newspapers, I felt the traditions and the future of the Fairfax publications would be safe in his hands.

As I complete this postscript the Parliamentary Committee on the Print Media, headed by Mr Michael Lee, has issued its report. I would propose to comment on it and any other relevant issue in another book which I shall begin writing in the second half of this year. This book will also comment on the new ownership of Fairfax, continue my descriptive chapters on the theme: 'Some Art, Some Travel and Some People' and might include some more family and autobiographical material. A quick perusal of the committee's report reveals that it found 'insufficient evidence' to conclude that the present concentration of ownership has led to 'biased reports, news suppression or lack of diversity'. This conclusion has not unnaturally been taken up with enthusiasm by the Murdoch press. This support for maintenance of the status quo is, however, accompanied by proposals that future changes of ownership should be made subject to a tougher merger test embracing the old lessening-of-competition test rather than the current domination-of-a-substantial market one.

Fred Brenchley in the *Herald* makes the point that while the report gets News Corp 'off the hook', it could well block any further acquisitions by Fairfax. The committee also exempted national magazines from inclusion with newspapers in the cross-ownership provisions — a move which would be much welcomed by Kerry Packer. It is interesting to note that the Trade Practices Commission emphasises the point that had the tougher merger test still existed in 1987, it could have brought greater force to bear in its examination of the H&WT takeover by News Ltd. Peter Robinson writes in the *Financial Review* that if the Print Media Committee's recommendations become law, Conrad Black will be precluded from raising his holding above 15 per cent.

Mr Black is in a cleft stick since the more successful he is in turning Fairfax into an even greater money-spinner than it has been (an eventuality which is highly likely), the more attractive the company will be to a takeover bid.

The market for such a bid, however, has been totally skewed by government regulation. It cannot come from a foreigner, for the same reasons which preclude Mr Black from increasing his holding, and it cannot come from Mr Kerry Packer, who is precluded by his other media holdings.

Such a bid could only come from some Australian group totally inexperienced in newspaper management but greedy for a perceived money-making machine.

Is this environment, supposedly preserving the national interest, actually protective or destructive?

However, to include a final comment from the *Financial Review*, with which I entirely agree:

The inquiry has taken a very small step towards fostering greater press diversity in Australia by conceding that foreign investment in the newspaper industry is one way of bringing new capital and ideas to what is a highly concentrated industry.

The problem is that it has not properly followed through on this concession by calling for a much more liberal approach to foreign investment. Nevertheless, the concession that foreign investment beyond 20 per cent be allowed when it is in the national interest may provide for more foreign participation in future.

Now the wheel put into motion by Warwick's takeover bid has turned full circle with the announcement on 24 March of a Fairfax public flotation — an offering of 173.25 million shares at $1.20 a share (with up to 10 million available to staff at a 7.5 per cent discount). After the float, Mr Black's company will own 15 per cent, Hellman and Friedman 5 per cent, Australian institutions and former US investors in junk bonds 55 per cent, and the Australian public 25 per cent. At time of writing, the company is due to be listed on the Australian Stock Exchange of 7 May. The result of Warwick's privatisation attempt has been to return the family company to public ownership, but with overseas interests as the leading shareholders instead of his own family.

APPENDICES

APPENDIX I
FAIRFAX FAMILY TREE

JOHN FAIRFAX
1805–1877

SARAH READING
1808–1875

CHARLES JOHN FAIRFAX
1829–1863
=
ANNE FAIRFAX

EMILY FAIRFAX
1831–1871
=
JOSEPH GRAFTON ROSS

JAMES READING FAIRFAX
1834–1919
=
LUCY ARMSTRONG

RICHARD POPE FAIRFAX
1838–1839

EDWARD ROSS FAIRFAX
1842–1915
=
CATHERINE MACKENZIE

MARY ELIZABETH FAIRFAX
1858–1945

CHARLES BURTON FAIRFAX
1859–1941
=
MARIE FLORENCE FRAZER

GEOFFREY EVAN FAIRFAX
1861–1930
=
LENA MARY HIXSON

JAMES OSWALD FAIRFAX
1863–1928
=
MABEL ALICE HIXSON

HAROLD WALTER FAIRFAX
1869–1913
=
ELSIE DORA CAPE

JOHN HUBERT FRASER FAIRFAX
1872–1950
=
RUTH BEATRICE DOWLING

EDWARD WILFRED FAIRFAX
1874–1952
=
MARY MARGUERITE LAMB

JAMES GRIFFYTH FAIRFAX
1886–1976
=
ROSETTA MARY GLOVER

WARWICK OSWALD FAIRFAX
1901–1987
=
3. MARY WEIN
2. HANNE BENDIXSON
1. MARCIE ELIZABETH WILSON

VINCENT CHARLES FAIRFAX
1909–
=
NANCY HEALD

JOHN FITZGERALD FAIRFAX
1904–1951
=
2. GWENDOLINE ANABEL
1. VALERIE MOULE

HUBERT DESMOND (MICK) FAIRFAX
1909–
=
SUZANNE STOGDALE

MARGARET MARY FAIRFAX
1842–1915
=
3. ARTHUR WILLIAM MORROW 1903–1977
2. CLARENCE EDWARD CHAUVEL 1909–1968
1. ARTHUR PETER MOORE 1907–1941

BENITA LEONORA

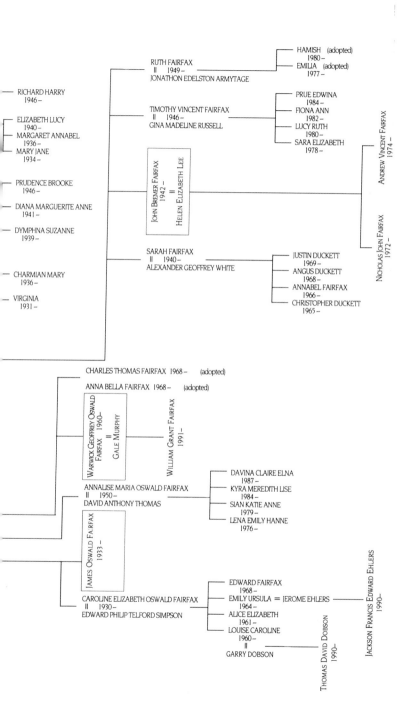

CHRONOLOGY OF KEY EVENTS

1928	27 March	Parents (Warwick Oswald Fairfax and Marcie Elizabeth Wilson) marry.
1930	27 March	Father appointed managing director of John Fairfax & Sons Ltd.
	6 October	Caroline Fairfax (sister) is born.
1933	27 March	James Oswald Fairfax is born.
1938	17 August	Rupert Henderson appointed general manager.
1941	February	JOF attends Edgecliff Preparatory School.
1944		Father acquires Harrington Park at Narellan, near Camden, 60 kmfrom Sydney.
	February	JOF attends Cranbrook.
	December	The last family Christmas celebrated at Ginahgulla.
1945		Parents divorce.
		JOF buys first painting (from Macquarie Gallery, a Paris street scene by Eric Wilson).
1946	February	JOF attends Geelong Grammar.
	March	Mother marries Pierre Gilly.
1947	December	JOF travels to Japan to join mother and stepfather Pierre.
	21 December	Edward Gilly (half-brother), born to mother and Pierre.
1948	1 May	Father marries Hanne Anderson.
	December	JOF visits mother and Pierre in Paris
1949	29 June	Henderson appointed managing director and Angus McLachlan appointed general manager.
1950	15 November	Annalise Fairfax (half-sister), born to father and Hanne.
1951	March	JOF attends Sydney University.
	June	JOF travels to Paris to visit mother. Mother and Pierre separate.
1952	16 August	*Australian Financial Review* launched (weekly)
	October	JOF attends Balliol College, Oxford.

1953	1 January	John Pringle appointed editor of *Sydney Morning Herald*.
1955	September	JOF returns to Australia.
	October	JOF joins the company, under John Pringle.
1956	January	The company's move from Hunter Street to Broadway is complete.
	27 March	Board ratifies family empire becoming a public company (John Fairfax Limited).
	August	JOF moves to Scotland to work on the *Glascow Herald*.
1957		JOF buys Henry Moore silk-screen print, his first major acquisition. Purchases flat at Retford Hall.
	4 March	R. P. Falkingham appointed treasurer.
	April	JOF returns to Australia.
	9 May	JOF appointed a director.
1958	May	Angus Maude becomes editor of the *Herald*.
1959	February	Father and Hanne divorce. Cedric Symonds issues Supreme Court writ against father.
	4 July	Father marries Mary Symonds.
1960	February	JOF purchases Bilgola beach property.
	2 December	Warwick Fairfax (half-brother), born to father and Mary.
1961	January	Father resigns temporarily.
	March	Father reappointed as chairman.
	May	Angus Maude resigns. Succeeded, in June, by Colin Bingham.
1964	January	JOF purchases Retford Park at Bowral. Donald Friend commissioned to paint murals at Retford Park.
	October	Ranald Macdonald (great-grandson of David Syme) appointed managing director of David Syme and Co Ltd.
	21 October	*Australian Financial Review* published daily.
	December	Henderson retires as managing director of JFL, succeeded by McLachlan.
1965		JOF purchases first Old Master drawing of Hon. Frederick North by Ingres (Rome, 1815).
	June	John Pringle succeeds Colin Bingham as *Herald* editor.
1966	May	JOF purchases property at Lindsay Avenue, Darling Point.

1967		Father knighted. Sir Warwick and Mary travel to UK.
1968	December	Sir Warwick and Mary return from UK.
1969	January	McLachlan suffers heart attack.
	December	McLachlan retires, Falkingham becomes general manager and Sir Warwick assumes executive powers as a 'Committee of One'.
1970	April	John Pringle departs the *Herald* eight months earlier than expected, succeeded by Guy Harriott in July.
1971	7 February	*National Times* launched with Trevor Kennedy as editor.
1972	November	Max Suich succeeds Trevor Kennedy as *National Times* editor.
1973		JOF first purchases Old Master oil painting — *Pastoral Landscape* by Claude Lorrain.
1975	January	JOF becomes chairman of ATN-7.
	1 December	Greg Gardiner appointed administration manager.
1976	August	Sir Warwick asked to step down as chairman of JFL.
	1 September	Board ratifies August decision, JOF becomes deputy chairman.
1977	March	JOF becomes chairman of JFL. David Bowman appointed *Herald* editor.
	December	Board decides to appoint Sir David Griffin and Arthur Lissenden to the board as the first 'outside' directors.
1978	October	Henderson retires from the board.
1979	February	John B. Fairfax appointed a director.
	November	Rupert Murdoch launches first bid for the Herald and WeeklyTimes (H&WT), JFL buys 14.9% of H&WT.
1980	July	Max Suich becomes the *Herald* chief editorial executive.
	October	Falkingham succeeds McLachlan on the JFL board. Vic Carroll succeeds David Bowman as *Herald* editor.
	November	Greg Gardiner succeeds Falkingham as chief executive of JFL.
1981	February	Norris inquiry into the ownership of Victorian newspapers. David Marr succeeds Evan Whitton as editor of *National Times*.
	April	*Business Review Weekly* is launched.
	April	Sesquicentenary of the *Herald*.

	July	JFL sells H&WT shares to Queensland Press. Sungravure is closed.
	October	Falkingham retires as a director of JFL.
1982	February	Chris Anderson appointed *Herald* editor.
	March	Brian Toohey succeeds David Marr as editor of *National Times*.
1983	September	Macdonald retires from David Syme, Syme family sells their shares (13.54%) to JFL, which now owns 75%.
1984	February	Chris Anderson succeeds Vic Carroll as *Herald* editor-in-chief.
	July	Eric Beecher appointed *Herald* editor.
	August	JFL board adopts PIPS proposal. Jefferson Penberthy appointed managing editor of *National Times*.
	October	JFL withdraws PIPS share issue after Stock Exchange refuses to grant listing.
1985	January	JFL buys the *Spectator* (UK).
	March	Arthur Lissenden dies.
	July	JFL acquires 100% of David Syme.
1986	August	Eric Neal is appointed a director.
	August	*National Times* relaunched as *National Times on Sunday* with Robert Haupt as editor.
	December	Both Robert Holmes à Court and Rupert Murdoch launch bids for the H&WT. Sir Rupert Clarke appointed alternative director to Sir Warwick.
1987	4 January	JFL launches bid for Queensland Press.
	9 January	H&WT accepts Murdoch's bid.
	14 January	Sir Warwick dies.
	15 January	Holmes à Court drops his bid and Queensland Press accepts Murdoch's bid.
	16 January	JFL withdraws bid for Queensland Press.
	20 January	JFL launches bid for H&WT.
	22 January	Broadcasting Tribunal into foreign ownership announced.
	5 February	H&WT holds one-day auction of electronic assets to allow Murdoch's bid to succeed. JFL acquires, among other media properties, HSV-7.

	5 February	John Alexander appointed *Herald* editor. Newco scheme proposed to JFL board to deal with television assets and raise capital. Warwick engages Baring Brothers Halkerston to advise on Newco. Warwick purchases 1.5% of JFL's capital.
	March	Valerie Lawson appointed editor of *National Times on Sunday*.
	18 March	H&WT shares delisted from Melbourne Stock Exchange.
1987	May	Warwick returns to Sydney from Harvard and begins work as assistant to Peter Gaunt, publisher of the *Herald, Sun* and *Sun-Herald*. Attends board meetings although refuses to take up position as a director.
	August	JFL board approves sale of Seven Network to Christopher Skase's Qintex for $780 million.
	30 August	Warwick visits JOF, John B. Fairfax and Greg Gardiner at their homes to advise them of his takeover bid.
	31 August	Warwick moves from Broadway to Rothwell's Sydney office. News of Warwick's proposed takeover first announced on John Laws's radio program, 2UE.
	28 September	JOF and John announce their intention to sell to Warwick.
	19 October	World stock market crash.
	5 November	Tryart's bid declared unconditional.
	4 December	Resignations of Gardiner, Such and Fred Brenchley announced.
	8 December	Final JFL board meeting at which Tryart team takes over with Warwick as proprietor, Martin Dougherty as managing director (editorial), Ron Cotton as managing director (finance) and Peter King as chief executive.
	9 December	JOF departs Broadway.
1988	11 January	Sale of Fairfax Magazines and *Canberra Times* to Mr Kerry Packer's Consolidated Press Holdings concluded.
	3 February	Negotiations to sell *Australian Financial Review, Times on Sunday*, Macquarie Radio Network and New Zealand's *National Business Review* to Robert Holmes à Court abandoned by mutual consent.
	10 February	Anderson resigns as editor in chief of the *Sydney Morning Herald,* is replaced by Andrew Clark. John Alexander, editor, and several assistant editors resign. Journalists strike to express lack of confidence in management.

	15 February	Warwick Fairfax terminates Dougherty's employment.
	18 February	Anderson returns as group editorial director and member of the board in place of Dougherty. Alexander made editor in chief of the *Sydney Morning Herald* in place of Clark (later appointed as London editor). Resignations withdrawn.
	14 March	The *Sun* and *Times on Sunday* closed. Laurie Connell resigns as director at Warwick's request.
	15 March	Fairfax sells its 50 per cent of Australian Newsprint Mills to Fletcher Challenge Ltd, of New Zealand.
	April	Fairfax sells *The Spectator*, London, to the London Daily Telegraph group.
	May	Fairfax sells *Ms.* and *Sassy* in US to Matilda Publications Inc., *Money Magazine* in London to Stonehart Magazines Ltd, 50 per cent of Fourth Estate Group, NZ, to Liberty Publishing Ltd, and the 44.65 per cent Fairfax holding in Australian Associated Press Pty Ltd to Reuters Holdings plc. Warwick rejects offer of $1.8 billion by Alan Bond for the whole Fairfax company.
	June	Tryart refuses to pay $100 million fee claimed by Rothwells Ltd for Connell's role in takeover of JFL. Bond Media, to whom Rothwells assigned the fee, announces joint legal action to recover it from Tryart.
	August	Tryart in cross action seeks damages of at least $160 million from Bond and Rothwells.
	8 September	Cross claim widened to include Dougherty and Bert Reuter, alleging they breached duties owed to Tryart during the takeover.
	20 September	JFL announces basic terms agreed with Citibank, ANZ and Drexel Burnham Lambert Inc. for long term financial package to restructure its debt.
	17 October	Hearing of Bond Media v John Fairfax Group Pty Ltd (formerly Tryart) opens in NSW Supreme Court.
	16 December	After 38 hearing days, case stood over to 31 July 1989.
1989	January	Bond and King negotiate settlement. JFL to pay Bond Media $27 million, drop claims against Dougherty, Reuter and Rothwells. Warwick rejects renewed, higher offer of $2.1 billion by Bond for whole Fairfax company.

27 January	Fairfax announces $1.6 billion refinancing of debt through Citibank, ANZ and Drexel, including $450 million issue of junk bonds in US.
March	Ron Cotton resigns as group managing director.
20 April	Management restructure. Anderson elevated to NSW managing director and deputy to King.
13 July	Bryan Kelman, former chief executive of CSR, appointed chairman of John Fairfax Group. William Simon, former Secretary of US Treasury, appointed director.
31 July	Bob Johnston, retired Governor of Reserve Bank, joins board.
October	Simon resigns from board.

1990
August	Fairfax fails to make $13.9 million interest payment to US junk bond holders.
9 August	King resigns as chief executive officer, is replaced by Anderson.
23 August	Anderson, Kelman and Johnston resign from board after disagreeing with Warwick on strategy for financial restructuring. Keith Halkerston appointed chairman, Bill Beerworth a director.
24 August	Warwick assumes role of chief executive.
2 October	John Fairfax Group announces $73.4 million operating loss in 1989-90, warns that it may breach covenants on undrawn credit facilities as early as December if tough trading conditions continue.
10 December	Banks place Fairfax Group in receivership. Des Nicholl, of Deloitte Ross Tohmatsu, appointed receiver and manager.

1991
May	Greg Taylor, chief executive of Syme, made chief of executive committee of John Fairfax Group.
June	Kerry Packer emerges as a bidder for Fairfax in conjunction with Conrad Black. ALP national conference agrees to federal parliamentary inquiry into concentration of ownership of print media.
July	Sir Zelman Cowen agrees to be independent chairman of Fairfax if bid by Black's Tourang consortium succeeds.
18 September	Baring Brothers Burrows, advisers to banks, set 15 October deadline for bids.
15 October	Trevor Kennedy resigns as managing director of Tourang.

	4 November	Packer before Parliamentary Print Media Committee, denies he would wield influence on Fairfax beyond his 14.9 percent shareholding.
	12 November	Trade Practices Commission warns all three bidders they may contravene the takeover provisions of the Trade Practices Act, begins 'normal market inquiries'.
	14 November	Australian Broadcasting Tribunal issues questions to members of the Tourang group.
	26 November	ABT announces it will hold public inquiry into the Fairfax sale after receiving last-minute information on the Tourang bid.
	28 November	Packer quits Tourang.
	29 November	Turnbull resigns from Tourang after differences with Packer and Black.
	6 December	John Kerin, Federal Treasurer, rejects Tourang bid as contrary to national interest.
	11 December	Final offers close.
	13 December	Revised bid by Tourang cleared by new Treasurer, Ralph Willis.
	16 December	Tourang bid wins.
	23 December	Black takes control of Fairfax as contracts for sale completed.
1992	24 March	Prospectus issued for public flotation of John Fairfax Holdings Ltd.

APPENDIX III

MAJOR SHAREHOLDINGS IN JOHN FAIRFAX LTD

SUBSTANTIAL SHAREHOLDERS

The substantial shareholders shown in the Company's register of substantial shareholders at September 10, 1987 were as follows:

NAME OF SUBSTANTIAL SHAREHOLDER	NUMBER OF SHARES IN WHICH THE SUBSTANTIAL SHAREHOLDER IS DEEMED TO HAVE A RELEVANT INTEREST
Cambooya Pty Limited	43,965,498
James O. Fairfax	51,297,855
John B. Fairfax	41,843,340
Timothy V. Fairfax	31,937,769
Sir Vincent Fairfax	31,243,359
Warwick G.O. Fairfax	33,994,116
George E. Foster	35,217,230
Inta Pty Limited	33,994,116
Kinghaven Pty Limited	33,994,116
Marinya Pty Limited	43,965,498
Old South Pty Limited	33,994,116
The Rockwood Pastoral Company Pty Limited	38,521,080
Rupertswood Nominees Pty Limited	31,286,658
Serpentine Pty Limited	33,994,116
Tailer Investments Pty Limited	35,619,750

DIRECTORS' SHAREHOLDINGS

In compliance with Section 3C(3)(c) of the listing manual of the Australian Stock Exchange Limited the following statement shows the interest of the Directors in the share capital of the Company as at September 17, 1987.

Interest in John Fairfax Limited

(fully paid ordinary shares of 50¢ each)
Held beneficially

Mr J.O. Fairfax	7,027,566
Sir Vincent Fairfax	1,636,542
Sir David Griffin	30,000
Mr J.B. Fairfax	6,534,639

Mr J.O. Fairfax, Sir Vincent Fairfax and Mr J.B. Fairfax are also deemed by virtue of Section 8 of the Companies Act 1981 to have a relevant interest in the following shares:

Mr J.O. Fairfax	44,270,289
Sir Vincent Fairfax	29,606,817
Mr J.B. Fairfax	35,308,701

JOHN FAIRFAX LIMITED ANALYSIS OF INDIVIDUAL ORDINARY SHAREHOLDINGS

as at September 10, 1987

HOLDING	NO. OF-SHAREHOLDERS	PERCENTAGE OF TOTAL	NO. OF SHARES	PERCENTAGE OF ISSUED CAPITAL
*1 – 1,000	673	14.52	304,180	0.10
1,001 – 5,000	1,707	36.83	4,662,863	1.55
5,001 – 10,000	1,177	25.39	8,536,339	2.85
10,001 & over	1,078	23.26	286,496,618	95.50
Total Holdings	4,635	100.00	300,000,000	100.0

* III Shareholders registered with less than a marketable parcel.

Transfers

During the year ended June 28, 1987, the Company handled 7,788 transfers, for a total of 20,415,427 ordinary shares in John Fairfax Limited.

Voting

Each shareholder present at a meeting, either personally or by proxy, attorney, or in the case of a corporation, by a representative shall have:

(a) on a show of hands, one vote only.

(b) on a poll, one vote for every share of which he is the holder. A member entitled to more than one vote need not, if he votes, use all his votes or cast all the votes he uses in the same way.

JOHN FAIRFAX LIMITED
TWENTY LARGEST SHAREHOLDINGS

as at September 10, 1987

	Number of Shares Held	Percentage of Total Shares Issued
The Rockwood Pastoral Company Pty Limited	38,521,080	12.84
Kinghaven Pty Limited	33,994,116	11.33
Vident Pty Limited	28,898,630	9.63
Marinya Pty Limited	20,808,213	6.94
Australian Mutual Provident Society	15,655,712	5.22
Marinya Pty Limited No. 2 A/c	12,449,124	4.15
Bridgestar Pty Limited	9,558,423	3.19
Public Authorities Superannuation Board	7,611,006	2.54
Mr J.O. Fairfax	7,027,566	2.34
Mrs M.E. Fairfax & Mrs C.E.O. Simpson	6,759,219	2.25
Lockville Pty Limited	6,288,030	2.10
Beaglemoat Nominees Pty Ltd	5,773,500	1.92
J.N. Taylor Securities Pty Ltd	5,355,386	1.79
Primera Pty Ltd	4,315,050	1.44
Swan River Nominee Corporation Pty Ltd	4,230,000	1.41
Sir Vincent Fairfax, N. Fairfax, J.B. Fairfax & P.W. Fisher	3,720,432	1.24

	Number of Shares Held	Percentage of Total Shares Issued
Acrux Holdings Pty Limited	3,333,333	1.11
The Prudential Assurance Co. Ltd.	3,147,564	1.05
Australian Mutual Provident Society No. 2 Account	3,037,690	1.01
Bank of New South Wales Nominees Pty Limited	2,209,016	0.74
	222,693,090	74.24

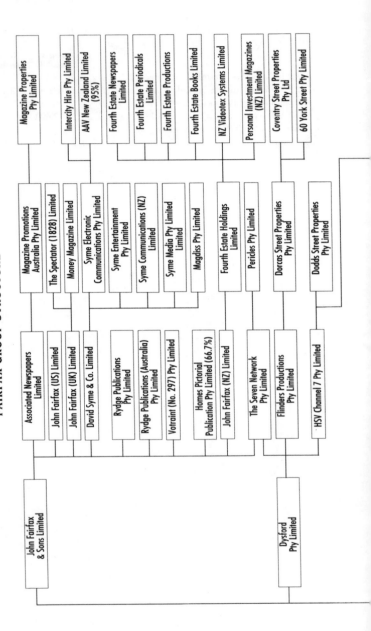

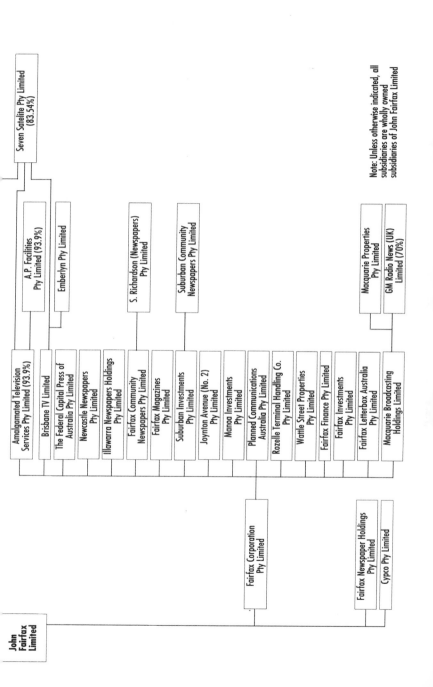

John Fairfax Limited

Seven Satellite Pty Limited (83.54%)

A.P. Facilities Pty Limited (93.9%)

Amberlyn Pty Limited

Amalgamated Television Services Pty Limited (93.9%)

Brisbane TV Limited

The Federal Capital Press of Australia Pty Limited

Newcastle Newspapers Pty Limited

Illawarra Newspapers Holdings Pty Limited

S. Richardson (Newspapers) Pty Limited

Fairfax Community Newspapers Pty Limited

Fairfax Magazines Pty Limited

Suburban Investments Pty Limited

Suburban Community Newspapers Pty Limited

Joynton Avenue (No. 2) Pty Limited

Manoa Investments Pty Limited

Planned Communications Australia Pty Limited

Rozelle Terminal Handling Co. Pty Limited

Wattle Street Properties Pty Limited

Fairfax Finance Pty Limited

Fairfax Investments Pty Limited

Fairfax Letterbox Australia Pty Limited

Macquarie Broadcasting Holdings Limited

Macquarie Properties Pty Limited

GM Radio News (UK) Limited (70%)

Fairfax Corporation Pty Limited

Fairfax Newspaper Holdings Pty Limited

Cypco Pty Limited

Note: Unless otherwise indicated, all subsidiaries are wholly owned subsidiaries of John Fairfax Limited

SCHEDULE OF HOLDING COMPANY'S INTEREST IN SUBSIDIARIES

COMPANY	NUMBER OF SHARES	CLASS OF SHARE (FULLY PAID)	INVESTMENT GROUP AMOUNT $	INVESTMENT GROUP PER CENT INTEREST	PLACE OF INCORPORATION	CONTRIBUTION TO GROUP NET PROFIT (D) 52 WEEKS ENDED JUNE 28, 1987 $000	52 WEEKS ENDED JUNE 29, 1986 $000	PRINCIPAL ACTIVITY
INVESTMENT BY HOLDING COMPANY JOHN FAIRFAX LIMITED IN:								
John Fairfax and Sons Limited	394 990	Ordinary $2	664 200 000	100.0	N.S.W.	19 550.2	7 696.8	Newspaper publishing investment and printing
Fairfax Corporation Pty Limited	3	Ordinary $2	30 000 000	100.0	N.S.W.	3 774.4	681.7	Investment in Subsidiaries, other securities and advances
Cypco Pty Limited	2	Ordinary $1	2	100.0	A.C.T.	—	—	Non trading
Dysford Pty Limited	2	Ordinary $1	2	100.0	A.C.T.	(8 413.9)	—	Investment in subsidiaries, other securities and advances
Fairfax Newspaper Holdings Pty Ltd	2	Ordinary $1	2	100.0	A.C.T.	—	—	Non trading
Other Subsidiaries of the Holding Company Consolidated into these accounts		Class of share (fully paid)						
Amalgamated Television Services		Ordinary $2		93.9	N.S.W.	3,511.2	6,544.9	Television broadcasting
AAV New Zealand Limited		Ordinary $NZ1		95.0	New Zealand(c)	6.8	—	Video cassette duplication
A.P. Facilities Pty Limited		Ordinary $2		93.9	A.C.T.	305.1	90.5	Film Production
Associated Newspapers Limited		Ordinary $2		100.0	N.S.W.	58,867.9	8,194.1	Investment in subsidiaries and other securities
Brisbane TV Limited		Ordinary 50¢		100.0	QLD.	3,152.6	3,043.5	Television broadcasting
Coventry Street Properties Pty Limited Formerly Second Herald Development Pty Limited		Ordinary $1		100.0	VIC.	276.5	—	Property owner
Creative Video Pty Limited		Ordinary $1		100.0	VIC.	—	64.5	Video cassette rental
David Syme & Co Limited		Ordinary 50¢		100.0	VIC.	45,679.0	29,481.7	Newspaper publishing
Dodds Street Properties Pty Limited formerly Herald Development Number One Pty Limited		Ordinary $1		100.0	VIC.	29.5	—	Property owner
Dorcas Street Properties Pty Limited formerly Herald Development Pty Limited		Ordinary $1		100.0	VIC.	(475.1)	—	Property owner
Emberlyn Pty Limited		Ordinary $1		100.0	QLD.	4.0	0.5	Production of television commercials
Fairfax Community Newspapers Pty Limited		Ordinary $2		100.0	N.S.W.	715.4	(2,221.5)	Newspaper publishing
Fairfax Finance Pty Limited		Ordinary $1		100.0	N.S.W.	—	—	Non trading
Fairfax Investments Pty Limited		Ordinary $1		100.0	N.S.W.	313.0	—	Investment in securities
Fairfax Letterbox Australia Pty Ltd		Ordinary $2		100.0	N.S.W.	(798.2)	—	Letterbox distributors
Fairfax Magazines Pty Limited		Ordinary $1		100.0	N.S.W.	3,664.5	88.3	Magazine publishing
Flinders Productions Pty Limited		Ordinary $1		100.0	VIC.	(369.0)	—	Production of television commercials
Fourth Estate Holdings Limited		Ordinary $NZ1		100.0	N.Z.(c)	(763.7)	—	Newspaper publishing
Fourth Estate Newspapers Limited		Ordinary $NZ1		100.0	N.Z.(c)	—	—	Non trading
Fourth Estate Periodicals Limited		Ordinary $NZ1		100.0	N.Z.(c)	—	—	Non trading
Fourth Estate Productions Limited		Ordinary $NZ1		100.0	N.Z.(c)	—	—	Non trading
Fourth Estate Books Limited		Ordinary $NZ1		100.0	N.Z.(c)	—	—	Non trading
GM Radio News (UK) Limited		Ordinary £Stg1		70.0	U.K. (a)	(248.0)	—	News service
Homes Pictorial Publication Pty Limited		Ordinary $1		66.7	N.S.W.	—	—	Trustee company
H.S.V. Channel 7 Pty Limited		Ordinary $2		100.0	VIC.	(880.9)	—	Television broadcasting
Illawarra Newspapers Holdings Pty Limited		Ordinary $2		100.0	N.S.W.	301.1	895.9	Newspaper publishing
Intercity Hire Pty Limited		Ordinary $1		100.0	VIC.	—	—	Non trading
John Fairfax (UK) Limited		Ordinary £Stg1		100.0	U.K. (a)	366.4	247.9	London representation

John Fairfax (US) Limited	Ordinary U.S.$100	100.0	U.S.A. (b)	61.3	63.4	North American representation
John Fairfax (NZ) Limited	Ordinary NZ$1	100.0	New Zealand(c)	51.2	244.2	Investment in securities
Joynton Ave No. 2 Pty Limited	Ordinary $1	100.0	N.S.W.	59.1	125.0	Property owner
Jumbuck Productions Pty Limited	Ordinary $1	100.0	QLD.	(196.2)	(424.6)	Sold during the year
Macquarie Broadcasting Holdings Limited	Ordinary 50¢	100.0	A.C.T.	980.6	2,035.2	Radio broadcasting
Macquarie Properties Pty Limited	Ordinary $2	100.0	N.S.W.	184.2	156.2	Property owner
Magazine Promotions Australia Pty Limited	Ordinary $2	100.0	N.S.W.	(202.8)	3,758.0	Now ceased trading
Magazine Properties Pty Limited	Ordinary $1	100.0	N.S.W.	696.1	1.1	Property owner
Magdiss Pty Limited	Ordinary $2	100.0	VIC.	6.1	7.0	Distribution of magazines
Manoa Investments Pty Limited	Ordinary $2	100.0	N.S.W.	123.5	125.1	Property owner
Money Magazine Limited	Ordinary £Stg1	100.0	U.K. (a)	(110.4)	—	Magazine publishing
Newcastle Newspapers Pty Limited	Ordinary $1	100.0	N.S.W.	1,670.3	929.5	Newspaper publishing and investment
NZ Videotex Systems Limited	Ordinary NZ$1	100.0	New Zealand(c)	—	—	Non trading
Pericles Pty Limited	Ordinary $1	100.0	A.C.T.	—	—	Non trading
Personal Investment Magazines (NZ) Limited	Ordinary NZ$1	100.0	New Zealand(c)	(298.9)	—	Magazine publishing
Planned Communications Australia Pty Limited	Ordinary $2	100.0	A.C.T.	174.2	25.0	Provision of functional music
Port Macquarie Newspapers Pty Limited	Ordinary $2	100.0	N.S.W.	(85.2)	12.2	Sold during the year
Radio 4AY Pty Limited	Ordinary $2	100.0	QLD.	—	(13.6)	Radio broadcasting
Rozelle Terminal Handling Co Pty Limited	Ordinary $1	100.0	N.S.W.	(10.5)	16.8	Operation of newsprint stores
S. Richardson (Newspapers) Pty Limited	Ordinary $2	100.0	N.S.W.	16.5	63.3	Newspaper publishing
Rydge Publications Pty Limited	Ordinary $2	100.0	N.S.W.	—	—	Magazine publishing
Rydge Publications (Australia) Pty Limited	Ordinary $1	100.0	N.S.W.	(149.5)	—	Magazine publishing
60 York Street Pty Limited	Ordinary $1	100.0	VIC.	—	—	Property owner
Seven Satellite Pty Limited	Ordinary $1	83.5	N.S.W.	—	—	Satellite network
Suburban Community Newspapers Pty Limited	Ordinary $1	100.0	N.S.W	(69.8)	(106.2)	Now ceased trading
Suburban Investments Pty Limited	Ordinary $2	100.0	A.C.T.	—	0.8	Investment in securities and advances
Syme Electronic Communications Pty Ltd	Ordinary $2	100.0	VIC.	(500.8)	2,453.8	Operation of recording studios and cassette duplication
Syme Entertainment Pty Limited	Ordinary $2	100.0	VIC.	(0.3)	(17.6)	Video cassette distribution
Syme Communications (NZ) Limited	Ordinary NZ$1	100.0	New Zealand(c)	2.6	—	Video cassette distribution
Syme Media Pty Limited	Ordinary $1	100.0	VIC.	1,043.5	1,137.8	Newspaper and magazine publishing
The Federal Capital Press of Aust. Pty Limited	Ordinary $2	100.0	A.C.T.	901.3	1,310.3	Newspaper publishing and commercial printing
The Spectator (1828) Limited	Ordinary £Stg1	100.0	U.K. (a)	(274.5)	(277.6)	Magazine publishing
The Seven Network Pty Limited	Ordinary $2	100.0	A.C.T.	38.5	—	Television program distribution
Votraint (No. 297) Pty Limited	Ordinary $1	100.0	A.C.T.	—	—	Investment in securities and advances
Wattle Street Properties Pty Limited	Ordinary $2	100.0	A.C.T.	8.6	10.9	Property owner
				502.1	230.3	
Contribution to group profit after tax by holding company, John Fairfax						
Consolidated net profit of group after provision for income tax				133,189.6	66,675.1	

NOTES:
(a) Indicates carries on business in the United Kingdom
(b) Indicates carries on business in the United States of America
(c) Indicates carries on business in New Zealand
(d) The contributions to the group net profit by subsidiaries and the holding company shown above are after elimination of inter-company transactions. The contributions to group net profit by subsidiaries are after deducting interest of outside shareholders in subsidiary companies.
(e) The percentage interest of outside shareholders in each subsidiary in the group's structure can be calculated by deducting the group percentage interest shown in the above table from 100 per cent.
(f) The final net profit of each subsidiary takes into account, in the case of subsidiaries acquired during the period, only profits since the date of acquisition to the end of the financial period, and in the case of subsidiaries sold during the year the profit up to the date of sale.

JOHN FAIRFAX GROUP PRODUCTS
AT 30 JUNE 1987

METROPOLITAN NEWSPAPERS

Sydney Morning Herald
Sun, Sydney
Australian Financial Review
Canberra Times
Illawarra Mercury
Times on Sunday

Age, Melbourne
Sun-Herald
Sunday Press, Melbourne
Newcastle Herald
Melbourne Winners

COUNTRY, REGIONAL, INTERNATIONAL NEWSPAPERS

Morisset Courier
Trafalgar News
Warrnambool Standard
National Business Review (NZ)

South Gippsland and Sentinel Times
Warragul Gazette
West Gippsland Trader

SUBURBAN NEWSPAPERS

Auburn Review Pictorial
Blacktown City Star
Canberra Chronicle
Dandenong Regional Journal
Express Bacchus Marsh
Frankston Peninsula News
Liverpool/Fairfield Champion
Melton Mail-Express
Newcastle and Lake Macquarie Post
St George and Sutherland Shire Leader
Sunshine Advocate
Werribee Banner
Williamstown Advertiser

Bankstown/Canterbury Torch
Bondi Weekly Courier
Cranbourne Sun and Berwick-Pakenham Times
Dandenong Springvale Journal
Footscray Mail
Free Press Camberwell
MacArthur Advertiser
Mercury
Penrith City Star
Southern Courier
Wentworth Courier
Western Suburbs Courier
Wollongong/Shellharbour Advertiser

MAGAZINES

Business Review Weekly
Dolly
Good Weekend
Amateur Radio Action
Australian Auto Action
Australian Motor Cycle News
B.C.M.E
Car Australia

Cosmopolitan
Good Housekeeping
Harper's Bazaar
ANZ Blue Ribbon Bulletin
Australian Golf
Australian Property News
Business Review Weekly Annuals
Car Tests

Caravan Buyers Manual
Caravan World and Outdoor Life
Countdown
Cricketer
Custom 4 Wheel Drive
Electronics Australia
Handmade
Inside Football
Juke
Lifestyle Series
Modern Fishing
Personal Investment
Spectator (London)
Woman's Day
Money Magazine (UK)
National Greyhound News
NZ Business Who's Who
Overlander
Personal Investment Australia
Portfolio International (U.K)
Rev's Motor Cycle News
Sonics
Standardbred Stallion Register
Tourist Park Guide
Trail and Track Buyer's Guide
Triple A (incorporating Asia Banking)
Turbo Australia
Victorian Greyhound Weekly
4 x 4 Australia
4 x 4 Treks

Caravan Tests
CB Action
Creative Handbook
Cricketer Special
Eazyriders
Electronics Today International
Homes Pictorial
Investment Action
Let's Travel
Modern Boating
People
Smash Hits
Time Australia
Money International (UK)
Money Management
National Trotting Weekly
On Video
PC Australia
Portfolio
Prevention
Soccer Annual
Sonics Yearbook
The Capital Letter
Trail and Track
Trendex
Truckin' Life
Two Wheels
Your Computer
4 x 4 Roadtests

TELEVISION STATIONS

ATN7 (Sydney)
BTQ7 (Brisbane)
HSV7 (Melbourne)

RADIO STATIONS

2GB Sydney
2WL Wollongong
4BH Brisbane
5DN Adelaide

2CA Canberra
3AW Melbourne
4RR Townsville
IBS News (UK)

APPENDIX VI

THE TRYART COURT CASE

The dispute in the Tryart court case centred on the $100 million success fee which, under the Tryart agreement, Warwick had agreed to pay Laurie Connell's Rothwells bank in return for services rendered in the planning and execution of the JFL takeover. In an agreement with Alan Bond, on 9 November 1987 Connell discounted the fee for $68 million with Bond Media, payable on 28 June 1988. It wasn't paid.

Early in July 1988, Bond Media and Rothwells filed a writ seeking to recover the $100 million. Tryart's response to the writ, which later formed the basis of its defence and cross claim, was that Rothwells had 'neither fully nor properly performed the obligations under the agreement'. Tryart claimed in a letter to Bond Media that some aspects of the services were seriously defective, and others were not rendered at all or were not completed. 'It follows that the fee of $100 million referred to in the agreement has not been earned, and is not owing.'

In a cross claim filed a month later, Tryart sought, among other things, damages of at least $160 million from Rothwells. It claimed that Rothwells had based the takeover on assumptions which were 'without any proper basis'.

The case opened to a crowded courtroom before Justice Roger Giles in the New South Wales Supreme Court on 17 October 1988, with Tom Hughes, QC, representing Bond Media, Neil McPhee, QC, representing Warwick/John Fairfax Ltd/Tryart and George Palmer, QC, representing Martin Dougherty. The thirty-eight days of the hearing gave Sydney one of its most sensational courtroom dramas in years.

Very briefly, there were three bases for Tryart's professed outrage about the fees:

1. its size — many considered $100 million outrageous when the benchmark fee for the kind of services offered was more like $10 million. (But Warwick had agreed to it.)
2. the contention that it was not earned — the scenarios presented by Rothwells, particularly in relation to assets sales and profit projections, had little to do with reality as it turned out.
3. its secret distribution by Rothwells between Reuter and Dougherty — Warwick claimed he was unaware of the cut being given to Dougherty.

The irony of Tryart's case on the advice issue was that to present Rothwells in the worst possible light, Warwick also had to be presented as a less-than-proficient businessman — in fact, as a complete novice who had very little idea during the takeover of what he was doing and how he was doing it. Hughes made much of the apparent contradiction between Warwick's claims to financial illiteracy and the fact that he was a Harvard MBA graduate. He also attacked Warwick for failing to tell the family about the success fee, considering he had planned to structure it into JFL, thereby partially diminishing their equity if they had stayed in. Warwick denied that this had been 'dishonourable to blood relations'.

Likewise, Warwick was by implication responsible for instances of deception on JFL's part during the takeover: failing to disclose the success fee to the ANZ; excluding provision for the fee from financial forecasts supplied to the National Australia Bank; and representations made by Cotton to the National Australia Bank that Warwick, not the company, was liable for the fee.

Another irony of John Fairfax's case was that, for it to be successful, the onus was on the company convincingly to expose itself as a failure — in direct contradiction to its best public relations effort of the previous year.

The two sides adopted different definitions of success. John Fairfax contended that a successful bid was one which resulted in a financially viable company. Rothwells/Bond Media defined success more narrowly as attainment of the minimum acceptance number (36.15 per cent) as stipulated in the Tryart agreement.

The dilemma for John Fairfax's lawyers was, just how far could it push the argument that the company was not financially viable without exacerbating the alleged lack of viability? This was a matter of acute sensitivity given that, even as the case was running, John Fairfax executives were touring the world trying to persuade investors to back the company through junk bonds. In fact the assertion of non-viability compromised the basis of all the company's post-takeover borrowings, for which lenders must have been persuaded that JFL was a viable concern and hence a good risk.

In court, Warwick projected as a solemn, calm and very measured witness. All his answers were delivered only after careful consideration, usually spanning exceptionally long pauses. Despite Hughes' considerable efforts, Warwick conceded very little. The most he gave away when an allegation was made which was not helpful to his case was that he did not deny it. Seldom did he recall the basis for such allegations. The court was left to judge whether he had an appalling memory, or whether he was extremely skilled in the art of truth manipulation.

The out-of-court settlement, details of which emerged in early February 1989, left this question hanging. John Fairfax agreed to pay Bond Media $27 million, instead of the $110 million-plus it might have had to pay had the court action failed. All claims against Reuter and Dougherty were dropped. Each party had to pay its own legal costs estimated between $6 million and $10 million.

While John Fairfax could fairly regard the settlement as a win, since it reduced its potential liability to Rothwells by some $73 million, there was no doubt immeasurable cost to the company, its reputation and financial standing as a result of the court case revelations.

SPEECH BY JAMES FAIRFAX
AT THE SYDNEY MORNING HERALD
150TH ANNIVERSARY DINNER
APRIL 15,1981

Your Excellencies, ladies and gentlemen, it is a great honour, Sir, to welcome you and Lady Cowen here tonight at this, the high point of our celebration of the 150th anniversary of the *Sydney Morning Herald*.

Your Excellency brings to the high office, which you have now occupied with distinction for three years, a multitude of qualities which have become apparent throughout Australia over this period.

These qualities, if I may say so Sir, are not only related to your eminent career in both legal and academic spheres, but embrace an interest and involvement in a wide range of activities covering many fields in our civic and cultural life.

We are delighted to have you and Lady Cowen with us tonight.

Among our special guests I should like to welcome are:

The New South Wales Attorney General and Minister for Justice, Mr Frank Walker, representing the Premier, and Mrs Walker.

The Federal Minister for Communications and Leader of the House of Representatives, Mr Ian Sinclair and Mrs Sinclair.

The Lord Mayor of Sydney, Alderman Sutherland, and the Lady Mayoress, Miss Feodosiou.

The Chief Justice of the Federal Court of Australia, Sir Nigel Bowen and Lady Bowen.

The President of the ACTU, Mr Cliff Dolan and Mrs Dolan.

The Chairman of the Advertising Federation of Australia, Mr Keith Cousins and Mrs Cousins.

The Leader of the New South Wales Opposition, Mr John Mason and Mrs Mason.

The Chairman of the Australian Broadcasting Commission, Sir Talbot Duckmanton and Lady Duckmanton.

The Chairman of Australian Consolidated Press, Mr Kerry Packer and Mrs Packer.

The Managing Director of News Ltd, Mr Ken Cowley and Mrs Cowley.

Mrs E. H. B. Neill, representing the board of David Syme and Co. Ltd.

We very much regret that the Chairman of the Herald and Weekly Times, Sir Keith Macpherson and Lady Macpherson were prevented from coming by an airline strike.

Finally I should like to say how pleased we are to have with us two former managing directors, Mr R. A. Henderson and Mr A. H. McLachlan.

Since becoming chairman of this company four years ago I have been very much aware over this time of the approach of the event we are celebrating tonight — the one hundred and fiftieth anniversary of the *Sydney Morning Herald*. The then *Sydney Herald* actually first appeared on 18th April, 1831.

Before turning to the event itself I think it would be appropriate if I made a few remarks about the Fairfax family, for this is in many ways a family occasion. If I may borrow an expression which users of the *Michelin Guide* in Europe will know, 'un peu d'histoire' — a little history. Unlike the *Michelin Guide* which, having lulled its readers into a false sense of security by this gentle suggestion, then proceeds to cram a truly astonishing amount of information about every aspect: historical, cultural, genealogical, architectural and so on, of the particular town into the bewildered head of the tourist — it is probably being read to him by his wife as he negotiates a traffic jam in the town square — unlike, as I say the *Michelin Guide* — my remarks will simply be a few personal observations.

It is never easy to talk about your own family — it is even less easy when they all happen to be sitting around you. Even in the days of the family Christmas lunch at Ginahgulla, presided over by Miss Mary Fairfax, eldest child and only daughter of James Reading Fairfax, second son of John, no one was required to make a speech, although we used to drink Aunt Mary's health. My role then was to dress up as Father Christmas.

The family, since the arrival of John Fairfax in 1838, have diversified into many different areas; succeeding generations have developed interests and talents in fields remote from the world of newspapers. This is perhaps best seen in the third and fourth generations, John Fairfax's sons being mainly involved in the *Herald*. Of the six sons of James Reading Fairfax, the second and third, Geoffrey and my grandfather, James, entered the Herald, while the fifth, Hubert, developed extensive pastoral interests and the sixth, Wilfred, was a G.P., having served as Senior Physician to the 1st Australian General Hospital at Rouen in the First World War.

The fourth generation is represented here tonight by my father, Sir Warwick, and my cousins, Lady Morrow, Sir Vincent and Mr H. D. Fairfax. Here, indeed, we find a diversity of talents. In spite of possible blushes I feel I must refer to them. My cousin, Margaret, had many years' service as State Commissioner for Girl Guides in New South Wales. My father, in addition to a distinguished career spanning some fifty-six years with the company, has published *The Triple Abyss*, a work on philosophy and religion which has received much acclaim; also *Men, Parties and Politics*, and has had three plays publicly performed. My cousin Vincent's career has extended from the newspaper world to that of commerce, the Royal Agricultural Society and rural interests. He headed the Scout movement in New South Wales at the same time as his first cousin headed the Guide movement. My cousin Mick's career has been devoted to country interests, where he is a pillar of the community. Of the fourth generation no longer with us, we remember John, war correspondent and author (not only of the life of John Fairfax) but of four small volumes depicting scenes and characters of the Australian countryside together with wartime reminiscences which I think will live forever. We remember too, Jim (James Griffyth Fairfax), a distinguished poet and one-time member of the British House of Commons.

I feel it is too soon to make any comment on the fifth generation — being one of them, it is certainly not for me to do so except to say we are delighted that so many were able to be here, including my brother Warwick, who has come back from Oxford for the occasion. The sixth generation, including two young Fairfax boys, is making its impact elsewhere, but we do have two representatives, Louise Simpson and Peta Boyce.

But in its diversity the family has been united. It springs from the one source and supports the traditions and principles established by John Fairfax and followed by his successors for 140 years. As with many families there have been divisions and disputes — some have caused bitterness — none have failed to be healed. As long as the family sticks together — in this context it is perhaps worth mentioning that they control some 50 per cent of the shareholding — I believe the future of the company is assured.

In the course of an article in Tuesday's Supplement I said that the significance of this sesqui-centenary to those celebrating it can be such that the event itself can be in danger of becoming an exercise on self-congratulation while the physical forms it takes can obscure the real meaning.

These physical manifestations such as Herald Square at Circular Quay, Fairfax Lookout at North Head and the Zofrea mural at the Broadway office are most important as a permanent commemoration and are intended as a positive enrichment to the lives of the citizens of Sydney whose forebears gave the *Herald* its first support.

But when the subject of commemoration happens to be a daily newspaper, controversy surrounding the media in this day and age makes an objective view of its meaning even more important.

What is the real meaning? It could mean many things to many people and the more involved one gets with the organisation, the greater the diversity of views one would find. To me, one question keeps recurring — whether it is possible at this time to own a newspaper and not only to run it in the interests of the community and the nation, but to be seen to be running it in those interests. Like justice, as well as being done, it must be seen to be done. This goes further than simply providing to the best of one's ability a comprehensive and unbiased news coverage combined with fair and authoritative comment. It raises the spectre of the potential conflict between editorial independence and a measure of proprietorial or board control. It involves the integrity of the newspaper and those running it.

In John Fairfax's time, integrity I think was rather taken for granted — the great issues of the day were fiercely fought over and trenchantly commented on, but generally speaking motive was not suspect. I doubt if it would have occurred to him or indeed to his sons and grandsons that anyone would have questioned their motives. In my father's time and my own this has not been so. We have been and are constantly being told by people from one end of the political spectrum to the other that we have some political axe to grind or some particular view to force down the throats of an unsuspecting public — that we are only giving people what we want them to know. There have been several recent examples of attacks on the media — an eminent novelist, a trade union leader, and sundry members of parliament — both sides of the house: Federal and State. My first reaction always is — can this really be Fairfax they are talking about?

There is another substantive charge: that the media and Fairfax, because it is an important part of the media, sets the agenda for discussion of the great public issues of the day. This of course has a great deal of truth in it. The job of the media is communications and in communicating ideas and setting our own priorities, we do influence public perceptions. But the media cannot be too far ahead of public opinion, nor can it ignore its markets without peril. There are important constraints in the media arbitrarily limiting the agenda or setting dubious or phoney priorities. Nowhere is this truer than in the Fairfax group, which, with its diversity of products with distinctive regional markets and very different specialist audiences, can ill afford to exercise arbitrary power over the dissemination of ideas. The evidence is in front of our face in the Channel Seven Network, the Macquarie Radio Network and the great newspapers we publish. If there is an agenda it can hardly be called a distinctively Fairfax agenda. Our obligations to our different audiences demand a diversity which we now acknowledge as company policy.

I try to see myself and my colleagues as some of the critics I have referred to must see us. I look in vain for secret deals with cabinet ministers — in point of fact I can only recall two major issues in the last four years on which I had discussions with cabinet ministers and they both involved television. One was the televising of the Moscow Olympic Games, the other the film of an execution in Saudi Arabia called Death of a Princess — you will recall that in both cases we rejected the government's advice. They were just as entitled to press their view as we were to reject it.

I search my mind too for instances during my regular discussions with editors when I have forced a view on them backed by the authority of the board. In theory it is quite possible — in fact it does not happen.

I look too for evidence of journalists cowed by threats — real or imagined — against their employment, into following a line which they think would meet with the proprietors' approval.

The suggestion either made or implied that I, as chairman, or my colleagues as directors in any way influence or manipulate the selection or presentation of news is totally false and cannot be repudiated too strongly.

As far as editorial comment is concerned, I said in the Tuesday article that the editors of all our publications operate with remarkably few restraints: the ultimate authority of the board is present but the emphasis is on discussion and consultation. The choice of topics for discussion in the papers is totally their own — from time to time I make suggestions which may or may not be taken up.

In yesterday's article I used the expression 'exercise a guiding hand' and here I would like to say that I profited from the example of my father.

Gavin Souter's book, A Company of Heralds, describes some dramatic clashes between proprietors, chief executives and editors from the 1940s through the 1970s — it would be surprising, the participants being men of talent with strong views, if this had not occurred.

However, I believe the concept of editorial freedom was always present and there was no instance of an editor either resigning or losing his job because of such clashes. Today, the board of this company sets certain standards and lays down a framework within which our newspapers operate, as in pre-public company days the family proprietors did more directly. This is the tradition that has been handed down.

One can, of course, be criticised just as much for non-interference as the reverse and in the preservation of editorial independence you are going to annoy just as many people who feel you should be plugging a particular line or supporting a particular political party more strongly. You end up at one time or another in irritating and annoying almost everybody and this in an odd way — this sort of provocation is one of the things a newspaper is all about.

On a somewhat lighter note and perhaps alluding to another of the Herald's mottoes which for many years occupied the space below the masthead, 'In moderation placing all my glory, while Tories call me Whig and Whigs a Tory,' I am reminded of a comment of my mother. She unfortunately cannot be here tonight as she is in London. She said to me early in December last year, 'All my friends tell me the Herald has gone Labor, but then they always say that at election time.'

Certainly at one or two parties I went to, it was as though the chairman of the Sydney Red Flag had walked in — needless to say we were still being assailed in other circles as the capitalist press.

Returning to the original question on running newspapers in the national and community interest I suppose the short answer is that there is no way of convincing some people of one's good intentions — and even if there was, one would quite rightly get no credit for good intentions alone. It would indeed be depressing if such a group formed the bulk of one's readers but of course they do not. If they did there would be a massive rejection of the product by the consumer. Sometimes an individual voice carries an influence out of proportion to the knowledge and experience of the speaker — for that, we must bear some of the blame.

We will go on producing newspapers as long as there is breath in our bodies and money in the till because we are convinced that we do have the trust and confidence of the bulk of our readers.

No amount of ill-considered talk of over-ambitious, grasping proprietors, of editors who are either out of control or under too much control or of arrogant or down-trodden journalists is going to shake our confidence in our editors and journalists.

We will know soon enough if we lose old readers' trust — but we shall go on providing the service to the public which we have been providing for 150 years to the best of our abilities. It is a team effort and everyone who plays his or her part in the organisation as the overwhelming majority do, is entitled to a share of the credit.

I believe, Sir, that would be an appropriate note on which to end.

NOTES

Place names mentioned in the text: Bellevue Hill, Darling Point, Double Bay, Edgecliff, Elizabeth Bay, Rose Bay and Woollahra are all inner eastern suburbs of Sydney, within 10 km of the city centre. Bowral, Bundanoon and Moss Vale are in the southern highlands, approximately 120 km south of Sydney. Leura is situated in the Blue Mountains, about 160 km west of Sydney, while Bilgola Beach and Palm Beach are around 50 km north of Sydney.

CHAPTER 1

1. The Warwickshire Fairfaxes were distantly connected with the well-known Yorkshire Fairfaxes whose best known member was Thomas, 3rd Lord Fairfax (Black Tom), commander in chief of the Parliamentary Army during the greater part of the Civil War in England (1645-1650).

2. A federal electorate has been named after the family in Queensland largely through Aunt Ruth's activities with the CWA. At the time of the 1990 election, the seat was held by National Party member John Stone, who had taken it over on the retirement of Evan Adermann. However, John Stone lost the seat to Liberal candidate Alex Somlyay.

3. Edward Philip Telford Simpson and Caroline married in 1959. Philip was born in 1924. Educated at Tudor House, Moss Vale, and The King's School, Parramatta, he joined the RAAF in 1942, and was discharged in 1945 with the rank of Flying Officer. After taking his Law degree at the University of Sydney, he joined the family firm, Minter Simpson and Company (now Minter Ellison) as a partner in 1951, eventually retiring on New Year's Eve 1989. He now farms at Newbury, Sutton Forest, a property held by the Simpson family since 1934.

4. John was a war correspondent and wrote several books including *Laughter in the Camp*, *Drift of Leaves*, *Run O' Waters*, *Historic Roads Round Sydney*.

CHAPTER 2

1. Now demolished, Llanillo was built by Sir Colin Stephen, father of my godmother Helen Rutledge, and features in her book *My Grandfather's House*.

2. Louise Meyer de Bovyl came to Sydney with Mr Adrian Knox (later Sir Adrian, Chief Justice of the High Court) and looked after his children Elizabeth, Margaret and Robert. She came to my father when he was aged seven and then became my grandmother's maid. She retired to France fifty-four years later, having been in employment at Fairwater from 1908 until 1962.

3. Lulworth is a nursing home attached to St Luke's Hospital where many well-known

inhabitants of Sydney have resided. The original house was owned by Mr and Mrs Victor White, parents of Patrick who describes it in *The Vivisector*.

4. Australia's best known paediatrician, Lorimer Dods discovered the Rubella syndrome. He also saved my life when I was three months old by diagnosing pyloric stenosis for which I was operated on

CHAPTER 3

1. Sir James Darling instituted Timbertop in 1953, near Mansfield in Victoria, for boys to live and work in bushland conditions. He was subsequently an enlightened chairman of the Australian Broadcasting Commission, and a member of the Broadcasting Control Board. He and his wife Margaret were to become good friends of mine and I have always greatly valued his advice and guidance. His autobiography, *Richly Rewarding*, was published by Hill of Content in association with Lloyd O'Neil in 1978.

2. Colleen was the only child of my grandmother's brother Harley Lord Hixson. She spent part of her childhood at Fairwater while her parents were in India and was a companion to my father who was the same age.

3. The Reading family were relations of ours through Sarah Reading's marriage to the first John Fairfax.

4. Now The Hon. Sir Laurence Street KCMG and Lady Street. Sir Laurence, recently Chief Justice of New South Wales and Lieutenant Governor of New South Wales, is a member of a well known Sydney legal family.

5. Sheila and Pierre still live just up the street. Pierre, who is past his 90th birthday, works actively for a number of charities.

CHAPTER 4

1. Later Lord Mockton of Brenchley, he was the Duke of Windsor's solicitor during the Abdication crisis and adviser to the last ruling Nizam of Hyderabad. He never mentioned the first of these two roles.

2. Hugh Stretton MA, FAHA, FASSA, Hon.D.Litt, Hon.LL.D., Resident Fellow in Economics, University of Adelaide, since 1990; Reader 1968-89; Professor of History 1954-68. Fellow, Balliol College, Oxford 1948-54.

CHAPTER 5

1. I refer to Rupert Henderson by his christian name although it was not until my return from Glasgow in 1957 that I was on those terms with him.

2. See Gavin Souter, *Company of Heralds*, Melbourne University Press, Carlton, 1981.

3. John Stephen Mansfield, a distant relation of the legal family, was the architect for the exterior of the building working with E.R. Bradshaw.

4. Warwick Fairfax, *The Triple Abyss: Towards a Modern Synthesis*, Geo. Bles, London, 1965.

5. Amalgamated Television Services was a consortium of broadcasting station 2GB, Macquarie Broadcasting Service Pty Ltd, Artransa Pty Ltd, AWA and Email Ltd with other investors, John Fairfax & Sons Pty Ltd, Associated Newspapers Ltd and its subsidiary, Radio 2UE Sydney Pty Ltd.

6. F. E. Trigg was senior partner in Price Waterhouse & Co and later financial adviser to John Fairfax Ltd, attending board meetings.

7. Later Sir Ian Potter and a leading financier in his own right having left the firm of Potter Partners.

8. Pringle wrote on 1 November: 'The speed and boldness — some might call it recklessness — with which Britain and France have acted in the Middle East have confounded their friends no less than their critics.' (Souter, *op. cit.* p.331)

9. Elliot Carnegy's father, Francis Joseph, son of Samuel Joseph MLC married Isabella Carnegy, who inherited the feudal barony of Lour (a cadet branch of the earldom of Northesk) in Angus in 1915 when the family took the Carnegy name. The Fairwater land, which adjoined the Geoffrey Fairfaxes at Elaine, was given to the Josephs as a wedding present by James White, MLC. Elliot's daughter Elizabeth, Baroness Carnegy of Lour, is a life peer and I visited her at Lour in 1988. The links between our two families have always been maintained.

CHAPTER 6

1. Alan Moorehead was a famous war correspondent and author. His books include *Cooper's Creek, Rum Jungle, Gallipoli, The Fatal Impact, The White Nile* and *The Blue Nile.*

2. A. T. Shakespeare, son of T. M. Shakespeare, and formerly a cadet on the *Sydney Morning Herald* with Rupert Henderson, was founder of the *Canberra Times.*

3. Bingham was a former war correspondent and newly appointed associate editor.

4. Maude was formerly with the London *Times* and the London *Daily Mail.*

5. For Kinghaven shares, see chapter 19, note 1.

6. Sue Du Val is my brother-in-law Philip's first cousin. His father, Telford, and her mother, Vera, married to Newcastle solicitor Archibald Rankin, were brother and sister.

7. Bridgestar was a similar arrangement to Kinghaven in its original form.

8. Souter, *op. cit.* pp.386-7.

9. In 1944 the four Sydney newspaper proprietors, due to a wildcat printers' strike, printed composite papers following a strike by production workers and, subsequently, journalists.

CHAPTER 7

1. Among other positions held, the forceful and competitive Lindsay Clinch had been an editor of the *Sunday Sun* (1947-53) and executive editor of the *Sun* (1953-59 and 1961-65).

2. For Pringle's leader, see Souter, *op. cit.*, pp.435-6.

3. Irene Thirkell had joined the company in the 1930s and worked as secretary to both Rupert and McLachlan until her retirement in 1971. She continued with McLachlan in Hamilton Street and assists him to this day.

4. Article 91: The Directors may delegate any of their powers to committees consisting of such member or members of their body as they think fit; and a committee so formed shall in the exercise of the powers so delegated conform to any regulations that may be imposed on it by the Directors. A committee may elect a Chairman of its meetings. If no such Chairman be elected or if at any meeting the Chairman be not present within fifteen minutes after the time appointed for holding the same or refuse to act the members present may choose one of their number to be Chairman of the meeting. The meetings and proceedings of any such committee consisting of two or more members shall be governed by the provisions of these Articles regulating the meetings and proceedings of the Directors so far as the same are applicable and are not superseded by any regulations made by the Directors.

5. The late Dr Ian Lyall Thompson was a former tutor in medicine, University of New South Wales; RMO Sydney Hospital 1954-55; Res. Boston City Hospital 1956-58; Consultant Physician from 1966; Visiting Medical Officer, St Vincents and St Luke's Hospital, Darlinghurst.

6. Santamaria was President of the National Civic Council from 1957. He was also former Director, National Secretariat of Catholic Action; President, Catholic Social Movement; Secretary, National Catholic Rural Movement.

7. The Syme-Fairfax deed states the partnership principles as '. . . to maintain the independence of the company, to sustain and foster the traditions of the late David Syme as developed and expanded by his heirs and in particular to maintain the influence of the Syme family in the affairs of the company as publisher of 'the Age', to maintain 'the Age' as an independent newspaper of high quality and responsibility in competition with other newspapers circulating mainly in Victoria, to ensure the continued dissemination through 'the Age' and other channels of news possessing a high degree of objectivity, and to enable the company to take advantage of the Associate's (John Fairfax & Sons Ltd) extensive experience in the publication of newspapers and allied activities.'

8. Richard had remarried a few years before. He, Sandie, their son Kristan (who is my godson) and their daughter Cressida are close friends of mine.

9. Souter, *op. cit.*, pp.563-4: The redundancy proposal was to remain in force at least until 31 December 1981. During that period there was to be no compulsory

retrenchment of permanent PKIU employees as a result of new technology, provided they were willing to be trained in and accept new or existing PKIU duties. Permanent employees were defined as those who had joined the company prior to 3 September 1975. Employees who had joined after that date were defined as temporary. As new production processes were introduced, permanent PKIU employees in redundancy areas would be invited to apply for transfer to new non-PKIU duties. All retraining would be carried out at company expense and in the company's time.

Permanent and temporary employees in redundant areas who did not offer to, or were not accepted for, transfer to alternative duties, could apply to the company for voluntary termination of their employment. The severance remuneration would be one week's pay for each year of service up to ten years, two weeks' pay for the eleventh to twentieth complete years of service and three weeks' pay for the twenty-first and subsequent complete years of service.

CHAPTER 8

1. Sir Vincent Fairfax was Chairman of the AMP Society 1966-82 and President of the Royal Agricultural Society 1970-79. He was a Director of the Bank of New South Wales 1953-82, a Director of the London *Times* 1962-67 and National President of the Scout Association of Australia 1977-86.

2. Souter, *op. cit.*, p. 571.

3. The exchange between Falkingham and Murdoch is quoted in Souter, *op. cit.*, p. 574.

4. Under the Broadcasting and Television Act at that time, a purchase of more than 5 per cent of the H&WT, which had a prescribed interest in HSV, would require Fairfax to sell its Canberra (CTC) and Brisbane (QTQ) television interests.

CHAPTER 9

1. The Syme/Fairfax agreement ended in March 1984 and the board was reconstituted with myself as Chairman (at Sir Warwick's suggestion), Bill Bland (former General Manager) as Deputy Chairman, Greg Taylor as Managing Director and Dacre Smith (representing the Syme family) and Professor D. A. Denton (Director of the Howard Florey Institute) making a majority of Victorian directors.

2. Subsequent to the Norris enquiry and after six years' resistance, John Fairfax Ltd joined the Australian Press Council. Inspired largely by Ranald Macdonald, a number of newspaper publishers and the Australian Journalists' Association formed the council in 1976 as a voluntary watchdog on press behaviour and a defender of press rights. Fairfax was the one major press group to stand out at the time, directors and management agreeing with Sir Warwick, then chairman, that we should make no concession to press regulations, even voluntary regulation. There was a fear that

the council's establishment could encourage moves towards official controls, and a confidence that the Fairfax company, custodian of a tradition of 145 years of decent journalism, was better equipped than any council to see to fair play in its newspapers. Nevertheless, Fairfax papers fully reported any criticism of them by the council and reported extensively on the council's activities.

In August 1980 the decision to stay out was reaffirmed, but views were ready to change when a new invitation came early in 1982. Recommending that we join, Suich said there were now more advantages than disadvantages. If the present council collapsed there was a danger a statutory press council would be formed. He was anxious that we should join before any decision by the News group to return, but that first we should be satisfied that a suitable chairman would be found to succeed Sir Frank Kitto, who was about to retire. The recommendation found general support among directors, Sir Warwick taking it as a strong point that our joining would make it harder for a Federal or State government to establish a press control commission. The choice of chairman having fallen on Professor Geoffrey Sawer, constitutional authority and a commentator on the press, we announced our decision to join on 9 July 1982.

CHAPTER 10

1. Malcolm Fraser was both Prime Minister and Minister Without Portfolio. In the latter capacity he could intervene on a minister's terrain and become the de facto minister, taking over negotiations, making public statements and determining policy. This he did in the case of Andrew Peacock's negotiations with ICI over a shorter working week, part of a log of claims served on the company by the Federated Ironworkers' Association. The Prime Minister's approach was very different to his minister's, and appeared to undermine promises that Peacock had already made (Paul Kelly, *Sydney Morning Herald*, 3 April 1981, p. 7).

CHAPTER 12

1. Arthur Calwell's reference to Henderson as 'that quilp-like creature', quoted in Souter (pp. 251) and recorded in *Hansard*, occurred during a parliamentary debate, on 13 March 1946, over the fate of Japanese, Formosan and Korean prisoners of war and internees returning north from Sydney in the Japanese destroyer *Yoizuki*. The *Herald*, among other newspapers, had protested at the appalling conditions on board, which Calwell felt was an unpatriotic stance. The term 'quilp' was a reference to Daniel Quilp, the atrocious villain of Dicken's *The Old Curiosity Shop*: 'an elderly man of remarkably hard features and forbidding aspect, and so low in stature as to be quite a dwarf, though his head and face were large enough for the body of a giant.'

2. David Bowman, *The Captive Press*, Penguin, Ringwood (Victoria), 1988, pp. 127-9. It is a salutary, though sometimes disconcerting, experience to see ourselves as others see us and I have indeed profited from Bowman's comments. In chapter 5,

entitled 'Fairfax', Bowman gives a generous assessment of my years as chairman and what I was trying to achieve — which to me is all the more gratifying, coming from the man whose removal from the editorship I had recommended to the board following the Suich report.

CHAPTER 13

1. In late November 1986 the Federal Government announced its cross-media legislation of which the two main proposals were: that there would be no restriction on the number of television stations a single proprietor might own, provided they did not have access to more than 75 per cent of the market; secondly, ownership of a newspaper and a television station in the same area was not permitted if more than 50 per cent of the newspaper's circulation was within the viewing area. In Treasurer Paul Keating's colourful expression, proprietors could be 'Princes of Print or Queens of the Screen'.

The legislation ultimately achieved what every Federal Government since that of Menzies had attempted in one form or another (reducing, in the process, the Broadcasting and Television Act to an impossible mess): a restriction on the print media's ownership of the electronic media which might lead to total separation of the two industries. Even though there was the usual 'grandfather' clause protecting existing holdings, the Keating legislation was to result in such a separation because it increased the vulnerability of the H&WT group, particularly to Murdoch who had a clear indication that he could proceed without let or hindrance along one path or the other. He also had the advantage of prior consultation with Keating together with Packer, something that was denied the H&WT and ourselves, who were regarded as 'enemies'. Even though the *Sydney Morning Herald* and, to a lesser extent, the *Financial Review*, had been generally supportive of the Hawke Government, the investigative activities of the *National Times* put us firmly in this category; the Melbourne *Herald* was regarded by Hawke as being historically and sometimes violently anti-Labor.

2. To get to the $111 million surplus, the Macquarie Hill Samuel scenario was:

Purchase H&WT including Qld Press and Adv...........2,250,000,000
Sale of D. Syme and other assets by Cash...................... 798,000,000
Borrowing 176,000,000
Rights issue 226,000,000

....(1,200,000,000)
....1,050,000,000
Sale of other H&WT assets ....(1,485,000,000)
Surplus 435,000,000
Less existing Fairfax and H&WT borrowings...............(211,000,000)

less subscribe for rights issue..(113,000,000)
Surplus 111,000,000

3. Tryart was the bid vehicle that Warwick used to take over John Fairfax Ltd in November 1987. Early the following year, a legal battle ensued between Warwick, Tryart's other directors (Laurie Connell and Bert Reuter), Martin Dougherty and Bond Media. Details of the court case are given in Appendix VI.

CHAPTER 14

1. The difficulties than can arise in the pursuit of investigative reporting are illustrated by the involvement of the *National Times* in Kerry Packer's defamation action against it, following its publication of material relating to the Costigan Commission in August and September 1984. While I have no wish to shelter behind legal advice, the fact remains that the advice I have been given is to restrict my comments to matters published in relation to the settlement of the action which took place in April 1985. The following statement of apology to Packer was published in the *National Times* in the issue April 26-May 3 1985.

APOLOGY TO KERRY PACKER

On September 14, 1984, John Fairfax & Sons Limited published in the *National Times* a long feature article setting out a number of confidential 'case summaries' from the Costigan Royal Commission.

The case summaries made a number of very grave allegations against a person called 'the Goanna'.

John Fairfax & Sons Limited recognises that 'the Goanna' was identified by many people as being Mr. Kerry Packer.

At the time of publishing the case summaries, John Fairfax & Sons Limited had no knowledge of its own as to the truth of the allegations and did not endorse them. Mr. Packer has at all times publicly and strenuously denied these allegations.

Mr. Packer commenced proceedings against John Fairfax & Sons Limited claiming damages for defamation for the publication of this article.

These proceedings have been resolved.

John Fairfax & Sons Limited accepts and recognises that it has no evidence nor is it aware of any evidence to support the allegations in the Costigan case summaries.

John Fairfax & Sons Limited sincerely regrets and apologises for the embarrassment and hurt caused to Mr. Kerry Packer and his family by the article.

Gavin Souter has covered these events in *Heralds and Angels*, Melbourne University Press, 1991.

2. Journalists' worst fears were confirmed with the closure of the *Sun* and the *Times on Sunday* on 14 March 1988. The closure of the two newspapers cost five hundred jobs. Low morale and uncertainty in the aftermath of Warwick's takeover led to a great deal of dissatisfaction and industrial unrest, not least the resignation of Chris

Anderson on 9 February, soon after his return from a month's holiday in England. Martin Dougherty appointed Andrew Clark, an outside journalist, in his place, prompting the next day's resignation of *Sydney Morning Herald* editor, John Alexander. Nine senior journalists — including the news editor, business editor, features editor and investment editor — followed suit.

A meeting called that afternoon to discuss the Fairfax Magazines redundancy dispute, already the cause of strike action in January, quickly turned into an emotional debate about apparent threats to the Fairfax tradition of editorial independence. The meeting voted to strike for seventy-two hours. It also passed a motion of no confidence in the company's management, and specifically Martin Dougherty. A later strike meeting passed a motion deploring Warwick Fairfax's failure to face the staff and answer for the consequences of his actions. (It later emerged that he was in the United States attending a presidential prayer breakfast at the time.)

Subsequently, on 15 February, Dougherty was asked to resign, taking with him a pay-out of $3 million, and the journalists who had resigned were reinstated.

Chapter 16

1. For details of the Tryart court case, see Appendix VI.

2. The Rockwood Pastoral Company Pty Ltd held a total of 11,354,732 shares in John Fairfax Ltd. It was generally thought that Warwick controlled Rockwood and therefore its JFL shares, but in fact at the time of the takeover it was jointly controlled with Mary Fairfax.

3. Clive Evatt, QC, former Minister for Housing in the New South Wales Goverment, was the younger brother of the renowned Dr H.V. Evatt, former Minister of External Affairs and President of the United Nations General Assembly.

4. Rothwells was the merchant bank established in 1981 by Laurie Connell, Warwick's main adviser — for a fee of $100 million — on the takeover of John Fairfax Limited. It became the headquarters of the takeover team which consisted, in the early stages, of Connell, Martin Dougherty and Bert Reuter.

Chapter 17

1. Ernie Fairbrother and his wife had been cultivated by Mary Fairfax to a degree I think they sometimes found embarrassing. Her invitations issued to Fairfax staff to Fairwater often had an ulterior motive.

2. Peter King was Executive Director of Van Leer, a Dutch packaging multinational.

3. Formerly senior finance executive of the Fairfax group and at that time general manager of finance and administration with National Mutual Royal Bank. He had been close both to Sir Warwick and Mary Fairfax.

Chapter 19

1. I first broached the possibility of a share arrangement with my father towards the end of 1958 following a discussion with Rupert. I do not believe the prospect of his third marriage was a major consideration, although coincidentally the sale agreement was finally signed in June 1959, just before that marriage in July.

The ownership and ultimate destination of my Kinghaven shares could have had a bearing on family attitudes in the years leading up to the takeover. Sir Warwick sold 500,000 one pound ordinary stock units in JFL to Kinghaven Pty Ltd in March 1959 for two pounds five shilling each (market price) for a total of 1.125 million pounds. Repayments were at the rate of 25,000 pounds per annum interest-free and the shares could not be sold without the consent of Sir Warwick while any part of the purchase price remained unpaid. The voting rights passed to Kinghaven, of which I was the beneficial owner, as payments were made. This transfer of shares, urged for by Rupert Henderson to avoid the costly burden of death duties, was agreed to by Sir Warwick — just before his marriage to Mary — only after some hesitation.

In 1961, after Warwick's birth, I agreed to provide in my will that if I had no male heirs, the shares would pass to a trust. The trustees, who would be appointed by Sir Warwick and myself, would have power to transfer the shares to Warwick or hold the shares on trust and pay him the income. The outcome of this was the Lorimer Dods settlement in 1973, under which the trustees I appointed would have the power to decide when to vest the shares or pass control of them to Warwick. The intention was to vest the shares in Warwick providing certain criteria were met. These related to Warwick's interest and involvement in the affairs of JFL and his understanding of the control of JFL by the Fairfax family and the continuation of that control. This was particularly important during the period of estrangement from 1976-80, as during that time I was endeavouring, through a stiff and formal correspondence with Sir Warwick, to ascertain what his own arrangements were and what part Mary would play in them. After the reconciliation I was given information on this, but it was alleged (Tryart Case) that Sir Warwick's will was changed not long before his death to restore Mary's 50 per cent control over his shares, because of her uncertainty about her influence over Warwick. This control enabled her to negotiate the astonishing 2.9 million indexed and tax-free annual income from Warwick in October 1987. As Sykes says, it must be a unique financial deal between a son and his mother in Australia. It does not explain her supposed inaction during the final months of the takeover plans.

Returning to Kinghaven, in November 1983 a series of meetings began, firstly between Sir Warwick and me and then between Halstead and Robinson (for me) and Fieldhouse (for Sir Warwick). These meetings were held because Sir Warwick had expressed concern that my trustees were not obliged to exercise their discretion to vest the shares in Warwick immediately upon my death but rather, if in their opinion he was not a suitable custodian of the shares, they could be vested in other members of the family. Also, the trustees would obtain the voting rights. It should be added that the trustees were concerned about the responsibility of exercising this judgment and preferred that the obligation not rest with them.

These discussions resulted in the establishment of the Guilford Bell settlement in August 1985, which provided that I would have the income and voting rights of Kinghaven for life and that Warwick would be entitled to the capital rights to the shares on my death. If Warwick did not survive me and left no living issue, they would pass to the descendants of Sir Warwick's other issue and thence to those of Sir Vincent. The deed could only be amended or the shares sold with the consent of both Warwick and myself.

It will readily be appreciated that the key to the whole process was my confidence and trust in Warwick as the future controller of the company — he would have two-thirds of the family holding to John's one-third. Sir Warwick thanked me for this trust at a meeting in Halstead's office at which Warwick was present. To the best of my recollection the latter said nothing and my trust was to be sadly misplaced. In a deed dated 4 December 1987, I assigned all rights under the settlement to Warwick for a consideration of $22,700,000. There has been a degree of misconception and inaccuracy about this settlement. Connell is quoted as saying I was mad to accept $22.7 million for it and I must make several points in relation to this. The sum negotiated with Tryart was based actuarially on dividends receivable over a period of years, which was all I sought. I did not seek to use the shares as a bargaining counter, because I had undertaken to my father to pass them on to Warwick in the same form as they had been passed to me. I did not regard Warwick's actions as in any way releasing me from this obligation — an attitude some of the Tryart directors might find hard to understand.

There was, too, the secondary point that I was bound to consider: failure to reach agreement with Tryart on an appropriate sum could mean that the Kinghaven shares would be locked in to Tryart without any prospect of future dividends. I recognise that I could indeed have negotiated a higher figure than $22.7 million had I chosen to do so.

In a radio interview with David Koch of 2GB following the receivership appointment, Mary once again trotted out the old canard that by closing the Kinghaven deal with me, my father halved his income. The fact was that by the terms of payment his income did not change. Where I did benefit was in obtaining further share issues and dividend increases for the total holding. This, of course, was one of the purposes of the deal in passing on the holding intact, thus avoiding death and gift duties. In the same interview she describes her 'distaste' at my use of the shares to eject Sir Warwick in 1976, the implication being that his generous gesture (which was primarily for the benefit of the family and the company) had bought my support in all circumstances for the rest of his life.

2. Vic Carroll's *The Man Who Couldn't Wait* was published, by William Heinemann Australia in 1990, while this book was in the last stage of completion. I purposely completed my account of the takeover before reading it.

CHAPTER 23

1. Bill Beerworth was a lawyer who left Wardley's in November 1989 to set up his own consultancy with the backing of Keith Halkerston who had moved to England. Beerworth became a director of John Fairfax Group in August 1990 following the forced resignation of Kelman and Johnston and subsequent resignation of Anderson.

2. Dr Tony O'Reilly is Chairman, President and Chief Executive Officer of H.J. Heinz Co Inc, and Chairman, Independent Newspapers.